European Developments in Corporate Criminal Liability

When corporations carry on their business in a grossly negligent manner, or take a cavalier approach to risk management, the consequences can be catastrophic. The harm may be financial, as occurred when such well-regarded companies as Enron, Lehman Brothers, Worldcom and Barings collapsed, or it may be environmental, as illustrated most recently by the Gulf oil spill. Sometimes deaths and serious injuries on a mass scale occur, as in the Bhopal gas disaster, the Chernobyl nuclear explosion, the Paris crash of the Concorde, the capsize of the Herald of Free Enterprise, and rail crashes at Southall, Paddington and Hatfield in England. What role can the law play in preventing such debacles and in punishing the corporate offenders?

This collection of thematic papers and European country reports addresses these questions at both a theoretical and empirical level. The thematic papers analyse corporate criminal liability from a range of academic disciplines, including law, sociology/criminology, economics, philosophy and environmental studies, whilst the country reports look at the laws of corporate crime throughout Europe, highlighting both common features and irreconcilable differences between the various jurisdictions.

James Gobert has been a Professor of Criminal Law at the University of Essex since 1989, and before that at the University of Tennessee. He has also taught at the University of Michigan, Vanderbilt University, and the University of Notre Dame (London). His specialist areas of research are corporate crime and white collar crime and he has spoken on these topics at universities and conferences throughout Europe, Australia and North America.

Ana-Maria Pascal is MBA Programme Director at London College of Business, having previously been a Lecturer and Senior Researcher at the University of Essex. She holds a PhD in Philosophy and an MBA in International Finance. Her recently published PhD thesis, *Pragmatism and 'the End' of Metaphysics* (2009) won the Aurel Leon award for debut.

Routledge Advances in Criminology

European Developments in Corporate Criminal Liability

Edited by James Gobert and Ana-Maria Pascal

Routledge
Taylor & Francis Group

LONDON AND NEW YORK

First published 2011
by Routledge
2 Park Square, Milton Park, Abingdon, Oxon OX14 4RN

Simultaneously published in the USA and Canada
by Routledge
711 Third Avenue, New York, NY10017

Routledge is an imprint of the Taylor & Francis Group, an informa business

First issued in paperback 2014

British Library Cataloguing in Publication Data
A catalogue record for this book is available from the British Library

Library of Congress Cataloging in Publication Data
A catalog record for this book has been requested

ISBN 978-0-415-62066-6 (hbk)
ISBN 978-1-138-01987-4 (pbk)
ISBN 978-0-203-81920-3 (ebk)

Typeset in Baskerville by
HWA Text and Data Management, London

Contents

Contributors

Anne Alvesalo-Kuusi is a Senior Researcher in the Finnish Institute of Occupational Health, where she is currently investigating the effects of a new Finnish Act on the obligations and liability of contractors when work is contracted out. She has studied extensively the area of crime control and the problems of policing health and safety crimes in Finland, and has spoken widely on the topic of investigations in the health and safety arena.

Pascal Beauvais is a Professor of Criminal Law at the University of Poitiers. He graduated from Ecole Normale Supérieure (Cachan), and holds a Master from Paris Institut d'Etudes Politiques (Sciences-po Paris), a DEA in International Economic Law from the University of Paris Sorbonne, a PhD from the University of Paris X Nanterre, and Agregation de Droit Privé. He is the author of numerous articles on European criminal law and has taught criminal law and related subjects at several leading law schools in France.

Steven Bittle is an Assistant Professor of Criminology at the University of Ottawa. His recently completed PhD ('Still Dying for Living: Shaping Corporate Criminal Liability After the Westray Mine Disaster') examines the history and development of corporate criminal liability in Canada. In addition to his publications in the area of corporate crime, he has written on hate crime and child prostitution.

Cristina de Maglie is a Professor of Criminal Law at the University of Pavia and a fellow of the Institute for Legal Research at the University of California, Berkeley. She is a member of the scientific board of *Criminalia* and of the Centro Studi Federico Stella. She serves on the editorial board of the *Journal of Private International Law and Procedure*. She has published extensively in both Italian and foreign journals and is the author of 'Models of Corporate Criminal Liability in Comparative Law' (2007) 4 *Wash. U. Global Stud. L. Rev.* 547.

Janis Dillon is a postgraduate student at the City Law School, London.

Edward Fitzgerald is a postgraduate student at the City Law School, London.

Neil Foster is a Senior Lecturer in the School of Law at the University of Newcastle, New South Wales, Australia. His undergraduate Arts/Law degree was from the University of NSW in Sydney (1982), and his research-based LLM from Newcastle (2004). His LLM thesis explored the personal liability of company officers for company workplace safety breaches, and he has published a number of articles on this topic. He is an Associate Member of the National Research Centre for Occupational Health and Safety Regulation, and has worked for the Commonwealth Attorney-General's Department in Canberra on issues of legal policy in respect of corporate crime.

James Gobert is a Professor of Criminal Law at the University of Essex. Among his more recent publications in the field of corporate crime are *Rethinking Corporate Crime* (Butterworths 2003) (with M. Punch); 'The Corporate Manslaughter and Corporate Homicide Act 2007 – Thirteen Years in the Making But Was It Worth the Wait?' (2008) 71 *Modern Law Review* pp. 413–433; 'The Evolving Legal Test of Corporate Criminal Liability', in J. Minkes and L. Minkes (eds.), *Corporate and White Collar Crime* (Sage 2008) pp. 61–80; 'Because They Can: Motivations and Intent of White-Collar Criminals' (with M. Punch) in H. Pontell and G. Geis (eds.), *International Handbook of White-Collar and Corporate Crime* (Springer 2006) pp. 98–122; 'The Politics of Corporate Manslaughter – The British Experience' (2005) 8 *Flinders Journal of Law Reform*, pp. 1–38; and 'Corporate Killings at Home and Abroad – Reflections on the Government's Proposals' (2002) *Law Quarterly Review*, pp. 72–97.

Michael Levi is a Professor of Criminology at Cardiff University. He has been conducting international research on the control of white-collar and organised crime, corruption and money laundering/financing of terrorism since 1972, and has published widely on these subjects as well as editing major journals, including *Criminology and Criminal Justice*, for which he edited a special issue on organised crime in November 2008. He was granted a DSc (Econ.) from Cardiff University (2007) and elected to the Academy of Social Sciences in 2006. In 2007, he was awarded a 3-year Professorial Fellowship by the UK Economic and Social Research Council to develop research on transnational economic and organised crime and on responses to it. In 1992–3 he carried out a review of the Investigation, Prosecution and Trial of Serious Fraud for the Royal Commission on Criminal Justice.

Ingrid Mitgutsch is an Assistant Professor at the Institute for Criminal Law at Johannes Kepler University Linz. Previously, she was a legal assistant at the Institute for State Law and Political Sciences (1991–1994) and the Institute for Criminal Law (1994–2005). She regularly lectures at European universities, most recently Trinity College Dublin and Mykolas Romeris University (Lithuania). Among her publications are *Casebook Criminal Law General Partition II*, edns 1 (2007) and 2 (2009) (with W. Wessely) and 'The New Offences of Corruption in the Public Sector and Their International Guidelines' (2009), in Mitgutsch and Wessely (eds.), *Yearbook of Criminal Law* Special Partition 39.

Ana-Maria Pascal is MBA Programme Director at London College of Business, having previously been a Lecturer and Senior Researcher at the

University of Essex. Her recently published PhD thesis (*Pragmatism and 'the End' of Metaphysics*, 2009) won the Aurel Leon award for debut. Prior to her time at Essex, she was the UK Director of the Centre for Corporate Accountability, a London-based NGO promoting legal reform on corporate crime and better law enforcement. In 2003, she was a Research Fellow at the New School for Social Research, New York. Her main research interests are in corporate crime, jurisprudence, ethics, and political philosophy. In addition to *Pragmatism and 'the End' of Metaphysics* (2009), Dr Pascal's recent publications include 'Corporate Governance, Shareholder Value and Societal Expectations' (with R. Tudway), in *Corporate Governance: The International Journal of Business in Society*, Vol. 6, No 3, 2006, pp. 305–316 (Emerald Publishing Group, Oxford); 'Beyond the Ivory Tower: From Business Aims to Policy-Making' (with R. Tudway), in *Public Administration and Development*, Vol. 26, No 2, 2006, pp. 99–108 (John Wiley & Sons, London); 'International Aid: From the Moral Case, to Everyday Life Experiences', in *International Journal of Philosophy of Culture and Axiology*, Iasi, No 4, 2005, pp. 154–71.

Maurice Punch is a Visiting Professor at King's College, London. He has also taught at the University of Essex, the University of Utrecht, the State University of New York (SUNY) Albany, and Nyenrode University (the Netherlands Business School). Among his published monographs are *Police Corruption* (Willan 2009), *Rethinking Corporate Crime* (Butterworths 2003) (with J. Gobert), and *Dirty Business* (Sage 1996). He has also written many articles on corporate crime, including 'The Organisation Did It: Individuals, Corporations, and Crime' in J. Minkes and L. Minkes (eds.) *Corporate and White Collar Crime* (Sage 2008) pp. 102–121; 'Tackling Business Crime Within Companies' (1999) *Security Journal*, 2: 2, pp. 39–52; 'Because They Can: Motivations and Intent of White-Collar Criminals' (with J. Gobert) in H. Pontell and G. Geis (eds.), *White-Collar and Corporate Crime Handbook* (Springer 2006) pp. 98–122; and 'Whistle-blowing and the Public Interest Disclosure Act' (2000) *Modern Law Review*, 63: 1, pp. 25–54 (with J. Gobert).

Melanie Ramkissoon is a postgraduate student at the City Law School, London.

Klaus Rogall is a Professor of Law at Freie Universität Berlin. He studied law at the University of Bonn from 1969 to 1974, passed his First State Examination in 1974 and obtained his doctor's degree in 1976. In 1977 he passed his Second State Examination. From 1974 to 1978 he was employed as a research assistant at the Law Faculty of the University of Bonn. In 1978 he was appointed public official at the Federal Ministry of Justice in Bonn, where he served as a counsellor (Referent) until 1987. In 1986 Professor Rogall attained his habilitation, after which he taught at the University of Cologne (1987–1990) before being appointed as Professor of Criminal Law and Criminal Procedure Law at Freie Universität Berlin in 1990. At Freie University he has served, first, as Deputy Dean of the Faculty of Law (2004–2006) and then as Dean (2006–2007).

Rick Sarre is Professor of Law and Criminal Justice at the University of South Australia, where he has a joint appointment with the School of Law and the School of Commerce. He currently lectures in criminal justice, policing, media law and commercial law. Among his many publications in the field of corporate crime are: 'Responding to Culpable Corporate Behaviour: Current Developments in the Industrial Manslaughter Debate' (2005) in 8 *Flinders Journal of Law Reform*, 93-111 (with J. Richards); 'Criminal Manslaughter in the Workplace: What Options for Legislators?' (2004) in *Law Institute Journal*, 78, (1-2), 58-61 (with J. Richards); 'Corporate Governance in the Wake of Contemporary Corporate Collapses: Some Agenda Items for Evaluators' (2003), in *Evaluation Journal of Australasia*, 3 (new series) (1), 48-55; 'Responding to Corporate Collapses: Is There a Role for Corporate Social Responsibility?' (2002) in *7 Deakin Law Review* 1-19; 'Reducing the Risk of Corporate Irresponsibility: The Trend to Corporate Social Responsibility', (2001) in *25 Accounting Forum* 300-317 (with M. Doig & B. Fiedler) and 'Preventing Disaster by Building a Risk-Prevention Ethic into Corporate Governance' (2000) in *15 Australian Journal of Emergency Management* 54-57 (with M. Doig).

Michael Smyth is sometime head of Clifford Chance's public policy practice. He retired as a partner in the firm in October 2010. He has extensive experience in commercial litigation and dispute avoidance, including media litigation and public law, where he has regularly received high marks in industry surveys for his expertise in administrative law, public policy and defamation. He is the author of *Business and Human Rights Act* (2000) and has been a Consulting Editor of UK Human Rights Reports. Currently he is the Chairman of Public Concern at Work, a charity established to protect whistleblowers. In 2009 he was made a Commander of the British Empire (CBE).

Laureen Snider is a Professor of Sociology at Queen's University in Kingston, Ontario. Her major research interests are in corporate crime and regulation. Recent articles include an examination of regulatory responses to the 2002 stock market meltdown (*Social & Legal Studies*, 2009: 18:179–97), a study of government attempts to strengthen criminal corporate liability (Bittle & Snider, *Journal of Law & Policy*, 2006: 28 (4): 470–97); and an analysis of water privatisation and its subsequent re-regulation following a major poisoning disaster (*Social and Legal Studies*, 5 (2): 27–47). Among Professor Snider's many publications in the field of corporate crime are: *Corporate Crime: Contemporary Debates* (1995), Toronto: University of Toronto Press (co-edited with F. Pearce); 'Researching Corporate Crime', in S. Tombs and D. Whyte (eds.), *Unmasking Crimes of the Powerful: Scrutinizing States and Corporations* pp. 49–69 (2003 Peter Lang, London); 'Corporate Crime: Business as Usual?' in B. Schissel and C. Brooks (eds.), *Critical Criminology in Canada: Breaking the Links between Marginality and Condemnation* (2002 Fernwood Press Toronto); 'Abusing Corporate Power: The Death of a Concept', in S. Boyd, D. Chunn, R. Menzies (eds.), *(Ab)using Power: The Canadian Experience*, pp. 112–130 (2001 Fernwood Press, Halifax); *Bad Business: Corporate Crime in Canada*, (1993 Nelson, Toronto); 'Regulating

Corporate Behaviour', in M.B. Blankenship (ed.), *Understanding Corporate Criminality* pp. 177–210 (1993 Garland Press, London); and 'Theory and Politics in the Control of Corporate Crime', in F. Pearce and M. Woodiwiss (eds.), *Global Crime Connections: Dynamics and Control*, pp. 212–240 (1993 University of Toronto Press).

Deividas Soloveičikas is a practising Attorney in Vilnius and an Adjunct Professor at Vilnius University. Dr Soloveičikas holds a Masters (2001) and PhD in Law (2005) from Vilnius University. He also studied at the Faculty of Law of Lund University, Sweden (1999) and the University of Essex, where he obtained a Master of Law (LLM) in European Community Law (2004). He was Reader in International Comparative Company Law at Vilnius University (2004–05) and Reader in Business Law at the ISM University of Management and Economics (2004–07). He has also taught European Community Law at the University of Mykolas Romeris (2005–08). Since 2008, he has taught public procurement law at Vilnius University. He is co-author of the Commentary on the Criminal Code of Lithuania, and a member of the editorial staff of the legal magazine *Juristas*.

Nigel South is a Professor of Sociology at the University of Essex. Following roles as Director of the Health and Social Services Institute and then Head of the Department of Health and Human Sciences, he is currently Pro Vice Chancellor (Academic and Regional Development) at the University of Essex. He has served on the editorial boards of *Sociology, The International Journal of Drug Policy*, and *The Howard Journal of Criminal Justice*. He continues to serve on the board of *Critical Criminology* and as an Associate Editor of the US journal, *Deviant Behavior*. His research interests include: illegal and legal drug use, related health and crime issues, drug treatment programmes involving vocational and educational opportunities, drugs (and wider) illicit markets; crime, inequalities and citizenship; the environment and related health and crime issues; theoretical and comparative criminology; public health; and interdisciplinary health and community safety initiatives. Recent books include *Criminology: A Sociological Introduction* (Routledge 2004) (with E. Carrabine, P. Iganski, M. Lee and K. Plummer); *Drug Use and Cultural Contexts – Beyond the West* (2004, Free Association Books) (with R. Coomber, eds.); *Crime in Modern Britain* (2002, Oxford University Press) (with E. Carrabine, P. Cox and M. Lee).

Steve Tombs is a Professor of Sociology at Liverpool John Moores University, having previously taught at the University of Wolverhampton. His main research interests focus on the incidence, nature and regulation of corporate crime, and in particular the regulation and management of health and safety at work. Recent publications include: *State, Power, Crime*, (Sage, 2009) (with R. Coleman, J. Sim and D. Whyte); *A Crisis of Enforcement: The Decriminalisation of Death and Injury at Work* (Centre for Crime and Justice Studies, 2008) (with D. Whyte), *Safety Crimes* (Willan, 2007) (with D. Whyte), and the co-edited texts: *Beyond Criminology? Taking Harm Seriously* (Pluto Press, 2004) (with D. Gordon,

P. Hillyard and C. Pantazis) and *Unmasking the Crimes of the Powerful: Scrutinising States and Corporations* (Peter Lang, 2003) (with D. Whyte). He is the co-author of *Corporate Crime* (Longman, 1999) (with G. Slapper), *Toxic Capitalism* (Ashgate, 1998; Canadian Scholars' Press, 1999) (with F. Pearce), *People in Organisations* (Blackwell, 1996) and *Risk, Management and Society* (Kluwer-Nijhoff, 2000).

Celia Wells is a Professor of Criminal Law at the University of Bristol and Head of the Law School. Before her current appointment she taught at Durham University (2006–08). In 2006 she was awarded the OBE for services to legal education. She was president of the Society of Legal Scholars of Great Britain and Ireland (2006–07) and served as Chair of the law panel for RAE (Research Assessment Exercise) 2008. She has provided expert advice on corporate criminal responsibility to a number of national and international bodies including the OECD Bribery Convention Working Group; the Crown Prosecution Service (in relation to the Ladbroke Grove rail crash); the House of Commons Select Committee Inquiry into the Draft Corporate Manslaughter Bill (2005); and the International Commission of Jurists' Expert Legal Panel on Corporate Complicity in International Crimes (2006). Among her many publications are *Corporations and Criminal Responsibility* (2nd edn. OUP 2001); 'Catching the Conscience of the King: Corporate Players on the International Stage', in *Non-State Actors and Human Rights* (2005) Ed. Alston, Oxford University Press, pp. 141–175 (with J. Elias); 'Corporate Criminal Responsibility', in *Research Handbook on Corporate Responsibility* (2005) Ed. Tully, S. Edward Elgar Press, pp. 147–159; 'The Corporate Manslaughter Proposals: Pragmatism, Paradox and Peninsularity' (1996), in Criminal LR 545; 'Corporate Manslaughter: A Cultural and Legal Forum' (1995), in Criminal LR 45; 'The Decline and Rise of English Murder: Corporate Crime and Individual Responsibility' (1988), in Criminal LR 788; and 'Corporations, Culture, Risk and Criminal Liability' (1993), in Criminal LR 551.

Foreword

Attitudes to big business have become increasingly binary in nature. Chicago-school monetarists assert that corporations should be left to 'get on with the job', contending that the only contribution capitalism should make towards the achievement of progressive social goals is to generate profit.

Not that any multinational, sensibly advised, would itself put it like that in the modern era. The point is invariably made by proxies.

On the contrary, when companies speak these days of the public interest, they are quick to acknowledge their obligations to a slew of stakeholders other than those on their share register. Firms now invest significant sums in good works and are not coy in saying so. Rare indeed is the day which goes by without the publication of a blue-chip stock's sustainability report. Corporate social responsibility or CSR has been elevated into a term of art in less than a generation.

There is, however, an equal and opposite view. If, as *The Economist* said in 2005, corporate social responsibility is 'the tribute that capitalism everywhere pays to virtue' it comes with an increasingly expensive price-tag, for the denunciation of perceived corporate vices has never been louder. Union Carbide, Toyota, McDonald's, Enron and (as I write) BP: in the popular consciousness these have all at one time or other been part of a rogues' gallery of corporate villainy, susceptible to excoriation at every turn, albeit in each case for different reasons.

So global business is in the dock. More often than not, however, the charge sheets have been based on rhetoric rather than substance. NGOs have for years held up the US Alien Torts Claims Act as a tool whereby corporate crimes anywhere in the world may be impeached in a US court, and true it is that this 1789 statute has by turns been invoked against Shell, Exxon-Mobil, Pfizer and others. But Professor John Ruggie, Special Representative on Business and Human Rights for the United Nations Secretary General, several years ago concluded that ATCA's relevance was largely 'existential' and it is not clear that it can bear the burden of expectation placed upon it by those anxious to constrain and punish corporate misconduct.

Time was when corporate entities, at least in England, were considered to be incapable of committing crimes, because they lacked the requisite intent, even though their members could be liable. This gave way to a 'directing mind' theory whereby a company was likened to a human body with a 'brain and a nerve centre' and 'hands which [held] the tools and [acted] in accordance with directions from the centre'.[1]

The 'directing mind' idea has proved no more adequate to the task in the modern era than has ATCA in the US. In recent years specific statutory measures have been introduced in this country to make the four corners of corporate liability less opaque, not least in the manslaughter context, while the UK Bribery Act 2010 will substantially extend the potential culpability not only of firms corporately but also their leaders individually.

Scrutiny of corporate conduct appears unlikely to diminish any time soon. Professor Ruggie will report next year on the instrumentalities which might conceivably underpin the *protect, respect, remedy* framework that he has devised and as a result the terrain across which companies may be at risk of liability may grow larger.

It was against this dynamic background that my firm was delighted to host the conference the papers for which appear in this book. There is much learning to be found here, which will be of interest not only to students and scholars but also to practising lawyers and their clients in the field.

Michael Smyth CBE
Partner, Head of Public Policy, Clifford Chance LLP,
18 June 2010

---

1 *HL Bolton (Engineering) Co Limited v T.J. Graham & Sons Ltd* [1957] 1 QB 159 at 172.

Introduction

James Gobert and Ana-Maria Pascal

On September 18–19, 2009, a conference entitled 'European Developments in Corporate Criminal Liability' was held in London. Organised by the editors of this volume and supported by grants from the Arts and Humanities Research Council (AHRC) and the British Academy (BA), the conference was hosted by and held at the offices of Clifford Chance, LLP. At the outset the editors would like to express their appreciation of the generous support provided by the AHRC, the BA, Clifford Chance and the University of Essex. Videos of conference presentations can be found on our Corporate and White-collar Crime website: www.essex.ac.uk/CWCN/.

Our speakers included distinguished scholars and practitioners from the UK, ten different European countries, Canada and Australia. The geographic diversity reflected a widespread recognition that corporate crime has become a global challenge. Both large industrialised nations where corporations have their headquarters and small developing countries where they locate their subsidiaries are affected by corporate crime, even if the crimes may be of a different nature.

The speakers also varied in their range of academic backgrounds. These included law, sociology, criminology, philosophy, economics and the environment. This diversity of speaker background was not accidental. Corporate crime is a multi-dimensional problem. The very concept of a company needs to be understood in legal, philosophical and economic terms, and in light of the pragmatic policies which gave rise to the concept of a limited company.

The roots of corporate criminality are economic, sociological and criminological; human psychology also plays a major role in shaping the sources and forms of corporate crime. Addressing this multi-faceted challenge requires resort to laws underpinned by an appreciation of the ethical, economic and social policies at stake. An understanding of specific substantive areas is essential to craft individual laws that can address each of the variety of harms that corporate misconduct may cause.

In the absence of a polymath versed in the multitude of academic disciplines necessary to understand corporate crime, it makes sense to pool our collective knowledge. That is why the conference and this book have taken a multi-disciplinary approach to the topic. The book consists of the thematic papers presented at the conference and country reports setting out the law of corporate criminal accountability throughout Europe. It is the latter dimension of our project that led us to include 'European' in the title of the conference, but in truth the thematic papers are of more general applicability. The book is divided into four parts. Parts I–III contain the thematic papers from the conference, and Part IV consists of country reports which were mainly prepared in the year leading up to the conference.

The chapters in Part I address theoretical issues, largely divorced from particular crimes and the specific laws of any country. The themes are social, political and philosophical, and the authors bring to their task a diverse range of backgrounds – Celia Wells, James Gobert and Rick Sarre are professors of law; Steve Tombs, Laureen Snider and Steven Bittle are sociologists/criminologists; and Dr Ana-Maria Pascal holds both a PhD in Philosophy and an MBA in International Finance. Professor Wells' keynote speech touches on a wide range of issues and sets the stage for some of the more in-depth analysis contained in subsequent chapters.

Part II addresses the question of whether the blame for corporate misconduct rests primarily with companies or with their directors/officers/senior managers. Maurice Punch presents the case for focusing on organisational liability, while Neil Foster argues why the focus should be on individuals' duties. Both would agree that individual and organisational liability should not be mutually exclusive; their papers reflect more a difference of emphasis than a disagreement as to where fault lies. James Gobert, too, begins from the premise that organisational and individual liability are not incompatible. His chapter offers a legal analysis of the relationship between individual and organisational fault and, more specifically, how individuals can be held liable as accessories to the offences of their companies, and companies as accessories to the offences of their directors and officers.

Part III provides an empirical analysis of some discrete dimensions of corporate liability in different areas. Nigel South examines environmental offences; Michael Levi, white-collar and organisational fraud; and Anne Alvesalo-Kuusi, health and safety violations. This selection of topics barely scratches the surface of the breadth of different offences that companies can commit. As it would have been impractical to cover all corporate crimes in this book, we have chosen to present a representative sample of subject matter areas that feature the problems commonly encountered when states attempt to hold companies to legal account.

Part IV of the book examines the laws of corporate criminal liability throughout Europe. In the year preceding the conference, the editors, supported by a grant from the British Academy, commissioned reports on the law of corporate criminal liability throughout Europe. The reports were written by a mix of academics, practitioners and students. We tried to recruit authors from each country about whose laws we were concerned, but this was not always possible and some of the reports were written by postgraduate students from City University, London, researching the law of a foreign country as best they could without direct access to primary sources. The reports provided the foundation for what turned out to be a wide-ranging and lively roundtable discussion at the conference, with significant input from members of the audience setting out the specific problems relating to corporate crime encountered in their home states.

Although our original aim was to write a report on the law of each European state, we quickly discovered that in some states corporations were not deemed to be appropriate subjects of criminal law, while in others existing laws seemed to be limited to a narrow range of offences (i.e. bribery) and too little information was available beyond that. In-depth reports could only be written about countries where companies are potentially liable for a wide range of offences.

Several caveats about the country reports should be made. The law of corporate criminal liability frequently is in a state of flux: long-standing laws prove inadequate and are replaced by new statutes; legislation is enacted in states which previously had no laws on point; and amendments to existing laws are passed as states come to recognise the loopholes and gaps in their legislation. International treaties and EU directives force states to consider new laws in areas which were not previously the subject of legal regulation, and dramatic harm-causing events traceable to corporate fault can give rise to new legislation. In the latter category, for instance, the impetus for the enactment of the Corporate Manslaughter and Corporate Homicide Act 2007 can be traced back to the capsize of the Herald of Free Enterprise some 20 years earlier.

Because the scope of corporate criminal liability often resembles an accordion, expanding or contracting, one cannot do much more than present a snapshot of the law at a particular point in time. Ours is a snapshot of the laws circa mid-2009. Even then, in some instances the research of our contributors was constrained by a lack of access to original sources, ambiguous translations, and an inadequate appreciation of how laws in various states had been classified (as an example, in the UK laws imposing criminal penalties on corporations can be found in many regulatory statutes and Company Law provisions).

The editors have reluctantly accepted that a completely up-to-date, comprehensive compilation of European statutes on corporate criminal liability would be a virtually impossible task. Our more modest aim in Part IV is to give the reader a sense of the diversity of laws that have been enacted with the hope that these can serve as a catalyst for legislators and policy-makers who seek to reform their own state's laws. As indicated previously, all countries are faced with the damages wrought by corporate misconduct and it is invaluable to see and learn from solutions that have been tried in other jurisdictions, whether they have succeeded or failed, with an eye to adapting the laws of these other states to one's own country's legal system and culture.

We hope that our collective research has produced a rich tapestry from which corporate directors and officers; lawyers and criminal prosecutors; workers and trade unionists; NGOs and public interest groups; legislators and policy-makers in the fields of business, government and regulation; academics and students; and members of the public can all benefit.

Background

Events in recent years have heightened awareness of the harm that companies which carry on their business in a reckless or grossly negligent manner can cause. The result of substandard risk management may be economic loss on a massive scale, as evidenced by the collapse of such previously well-regarded companies as Enron, Lehman Brothers, Bear Stearns and Barings Bank. Highly risky decisions by financial institutions have plunged the world into a fiscal crisis not seen since the Great Depression.

Sometimes, however, the costs are measured not in financial loss, but in loss of life and serious injuries. One need only look at the casualties that occurred as a result of Bhopal, Chernobyl, the crash of the Concorde, the capsize of the Herald of Free Enterprise and innumerable rail 'accidents' in Britain to see that companies can cause far more harm than a serial killer or lone gunman on a rampage.

Multi-national companies (MNCs), once seemingly impervious to legal constraint, such as the Ford Motor Company, Continental Airlines, and Goldman Sachs, now find themselves in the criminal spotlight. Once culpability is recognised, however, prosecuting authorities have discovered that traditional criminal laws are often inadequate to lead to a successful prosecution. Legal concepts such as *actus reus*, *mens rea* and causation were developed with natural persons in mind and do not easily lend themselves to fictitious (in law) entities such as corporations. Even today, there remain state legislatures and courts which do not accept that an inanimate entity such as a company can commit a criminal offence because it lacks a 'guilty mind' in the conventional legal sense of the term. What is indisputable, however, is that companies are capable of both causing immense social harm and preventing such harm. The challenge is to create laws that address the former and encourage the latter.

Failed prosecutions, and the practical problems involved in mounting a prosecution, have prompted many states to re-think their criminal laws as they relate to companies. The diversity of approaches taken by European countries bears witness to the complexity of the problem. Finding a suitable doctrinal basis for holding companies to account has proved elusive.

Many states impose vicarious liability, imputing to companies offences committed either by *any* of their employees (e.g., the US) or by *only* their directors, officers and senior managers (e.g., the UK). Vicarious liability, however, lacks a principled basis. A company can be convicted despite having taken not only reasonable but exemplary steps to prevent the offence in question.

Some states, such as Germany and Sweden, have eschewed criminal liability in favour of an administrative approach to liability. However, even here one can discern differences in the form that administrative liability takes. Other states, such as France and Italy, have developed hybrid models, or a *tertium genus*, that draws on both administrative and criminal law principles.

'Designer' statutes, addressed specifically to the unique situation of companies, have also been enacted. Frequently the relevant offence will impose strict liability, thereby sidestepping the need to prove *mens rea*. However, strict liability offences also pose the danger of liability without fault, and may have little deterrent effect if the fine for violating the law can effectively be passed on to the company's customers. Regulatory offences, another alternative, may lack the stigma associated with a conviction for a crime.

Legal reform often raises as many questions as it answers. Indeed, the law may be a 'red herring', the real obstacle being the lack of political will to bring criminal charges against powerful companies. In the country reports included in this volume we have, where statistics are available, sought to show the extent to which laws addressed to corporate criminal liability are enforced, and the level of penalties imposed in cases when a conviction is obtained. The record on these matters does not instil confidence in the ability of criminal justice systems to tackle corporate crime.

If there is to be criminal liability, the ancillary question arises as to whether the focus should be on the liability of the organisation, or the liability of individuals. The Corporate Manslaughter and Corporate Homicide Act 2007 (UK) specifically absolves individuals from criminal liability for complicity in their company's offence. Conversely, many European states focus exclusively on prosecutions of individual directors and managers while rejecting prosecution of their companies.

These are but some of the many questions which will be explored in this book.

Book outline

Part I: Thematic issues

1. Celia Wells – Containing corporate crime: civil or criminal controls?

This chapter (the keynote address at the conference) examines the often skewed thinking that corporate crime can engender. One of the reasons that corporate criminality is so challenging a field is that the law must deal with businesses of different sizes, variety and reach. Economic logic and political imperatives affect both *the nature* of corporate wrongdoing and *the legal responses* to it. The chapter begins with a short account of the kinds of wrongdoing with which the debate about corporate liability has been infused and then looks at the range of legal mechanisms commonly used to address such wrongdoing. In the course of her analysis Professor Wells offers insights into the nature of the corporation as a legal person. This foundation paves the way for the last part of the chapter where different models of corporate criminal liability are critically examined.

2. Ana-Maria Pascal – A legal person's conscience: philosophical underpinnings of corporate criminal liability

Criminal liability, unlike administrative liability, carries a deep moral weight, thereby suggesting the presence of moral agency. This chapter examines the qualities that allow an abstract entity (such as a 'legal person') to qualify as a moral agent and identifies three potentially *sine qua non* conditions: a sense of the self, a free will, and a moral conscience. Dr Pascal provides an in-depth analysis of the extent to which legal persons (companies) have these characteristics, asking whether this might depend on the size and structure of the company, and whether the 'moral conscience' of a parent company can be transferred to its subsidiaries and franchises. The ultimate question of whether a company should be criminally liable if it fails to display any or all of the three *sine qua non* characteristics of moral agency leads to an alternative hypothesis – that perhaps the criminal justice system should revise its understanding of what 'criminal' means.

3. Laureen Snider and Steven Bittle – The challenges of regulating powerful economic actors

In the aftermath of yet another fiscal crisis, this chapter explores the difference in public and legal attitudes to corporate crime and traditional offences such as theft, assault and homicide. The authors examine a triangle of mutually constitutive forms of dealing with offending organisations – through regulation, criminal law and concepts of corporate social responsibility (CSR). The struggle between these three approaches produces a precarious, ever-changing dialectic. The authors conclude that increased corporate accountability requires a re-evaluation of our attitudes to corporate fault – and the value it places on financial and economic power – and argue that, without a radical change in the way society views Wall Street, the status quo favouring the corporate capitalist ethic is likely to persist.

4. Steve Tombs – State complicity in the production of corporate crime

There are a series of ways, some well recognised, others less so, in which states are complicit in the systematic, routine production of corporate crimes. First, states are complicit in corporate crime production through their failure to put into place more effective legal regimes, to enforce adequately existing laws, or to respond effectively to violations of such laws, with respect to corporate activity. More actively, states are complicit in their relationships with the corporate sector – as partners in economic activity, as outsourcers and sub-contractors, as purchasers of corporate goods and services – and thus in the production of illegal activities. Finally, and perhaps least recognised, is the fact that once one departs from a view of state–corporate relations as characterised by externality, then it becomes clear that 'the' state – at its various levels – is implicated in the production of corporate crime through the complex inter-dependence of these apparently separate sets of entities. This chapter considers each of these forms of state complicity in turn, with an empirical reference point of safety crimes in the UK. On the basis of this exploration of the role of states in the production of corporate crime, Professor Tombs seeks to develop a more realistic view both of the extent to which illegal and harmful corporate activities can be more effectively controlled, and of the limits upon such control efforts.

5. Rick Sarre – Penalising corporate 'culture': the key to safer corporate activity?

In 2004, the Australian Capital Territory became the first – and to date the only – jurisdiction in Australia to adopt the recommendations of a national legislative criminal code officers group by enacting an offence of industrial manslaughter by recklessness or gross negligence. Significantly, one way that the fault element of the offence can be established is through proof that a 'corporate culture' existed within a corporation that 'directed, encouraged, tolerated or led to noncompliance with the contravened law'. Culpability can also be demonstrated if a corporation 'failed to create and maintain a corporate culture requiring compliance with the contravened law'. This concept of a criminogenic corporate culture has drawn increasing attention in both the academic literature and legislative committee rooms. Corporate directors and executives have also become self-reflective as to their own company's culture or ethos. In this chapter Professor Sarre explores the usefulness of the concept of corporate culture as a means by which corporations can be called to account for deaths in the workplace.

Part II: Organisational v. individual liability

6. Maurice Punch – The organizational component in corporate crime

Professor Punch offers a sociological account of deviance in organisations, seen as organisational or institutional crime. Two main issues are discussed: the challenging aspect of empirical analysis of corporate criminality, and the fact that the law typically focuses on individual rather than organisational liability. Several case studies are presented which illustrate the theme of organisational fault. Too many prosecutions of companies, however, seem to end with a failure to secure a conviction. Professor Punch examines the reasons for these apparent breakdowns in the criminal justice system and concludes that the problem may lie in the criminal law's inability to recognise collective guilt and its difficulty in applying conventional legal concepts to an organisation. His message is that organisations need to be put firmly in the frame of criminal liability.

7. Neil Foster – Individual liability of company officers

Companies are run by their directors, officers and managers. It has been recognised for some time that a key strategy in changing corporate behaviour is by holding out the possibility of personal liability for individuals who have the authority to influence corporate policy. This chapter argues for laws imposing such personal liability, and compares the operation of laws imposing such liability in the field of occupational health and safety in the UK and in the Australian State of New South Wales. The comparison and review of the fairly extensive case law which has developed under the NSW provisions illuminates the optimal mix of corporate and individual responsibility in criminal legislation.

8. James Gobert – Squaring the circle: the relationship between individual and organisational fault

Building on the previous two chapters, Professor Gobert agrees with their authors that organisational and individual criminal liability are not and should not be mutually exclusive. He then takes this analysis to the next level, addressing the legal relationship between organisational and individual fault. Through an analysis of principles of criminal complicity, he concludes that individuals can be accessories to the offences of their companies, and that companies can be accessories to the offences of individuals. However, the law of complicity as currently structured throws up several analytical and precedential obstacles to a successful prosecution, which he proceeds to analyse.

Part III: Particular offences

9. Nigel South – Environmental offending, regulation and 'the legislative balancing act'

One consistent theme in political and economic considerations of concern about the environment is the search for a reasonable balance between environmental protection and the practical costs of providing such protection. This is particularly evident in legal and regulatory approaches to environmental crimes. Mindful of the difficulties in addressing the relevant issues through regulatory laws, Professor South provides examples of particularly troubling environmental or 'green' crimes and then proceeds to examine issues and problems relating to regulation, prosecution and punishment. The chapter concludes with concerns regarding climate change, and the emphasis it places upon the prospects and problems of a more resource-hungry world.

10. Anne Alvesalo-Kuusi – Investigating safety crimes in Finland

In this chapter Dr Alvesalo-Kuusi examines how police deal with safety crimes and their effectiveness in combating such offences. Safety crimes fall between the stools of 'violent' crimes on the one hand and 'economic crimes' on the other. Furthermore, a zone of discretion permits police to interpret those crimes in a way that may marginalise their seriousness. The empirical evidence upon which this chapter builds is derived from an analysis of data gathered as part of a survey of police safety crimes in Finland which focused on the perceptions of the police regarding occupational safety incidents and their investigation. The data reveal a marked reluctance to treat such incidents as criminal events. Rather, they are seen as 'accidents', on the one hand, or 'unworthy in terms of legitimate police work' on the other. The result is that 'safety criminals' are not recognised as appropriate targets of police intervention. The author also discerns from her empirical research a tendency of the police to engage in 'victim blaming'.

*11. Michael Levi – Political autonomy, accountability and efficiency in the
prosecution of serious white-collar crimes*

This chapter examines the tensions involved in the prosecution and non-prosecution of serious economic crimes, focusing principally upon the UK but referring briefly to other jurisdictions in Europe and the US. It describes the history of serious fraud prosecutions in England and Wales since the 1970s and the attempts to make them more efficient, and examines the organisational and political tensions surrounding this process. Using some case illustrations, Levi reviews the political dimensions surrounding prosecutions and non-prosecutions and asks how and whether we can develop a system that is – and is seen to be – politically impartial, vigorous and fair to defendants.

Part IV: Country reports

IVa Countries with criminal liability

Austria: Ingrid Mitgutsch, Johannes Kepler University, Linz
Belgium: Melanie Ramkissoon, City University, London
Denmark: Ana-Maria Pascal, London College of Business
Estonia: Ana-Maria Pascal, London College of Business
Finland: James Gobert, University of Essex
France: Pascal Beauvais, University of Poitiers
Ireland: Edward Fitzgerald, City University, London
Italy: Cristina de Maglie, University of Pavia
Lithuania:Deividas Soloveičikas, Vilnius University
Luxembourg: Ana-Maria Pascal, London College of Business,
    and Janis Dillon, City University, London
Netherlands: Melanie Ramkissoon, City University, London
Poland: Ana-Maria Pascal, London College of Business
Portugal: Ana-Maria Pascal, London College of Business,
    and Melanie Ramkissoon, City University, London
Romania: Ana-Maria Pascal, London College of Business
Slovenia: Janis Dillon, City University, London
Spain: Melanie Ramkissoon, City University, London
UK: James Gobert, University of Essex

IVb Countries with administrative liability

Czech Republic: Melanie Ramkissoon, City University, London
Germany: Klaus Rogall, Freie University, Berlin
Sweden: Ana-Maria Pascal, London College of Business

Acknowledgements

The editors would like to thank their collaborators, in particular the students who contributed to Part IV of the book: Melanie Ramkissoon, Janis Dillon,

Edward Fitzgerald, and Tom Alexander Burden from City University. Special thanks go to our colleagues who have read and made valuable comments on our respective thematic chapters: Celia Wells and Steve Tombs. Our deepest gratitude also to Sally Painter, who was always helpful with administrative matters. On a personal note, Ana-Maria would like to thank her partner, Luca, for all his love, understanding and unwavering support on this, and every other project.

Part I
Thematic issues

1 Containing corporate crime

Civil or criminal controls?

Celia Wells

Introduction

Everything about corporations and corporate liability seems to involve paradoxes and two-way mirrors. The title of this paper aptly demonstrates the skewed thinking that corporate crime can involve. If it is 'crime' then surely it should be controlled via 'criminal' law? But not everyone thinks so. Khanna for example argues that

> If we start with the notion that corporate wrongdoing is not sufficiently deterred at present, then we would want to argue for curtailing corporate criminal liability and increasing the focus on corporate civil liability and managerial liability. This raises serious questions about how we regulate this area.[1]

This is surprising on the face of it and we might question whether we are concerned solely with deterrence, but it is difficult to disagree that there are serious questions about how we regulate corporate wrongdoing. We appear to be moving in the direction that Khanna advocates, that enforcement of criminal law against corporate crime increasingly uses classic regulatory techniques of negotiation and settlement. One of the reasons that this is such a challenging area is of course because we are dealing with a construct of infinite size, variety and reach. Two recent commentators sum this up nicely:

> The company has always shown a remarkable ability to evolve ... [that is] 'the secret of its success'. With its 'amoebic' qualities it can change again, those changes depend on economic logic and political imperatives.[2]

Economic logic and political imperatives affect both *the nature* of corporate wrongdoing and *the responses* that are made to it. I will start with a short account of the kinds of wrongdoing that the debate about corporate liability has been concerned with. Then I will briefly look at the range of legal mechanisms commonly used before turning to say something about the nature of the corporation as a legal person. This will then pave the way for the last section in which I describe the models available for criminal liability.

Wrongdoing: What makes us concerned about corporate liability?

The corporation is itself a means *by and through which* some crime is committed. The corporation may be our primary target because as a legitimate organisation it has committed a wrong. Or it may be a front for the activities of individuals already committed to fraud. To quote again, the corporation is for white-collar criminals 'what the gun or knife is for the common criminal'.[3]

From the 1980s the debate in the UK was mainly about corporate manslaughter, about the negligently caused deaths and injuries from transport disasters and from poor safety standards in construction and other industries. At the same time, there was a quieter rumble about fraud. Much of this was about fraud within organisations, what might be called intra-organisational fraud, embezzlement and so on. This was eclipsed by the massive inter-organisational frauds that have unravelled since the Enron scandal in 2002. From being the seventh most valuable company in the USA, Enron lost 100 billion dollars in shareholder equity. By 2004, 31 people had been indicted; not only Enron fell but also Arthur Andersen, one of the world's largest accounting firms, was reduced to a mere shadow of its former self. Then as we know there was Worldcom, followed by Parmalat and so on. And all this before the events of the last two years with the whole financial edifice of investment banking almost shaken to its knees by corporate collapses caused by absurd risk repackaging strategies as well as by some outright dishonesty, as in Bernie Madoff's Ponzi scheme.[4]

But before we get too excited about the novelty of these issues, it is salutary to go back to Edwin Sutherland's 'discovery' of white-collar crime. Gilbert Geis and Colin Goff, in their introduction to the 1983 reprint of Sutherland's classic 1949 work, remind us that sociologists had identified crimes by the powerful as early as 1901. Sutherland's main message, radical at a time when causal explanations via various forms of deprivation (poverty, absent parenting etc.) were prevalent, was that crime is essentially about social values, that the violation of trust is more important than the financial cost.[5] Despite this, Geis and Goff speculate that the revival of interest in Sutherland's work in the 1980s was prompted by the economic downturn after a long period of post-war prosperity. They do not make the further point but it seems to follow naturally, that the timing of Sutherland's seminal speech at the 1939 meeting of the American Sociological Society, when he first coined the term 'The White-collar Criminal' came just after the Great Crash. This may well explain why this objective, scientifically minded criminologist became the evangelist in relation to exposing the crimes of the powerful.

We are again emerging from a global financial crash with questions about corporate responsibility and corporate control in the headlines not just of criminology journals but also in the daily press. It is timely to think further about how best not just to regulate but to control corporations and their directors, whether to use and in what combination, administrative, civil, or criminal laws to address corporate misconduct. These are in many ways perennial questions. What is the argument for revisiting them? Corporate criminal liability tends to fall between the two legal specialisms of criminal and corporate law in each of which it is somewhat marginal. A double marginalisation then occurs given that the literature on specialised regulation often bypasses that on corporate criminal liability. This prompts the first theme of this chapter which explores the interface of regulation and criminal law.

Two other developments have contributed to the continued search for appropriate mechanisms for holding corporations to account. One is the transnational move through the OECD to standardise sanctions against bribery of public officials.[6] A second is the strong force within the international human rights movement to bring corporations within the realm of international law in relation to their complicity in human rights abuses.[7] Both of these moves require us to think about the core principles of corporate liability and how they can translate across different legal traditions. This has implications for the development of appropriate models of liability as well as for effective comparative work.[8] This then provides the second theme.

Throughout the chapter I assume that we endorse some form of corporate liability. Of course, in many cases senior officers or managers of a corporation are to blame for illegal corporate behaviour and it is important that any system provides for this. There may have been little point in prosecuting Bernard L. Madoff Investment Securities rather than Bernie Madoff himself. The judge's comment in sentencing him to 150 years in prison that his crimes were 'extraordinarily evil' would have sounded odd if applied to the company, although the follow-up remark that 'this kind of manipulation of the system is not just a bloodless crime that takes place on paper, but one instead that takes a staggering toll'[9] would not have been so out of place. But of course sometimes there is no functioning corporate entity to pursue – as was the case once Enron and Worldcom became bankrupt.

Mechanisms

One possible legal mechanism for dealing with corporate wrongdoing is by resort to *private law* – let the parties sort this out themselves. I don't think anyone seriously suggests this as the only option. Even Khanna emphasises the importance of public enforcement.[10] Sutherland noted that many white-collar violations are prosecuted under non-criminal (in other words, regulatory) statutes. *Regulation* can involve civil or criminal penalties. It is distinguished from *criminal law* – which applies across the board – in two ways: it targets those engaged in specialised activities and its underlying purpose is said to be different in that regulation is concerned to mould or encourage behaviour rather than to condemn it. While these distinctions have always been open to some debate, regulation and criminal law have for a long time been seen as a binary divide. My thesis is that the lines between regulatory and criminal procedures are becoming more tangled and blurred. This is not a new insight of course and partly builds on Karen Yeung's work on the public law aspects of regulatory enforcement.[11] But I am turning the lens in the opposite direction, looking at the implications of using regulatory mechanisms in the criminal law sphere, and training the focus more specifically on the corporate defendant. This is a (possibly subtle) variation on a familiar theme that crimes of the powerful tend to be downplayed or marginalised. Whereas it has been argued that their wrongdoing is either differently labelled or selectively enforced, the argument here is that it is being *differentially* enforced. The rhetoric is of clampdown and control but the method is more benign. Or at least that is the question.

Let me give some more detail to this abstract argument. Whether a civil or criminal regulatory penalty or a criminal sanction is imposed, the bottom line is generally a monetary fine. The 'civil' penalties imposed by some regulators are supplanting the criminal enforcement powers that are available to them. On the one hand this appears to be a tougher stance, enabling large fines to be administered (and administered seems the right word rather than imposed) but on the other the negotiation that this process allows appears to give the targeted corporation considerable bargaining power. In addition, the reputational and legal or transaction costs may vary considerably between regulatory and criminal law procedures.[12]

Fines are often accompanied by some form of operating restriction – suspension or removal of a licence to practise in the relevant area.[13] A further development is the pre-emptive Order, part of a more general move towards preventive justice chronicled by Ashworth and Zedner.[14] The recently introduced Serious Crime Prevention Order (SCPO) can be imposed for up to 5 years either on *conviction* of a serious crime or on *proof of involvement* in such a crime in civil proceedings.[15] The first use of this was against a fuel fraud conspiracy; the Order banned the defendants from dealing in fuel oils for 5 years.[16]

Civil recovery of proceeds of crime is another significant weapon. Powers introduced in 2008 give the Serious Fraud Office power to recover property without the need to establish a specific offence against any particular company or individual, merely that the property sought is the proceeds of unlawful conduct. Combined with the use of negotiated settlements, these civil sanctions are on the rise and arguably supplanting formal criminal law enforcement.[17]

To illustrate these different approaches, I have compiled a brief case file, a pen portrait, on one particular international construction company, Balfour Beatty, which describes itself in this way:

> Balfour Beatty is a world-class engineering, construction, services and investment business. We create and care for essential assets: hospitals, schools, road, rail, utility systems and major structures.
>
> We work in partnership with sophisticated customers who value the highest levels of quality, safety and technical expertise – applying our skills to meet their individual needs.

The company has an annual turnover of £9.5 billion (with a £270m pre-tax profit in 2008), proclaims its commitment to corporate social responsibility and sustainability and has won the award 'Most Admired Major Construction Company' several years running.

The Balfour Beatty story is a cautionary, and I hope illuminating, tale:

In 1993, the company was fined £17,500 for breaching safety rules at its Derbyshire foundry, where a worker was crushed to death.

Balfour Beatty (BB) was one of five UK companies contracted to build the Channel Tunnel, linking England and France, and found guilty in 1993 of failing to ensure the safety of seven workers who were killed during the construction period. The companies were fined between £40,000 and £125,000. In one case, the prosecutor claimed that the breaches were a continuing danger that the contractors had done nothing to prevent. Commenting on the circumstances surrounding the death of a 26-year-old worker, the judge said,

> The failure in this case is one of the worst this court has heard about in the past years. This accident happened because the safety procedures in place were not properly supervised and carried out.

In 1999, BB was fined a record £1.2 million for health and safety breaches during the construction of Heathrow Express. The fine was the highest ever meted out for incidents involving no loss of life. The judge called the incident 'one of the worst civil engineering disasters in the United Kingdom in the last quarter of a century. It is a matter of chance whether death or any serious injury resulted from these very serious breaches.'

In 2005, BB was fined £10 million for its part in the Hatfield rail crash in which four people died. This was reduced on appeal to £7.5 million in 2006 (on the grounds that it was disproportionate compared with the £3.5 million fine on Railtrack, now Network Rail).

We can speculate that this escalation in fine severity reflected the public outcry in relation to these well-publicised transport disasters. This hypothesis is supported when we see the much lower fines when rail workers are killed, sadly a far less newsworthy event. Thus in 2007, Balfour Beatty was fined £180,000 following the fatal electrocution of a track worker. This was not an aberration. Between 1997 and 2001, Balfour Beatty companies were fined amounts of less than £12,000 for health and safety offences on six occasions. In 2005, they incurred two fines of £3,000 and reached an all-time low, a fine of £400 in relation to a fatal accident in the same year.[18]

Moving away from health and safety, in the first civil settlement as part of a foreign bribery investigation, the Serious Fraud Office reached a £2.25m settlement with Balfour Beatty plc in October 2008. This was for 'inaccurate accounting records' during one of its subsidiaries' projects in Egypt (bribes, in other words). The settlement came only six months after the SFO was given the powers to make a civil recovery of the proceeds of crime.[19]

If you are a shareholder or director of this company, there is nothing to fear in the light of the recent announcement that Balfour Beatty Construction US has just been awarded $480 million of new contracts, including the Mecklenburg County Jail expansion project. The facility will contain an estimated 1,300 to 1,700 beds. Should Balfour Beatty's recidivism ever trigger a 'three strikes and you are out' sentence, as would be applied to any common-or-garden burglar, it can rest assured of a comfortable jail with all mod cons.

In a pattern that is hard to discern, Balfour Beatty has experienced a selection from the UK regulatory buffet: large fines, derisory fines and civil sanctions. The Balfour Beatty story reveals a roller-coaster, far from a clear and neat enforcement pyramid[20] and raises in stark form the dilemmas facing those seeking to control corporate wrongdoing. The civil penalty agreed by the Serious Fraud Office cut short a long investigation; it meant the UK could demonstrate to the OECD that it was applying dissuasive sanctions in relation to bribery and it reinforced a compliance ethos. The emphasis was on Balfour Beatty both having self-reported the discrepancy and taking steps to prevent recurrence. But of course the £2.25 million penalty was still relatively low and the reputational damage was minimal.[21] It has been pointed out that Balfour Beatty were obliged under the Proceeds of Crime Act 2002 to make the report. This suggests that their 'self-reporting' to the SFO was not indicative of contrition so much as of damage limitation.[22]

The SFO is not alone in deploying these new techniques. The Financial Services Authority is also being more proactive.[23] This renewed activity reinforces Snider's comment that:

> Crackdown periods following stock market disasters empower regulators – particularly staff charged with prosecuting and sanctioning offenders – to act on the always simmering internal contradictions between the compliance mission of the agency overall and the enforcement missions of Enforcement/ Litigation branches.[24]

But I do not think the reaction to recent events is the sole explanation. The Balfour Beatty CD may well be playing to Khanna's tune: the criminal penalties they incur hardly touch them. The overall impact may have little effect on the corporation or its market performance but undoubtedly reinforces the desired political message that corporations *are* controllable. Companies influence the form, shape and meaning of regulatory law and enforcement policies.[25] The sums are generally small and if you operate a major construction company you do not need to worry about consumers at the till, your customers are other big businesses or public bodies. If you are one of only a handful of companies with the specialised equipment needed to maintain railways, then you are already more than half way there in retaining your market position. And the story may support Khanna's argument that punitive responses which come about as a result of public outcry – as is the case with the pressure to increase health and safety fines and to introduce corporate manslaughter – have less deterrent effect than highly targeted civil penalties. The SFO as a specialist prosecutor with increased powers of civil recovery and settlements may be as effective an option.[26]

Three implicit points can be identified in this account of the emerging use of regulatory techniques. The first is that in relation to any or all of these mechanisms, on a spectrum of negotiation and compliance, enforcement strategies will fall somewhere at one end and strict punitive prosecutions at the other. A subhead of this is to acknowledge the opportunities for what Doreen McBarnet calls 'creative compliance', in other words working out the best way to stay just on the right side of legal.[27] This leads to a second point, that we cannot simply look at comparative differences in the *substantive* law. The procedural dimension is all important such as who investigates potential offences, who decides on prosecution and on what grounds, and what possibilities there are for bargaining. We can see this most clearly in the USA with its very strict formal regime mitigated by prosecution settlements. We also increasingly see elements of convergence between different jurisdictions, of which an example is the recently introduced Plea Negotiation Framework for Fraud Cases.[28] And lastly, lurking within and behind these different approaches are complex and changing ideas about jurisdiction. The territorial principle that underpinned criminal law for so long has had to adapt, but like all legal adaptations the force and pace of change has been inconsistent.[29] It is clear that we have moved from the 'last act' doctrine which assumed that jurisdiction was an all-or-nothing affair – it was either in the UK or it was not. We now recognise that jurisdiction can be assumed where the offence has a substantial connection with that State[30] and that, in cases of transnational crime, this requires co-operation between States. It can be noted that Serious Crime Prevention Orders are available in relation to conduct committed abroad that would amount to an offence both in its place of commission and in England and Wales.[31] As the Director of the SFO has said, '[i]f we believe that a corporate is engaged in fraud or corruption in a particular country, then we can apply to the High Court for an order preventing that corporate from continuing to operate in that territory. This would be a very effective weapon for us'.[32] More explicitly, there remain unanswered questions about the boundaries of regulation, about who determines the 'public interest', about how 'civil' is a civil penalty or how 'criminal' is a criminal regulatory penalty. The landscape has been redrawn. The SFO is not a specialist regulator as such; its remit is to investigate and prosecute serious frauds. Yet the powers it has acquired and the way it is using them looks 'regulatory'. According to its own account, the SFO decided that Balfour Beatty did not warrant prosecution in relation to the accounting irregularities, but Mabey Johnson did. The latter then pleaded guilty, while the former settled. It is not entirely clear where the difference lies, or on what grounds the decisions were made.[33]

I want now to move to my second theme, to consider the models of liability that are available if we are to impose criminal sanctions, with higher standards of proof. It is most likely that a combination of legal responses will continue to apply to corporate wrongdoing.[34] But as we all know, the particular challenge has been in how to apply criminal law to the corporation. It is time then to turn to look at the nature of the legal person and at the ways criminal law might be adapted if that is the chosen mechanism.

The legal person – back to basics

My aim here is to identify the key features that recur in any discussion of corporate criminal liability: these include corporate personality, corporate responsibility and corporate culture.

Corporate personality

Corporate liability proceeds from the assumption that a corporation is a separate legal entity, in other words that it is a *legal* (as opposed to human) person. The term 'legal person' can include States, local authorities, and universities. We should clarify what it means to say that an entity is a legal person.

H.L.A. Hart opened his inaugural lecture with these words: 'In law as elsewhere, we can know and yet not understand.'[35] We use the word corporation but we find it hard to say what it means. It does not correspond with a known fact, or possess a useful synonym. Lying behind the question 'what is a corporation?' is often the question 'should they be recognised in law?' It is the *context* in which we use words that matters. Even if we cannot find a satisfactory synonym, we can explain what the term means and this in its own way can be a definition. Sometimes we want to describe (and therefore ascribe responsibility to) a corporation as a collection or aggregation of individuals and sometimes as a unified whole. Thus Hart suggests the better question is not 'what *is* a corporation?' but 'under what conditions do we refer to numbers and sequences of men as aggregates of individuals and under what conditions do we adopt instead unifying phrases extended by analogy from individuals?'[36]

This then leads to the conclusion that we cannot deduce whether, why or how, to hold a corporation liable for criminal conduct by defining what a company is. If we state that it is a mere fiction, or that it has no mind, and therefore cannot intend, we 'confuse the issue'.[37] Nor does it help to decide whether a corporation is either a person or a thing. A corporation is neither exclusively a 'person' nor a 'thing'.[38] As Katsuhito Iwai argues, the corporation is both a *subject* holder of a property right – its assets – and an *object* of property rights – the interests of its shareholders, its owners. And it is the 'person/thing duality' that accounts for most of the confusion about the essence of a corporation.[39]

Organisations – of which corporations are an example – usually begin with a single instrumental purpose, they are a means to an end.[40] That end might be to further some political aim, to protect workers, or to make money from a particular activity. But they often become more like *an end in themselves*, preserving their existence in order to survive, and importantly acquiring an autonomous character, or, as some have put it, taking on a social reality. This is important because it shows us the error in seeing all corporations, or organisations, in the same light. It does not help to say that a corporation is 'only' a shell, a nominalism, any more than that the opposite is true, to say that a corporation is necessarily 'real'. Sometimes they are one, sometimes the other.

Two examples illustrate the point that we should avoid being too rigid about defining organisations as separate legal persons.

The first example is the Scottish case of *Balmer*. Partnerships in Scotland are separate entities. Fourteen residents died following a fire in Rosepark Nursing Home near Glasgow. The Home was a partnership which was dissolved shortly after the fire. The partnership consisted of three members of the Balmer family. An indictment was laid against the partnership. The High Court of the Justiciary ruled that an indictment could not lie against the partnership as it had ceased to exist, even though its principal members were alive and well.[41] An attempt to indict the three partners individually failed. So the 'person' who existed at the time of the offence was immune because it no longer existed. The three individuals who comprised the legal person could not be prosecuted because they were not the legal entity that ran the home.[42] Here the ability to dissolve the legal person provided a very useful escape chute for the individuals who formed it in the first place. Applying Hart's wisdom might have avoided this problem – was this not a case for considering the partnership an aggregate of individuals?

The second example is an English decision that an *unincorporated* association can be a 'person'. An unincorporated association is not a separate *entity*, nor does it have separate legal personality, but that does not prevent its being prosecutable. As the Court of Appeal put it, the 'simple legal dichotomy' between the separate legal personality of the corporation and the unincorporated association is deceptive, concealing a more complicated factual and legal position.

> As to fact, many unincorporated associations have in reality a substantial existence which is treated by all who deal with them as distinct from the mere sum of those who are for the time being members. Those who have business dealings with an unincorporated partnership of accountants, with hundreds of partners world-wide, do not generally regard themselves as contracting with each partner personally; they look to the partnership as if it were an entity. The same is true of those who have dealings with a learned society, or a trade union, or for that matter with a large established golf club. Frequently, ... third parties will simply not know whether the organisation being dealt with is a company or some form of unincorporated association.[43]

And of course the reverse is true. We may think we are dealing with the woman who runs the garage down the road but find she is a limited company, as Salomon's creditors found over a hundred years ago.

What about the complicated legal position?

> As to the law, it no longer treats every unincorporated association as simply a collective expression for its members and has not done so for well over a hundred years. A great array of varying provisions has been made by statute to endow different unincorporated associations with many of the characteristics of legal personality.[44]

We can conclude that the notion of treating a collection of individuals *under one name* is neither new nor is it confined to organisations that are also separate entities. Thus the emphasis should probably be less on the *'separate'* part of the phrase 'separate legal person' and more on the *'legal person'* part.

This discussion paves the way to the next step in the argument, that of responsibility.

Responsibility

Responsibility is multi-layered too. Harding, in his recent authoritative monograph, reminds us that responsibility means accountability or answerability.[45] He notes that:

> In so far as norms and standards necessarily impose obligations, responsibility is the allocating device which attaches such obligations to particular persons or subjects of the order in question.[46]

Responsibility is however an umbrella term under which shelter four different senses or meanings: role responsibility, capacity responsibility, causal responsibility, and liability responsibility.[47]

Role responsibility is a useful concept in the context of corporate liability. There are two sides to this. One aspect is that individuals within organisations have specific roles or duties or individuals 'take responsibility'.[48] A second aspect is that individuals and organisations themselves may bear responsibility for an activity. An example here would be the owner of a ship or an aeroplane. Owners of ships, planes and trains have responsibilities.[49] Employers have responsibilities.

Capacity responsibility refers to the necessary attributes, rationality and awareness, to qualify as a responsible agent. This is often seen as the stumbling block to corporate or organisational liability for it appears to assume human cognition and volition. If we are to accept *the idea* of corporate responsibility, we must necessarily find a different way of expressing capacity than one that immediately precludes anything other than an individual human. While this is an argument that has underpinned the work of the increasing number of scholars in the field,[50] it is raised here in headline terms in order that it can be seen for what it is – an argument about one sort of thing (human individuals) applied to another thing (corporate 'persons'). For a corporate person to be liable, a form of capacity that is relevant to the corporate person is required. The fact that the capacities relevant to humans are inappropriate is neither here nor there.

The third dimension, *causal* responsibility, can be seen as the link between role and capacity responsibility and liability.[51] Thus if car driver X (role) has capacity (she is not attacked by a swarm of bees) and crashes into Y's property, she has caused damage, and she may be liable for causing damage. But on another view cause responsibility is more blurred, crossing into and affecting the assessment of capacity or role.[52] Car park attendant P negligently directs X to reverse into a parking place, causing her to damage another car. Has X caused that damage?

Or was her role responsibility affected by the supervision of the attendant? As Harding states, such 'causal complexity can be seen very clearly in a situation involving both individual and organisational actors'.[53]

Liability responsibility is the culmination of the three senses of responsibility outlined above. Because establishing liability is the allocating device referred to earlier, it provides the raison d'être for, and is the purpose behind, establishing role, capacity and causal responsibility.

Corporate actors and corporate culture

The third key feature is that of the organisation as an autonomous actor, one that 'transcends specific individual contributions'.[54]

> Theories of organizations tend to confirm that it is right to think of the corporation as a real entity; they tell us something about how decisions are made and the relationship between the individual, the organization, and wider social structures.[55]

Acceptance of the corporation as an organisational actor in its own right is similar to that of the State in international law.[56] Harding suggests four conditions for autonomous action: an organisational rationality (decision-making); an irrelevance of persons (that human actors occupy roles and can be replaced in those roles); a structure and capacity for autonomous action (physical infrastructure and a recognisable identity); and a representative role (that it exists for a purpose, the pursuit of common goals).[57]

Models of liability

I have devoted some space to a discussion of the corporate entity, of the meanings of responsibility and introduced the concept of corporate culture in order to lay the foundations for the final task of this paper, to explore models of liability that can be applied to corporations.

We have seen that corporations are not readily definable other than through an explanation of their context. This explains why they have often been subjected to metaphorical flights, likened to the functioning of human beings. The dangers with this arise if we then begin to treat them *as if* they were human beings. In order to work out the ways in which a corporation, or organisation, can be said to be responsible, to have capacity, to have intention or be reckless or negligent, we need stipulative definitions. We do not need to be driven by some unattainable idea of what a corporation actually *is*, for that, as Hart showed, is the wrong question.

The models are routes to liability for offences – they are not the offences themselves. Corporate liability provides tracks that enable legal actors that are not human beings to be answerable for criminal offences.

A report prepared for the UN (the Allens Arthur Robinson Report)[58] identifies a number of 'design issues' that any scheme should address. These include whether liability is generic or specific; the relationship between the physical actor and the corporation; on whose fault corporate liability is based; and the relationship between the prosecution of corporation and the/any individual.

Schemes

The following schemes can be identified: general liability schemes (which sub-divide into the generic and those where different rules apply to different offence types) and offence-specific schemes. Most jurisdictions adopt a general liability scheme. Many have a generic – one size fits all – model that applies to all types of offence. So for example Austria, Belgium, France, and South Africa apply the same model whatever the type of offence. Australia for federal offences and Canada on the other hand have a general liability scheme but apply different models according to the fault element of the offence. It is thus possible to develop a relatively simple scheme which caters for the full range of types of offences within it (as in Australia and Canada). This has the advantage that the jurisprudence in relation to corporate liability can develop independently of other principles of criminal liability.

England and Wales have a haphazard scheme combining both different liability models applying to types of offence together with some exempt offences to which specific rules apply.[59] Examples of the latter are the stand-alone offence of corporate manslaughter and the corporate offence in the Bribery Act 2010, section 7.

Conduct attribution

The second design issue – the relationship between the physical actor and the corporation – highlights the importance of establishing a link between the corporation and the physical or conduct element of any offence.[60] Large organisations, including corporations, implement their activities through employees, usually groups or teams.

A general provision, as in the Australian Criminal Code Act 1995 would cover all situations:

> If a physical element of an offence is committed by an employee, agent or officer of a body corporate acting within the actual or apparent scope of his employment, or within his or her actual or apparent authority, the physical act must also be attributed to the body corporate.[61]

The Canadian Criminal Code incorporates equivalent provisions in the sections dealing with, respectively, negligence and fault offences by corporations.[62] It is uncontroversial because it was implicit in the early vicarious/agency cases that the physical or conduct element was attributed to the corporation. It was also implicit in the anthropomorphic metaphor that underlay the identification doctrine which saw the 'directing mind and will' as the brains of the company and the workers as the body and hands.[63]

Fault attribution

The real stumbling block to corporate liability has been the perceived difficulty in releasing the fault element – whether it be intention, recklessness, negligence or knowledge – from its individualistic anchor. Three main forms of corporate criminal liability are recognised in common law (and in some civil law) jurisdictions: agency (alternatively styled vicarious or strict); identification (sometimes called direct) and organisational (or corporate culture).

Not only are the lines between these blurred but the labels are uncertain and descriptively misleading. Whether the corporation is liable through a doctrine of vicarious agency, or identification with senior officers or a corporate culture, or failure to supervise, it is *the corporation* that is being held liable. All organisational liability presupposes an organisational agent or actor. Holding a corporation liable is separate and distinguishable from any liability for the human actions that have contributed to the realisation of the organisational liability. In addition to the three main forms or pillars there are two cross-cutting concepts, one inculpatory, the other exculpatory: they are respectively, failure to supervise and the defence of due diligence.

Agency or vicarious liability, where a company is liable for any offences committed by any of its employees, is a broad principle. It is used for regulatory offences in England and Wales which do not require proof of mens rea, including many of those which have due diligence defences. It is used in some jurisdictions, notably for federal offences in the USA and in South Africa, for all offences. The strictness of vicarious liability can be tempered in a number of ways: procedurally – through prosecutorial and sentencing discretion, and substantively – through failure to supervise provisions, or due diligence defences.[64]

Identification liability applies to all mens rea offences in England and Wales (except manslaughter).[65] Under it the corporation will be liable only when the offence has been committed by one of its directors or officers. It is thus very narrow.

Organisational/corporate culture principles are those which do not require proof of fault by an individual human actor.[66] The leading example is found in the Australian Criminal Code Act (C'th) 1995 which applies to federal offences.[67]

A (very) weak version of it can be seen in the UK Corporate Manslaughter and Homicide Act 2007. This introduces the principle of 'senior management failure'. This retains an affinity with *identification* liability because the definition of senior management is those persons who play 'a significant role in managing or organising a substantial part of the organisation's activities'. It also has elements of 'organisational' liability in allowing the jury, when it decides whether there has been a gross breach of duty of care, to consider whether elements of corporate culture – attitudes, policies, systems or accepted practices – contributed to the failure to comply with health and safety legislation.[68]

Cross-cutting concepts: failure to supervise and due diligence

There are numerous ways in which the cross-cutting concepts of failure to supervise and lack of due diligence can be expressed. Jurisdictions that use one or other of failure to supervise or due diligence schemes include Australia, Canada, Finland[69] and Switzerland.

A combination of failure to prevent and a due diligence defence can be found in the Bribery Act 2010. Section 7(2) of the Act provides:

> [I]t is a defence for C (a commercial organization) to prove that [it] had in place adequate procedures designed to prevent persons associated with [it] from undertaking such conduct.

This approach is consistent with that taken to liability for breaches of health and safety duties under the Health and Safety at Work etc. Act 1974. Section 3 imposes on employers a duty 'to ensure, so far as is reasonably practicable, the health, safety and welfare at work of all his employees'. It is an offence under s. 33 'to fail to discharge' this duty.[70] The House of Lords last year had a rare opportunity to rule on the respective burdens on the prosecution and defence in such cases. Lord Hope made clear that the onus is on the employer/corporation to show that it was not reasonably practicable to prevent a breach of the duty – there is no obligation on the prosecution to give chapter and verse on the particulars of the breach of duty so long as a prima facie breach is established.[71] He pointed to three factors: that the Act's purpose was both social and economic; that duty holders were persons who had chosen to engage in work or commercial activity and were in charge of it; and in choosing to operate in a regulated sphere, they must be taken to have accepted the regulatory controls that went with it.[72]

This approach would seem to have considerable potential for development in relation to other criminal offences such as bribery which depend on the actions of individuals who operate under the cloak of organisational toleration. It strengthens the corporate culture model in that it places the burden of proof more squarely on the corporate defendant. The Criminal Code Act specifies two ways of establishing this type of liability: 'proving that a corporate culture existed within the body corporate that directed, encouraged, tolerated or led to non-compliance with the relevant provision';[73] or 'proving that the body corporate failed to create and maintain a corporate culture that required compliance with the relevant provision'.[74]

Summing up

The theme of this chapter has been one of continuity, change and convergence; transitions rather than transformations. How can criminal law accommodate the corporation? This question has been taxing lawyers for well over a century. When it was first asked, the business corporation was a much less sophisticated instrument than now and played a less central role in national and global economies. Nonetheless the legal adaptation has not kept pace. There remains, in the UK at least, a patchwork of answers, in fact more of a collection of cut-out pieces waiting to be sorted before being sewn together to make a coherent structure, than a joined-up article.[75]

We have a boxed set of mechanisms in the form of regulatory/civil and criminal penalties enforceable against the corporation itself and/or against its directors. I began with Khanna's observation that powerful corporations have not prevented a very strict regime of criminal liability in the USA. He speculates that criminal liability in fact suits corporations, it avoids civil sanctions and avoids managerial liability (though some jailed executives may think this a somewhat doubtful assertion). But his main point is that criminal liability satisfies public outcry while imposing relatively low costs on those demands.[76]

Part of an answer to Khanna is that deterrence is not the only object served by criminal liability.[77] Another answer is that we tend to talk quite loosely about regulation and crime, with the result that techniques developed for moulding behaviour through regulatory standards have been applied in the pursuit of serious white-collar and corporate crime such as fraud and bribery. A more reductive answer is that the distinctions between the different types and forms of control are perhaps more apparent than real – again much enforcement of crime against individuals deploys negotiation, discretion and selectivity. Bussmann and Werle concluded from their survey that despite the observed regional and cultural differences throughout the world, there are very similar patterns of economic crime and equally similar ways of handling it. Companies worldwide prefer internal settlements of cases when they have been victimised through economic crime, and business globally develops a set of strategies of prevention and control in the shadow of the criminal justice system.[78]

There is increased recognition that regulatory offences are concerned to prevent harms just as, often more, threatening to health and welfare than many so-called 'real' crimes. An unsafe mine or steelworks can damage employees and the public in ways that bear no comparison with Saturday night pub violence. A corrupt corporation can similarly wreak damage to the economy that places a professional shoplifter in the shade. Regulators and prosecutors have acquired (albeit opaque) more sophisticated and more punitive sanctions.

The variety in corporate form, reach and activity requires a flexible response both in terms of forms of regulation and in terms of corporate liability models. It is not a question of one or the other. Specialised regulatory bodies are better equipped if not to stay one step ahead of the cleverest corporations, at least not to be too far behind.[79] But the symbolic impact will be lost if criminal enforcement is replaced by regulatory techniques of persuasion and negotiation. And as Yeung points out, while the benefits of efficiency, responsiveness and predictability are clear, there are hidden risks in compromising values of transparency, accountability and proportionality, and above all due process.[80] In respect of full-blown criminal liability, the vicarious model assumes that all employees contribute to the corporate goal. This is a good starting point but a blunt instrument in terms of encouraging or rewarding the development of effective compliance policies. It is better combined with a due diligence defence. The identification model is not appropriate as a single model. On their own neither of these models is a solution. They are better conceived as part of a broader organisational model that is responsive to different forms of criminal offences.

Acknowledgements

This paper is an edited version of the keynote speech delivered at the European Corporate Liability conference at Clifford Chance, London, on 18 September 2009. I have benefited both from the conference deliberations that followed and from the discussions after I presented some of the ideas at a seminar during my time at the University of Queensland in November 2009.

Notes

1 Khanna 'Corporate Crime Legislation: A Political Economy Analysis' (2004) 82 *Wash. U. L.Q.* 95, p. 140. See also Ainslie 'Indicting Corporations Revisited: Lessons of the Arthur Andersen prosecution' (2006) 43 *Am. Crim. L. Rev.* 107 arguing that prosecution was disproportionate.
2 Micklethwait and Woodridge *The Company* 2003, pp 173–174; Ireland 'Property and Contract in Contemporary Corporate Theory' (2003) 23 *Legal Studies* 453.
3 Wheeler and Rothman, 'The Organisation as Weapon in White-Collar Crime' (1982) 80 *Michigan Law Review* 1403–26.
4 Reported to be $21.2 bn, *Financial Times*, 29 October 2009. Beale and Safwat 'What developments in Western Europe tell us about American critiques of corporate criminal liability' (2004) 8 *Buff. Crim. L. Rev.* 89; see the FBI investigation into insider dealing on Wall Street http://www.guardian.co.uk/commentisfree/2009/nov/08/will-hutton-wall-street-corruption/
5 Sutherland, p. 10.
6 OECD Anti-Bribery Convention 1997, http://www.oecd.org/daf/nocorruption/convention
7 International Commission of Jurists, Final Report of the Expert Legal Panel on Corporate Complicity, 2008 http://icj.org/news.php3?id_article=4405
8 Though we might bear in mind van Caenegem's reminder that domestic national laws are of relatively recent origin, *European Law in the Past and the Future*, CUP 2002.
9 Judge Chin, 29 June 2009. In contrast Jeffrey Skilling, Enron's former chief executive, is serving a 24-year sentence while former WorldCom head Bernard Ebbers was sentenced to 25 years in 2006.
10 Khanna 2004, p. 100.
11 Yeung *Securing Compliance* 2004.
12 There is of course a large law and economics literature in this area. See Faure and Tilindyte 'Towards an Effective Enforcement of Occupational Health and Safety Regulation' in Faure and Stephen, eds *Essays in the Law and Economics of Regulation*, 2004, pp 325–340, and Garoupa and Gomez-Pomar 'Punish Once or Punish Twice: A Theory of the Use of Criminal Sanctions in Addition to Regulatory Penalties' (2004) 6 (2) *American Law and Economics Review* 410–433.
13 E.g. Sections 66 and 123 Financial Services and Markets Act 2000 empower the FSA to impose financial penalties on corporations guilty of market abuse. See Ainslie, above n.1: automatic civil sanction of automatic disbarment from practise caused Arthur Andersen to fold, though the firm was later successful on appeal.

14 Ashworth and Zedner 'Defending the Criminal Law: Reflections on the Changing Character of Crime, Procedure, and Sanctions' (2008) 2 *Crim. Law and Philos.* 21–51.

15 Serious Crime Act 2007, s 1 (Sched 1 lists the serious crimes for which SCPOs can be given).

16 http://www.belfasttelegraph.co.uk/news/local-national/smashed-the-fuel-smugglers-secret-network-13876732.html

17 E.g. under the Financial Services and Markets Act 2000 settlements can be negotiated at any stage, appealable to Financial Services and Markets Tribunal: http://www.fsa.gov.uk/pages/About/Who/Accountability/FSAMT/index.shtml. These settlements do not require judicial approval, cf. Australian competition regulation, see Yeung, above n. 11, 96–101.

18 Trawled from the somewhat incomplete HSE online database, http://www.hse.gov.uk/Prosecutions/

19 See other recent SFO cases, such as Mabey and Johnson, http://news.bbc.co.uk/1/hi/uk/8275626.stm

20 Braithwaite and Ayres *Responsive Regulation: Transcending the Deregulation Debate* 1992 conceived a static pyramid while Yeung suggests it is fluid and dynamic, above n. 11, p 167.

21 See Corker 'Waiting for a Verdict: The Jury is Out on the SFO's New Prosecution Policy' 2009 *New Law Journal*, 1457.

22 The renewed pursuit of BAE is further evidence: The Serious Fraud Office has announced that it intends to seek the Attorney General's consent to prosecute BAE Systems for offences relating to overseas corruption and will prepare its papers to be submitted to the Attorney when the SFO considers it is ready to proceed. This follows the investigation carried out by the SFO into business activities of BAE Systems in Africa and Eastern Europe. SFO policy in relation to overseas corruption: http://www.sfo.gov.uk/media/28313/approach%20of%20the%20sfo%20to%20dealing%20with%20overseas%20corruption.pdf and see in relation to fraud generally, the Plea Negotiation Policy in Fraud Cases (n.28 below).

23 For example, Seymour Pierce were fined £154,000 for failing to prevent employee fraud, 8 Oct 2009.

24 Snider 'Accommodating Power: The "Common Sense" of Regulators' (2009) 18(2), *Social and Legal Studies* 179–197.

25 Snider, quoting Reichman 'Moving Backstage: Uncovering the Role of Compliance Practices in Shaping Regulatory Policy', pp. 244–268 in K. Schlegel and D. Weisburd (eds) *White-collar Crime Reconsidered,*1992, p.245.

26 The BB order was followed in October 2009 by a Civil Recovery Order of almost £5 million against AMEC plc, an international engineering and project management firm. Also see Ashley/JBB investigation *Guardian* 11 Sept 2009. http://www.guardian.co.uk/football/2009/sep/10/mike-ashley-faces-fraud-investigation.

27 Doreen McBarnet 'After Enron Will "Whiter Than White Collar Crime" Still Wash?' (2006) 46 *Brit. J. Criminol.* 1091 arguing that the *fraud* cases brought against Enron et al. may have indirectly endorsed the *creative compliance* strategies. The use of deferred prosecution agreements may have been equally or more effective in bringing about changes in corporate practice. This would only work of course where there was a functioning corporation available to persuade.

28 Announced in march 2009: www.attorneygeneral.gov.uk; see Nick Vamos 'Please Don't Call it "Plea Bargaining"' [2009] *Crim. LR* 617.

29 Tyler Hodgson 'From Famine to Feast: The prosecution of Multi-jurisdictional Crime in the Electronic Age' (2008)15 *Jnl Fin. Crime* 320–337.

30 *R v Wallace Duncan Smith* (no 4) [2004] EWCA Crime 631 and Criminal Justice Act 1993.

31 Serious Crime Act 2007, s. 2(5).

32 Richard Alderman, Director of the SFO, 'How the SFO and corporates can work together,' speech 11 March 2009 http://www.sfo.gov.uk/about-us/our-views/speeches/speeches-2009/how-the-sfo-and-corporates-can-work-together.aspx

33 Mabey and Johnson 'agreed to be subject to financial penalties to be assessed by the Court, to pay reparations and to submit their internal compliance programme to an SFO-approved independent monitor. A fine of £6.6 million was imposed'. Richard Alderman, 'Bribery Bill and Anti-Corruption' speech 10 November 2009 http://www.sfo.gov.uk/about-us/our-views/speeches/speeches-2009/bribery-bill-anti-corruption,-richard-alderman.aspx

34 Garoupa and Gomez-Pomar, above n.12, argue that in some circumstances both may be optimal.

35 H.L.A. Hart 'Definition and Theory in Jurisprudence' (1954) 70 L.Q.R. 37. See also Hoffmann, Foreword in Pinto and Evans *Corporate Criminal Liability*, Sweet and Maxwell, 2003, xiv.

36 At p. 56.

37 At p. 57.

38 Katsuhito Iwai 'Persons, Things and Corporations: the Corporate Personality Controversy and Comparative Corporate Governance' (1999) 47 Am. J. Comp. L 583.

39 At p. 593.

40 Harding *Criminal Enterprise: Individuals, Organisations and Criminal Responsibility*, Willan 2007, ch 2. Harding distinguishes organisations of governance and representation from organisations of enterprise, although the categories may overlap. Here I am talking more of organisations of enterprise.

41 *Balmer* v *HM Advocate* [2008] SLT 799.

42 High Court Justiciary 20 May 2009, http://www.firmmagazine.com/news/1502/Lord_Matthews_calls_for_law_change_as_third_Rosepark_indictment_falls_at_the_first_hurdle.html HSE guidance: http://www.hse.gov.uk/enforce/enforcementguide/investigation/identifying/insolvency.htm

43 *R.* v *L(R) and F(J)* [2008] EWCA Crim. 1970, per Hughes LJ.

44 The matter is not straightforward, however, and it is a matter of statutory interpretation whether an offence applies to an unincorporated association; the discussion excluded offences which require proof of mens rea.

45 Harding, ch. 5, quoting Hart *Punishment and Responsibility: Essays in the Philosophy of Law* OUP 1968, p 265.

46 Harding, p. 103.

47 From Hart, Ch IX. The discussion here is taken from Harding, note 40 Ch 5.

48 For example, Harlequins rugby club chairman resigned over a fake blood injury scandal, 'Ultimately this happened under my watch and the failure to control must fall at my door.' But he denied personal blame for the blood capsule scandal, 'We, Harlequins, failed to control Dean [Richards, the club's director of rugby]'. *The Guardian* 28 August 2009.

49 Interestingly, as Nick Gaskell has pointed out to me, much of the jurisprudence on the 'directing mind' of the company derives from civil maritime liability cases.

50 Leigh *The Criminal Liability of Corporations*, Weidenfeld and Nicolson 1969; Fisse and Braithwaite *Corporations, Crime and Accountability*, CUP 1993; Gobert and Punch *Rethinking Corporate Crime*, CUP 2003; Wells *Corporations and Criminal Responsibility*, OUP 2001.

51 Broadly the Hart and Honore view *Causation in the Law*, OUP 1968, see Harding p. 111.

52 Broadly the Norrie view, 'A Critique of Criminal Causation' (1991) 54 Mod LR 685.

53 Harding, p. 111.

54 See Harding, pp 226–227; Wells, ch 4.

55 Wells, p. 151.

56 Wells and Elias 'Catching the Conscience of the King: Corporate Players on the international stage', in Alston ed. *Non State Actors in International law*. Collected Courses of the Academy of European Law Vol XIII, Oxford University Press, Oxford (2005), 141, at 155.

57 Harding, ch 9.

58 Report prepared for the UN Special Representative of the Sec General on Human Rights and Business by Allens Arthur Robinson '"Corporate Culture" as a basis for the criminal liability of corporations' February 2008. http://198.170.85.29/Allens-Arthur-Robinson-Corporate-Culture-paper-for-Ruggie-Feb-2008.pdf, p. 62.

59 It could be argued that this is so in Australia too since the Australian Criminal Code Act's application has been exempted from a number of key federal statutes which have their own models of liability. However, the Australian Code does provide a broad unifying starting point for non-exempt federal offences.

60 The Report is ambiguous here between the physical (i.e. human) *actor* and the physical *act*. Here my emphasis is on the latter.

61 Part 2.5, s. 12.2. 'Physical element' is further defined in s.4.1(2) as including 'an act, an omission to perform an act or a state of affairs'.

62 S. 22.1 (a) and s. 22.2.

63 *HL Bolton (Engineering) Co. Ltd v T.J. Graham and Sons Ltd* [1957] 1 QB 159 at 172, per Lord Denning, MR.

64 In 2003 the US Department of Justice issued revised guidelines to prosecutors (the Thompson Memorandum). Relevant factors include the criminal history of the corporation, the likely collateral consequences of prosecution, the level and role of criminal conduct of the corporate employees, and the existence of an effective corporate compliance programme and placed particular emphasis on analysis of the concrete steps taken by the corporation to cooperate. Larry D. Thompson, Deputy Att'y Gen., to Heads of Department Components and United States Attorneys, Principles of Federal Prosecution of Business Organizations VII.B (January 20, 2003), available at http://www.usdoj.gov/dag/cftf/business_organizations.pdf

65 With some exceptions. One way of putting it is that identification liability applies where vicarious does not.

66 These fall broadly under the self-identity model described by Lederman 'Models for Imposing Corporate Criminal Liability: From Adaptation and Imitation Toward Aggregation and the Search for Self-Identity' (2000) 4 *Buff. Crim. L. Rev.* 641, at 677 et seq. See also Pettit 'Groups with Minds of their Own' in Schmitt ed. *Socializing Metaphysics*, Rowan and Littlefield, 2003, pp 167–193; and Rock 'The Corporate Form as a Solution to the Discursive Dilemma' (2006)162 *Journal of Institutional and Theoretical Economics (JITE)* 57–71.

67 Pt 2.5 This applies generally unless specifically exempted. For a list of statutes that have been amended in order to exempt offences, see Hill 'Corporate Criminal Liability in Australia: an Evolving Corporate Governance Technique?' (2003) J.B.L. 1, fn. 13.

68 Corporate Manslaughter and Corporate Homicide Act 2007, ss 1 and 8.

69 Penal Code of Finland, Chapter 9, s. 4.

70 Section 40 provides that the onus is on the employer to show that all reasonably practicable steps have been taken. See Weismann 'Why Punish? A New Approach to Corporate Criminal Liability' (2007) 44 *Am. Crim. L. Rev.* 1319 arguing that liability should follow where a corporation lacks adequate compliance.

71 *R v Chargot Ltd* [2008]UKHL 73 at para 21.

72 [2008]UKHL 73 at para 29.

73 s. 12.3 (2) (c).

74 s. 12.3 (2) (d).

75 The Law Commission has recently subsumed its work on corporate criminal liability originally scheduled for consultation in 2009 into a project on 'Regulation, Public

Interest and the Liability of Businesses'. Law Commission Consultation Paper No. 195 (2010).

76 Khanna 2004, p. 98.
77 See the strong argument for desert by Laufer and Strudler 'Corporate Intentionality, Desert, and Variants of Vicarious Liability' (2000) 7 *Am. Crim. L. Rev.* 1285; see also Yeung, above n. 11, 85–90.
78 Bussman and Werle 'Addressing Crime in Companies: First findings From a Global Survey of Economic Crime' (2006) 46 *Brit. J. Criminol.* 1128–1144.
79 See discussion of the new regulatory paradigm in Tomasic 'From White-Collar to Corporate Crime and Beyond: The Limits of Law and Theory' in D. Chappell and P. Wilson, eds., *Issues in Australian Crime and Criminal Justice*, pp. 252–267, LexisNexis Butterworths, 2005.
80 Above n.11, p 151.

2 A legal person's conscience

Philosophical underpinnings of corporate criminal liability

Ana-Maria Pascal

Introduction

Consider this. Two shopkeepers are treating their customers fairly – albeit for different reasons: one – out of prudence (because he is afraid of losing his business if he gets caught), the other – out of moral conviction. Only the latter can be said to behave morally, because he does so *for the right reason*. This is an example used by Kant, in order to make the point that it is not the result, but the motive of our actions, which determines their moral value.

What motivates people to behave responsibly – is it a true sense of morality, or mere self-interest? The question applies to companies at least as much as it applies to people. Indeed, one of my aims in this paper is to show that it applies to companies more. The reason for this (and something which I attempt to discuss at length later) is that legal persons lack a moral conscience – hence, there is an increased likelihood that they will act more out of interest than out of duty or conviction. This is not to say that companies cannot or will not act morally – ever – only that, if they do, they do so for a purpose, rather than out of sheer moral conviction.

Criminal liability is generally perceived as carrying a deep moral weight,[1] although the opposite is not true.[2] The direct implication of this is that criminal liability requires the presence of a moral agent. Is the company (this abstract entity called a 'legal person') a moral agent? What is needed for any entity, be that human or not, to qualify as a moral agent? I will argue that the following features are necessary: a sense of the self, a free will, and a moral conscience – or, what Charles Taylor calls 'a sense of the good'.

What we need to explore next is: a) do any or all of these apply to the legal person? and b) if the legal person lacks any of these features, does that mean it cannot or should not be held criminally accountable?

One note of caution may be in order. Readers who might rightfully expect this chapter to engage with the literature on business ethics will be disappointed. Although a whole range of theoreticians (from R. De George and M.G. Velasquez in the 1970s and '80s to J.K. Galbraith and J. Dobson in the '90s and A.J. Walsh, K. Greenfield, and T.R. Machan in the 2000s, to name but a few) have written widely on corporate ethics, their focus has rather been on moral problems arising in specific areas of business activity (from finance, marketing and property rights to corporate governance and human resources), whereas my focus is on a generic issue – namely, whether or not business organisations can or should be seen as moral agents *per se*, and how this impacts on the understanding and practice of corporate criminal liability.

Features of a moral agent

What does it mean to be a self?

My first assumption in this search for 'sources of the self' (to borrow Charles Taylor's title)[3] is that, in order to claim an identity, one must have a sense of oneself – that is, a notion of what it is to be a self, and a perception of oneself as such. In other words, being a self is not just a matter of having an identity; it also involves awareness of that particular identity of the self.

In order to understand what that awareness or self-perception might entail, let's take a few examples from the history of ideas, about the actual notion of the self, and see how (if at all) they might apply to 'legal persons'. Three examples spring to mind: Descartes' *ego cogito*, Locke's 'punctual self' (one capable of objectification), and Heidegger's *Dasein* (literally, the 'being here', largely identified with the self).

Descartes situates the moral sources within, rather than outside, of us. For Descartes, that in us which directs our conduct is the free will, which he equates with reason: 'freewill is in itself the noblest thing we can have'.[4] Making use of our free will wisely is the key to rational mastery: it is through understanding the matter and passions that one can control them. This is what mastery actually means, for the French philosopher: that reason is able to rule over passions, in all circumstances of our everyday life. Hence – an ethic of self-control.

At the heart of Descartes' ethics lies the conviction that the self has two dimensions – the mental and the material (*res cogitans* and *res extensa*) and that it is the former (more lasting and valuable side) which must control the latter. The essence of the self is its ability to reason – hence, *ego cogito* as the first principle of Descartes' metaphysics. In fact, the mind (the same as spirit, or soul) is so important for Descartes, that it becomes a synonym for the self. 'But what then am I? A thinking thing', says Descartes in his 2nd Meditation. And he continues: 'But what is a thinking thing? It is a thing that doubts, understands, [conceives], affirms, denies, wills, refuses; that imagines also, and perceives.' This is not to say that Descartes' 'self' is but a walking mind; rather, that its quintessence is the mind, through which it perceives and relates to everything else – material and immaterial substances alike. And it is the cogito, which has the ultimate ethical function as well, because only through reason can one gain control of oneself (i.e., of one's passions and doubts).

John Locke pushes this search for self-control much further, and talks about a disengagement (or 'objectification' as he calls it) of the self. The notion of this detachment stems from the regnant mechanistic outlook at the time, which saw the mind as disengaged reason. For Locke, the self is extension-less, and its primary function is to objectify things, to see them as objects, out there. And that in us which does this objectification is *consciousness*.

> For it is by the consciousness it has of its present thoughts and actions, that it is a self to itself now, and so will be the same self, as far as the same consciousness can extend to actions past and to come; and would be by distance of time, or change of substance, no more two persons, than a man wearing other clothes today than he did yesterday, with a long or short sleep between; the same consciousness uniting those distant actions into the same person, whatever substances contributed to their production.[5]

To what extent this picture of the self as pure consciousness is realistic and applicable to legal persons, should not require much debate at all. Quite obviously, legal persons lack self-awareness in the strict sense that Locke meant it, with reference to human beings; however, they do have what we could call a sense of identity with themselves, in space and time.

What is interesting in Locke's theory is, just as in Descartes, the notion of self-control. Locke's *person* 'is a forensic term, appropriating actions and their merit; and so belongs only to intelligent agents, capable of a law, and happiness and misery'.[6] The person who acts is the same person who will be rewarded or punished for its action: 'In this personal identity is founded all the right of reward and punishment.'[7] Hence – an ideal of responsible agency: Locke's person takes responsibility for his acts in the light of future retribution. This ideal of rational self-responsibility would dominate the Enlightenment, in conjunction with the notion of procedural reason, or disengagement and instrumental control.

It is precisely this notion of self-responsibility which is relevant for us here, in the context of our enquiry into whether or not companies (or 'legal persons' in general) can be said to have a moral self and, if so, what might this entail. To the extent that such collective entities are able to control themselves, their behaviour and their actions, in such a way that could be described as *responsible* action, then they do qualify as moral selves – in the rationalistic sense of the term that Descartes and Locke advocate.

Heidegger's ontology is the best example of a theory of the self which does not apply to non-human, collective entities such as legal persons. The reason for this is because all the main features of the German philosopher's *Dasein* are utterly individual, psychological and existential: being-together and being oneself; care, or anxiety (*Sorge*); fear; concern (*das Besorgen*); solicitude; understanding, as opposed to explanation; intuitive grasp (*Vorhabe*) and anticipation (*Vorgriff*); language (*Sprache*) and communication (*Mitteilung*). All these *existentialia* are ways of being in the world characteristic to human beings – and they all entail an emotional stance, as well as a certain openness or being-towards (*Erschlossenheit*), aiming beyond one's own boundaries.[8]

The reason why I thought Heidegger's theory worth mentioning, however, is that in his analysis of *Dasein*, the author emphasises the fact of being-in-the-world as one of the primary existential features of the self. There are two sides to this characteristic: being-together, and being-oneself (*Mit-* and *Selbst-sein*). This is no different when it comes to organisations or institutions. Their very presence in society has two facets: one is the way in which they perceive and portray themselves, the other is their behaviour, the way they choose to act amongst others. And it is only when these two mirror each other, that the basis for rational self-responsible behaviour is laid.

From reason to free will

This is arguably the second most important feature of an entity which claims to be not only a self with its own identity and rationality, but also a *moral* self – that is, a self with a sense of responsibility and the capacity to act accordingly. We have already seen how free will and reason are connected in Descartes, and provide the key to self-control. For Descartes, that within us which directs our conduct is the will, which is to say rational control (*phronesis*). But does having a free will automatically provide one with a sense of responsibility? What does it mean to be a responsible legal person? Let us briefly remind ourselves what another modern philosopher had to say on the subject of the free will, before we tackle these questions.

The French rationalist is not the only one who places such an emphasis on free will. Immanuel Kant is also keen to stress its moral value – indeed, this is paramount for his ethics. In the opening sentence of his *Foundations of the Metaphysics of Morals*, Kant says: 'Nothing in the world – indeed nothing even beyond the world – can possibly be conceived which could be called good without qualification except a *good will*'.

In loose terms, free will is the power to decide for oneself. However, for Kant, free will is more than that: it is the power to decide for oneself *according to universal laws*. Kant defines morality and *freedom* (or free will) in terms of each other. It is the motive, not the outcome of action that determines its moral value. (And the motive, of course, must be conforming to universal law.) We must choose to do the right thing, for the right reasons. Kant's example about the two shopkeepers, mentioned at the beginning of this chapter, illustrates the notion that only actions that conform to what the moral law requires can be described as moral. 'The moral person may lead the same external life as the non-moral one, but it is inwardly transformed by a different spirit. It is animated by a different end.'[9]

The second essential feature in Kant's ethics is *rationality*. Only rational creatures conform to moral laws, and that gives them a special status, which is incomparably higher than that of all other creatures. Here is how Kant describes this special status: 'Everything in nature works according to laws. Only a rational being has the capacity of acting according to the conception of laws, i.e., according to principles.'[10]

Finally, the paramount concept in Kant's ethical theory is his *principle of universal justice*: the imperative to act only by universal maxims and to treat all rational beings as ends in themselves. This is what the legal person lacks – the determination to act by universal laws alone.

Let us now return to our initial question in this section: does having an identity and a free will automatically provide one with a sense of responsibility? Human beings are self-aware, free and self-determining. But so are companies – with the qualification that self-awareness implies a sense of *sameness* in time and space, rather than in mental terms, as in the case of human beings, where self-awareness means perceiving oneself as a conscious being. Does that make them capable of behaving responsibly, thereby morally (and, at limit, criminally) liable when they don't?

The cornerstone to morality: consciousness

My short answer to the above question is 'no'. Something else is needed, over and above a sense of the self and a free will (that is, the capacity to decide for oneself in a rational manner), in order to make the person qualify as a *moral* agent. That third element is consciousness or, in this context, a moral conscience. Without it, one's rationality and self-control can only yield *seemingly* moral – indeed, calculative – behaviour. Only a moral conscience provides the basis for moral behaviour – i.e., the right motive, as we saw in Kant's example with the two shopkeepers. Without it, any apparently good action is not so in itself, but merely by accident.

Whether we call it soul, spirit, inner voice, or (in Plato's terms) *daemon*,[11] moral conscience is the key to defining our true self. Most philosophers agree that conscience requires rationality, but they disagree with regards to the principal aim and criterion for it. The main views are that conscience is to be judged as awareness and fulfilment of *utility* (J.S. Mill), *duty* (I. Kant, J. Rawls), or *virtue* (Aristotle, A. MacIntyre).

For J.S. Mill, utility is the main criterion for actions, and it is associated with individual freedom and happiness.

> The creed which accepts as the foundation of morals, Utility, or the Greatest Happiness Principle, holds that actions are right in proportion as they tend to promote happiness, wrong as they tend to produce the reverse of happiness. By happiness is intended pleasure and the absence of pain; by unhappiness, pain and the privation of pleasure.[12]

So according to this theory of morality, pleasure and freedom from pain are the only things desirable as ends; but some kinds of pleasure are more desirable than others, and the criterion for judging their quality is, oddly enough, a quantitative one: that pleasure to which more people give it a decided preference, is considered the most desirable one. In business terms, this can be translated as follows: that value, which most stakeholders prefer, is considered the most important one. The problem is – the reins of power for deciding the best means to that end (whatever it may be) are far less inclusive or democratically established.

There is, however, another facet to Mill's theory, namely, his liberalism – the post-Romantic notion of individual difference, of respecting another person's autonomy, which amounts to the demand that we give people the freedom to develop and manifest their personality in their own way, irrespective of whether we like those ways or not, as long as they do not impinge on the freedoms of others. For legal persons, this translates as competition – and the checks and balances for it have less to do with respect than they do with self-interest. From this point of view (and if we accept that acting out of interest and acting for one's own pleasure can be synonymous), Mill's theory of morality makes more sense when applied to organisations than to people.

For Kant, fulfilment of *duty* is the main test of moral behaviour. Let us remind ourselves of the three moral propositions that provide the framework for Kant's ethics:

1   To have moral worth, an action must be done from duty.
2   An action done from duty derives its moral worth not from its purpose, but from the maxim by which it is determined (i.e. the principle of the will by which the action has taken place).
3   '*Duty is the necessity of acting from respect for the law*', not just from inclination. 'The pre-eminent good which we call moral can therefore consist in nothing else than *the conception of law* in itself, *which certainly is only possible in a rational being*, so far as this conception, and not the expected effect, determines the will'.[13]

Acting this way (according to universal laws or principles) entails having a strong will, which for Kant is the same as practical reason. For something to be good, it has to be practically necessary, in conformity with universal principles. And categorical imperatives are those which show an action to be necessary in itself, not merely as a means to something else.

For many ethicists, including Aristotle, Martha Nusbaum, and Alasdair MacIntyre, the test of moral behaviour is *virtue*. MacIntyre talks of a 'heroic society' where 'a man *is* what he *does*', therefore 'morality and social structure are one in heroic society'.[14] This moral/social structure has three parts, namely, a conception of what each role requires; the virtues each role requires; and the human condition as 'fragile and vulnerable'. MacIntyre agrees with Aristotle in that the good is acting according to the right reason, which is about judgement and is governed by what the Greeks used to call *phronesis* (practical wisdom), but he ultimately rejects the Aristotelian notion of the unity of the virtues as purely metaphysical. For him, virtue is contextual; it is 'good *internal* to a practice'. Virtues can only be understood in relation to the communities which they come from. We must aim for something which is beyond (or 'after') virtue: this, for MacIntyre, should be the construction of 'local forms of community' which would stimulate intellectual and moral life. Talking about practices and communities should not commit us to relativism. MacIntyre illustrates his notion of 'practice' by means of an example: teaching a disinterested child how to play chess. At first, the child will be offered candy to play and win the game. MacIntyre points out that the result of this is that the child may learn how to win but without appreciating the beauty of the game in itself. After a while, the child may discover this intrinsic beauty, and come to enjoy developing the skills it requires. So he will become interested in playing the game for its own sake. In other words, the true value of the game is internal – win or lose. MacIntyre's distinction between internal and external goods (i.e. goods that can be achieved by participating in the practice, v. goods attached to it merely through social circumstance) is meant to teach us the value of participation and experience over that of property or money, and that only the former can benefit the whole community, rather than the individual alone: it is characteristic of internal goods 'that their achievement is a good for the whole community who participate in the practice'.[15]

How do these three criteria apply to collective entities – such as organisations? Can a company be said to act out of duty, or virtue? Or is it all about the utility of its actions? If, say, Royal Dutch Shell decides to invest $10,000 in schools for African children, is that a sign of generosity, responsibility, or self-interest? Before answering this question, one should consider the following: in the Niger Delta, oil deposits have generated an estimated $600 billion for the Nigerian government and multinational oil companies since the 1960s; 75 per cent of the 31 million people living in the area don't have access to clean water, much of which is polluted by oil spills; Shell has been the major oil producer in the Niger Delta for the last 50 years.[16] At best, I would say that Shell's decision to invest a fraction of its profits in local regeneration projects would be motivated by self-interest. None of the three criteria which would prove that a moral conscience lies behind the seemingly good behaviour can be tested in this case.

But let us take a positive example. If a local services business (say, an insurance company) decides to invest 1 per cent of its profits in green projects because its management genuinely cares about the 'save the environment' cause, can this be said to fulfil any of the three moral tests? Many ('the company' included) may agree that a cleaner environment can enhance the quality of life for everybody – so the project meets Mill's utilitarian criterion. (Of course, the assumption is that management's creed is genuine, and not a mere symptom of self-interest. This is no small assumption.) Furthermore, the environmental cause is a universal one and thus serving it can be viewed as a duty in Kantian terms. (Again, assuming the company's pro-environment projects are motivated by a genuine belief, rather than embarked on for a self-serving purpose.) Thus, at least two of the three moral tests seem to be fulfilled: those of utility and responsibility or duty.

What about virtue – can the company's actions be considered to be virtuous, as well as useful and responsible? The only case in which we could grant this is if it could be demonstrated that the company would act in this manner *no matter what*, in any circumstances, irrespective of its performance. There is no way that any such case could be made by any company, on any topic; a business' strategy and actions (and indeed those of any type of organisation) will always depend on time, place and performance. It would be foolish to imagine that any organisation would keep investing in corporate social responsibility (CSR) projects (no matter how genuine its commitment to those causes were) if its operations suffered or if it was in danger of making a loss. The same applies to a company's dutiful behaviour – so the second moral test is also contextual. And indeed, the same can be said about the utility criterion: no matter how useful a goodwill gesture on the part of the company may be, it is not going to be made in times of hardship. So the fulfilment of all three moral tests is contingent upon the wellbeing of the company. In the absence of a moral *conscience*, no entity will ever prioritise its 'beliefs' over its self-interest.

One last note about conscience, and how it may or may not apply to inanimate entities. So far we have talked about conscience in itself; but we could also talk about *self-consciousness* and how it stems from the dialectics between 'the self' and 'the other' – the master and the slave, in Hegel's terms.[17] Having an identity means having a *recognised* identity. In other words, self-consciousness requires the recognition of other selves whom we, in turn, recognise.

> Servitude is not only a phase of human history, it is in principle a condition of the development and maintenance of the consciousness of self as a fact of experience. Self-consciousness exists in itself and for itself, in that, and by the fact that it exists for another self-consciousness; that is to say, it is only by being acknowledged or 'recognized'.[18]

Ironically, it is only the slave that enjoys such recognition – not the master. Because one cannot gain recognition from a self one doesn't recognise. For companies, governments, and all other collective entities, this dilemma is evident: they only recognise other companies, governments etc. – equally conscious-less entities – so it is hard to see where a consciousness-backed acknowledgement might come from, for them.

To return to the issue of moral conscience (whether recognised by others or not), Charles Taylor extrapolates it, making it the very criterion of selfhood. For him, to have an identity, a sense of the self, is to have *a sense of the good*, a moral orientation: 'To know who you are is to be oriented in moral space, a space in which questions arise about what is good or bad, what is worth doing and what not, what has meaning and importance for you and what is trivial and secondary'. Taylor thinks of this moral orientation 'as essential to being a human interlocutor, capable of answering for oneself'.[19] He sees the relation between the self and the good as a crucial feature of human agency: it is essential to the self 'that it orient itself in a space of questions about the good, that it stands somewhere on these questions'.[20] To be a self, one needs to have an orientation to the good.

A sense of the good must also be present in self-perception, which for Locke is the key feature of the self. For Taylor, self-perception is insufficient, because neutral; we need to add self-concern, or engagement (on moral issues) to this rapport. Human beings 'are not neutral, punctual objects; they exist only in a certain space of questions, through certain constitutive concerns' which, in turn, 'touch on the nature of the good that I orient myself by and on the way I am placed in relation to it.'[21]

The question for us is, can this be the case insofar as legal persons are concerned – this essential connection between themselves and a sense of the good? Do companies have such a moral orientation? Can we say they are what they are because they have a certain moral sense, which they take to be right? I doubt it. If they do have such an orientation, it is merely contextual, rather than constitutive, as in the case of human beings.

A legal person's self, will, and conscience

To what extent can legal persons be said to have the three features that would qualify them as moral agents? Throughout the previous section, we looked at this issue in general, rather theoretical terms. I would now like to discuss it in relation to some specific cases, taking real companies of different size, structure, and type of organisation for example.

Companies of different sizes and structures

Everybody will agree that a big company organises itself (its policies, morals, and behaviour) differently from a smaller one. The question is – how significant is the difference, and does it have an impact on whether or not either of the two organisations can or should be held criminally accountable? How does the notion of corporate responsibility apply to each? What does it mean for a big/small company to behave responsibly – who exactly is it that behaves so? Who is the 'conscience', where should we look for the *mens rea*? Should we even try to apply such an old, anthropomorphic notion to abstract entities?

Let us take Transco PLC and Keymark Services for example. They were both involved in criminal cases for offences that caused people to lose their lives, and were both held to account: one at organisational level (the company as a whole was convicted), the other – both at organisational and individual levels (its directors were also prosecuted).

The utility firm Transco PLC received one of the most substantial fines ever imposed in the UK for a health and safety offence (£15,000,000 for breaches of HSW Act, section 3) for its failure to maintain a leaking gas main which resulted in a fatal explosion that killed a family whose garden lay above the main. According to the indictment, the firm failed to keep accurate records of the condition of its pipelines.

Who was to blame, where did the conscience lie? Should we even look for a 'controlling mind' inside the company, or is this an empty signifier with no empirical grounds whatsoever? Where are the sources of the company's identity in this case? Is there such a thing as 'the self' of this legal person that happens to have been held accountable for serious health and safety offences but might as well have been found guilty of corporate manslaughter? Indeed, the company was also prosecuted for manslaughter under the old common law, but the prosecution failed. Most of the time we find layers, rather than centres of responsibility in big companies. So how can we reconstruct the self of the organisation (let alone its moral conscience) from such a multi-layered structure, with so many intricate mechanisms of blame-shifting?

In the case of Transco, at least two different teams were involved in the failure that caused the offence: the records team and the maintenance team.

The communication channels between the two may also have been faulty. And certainly the maintenance would involve at least two levels: one for checking the status of gas mains, the other for updating it and fixing the problems. Yet another set of teams, of course, are those of finance and human resources, which decide the budgets and staff available for carrying out the work that needs carrying out. In total, there are at least four or five independent centres of action. Of course, there is a top layer of management, from where these separate centres should be coordinated and controlled. But is it fair to place all power and responsibility in the hands of only one person, or even two or three? Should we expect there to be a single controlling mind behind such a sophisticated structure? Is it fair to hold just one person to account for the mistakes of many, especially when there is so much scope for error in execution, rather than strategy and planning? The more we elaborate these questions, the harder it becomes to defend the position that there should be one identifiable centre of power in each big organisation, which should then be held liable when things go seriously wrong.

Moving on to our next case, in December 2004, company director Melvyn Spree, from Sheerness in Kent, admitted the manslaughter and unlawful killing of Neil Owen and Benjamin Kwapong in a car crash involving one of their company lorries. The company, Keymark Services, also pleaded guilty to the manslaughter of the two men. The crash on the M1 in Northamptonshire happened on 27 February 2002, when lorry driver Steven Law – who worked for Keymark Services – fell asleep at the wheel and crashed into seven vehicles. Northampton Crown Court heard how lorry drivers were told to falsify records so they could work longer hours. It also heard how working practices at the haulage company were 'an accident waiting to happen'. Sir Derek Spencer QC, prosecuting, said: 'Drivers drove as long as they could, failing to take daily rests and weekly rests.' The result was that there was a risk that any of them at any time might fall asleep at the wheel. At the time of the collision, Mr Law's tachograph actually showed his truck at rest at Keymark's depot on the Isle of Sheppey.

Following a police investigation, all of the company's ten full-time drivers were prosecuted and fined for a total of 400 different offences of breaching driving regulations and falsifying vehicle records. Three other part-time drivers received official cautions.

Spree's fellow director Lorraine March was jailed for 16 months for conspiracy to falsify driving records, while the company's secretary, Clare Miller, was given 160 hours of community service for the same charge. An inspection by the Vehicle Inspectorate led to Keymark's operators licence being revoked and Spree and March were banned for life from holding such positions.[22]

The two cases are similar in that the failure of the employer to protect members of the public (and, in the second case, its own employees, too) is obvious and gross. But where they differ is the extent to which the person(s) responsible for the causes of that failure could be identified. Transco ended with a conviction for health and safety offences rather than manslaughter – because for the latter offence the individual liability of a person who was a directing mind of the company would have had to be proved under the then prevailing law. As *mens rea* was a sine qua non for liability, the courts were faced with the prospect of hardly ever being able to hold a big, multi-layered company accountable for serious (criminal) offences.

In the Keymark Services case, the manslaughter prosecution was successful, because the company officials who had been guilty of gross negligence could be identified. As a result, the company could be convicted as well as the individuals.

Both companies arguably had a sense of their own identity; what differed was the extent to which their sources of self-identity were situated in themselves (thereby providing them with a strong sense of morality) or outside – in some fluctuating interest or influence (profit, competition etc.). As we have seen, according to most modern philosophers, what grounds our (human beings') moral conscience is our rationality, or practical reason – which, in moral terms, amounts to strong will and self-control. But for a company to display the latter, it would sometimes have to act against its own interests, because the very purpose of rationality and self-control is to keep one's interests (which, in philosophical jargon, are passions or desires) at bay. This entails the presence of a strong moral conscience, which legal persons obviously lack – so they cannot be said to act out of a moral law-based rationality, as humans are expected to.

Subsidiaries and franchises

The same question that we asked about the locus of moral responsibility in relation to companies of different sizes applies to companies with subsidiaries: is it the parent company, or the subsidiary that should be considered the moral agent and therefore be praised or blamed for the company's actions? Should we expect the moral conscience of a parent company to be automatically transferred to its subsidiaries? Let us take for example the Bhopal disaster, where thousands of people lost their lives in a gas explosion.

The question of where the burden of responsibility should lie – whether with the parent company or with its subsidiary – stands, however, irrespective of our views concerning Dow Chemical's liability. At the time of the disaster, UCC was a multinational corporation itself, and UCIL was one of its subsidiaries.[26] The parent company had several international facilities, and no consistent standards of safety. According to a case study undertaken by Trupti Patel from the School of International Service at American University, Washington, 'Carbide had dropped the safety standards at the Bhopal plant well below those it maintained at a nearly identical facility in West Virginia. It is also important to note here that Carbide was able to operate its deteriorating plant because industrial safety and environmental laws and regulations were lacking or were not strictly enforced by the state of Madhya Pradesh or the Indian government making them indirectly responsible for the tragedy at Bhopal.'[27] If this is true, then the locus of liability becomes more clearly demarcated – namely with the parent company – at least insofar as minimum standards are concerned. If the *mens rea* of the parent company cannot be said to be transferable to its branches and subsidiaries, its threshold for safety and its policies for ensuring it throughout its operations should be.

Perhaps what these cases show is not so much that companies have (or have not) a 'personal identity' of their own – regardless of their size and structure – and a moral conscience which they should be expected to pass on to their subsidiaries and franchises (or not), but that size and structure do matter when it comes to business behaviour. The ensuing question is, then, not who or how exactly a company is, by nature, and *whom to blame* when it acts unlawfully, but *what to do* to prevent it from doing so. We should therefore discuss socio-economic policies and regulatory mechanisms, rather than ponder upon the philosophical notions that might lie behind the distinction between individual v. organisational liability. This, however, will have to be addressed in a separate paper. For now, I would like to stick to the subject at hand in this chapter – the relationship between the metaphysical and the moral dimensions[28] of a (legal) 'person'.

Discussion

To resume our enquiry into the depth of moral responsibility of legal persons, and assuming agreement about the lack, in the latter, of at least one quintessential feature out of the three we looked at (namely, a moral conscience), let us now consider the effects of this realisation. If companies cannot be said to have a conscience, does it mean they cannot or should not be held criminally liable?

One option would be to say *no*, companies should be held accountable – and it is our understanding of 'the criminal' that should be revised instead, so that it becomes more pragmatic and less metaphysical (as in Susan Wolf or Michael Sandel, for example). Another option would be to suggest that we give up the idea of organisational liability altogether, and either choose to hold companies accountable vicariously (based on the liability of their directors), or continue with the traditional notion of individual liability alone, as the only appropriate form of criminal liability. Personally, I would opt for the former option – revising our understanding of 'criminal' liability. In what follows, I will try to explain what I think a more pragmatic version of criminal liability might involve.

The same question could be raised with respect to governments, societies, and trade unions, and it amounts to whether we choose to think of the individuals in charge of these collective entities (company directors, government ministers, etc.), rather than of the organisation seen as an abstract entity.

In this day and age, where companies are more powerful than nation states, being responsible for the fate of tens of millions of people and indeed the ecological equilibrium of the planet, the traditional case for individual liability is becoming very weak. As Maurice Punch puts it, those who argue that organisations don't exist outside of the perceptions and actions of individuals ignore the social nature of collective behaviour. It is equally 'short-sighted to think of decision-making at the top of a major corporation as that of "individuals"; the executives have been groomed in the corporate culture and have been selected and shaped to function as a unit that works in the best interests of the company … In a very real social sense there are no "individuals" in organisations. In business, managers slot into the corporation, "leave their conscience at home" and do what the collective demands of them'.[29] The problem is that the law does not recognise this reality – the collective guilt of organisations; instead, it prefers to apply liability to individuals, rather than institutions. Criminal law in particular remains largely focused on individual rather than organisational liability. Even in those rare occasions where attempts were made to hold companies responsible for their crimes, prosecutions failed: Barings Bank, Herald of Free Enterprise, Ford Motor Company, Union Carbide – all unsuccessful. The law should move away from its focus on the individual, towards an 'aggregation theory of corporate liability', where aggregation represents 'a first step towards an approach to corporate criminal liability where a company's liability is not derivative, and where the company is liable in its own right for its own fault'.[30] Ultimately, corporate fault should be seen as totally separate and distinct from individual fault.

Assuming this to be a matter of general agreement (that we should aim towards making corporate liability possible and distinct from the individual one), let us consider the ways in which we should alter our conception of the criminal (from that centred around the old, metaphysical notion of *mens rea*, towards a more flexible one), so that the legal person can be viewed as criminally responsible without needing to be a full-blown self, with a conscience of its own.

I would like to start this discussion with an analysis of the current notion of 'the criminal', as implicit in the distinction between criminal and administrative liability in the UK, and then move on to consider how the new theoretical framework would differ from the current, rather rigid, one.

Features of criminal liability

Criminal liability differs from civil liability in respect of both scope and substance. In a criminal prosecution the state is the accuser, and the aim is legal accountability (or justice), rather than mere compensation. In a civil case an individual brings an action seeking damages from the alleged wrongdoer.

Insofar as the test of liability is concerned, criminal law typically requires proof of both *actus reus* (where conduct is the substance) and *mens rea* (a mental state, which in most cases is intent). There are two relevant mental states: intention (the most serious one), and recklessness (i.e., awareness of the risk). A third test of fault involves proof of gross negligence, which although not a mental state, often entails an enquiry into the state of mind of the individual. Therefore, what is needed in order to establish criminal liability is, on the one hand, a subjective test concerning the state of mind of the individual, and on the other, an objective test concerning only the level of negligence.

In the UK, the move from 'recklessness' to 'gross negligence' insofar as manslaughter is concerned took place in 1995, with the Adomako case.[31] The test of gross negligence requires proof of a duty of care (in the law of tort), a breach of that duty, that the breach is gross, and that the breach was a significant cause of the death. All these elements must be proven beyond reasonable doubt, unlike in civil law where liability can be based on proof by a balance of probabilities (roughly, a greater than 50 per cent likelihood of fault).

Under the old common law, in order to prosecute a company for corporate manslaughter, the *identification* test needed to be satisfied, which entailed proof that a person who was part of the controlling mind of a company had committed an offence that could then be imputed to the company. There was no separate way of assessing the guilt of a legal person, other than by assessing the guilt of an individual therein. This explains why the only companies to have been convicted are small ones,[32] because it is much easier to identify a senior manager who failed in his/her duty; for large and medium companies, the responsibility is diffused over multiple layers, hence it is much more difficult to identify a senior manager.

Under the new CMCH Act 2007, the key elements of the test are the same as before (duty of care, causation, and gross breach), but there is one big difference: only a substantial element of the breach must be at senior management level, so there is no need to identify an individual as the 'controlling mind' of the company. It is important to recognise that under the new statute, one need not look at a person first and foremost, but at the senior management of the organisation as a whole. And there is a whole range of factors which may be taken into consideration by a jury when assessing the guilt of the company (i.e. 'corporate culture', 'culture of complacency'). This broader test should help shift the emphasis from an individual to an organisational level. Indeed, according to some, due to this change of focus from individual to corporate behaviour, some of the manslaughter prosecutions that failed (i.e. Balfour Beatty and Network Rail in the Hatfield rail crash case) would have resulted in a conviction, had the new CMCH Act been in place at the time.[33]

But does it even matter whether a company is convicted of, say, health and safety charges (as in respect of Corus, Transco, and companies involved in major rail crashes) rather than corporate manslaughter? The short answer is, of course it matters: everything (from the burden of proof, through the level of failure and sanctions – hence, the degree of accountability and deterrence) is different, in the two types of cases. Fines, the only sanction available for health and safety, are not a deterrent; under the new CMCH Act, there are other sanctions available, such as publicity orders and remedial orders.

John Dugard recognises the great impact these differences between civil and criminal liability have on our perception of moral (and implicitly, criminal) responsibility:

> Civil law jurisdictions have in the past been unwilling to allow criminal liability to be imposed upon legal persons. Criminal law expressed and enforced the moral commitments of society. It punished a person who had committed an ethical wrong. Such a wrong could be committed only by a moral agent, one that had the capacity to comprehend ethical norms but nonetheless violates them. Corporations did not possess this quality: a corporation was not an agent vested with a conscience, or with consciousness of its actions. Therefore, according to this theory of criminal justice, corporations cannot be held accountable for their actions.[34]

However, according to the same author, this approach has recently shifted dramatically, under the influence of, *inter alia*, globalisation, and the rise of multinational corporations. France, Spain, the Netherlands, Belgium, Switzerland, Austria, and Italy have all introduced criminal punishments for corporations. But 'there are still certain civil law systems that do not attribute criminal liability as such to corporations. For example, Germany has not introduced criminal liability as that concept is understood in the common law'; Germany's system of administrative penalties does not have 'the specifically moral character of criminal sanctions.'[35] The same could be said about Sweden and the Czech Republic. (See the respective country reports in Part IV of this volume.)

Different authors interpret the general reluctance to allow criminal liability to be imposed upon legal persons in different ways, but most of them trace it back to modern philosophy. 'All the way until the end of the eighteenth century, criminal liability of collective entities had been a well-recognized and frequently practised phenomenon under the law applicable on the territory that today is Germany ... It was only in the wake of Immanuel Kant's individualistic understanding of responsibility that the notion of the criminal guilt of a corporation lost credit.'[36] Indeed, 17th- and 18th-century modernity as a whole is generally considered to have influenced our understanding of the law and justice, as centred on the individual: 'we inherit from this century our theories of rights, the modern tendency to frame the immunities accorded people by law in terms of subjective rights. This ... is a conception which puts the autonomous individual at the centre of our system of laws.'[37] Regardless of how we interpret the philosophical roots of current legal theory, the fact remains that acknowledging collective, organisational responsibility has long been an important challenge for most criminal systems.

A 'sense' of the good

The more flexible conception of criminal justice that I referred to earlier (viewed as an alternative to the traditional, metaphysical one) would have to be based on a pragmatist conception of ethics in general. Charles Taylor could be considered one of the champions of such a theory. For him, having a sense of the self and having a sense of the good are closely interconnected. Self-identity presupposes a kind of moral orientation: 'To know who you are is to be oriented in a moral space, a space in which questions arise about what is good or bad, what is worth doing and what not, what has meaning and importance for you and what is trivial and secondary ... But to be able to answer for oneself is to know where one stands, what one wants to answer'.[38] And the questions to be answered are all moral ones.

One might argue that this conception, too, springs from deeply metaphysical beliefs in something like a human nature and the permanence of that, which gives substance and meaning to the self (moral values); and one of the main influences in Taylor is, indeed, Hegel's philosophy. However, these would-be metaphysical assumptions are not essential to his ethical view, whose silver lining remains the interconnectedness of our sense of the good with that of the self. For any person (be that natural or legal) to be aware of itself and coherent in its self-perception, it has to have a moral orientation, regardless of whether the latter can be seen to be grounded in a moral 'conscience'. This is the key difference between Taylor's conception and those of classic philosophers, whose views we looked at previously. And the reason why this is such a key difference is because it allows us to imagine an entity which, although it lacks the features of the modern self, has nonetheless a moral orientation – and thereby, can become subject to moral (possibly even criminal) liability.

If Taylor is the foremost proponent of pragmatist ethics, Michael Sandel is the one who puts it into practice by constantly discussing ethical issues in everyday contemporary life situations, while Susan Wolf applies it to the very issue of corporate criminal liability: 'The most obvious and most central question we need to answer is, Are organisations ever morally blameworthy themselves or is the apparent blameworthiness of organisations always more properly regarded as a function of the blameworthiness of some or all the individuals in it? The question could be rephrased as, Are organisations full-fledged, irreducible moral agents?'[39]

I don't believe this to be the answer to our dilemma, because I take the view that a company as a holistic entity is greater and more powerful than its directors, officers and staff. This is what Wells and Wolf call the *organic* view of organisational responsibility, which considers that the moral responsibility of an organisation is not reducible to that of its members (as opposed to the *atomic* view, which sees the responsibility ascribed to organisations as derivative – that is, a function of the responsibility of the members). General support is much stronger for the atomic view than for the organic, and Wolf herself supports the atomic view. If we take the organic view – as Celia Wells does – then we can apply criminal law directly to organisations, because they can be as guilty of crimes as individuals. If the atomic view is correct, then we shouldn't use criminal law against organisations.

Wolf's conclusion is that, although companies can't be held responsible in a *deeply moral* way because of their lack of consciousness, we can still hold them liable in a *causal* way (i.e. in the sense that we say the cat is responsible for the spilt milk). They can be practically responsible, and this matters more than whether they can be morally responsible or not. They can be held to assume the risks of possible costs of their actions, because 'although organisations lack the capacity to be motivated to adopt moral goals and constraints, they have the capacity to be guided by them. Since they have this capacity, there seems no reason not to insist that they exercise it. That is, it is not unreasonable to hold organisations practically responsible, to insist that they be liable for covering the costs and paying the consequences for the harmful and immoral actions they perform'.[40] They can be practically responsible because they have cognitive capacity (the capacity to be sensitive and responsive to complex reasons for and against various actions). In other words, one [legal person] can be morally responsible without necessarily having a moral conscience, but the implication of this is that we should only ascribe civil, rather than criminal liability to it. Personally, I don't find this a satisfactory solution to the issue of the relationship between moral and criminal responsibility, either in theory or in practice.

Wells has a more elaborate approach to this dilemma: first, she argues that organisations are indeed more than the sum of individuals working for them. Second, she notes the difficulties involved in using an anthropomorphic notion such as 'moral blame' in discussions about criminal liability, and suggests better alternatives. One such alternative way of framing corporate criminal liability would be to use the notion of 'accountability' instead of 'moral blame', and functional criteria for culpability, rather than a metaphysical association between the human mind and corporate rationality.[41] My only concern with this proposal is that, without appropriate policies and regulations to accompany it in practice, it could remain a mere theoretical exercise, without much impact on the perception and applicability of corporate criminal responsibility. But if we can find ways of putting it into practice (i.e., what I like to call 'pragmatist' criteria – see the conclusion below), it could lead to a better understanding and enforcement of criminal law applied to legal persons.

Conclusion

The key question raised in this chapter has been twofold: what are the main features of a moral agent, and, should an abstract entity (such as a legal person) fail to display those, would that mean it cannot or should not be held criminally accountable, given the general perception that there is a strong link between criminal and moral responsibility? Having identified three essential features of moral agency – a sense of the self, a free-will, and a moral conscience – and analysed the extent to which legal persons can be said to display these, we found that they lack at least one of them – namely, a moral conscience (1).

We then briefly considered Susan Wolf's proposition that, because (1) is the case, we should refrain from holding companies criminally accountable, and subject them to what she calls practical (that is, civil) liability only (2).

Since I don't agree, however, with proposition (2) above, I suggested that we should revise our understanding of 'the criminal' and what criminal liability entails, from an intrinsically moral notion with metaphysical implications (in particular, about its 'moral conscience' as a root of *mens rea*), to a more contextual one, in order to be able to apply it to collective legal entities such as organisations. In a way, this revision could be seen as something similar to what happened with our understanding of science during the Enlightenment, or with our understanding of language in post-modernity: we should bring it down to earth, make it contextual and susceptible to be constantly revised – rather than strictly dependent on some abstract mentalist notions that don't fit the reality of the corporate world.

Michael Sandel discussed the issue of markets' morals not in general, but with reference to examples from everyday life, such as the morality of paying people to do two kinds of work – fighting wars and bearing children. 'Thinking through the rights and wrongs of markets in these contested cases will help us clarify the differences among leading theories of justice.'[42] By invoking such controversial situations, the author highlights the weaknesses of two major conceptions of justice, which are normally used to support the case for free markets: the libertarian belief that free markets stimulate individual freedom, and the utilitarian view that free markets promote general welfare. What this kind of approach shows is that, while well and good in theory, such claims can prove problematic in relation to real-life situations: the case of the hired soldier makes us wonder how free are the choices we make in the so-called 'free market' society, while the issue of outsourcing surrogacy reminds us that some goods, values, and social practices are degraded if bought and sold for money, and they should be left out of the markets game.

The reason I mentioned Michael Sandel's way of thinking about justice theories is to show how important it is to keep questioning those concepts and theories that we take for granted, by putting them into practice and testing them in light of real-life case scenarios. This is similar with what Rawls referred to as 'reflective equilibrium',[43] the constantly flipping back and forth between theory and one's existing judgements, except in this case the suggested dialectic is between theory and real-world situations. The issue that we looked at in this chapter – to what extent organisations' criminal liability presupposes a deep moral responsibility, thereby the presence of a moral agent – should be discussed by reference to socio-legal circumstances, rather than old anthropomorphic notions such as *actus reus* and *mens rea*.

But what are the wider implications of the conclusion that legal persons don't have (or should not be described as having) a moral conscience? Does this mean we should not expect them to act in a moral way? One might argue that, on the contrary, collective entities need not be human like, to behave ethically, or else, all hope for responsible governments and moral institutions would be lost. And it may well be true that some of them do, sometimes, act in a responsible way. But is it in their nature to do so? I would think rather not. And we should cautiously assume that, because they are not human-like, they are not designed to behave morally. Since this is hardly a theoretical issue and can potentially have disastrous effects on society, we should have socio-economic and regulatory mechanisms in place to supervise their behaviour and put it right, where it errs.

References

Cooper, J.M., ed. (1997), Plato, *Complete Works*. Indianapolis, USA and Cambridge, UK: Hackett

Dugard, J. (2009), Amicus Brief on whether international law recognises corporate criminal liability, 22 December, http://www.essex.ac.uk/cwcn/humanrights.html

Hazarika, S. (1987), *Bhopal: The Lessons of a Tragedy*. New Delhi: Penguin Books

Hegel, G.W.F. (2003), *Phenomenology of Mind*. New York: Dover Publications

Heidegger, M. (1978), *Being and Time*. Malden, USA, Oxford, UK, and Carlton, Australia: Blackwell Publishing

MacIntyre, A. (1984), *After Virtue: A Study in Moral Theory*. Indiana: University of Notre Dame Press

Mill, J.S. (2007), *Utilitarianism*, Filiquarian Publishing, LLC

Rawls, J. (1978), *A Theory of Justice*. Oxford: Oxford University Press

Sandel, M.J. (2009), *Justice: What's the Right Thing to Do?* London: Allen Lane

Sterba, J.P., ed. (1998), *Ethics: The Big Questions*. Malden, MA and Oxford, UK: Blackwell

Taylor, C. (1994), *Sources of the Self: The Making of the Modern Identity*. Cambridge, MA: Harvard University Press

Weigend, T. (2008), 'Societas delinquere non potest? A German Perspective', *Journal of International Criminal Justice*, 6 (2008), 927–945

Wells, C. (1993), *Corporations and Criminal Responsibility*. Oxford: Clarendon Press

Wolf, S. (1985), 'The legal and moral responsibility of organizations', in Pennock, J.R. and Chapman, J.W., eds., *Criminal Justice: Nomos XXVII*. New York University Press

Notes

1   Some modern offences are completely unrelated to morality. There is nothing moral or immoral, for instance, in driving on the right rather than the left side of the road. Many corporate offences, such as the permissible maximum hours that one can work per week, and some health and safety offences, are based on social policy, rather than morality. Despite this, however, the general perception remains that there is a strong link between criminal and moral responsibility. 'The criminal law has a closer (or different) relation to morality than the civil law. In particular, the criminal law may be associated with moral blameworthiness in a way that civil law may not' (Wolf 1985: 268).

2   Although many *mala in se* crimes are grounded in morality (i.e. murder, theft, rape), some moral prohibitions (i.e. adultery, homosexuality) are no longer considered criminal.

3   Taylor 1994.

4   R. Descartes, *Letters to Elisabeth*, quoted by Taylor 1994: 147.

5   J. Locke, *Essay*, 2.27.10.

6   Ibid., 2.27.16.

7   Ibid., 2.27.18.

8   See Heidegger 1978: sections 12, 26–29, 31–34, 39–41.

9   Taylor 1994: 265.

10 I. Kant, *Foundations of the Metaphysics of Morals*, p. 412, cit by Taylor 1994: 364–5.

11 Plato's daemons are gods or children of the gods (*Apology* 27d-e) or messengers from the gods (*Symposium* 202e), who guide people. They are 'responsible for mediation between gods and humans, and should be highly honoured in our prayers for bringing words of good tiding' (*Epinomis*, 984e). 'Now those who were inspired by a good daemon during their lifetimes go to reside in a place for the pious' (*Axioclus*, 371c). As Socrates says, 'daemons are wise and knowing', so 'every good man (…) is daemonic' (*Cratylus*, 398b-c), because knowledge and morality go together. See Cooper 1997.

12 Mill 2007: 14.

13 I. Kant's 'Fundamental Principles of the Metaphysic of Morals' in *Critique of Practical Reason and Other Works on the Theory of Ethics*, 6th edn, London: Longmans, 1909, quoted in Sterba 1998: 173–4.

14 MacIntyre 1984: 122–3.

15 Ibid: 190–1.

16 More information is available on Amnesty International's website: http://www. amnesty.org/en/news-and-updates/news/oil-industry-has-brought-poverty-and-pollution-to-niger-delta-20090630

17 See section IV.A of the *Phenomenology of Mind*, 'The Independence and Dependence of Self-consciousness: Lordship and Bondage', in Hegel 2003: 104sq.

18 Ibid: 104.

19 Taylor 1994: 28.

20 Ibid: 33.

21 Ibid: 50.

22 For more information, go to http://news.bbc.co.uk/1/hi/england/4066331.stm
23 This record is now being challenged by the environmental disaster recently caused by BP.
24 See http://studentsforbhopal.org/learn
25 Sentencing took place on 7 June 2010 in an Indian Court. For further information see http://news.bbc.co.uk/1/hi/world/south_asia/8725140.stm
26 The former had a strong hold on the latter. 'The American firm held a majority ownership of the company. No major decisions could be taken without its consent and consultation. When UCIL wanted to sell its Bombay plastics unit in 1983, the decision had to be cleared by headquarters. Its annual budget had to be cleared by UCC as well. The fact that such close links existed between UCIL and the parent company UCC made the buck passing that ensued post Bhopal all the more unfortunate' (Hazarika 1987: 139).
27 http://www1.american.edu/TED/class/allcrime.htm#crime7
28 I am borrowing this distinction from P. French, cf. C. Wells: 'It is helpful initially to break down the notion of personhood, as French does, into three types: the metaphysical, the moral, and the legal' (Wells 1993: 86).
29 M. Punch, 'The Organisational Component in Corporate Crime' (Chapter 6 of this volume).
30 Ibid.
31 For an in-depth analysis of this case, see J. Gobert, 'Squaring the Circle: The Relationship between Individual and Organisational Fault' (Chapter 8 of this volume).
32 Only eight companies (all small) have ever been convicted of manslaughter in England and Wales; only one company was prosecuted, but not convicted, in Scotland: Transco PLC; no company has ever been convicted in Northern Ireland (Statistics as of 3 September 2008, available at: http://www.corporateaccountability.org/manslaughter/cases/convictions.htm).
33 Cf. Richard Lissack's talk at the CCA conference on 'Corporate Manslaughter, Directors Duties, and Safety Enforcement', Hamilton House, London, 19 November 2007.
34 Dugard 2009: 3.
35 Ibid: 3–4.
36 Weigend 2008: 930.
37 Taylor 1994: 195.
38 Ibid: 28.
39 Wolf 1985: 268.
40 Ibid: 282.
41 Wells 1993: 88–90.
42 Sandel 2009: 75.
43 Rawls 1978: 48–50.

3 The challenges of regulating powerful economic actors

Laureen Snider and Steven Bittle

In 2008 the latest financial bubble burst. One by one, the pillars of Wall Street and their equivalents in capitals around the world began to default on their debt obligations and collapse. As soon as the major financial institutions of the western world and its most esteemed and profitable corporations – J.P. Morgan, Lehman Brothers, Bank of Scotland, Merrill Lynch, Bank of America, Bear Stearns, Fanny Mae, Freddie Mack – were threatened with bankruptcy, governments leapt to the rescue, pledging billions of dollars of taxpayer monies to 'save' them from the consequences of their own mismanagement and fraud. The victims of their risky and illegal financial manoeuvres – the thousands who lost their homes to foreclosed mortgages, whose jobs disappeared, whose pension and savings were wiped out – received no such largesse. What explains this instantaneous – and generous – government response?

Sadly, this pattern of states rescuing corporations in trouble, forgiving their offences and awarding them second (and third and fourth) chances is anything but unusual. To study the regulation of business is to realize that equally harmful acts are not equally punished. While numerous studies have shown that the illegal acts of corporations cause more injury and death per year than 'garden variety' assault and homicide, and easily fifty times as much financial loss as the thieves and muggers who fill You-Tube videos and newspapers (Pearce and Tombs 1998; Slapper and Tombs 1999; Rosoff, Pontell and Tillman 2006; Snider 1993, 2009), the sanctions visited on business criminals are very different. Many researchers have tried to explain the relative absence of criminal sanctions for corporate offences, citing the complex nature of most corporate crimes, the lack of expertise and lenience of judges and juries, difficulties residing in the *mens rea* requirements of Western criminal statutes, the challenges of finding responsible parties and proving criminal liability in a multi-layered corporate structure, the expense of criminal proceedings, and more (Braithwaite 2005; Gunningham *et al.* 2003; Haines and Sutton 2003; Parker 2002; Shearing 1993; Shapiro 1984). Criminalizing the corporation – holding it and its executives accountable for fraud, theft, negligence, injury, and manslaughter and the economic and human damage caused – is expensive for governments in a number of ways. At the economic level, because corporations have entire legal departments poised to exploit every legal loophole, investigations may drag on so long that they consume the entire annual budget of the regulators. From a political perspective, prosecuting business, especially big business, can cost governments votes, donations and electoral support. Targeted businesses often threaten to close down or move to a less restrictive regime, putting crucial jobs and tax income at risk. And the business sector is well positioned to ensure that governments it sees as 'unreasonable' are publicly branded as 'anti-business' or (the worst slander of all) 'socialist'.

The special treatment accorded corporate crime can be seen in differential statutes and sanctions. If you kill someone accidentally in a car because you were speeding or failed to notice a car in your blind spot, you could be liable to criminal negligence charges which carry, on conviction, significant jail time and/ or fines. If you kill someone accidentally in a mine because you (or more typically a distant management committee) decided that installing safety equipment would jeopardize the quarterly profit statement, the chances are good that you will never be hit with criminal charges or serve any time in prison. The same holds true if your corporation killed or injured people by marketing an experimental drug prematurely. If corporate negligence is unambiguous and high profile, if the best efforts of your team of lawyers fail, if the responsibility-hiding complexities of hierarchy provide insufficient camouflage, if a *nolo contendere* or similar no-fault plea is not available, a couple of designated senior officers and/or the corporation itself may be fined. In most cases the fine will be minuscule compared with the profits generated and the injuries caused by the offence. And since most corporate offences – including acts that defraud, injure, and kill through dangerous working conditions or toxic dumps – are classified as administrative or regulatory acts and handled by special tribunals, corporate actors seldom have to face the degradation, stigma, and publicity signified by the criminal justice process.

Victims of corporate crime are also disadvantaged. Should you be defrauded in a Ponzi scheme, injured in the course of your job, sickened by illegally dumped toxic waste, inadequately regulated pesticides or unsafe food, it is unlikely you will ever face the offending party in court. Workers injured on the job may receive some compensation while recovering (only if they are covered by Workers' Compensation), but will have to make do with a fraction of their usual wages. Those who are not unionized and have no access to compensation have the right to sue their employers, but that is a costly route fraught with difficulties in terms of proving the company acted illegally and that the injury or illness is in fact work-related (a particularly daunting task in cases of industrial disease). If your losses are monetary rather than physical, you will find that getting your money back and having your day in court are equally unlikely (Kivenko 2010). Misleading investors or consumers through false advertising, refusing to pay the minimum wage or overtime are technically illegal (though not criminal) in all Anglo-American countries, but enforcement, if a police matter at all, is a very low priority. And if the fraudulent act was committed by a corporation, several liability-avoiding options are available to it, including bankruptcy, which typically favours other large corporations and governments as the secured creditors who receive the lion's share of what is available. In high-profile financial scams where a particular fraudster (an 'overenthusiastic' mutual funds seller, for example) can be identified and a scapegoat is required, the offender may face jail time – which returns no compensation to victims. In some jurisdictions (the United States being the most conspicuous example), class action suits are legal. If your 'side' is successful, you will be entitled to receive back some portion of what you lost – but expect years of appeals and watch your compensation shrink as lawyers' fees and court costs mount.

What causes these glaring inequalities between corporate crime and traditional theft, assault and homicide? This paper argues that the answer lies, in part, in understanding the triangle of mutually constitutive forms of discipline – regulation, criminal law and Corporate Social Responsibility (CSR) – that govern corporate crime. The struggle between these disciplinary forms produces a precarious, ever-changing juggling act, a regulatory dance (Snider 1991). Trigger events such as the fiscal disasters of 2000 (the bursting of the new technology bubble) and more recently the 2008–09 meltdown, have starkly illustrated the limits of the free market, putting increased pressure on regulators and governments to toughen regulation and criminal law, the disciplinary strategies they ostensibly control. But neo-liberal doctrines, which have dominated the corporate disciplinary landscape for the past twenty years, have promoted cooperative, non-punitive responses to corporate crime and seriously weakened these tools both ideologically and politically. The third corner of this triangle, the disciplining of corporations through strategies of CSR, is also a battleground of warring social movements, NGOs and businesses, each vying to promote its favourite remedies. This paper argues that variously constituted forms of resistance to disciplining the corporation have gained the upper hand, and shows how and why this has happened.

Shaping the triangle: understanding the 'common sense' of corporate crime

To understand how this triangle came to be, we must examine the historical practices that shaped western law and culture. Government reluctance to control and sanction the harmful acts of business is deeply rooted in the culture and belief systems of capitalist societies. When the first Factory Acts were debated in the 19th century in England, the very *idea* that any of the profit-seeking activities of business could be considered immoral or criminal was revolutionary. The business classes insisted the state had no right to oversee any element of business practice. In their view, this was an abrogation of the near-sovereign rights of ownership enshrined in English common law, where those who owned the factories and machines assumed their God-given right to control everything in that workplace. If the owner did not want to pay more than ten cents a day, put guards on machinery, provide safety equipment, lunch breaks or ventilation, this was his business (literally and figuratively). Nor did the employee have any right to protest, much less organize co-workers: he or she had 'freely' chosen to work here, which meant they agreed to the working conditions. When religious and political militants ('radicals' and 'socialists' to the employer classes) began pointing out that thousands of workers were losing arms, legs, and lives to unsafe machinery,

10-year-olds were deprived of their childhoods, and that 85-hour work-weeks in fibre-filled air and unventilated workplaces were producing women too unhealthy to reproduce, state leaders were in a quandary. Official policy throughout the 19th century was to celebrate the accomplishments of capitalism while ignoring its costs. This was made easier by the fact that law-makers themselves were seldom required, in their normal life-cycles, to acknowledge or experience the difficult lives of the working class. Criminal law, the prison and the workhouse were reserved for the feckless, inebriate, and larcenous – in other words, the poacher, prostitute, thief or drunken Irish immigrant who overfilled the institutions of Victorian England. And criminals were those who stole from propertied gentlemen, not the gentlemen themselves (Carson 1970, 1980; Thompson 1963; Paulus 1974; Tucker 1988).

But by the last quarter of the century, decades of activism – the tales of novelists such as Dickens, the reform efforts of Quakers and other clerics, early feminists keen to rescue the 'fallen' working class girl, socialists and the nascent union movement – had split the English bourgeoisie. And many who did not buy into humanitarian arguments were persuaded to go along because the political situation was becoming dangerous, with socialist notions gaining strength and unrest mounting. Thus laws were passed, initially laughably weak, but over time the idea that capitalism needed limits became established in common law and the public mind.

Because stock markets were originally established to serve corporate interests, stock market reform has a different history, though the reluctance to 'interfere' with business practice was equally strong. Three centuries ago, when the values and practices of a land-based aristocracy were still in place, the basic principles of stock markets – dispersed ownership and publicly sold shares through the vehicle of the corporation – aroused suspicion. Incorporation (limited liability) began as a privilege granted by the nation-state, a purchased privilege with specific obligations and responsibilities. Adam Smith himself warned against the dangers of the limited company and the perils of allowing control to be separated from ownership. Incorporation should only be allowed, he said, under circumstances where the interests of management coincided with those of investors/owners (Smith 1994/1776). At this time stock trading was viewed as suspect, disreputable, too closely related to gambling. The concepts that make up the basic understandings, the 'common sense' of the financial establishment today were seen then as incompatible with the moral and religious principles of the day. Decades of legal and ideological battles and the transformation of the land-based aristocracy into an industrial bourgeoisie changed the corporate form from a privilege into a right (Glasbeek 2002), and it quickly became something states compete to confer, a contest where each country promises the least amount of regulation – hence the present-day dominance of incorporation havens such as Liberia and the Cayman Islands. By the dawn of the twenty-first century, stock market exchange and the manipulation of money (financial capitalism) had ascended to the cultural and political apex: in 2006, before the latest bubble burst, the financial sector in the USA accounted for 40 per cent of total corporate profits (Foster 2010).

Predictably, then, government regulation of stock markets and the financial sector developed slowly, reluctantly, and only in response to financial scams and disasters. The culture, history and political economy of different states resulted in widely varying systems of regulation and control. In Canada, governments in the 19th and 20th centuries saw themselves as facing two conflicting realities: 'nation-building' required them to attract investment, seen as essential to develop natural resources and ensure growth and prosperity. However the industries involved, particularly the pivotal mining industry, showed a lamentable, repeated susceptibility to fraud. This threatened investor confidence and thus the very basis of the system. On top of this difficulty, the division of powers enshrined in the British North America Act (BNA Act) and the conflicts and rivalries of the provinces *versus* the federal government made it impossible for the central government to set up a federal regulatory regime (Condon 1998). Thus each province and territory established its own regulatory system. Today there are thirteen, each with its own laws, jurisdiction, powers, budget and capabilities. Not surprisingly, duplication of efforts and turf battles are endemic, despite the efforts of the umbrella organization, the Canadian Securities Administrators, at 'harmonization'. Scores of federal governments have attempted to persuade or coerce the provinces to cede power to one federal regulatory agency, creating something analogous to the American Securities and Exchange Commission. Indeed the most recent initiative, announced by federal Finance Minister Jim Flaherty on June 23, 2009, is ongoing. Alberta and Quebec (and British Columbia, until Flaherty appointed the Chairman of its Securities Commission Douglas Hyndman to spearhead federal efforts) are the most vociferous opponents.

While Canadian governments in the 1960s and 70s never took corporate theft and assault as seriously as 'ordinary' theft and assault, activist movements at that time succeeded in getting regulations governing business passed (such as provisions expanding the Combines Investigation Act), and new ministries established (such as the federal Ministry of the Environment). However, in 1980 the United States under Reagan and the United Kingdom under Thatcher brought in neo-liberal philosophies of government that advocated getting rid of as much business regulation as possible. In transportation, competition, finance and the environment, laws restricting business were weakened or abolished. Privatization and budget cuts further diminished regulatory oversight and destroyed agency capability – if there are fewer watchers, less will be seen. Under the aegis of 'regulatory reform', sovereign states throughout the developed world, while nominally fine-tuning their de-regulatory strategies to accommodate the socio-political realities in each country, reacted in similar ways. In a quest to lower taxes and (they said) remain competitive in a globalized world, 'Red Tape' Commissions or their equivalents were established to 'set business free'. The free market, free trade and competition, we were told, would set standards, determine prices and wages, and punish bad business behaviour more efficiently than governments, and at less cost.

Thus throughout the 1980s and 90s all the Anglo-American democratic states massively expanded punishment for thefts and assaults by individuals through mandatory minimum prison sentences, zero-tolerance rhetoric and 'three strikes' laws, while punishment for the harms caused by business decreased (Garland 2001; Wacquant 2001). While incarceration rates doubled and tripled for the mostly poor, mostly powerless thieves and consumers of illegal drugs and the nets of criminal justice expanded, business criminals were deemed to merit education, counselling and non-criminal, non-publicized administrative penalties. The cultural compulsion to punish, it appeared, stopped at the door of the executive suite. The illegal acts of those who misrepresent the risk level or profit prospects of the mines they are running or the stock market funds or houses they are selling have generally been presented to various publics as atypical 'bad apples' in a corporate barrel assumed to be overwhelmingly 'good'.

Blaming the victim, so out of fashion in cases of traditional crime where the victim is now entitled to compensation, counselling and his/her day in court, is still the most common response to its corporate equivalent. In law and in culture, '*caveat emptor*' discourses are employed to shift the blame for fraudulent practices from the institutions that profit from it to those who are swindled by it. This cultural, political and economic blindness is facilitated by many of the 'experts' in the area: it is common for lawyers and economists to present regulatory law and criminal law as justifiably different – offences covered under the former are designated as *mala prohibita* (wrong because prohibited) while traditional criminal offences are *mala in se* (wrong in themselves). The regulatory corner of the disciplinary triangle therefore fits well with the dominant notion of corporate wrongdoing: the notion that these acts were best dealt with through various forms of cooperation and self-regulation that would encourage corporate actors to see the error of their ways and voluntarily take the necessary steps to avoid future offending.

Updating the triangle: regulation, law and financial crises

In the deregulatory climate of the 1980s and 90s, banks and insurance companies in the United States, the centre of the global economy, lobbied heavily and ultimately successfully to rid themselves of rules restricting where and how each could invest, the products they could sell, and the capital cushion each had to maintain. New, highly profitable instruments to entice investors were invented and marketed around the world: derivatives, a class of trading assets, and hedge funds, a mode of trading beyond regulatory purview, were foremost among these. With risk hidden and regulatory oversight largely eliminated, money from foreign and domestic investments flowed in. Much of it went into mortgages, offered (in the United States) with no down payment and low but rapidly escalating interest rates. Rating agencies did their part by awarding many of these highly risky vehicles double- or triple-A ratings. Real estate prices soared. Bank executives, finance and investment firms reaped millions of dollars in fees, salaries and bonuses. Eventually, as is always the case, the cycle of prosperity slowed, the real estate bubble burst and the reckless investment decisions, mismanagement, fraud and shady accounting manoeuvres that made the boom possible were revealed. A global financial crisis resulted.

Suddenly, as with the dot-com crash of 2000, the Savings and Loans crisis in the 1980s, the junk bond crisis and many more, corporate crime became newsworthy. Electronic and print media buzzed with articles, blogs and video clips bemoaning regulatory failure, urging each of the three sides of the disciplinary triangle – regulation, criminal law and CSR – to crack down (from centre-left voices) or warning governments not to 'over-react' (from business and the right). Experts in law, criminology, accounting and business management promoted new remedies and touted new courses on CSR. The publishing industry swung into high gear with books and articles on fraudsters such as Bernie Madoff, the downfall of Lehman Brothers, the complicity of CitiBank, and more (Arvedlund 2009; Kirtzman 2009; McDonald 2009; Oppenheimer 2009). Legal experts, standard-setting bodies and professional associations sprung into action – or at least into rhetoric – pledging reforms that would fix the financial system once and for all.

Similar reform chatter, with similar promises to really crack down 'this time', has followed every such crisis. These efforts have generally been cyclical and weak. The cultural permission to institute meaningful regulation and structural reform typically lasts only as long as the media buzz. Resistance and anti-regulatory lobbying mount – champions of corporate interests are already accusing Obama, Brown, Sarkozy and Merkel of overreacting, despite the fact that the only definitive actions they have taken thus far have been to rescue these same corporations from the consequences of their own folly (Grace Benn 2010; Krugman 2010; McKenna 2010).

We can reasonably predict the results of the latest corporate meltdown and global crisis by looking at its predecessor, the 2001–02 dot-com stock market meltdown. Like all well-publicized corporate disasters, the systemic, routinized corporate frauds revealed by the collapse of Enron, WorldCom etc. produced state-sponsored 'crackdowns' in law, the relevant professions, standard-setting organizations and SROs (Self-Regulatory Organizations). In the United States, the pivotal Sarbanes–Oxley Act (SOX) was passed in 2002. SOX increased reporting requirements, penalties and oversight over audits, financial reports, corporate counsel, senior executives and Boards of Directors. The federal government of Canada was forced by its close ties to US markets, the passage of SOX and Canada's long-standing reputation for lenient enforcement, to take similar action. Cognisant of the provincial nature of regulation, the federal government in 2003 authorized the national police force, the RCMP (Royal Canadian Mounted Police), to establish Integrated Market Enforcement Teams (IMET) to 'detect, investigate and prevent' serious capital market fraud. Each multidisciplinary unit would have specialists in accounting, economics and law enforcement. On February 12, 2004, Bill C-13 was passed, criminalizing insider trading and 'tipping', and increasing maximum penalties for 'market manipulation'. Non-governmental self-regulatory and standard-setting bodies responded similarly. The Toronto Stock Exchange, the Investment Dealers Association, and the Canadian Venture Exchange (now the TSX Venture Exchange) issued guidelines 'urging' security analysts and mutual fund dealers to adopt new conflict of interest rules. The Canadian Bar Association tightened ethics rules for corporate counsel. The Canadian Coalition for Good Governance, formed in June 2002, recommended measures 'to provide more power, oversight and independence to boards of directors and audit committees'. In 2005, Ontario amended the Securities Act to facilitate investor suits in hopes of activating a civil law deterrent (Snider 2009; Glasbeek 2002).

What were the effects of this wholesale crackdown on corporate crime? Like reform bills today, SOX and Bill C-13 were aimed at rescuing business from its own excesses. Despite this, business resistance was protracted, unrelenting, and ultimately successful. By 2008, when the latest credit crisis/market meltdown occurred, a number of the 2002 reform measures had been rescinded: the reform-minded William Donaldson, appointed Chair of the Securities and Exchange Commission (SEC) in 2002, was replaced by a Wall Street insider more sympathetic to industry concerns, Christopher Cox. The pivotal Independent Public Company Accounting Oversight Board revised its auditing rules to 'lessen the auditing burden' on corporations. These 'burdensome', 'unnecessary' provisions had in fact revealed that more than 8 per cent of all listed companies, in the 2005 fiscal year alone, had previously issued 'misleading' (that is, false) earnings statements (McKenna 2007).

Canada also backtracked in response to corporate pressure. Shortly after a high-profile conviction on an insider-trading case was overturned on appeal, the largest and most influential securities regulator in the country, the Ontario Securities Commission, announced it was 'rethinking' its enforcement strategies, particularly the use of criminal law. As its Vice-Chair mused, 'it may be that you just cannot get insider trading convictions in a criminal court' because 'the standard of proof is so high'. Her preferred solution to this problem was not to persuade the government to reform the problematic statutes, it was to retreat. In interviews conducted in 2006 (Snider 2009: 184), another stock market regulator declared: 'the pendulum is now swinging back'; 'there's the belief ... that Enron measures went too far' (Snider 2009: 184; also see Tillman and Indergaard 2005).

The IMETs, the federal government's most visible and tangible initiative to increase convictions for financial fraud, also floundered. Although the IMETs had healthy budgets (compared with past efforts in this area), 'fenced funding' – monies were reserved exclusively for securities fraud investigations and the latest technological tools – PROOF (Priority Rating of Operating Criteria) to assess and prioritize cases, and MICA (Market Integrity Computer Analysis), with real time capabilities, no arrests were made for over two years, and their first arrest was a man with 'no fixed address' charged with selling 17 securities certificates from unclaimed accounts for $370,000 (RCMP News Release, May 13, 2004). Hardly a major financial player. Not until June 2008 were charges announced in any of their high-profile cases.[1] To date, only a handful of convictions have been registered.[2]

The third side of the triangle: constituting corporate social responsibility

The political, economic and ideological tsunami arising from fiscal crises also washes over disciplinary realms traditionally distanced from the state, Corporate Social Responsibility (CSR) foremost among them. Considered a virtue of good corporate citizenship, CSR has occupied a prominent role within the corporate disciplinary triangle, resonating well with preferred models of self-regulation and frequently promoted as a means of responding to corporate wrongdoing. As Glasbeek (2002: 187) reminds us, faced with calls for improved corporate discipline, stakeholders from the CSR movement will argue (desperately) that it is imperative to find ways to 'force corporations to behave more altruistically or else we are lost' (also see Christian Aid 2004; Corporate Watch 2006). This section of the paper will examine a number of the key constitutive factors at work. CSR, defined as the 'voluntary adoption by business of "responsible" practices beyond the demands of law' (McBarnet 2006: 1105), has grown exponentially over the past 15 years, not least at the rhetorical level (Athanasiou 1996; Lubbers 2002; Shamir 2004 and 2005; Burchell and Cook 2006).

Here again, the adoption of neo-liberal practices facilitated its expansion. As states retreated from their traditional responsibilities for citizen well-being, corporations came under increased pressure to pick up the slack. Problems were created when governments became unable or unwilling to force employers to provide benefits, pay adequate wages or obey environmental laws. To fill this regulatory void, business came under pressure to voluntarily take on these responsibilities. In the financial sector, state underfunding or abolition of universal pensions and health care forced many to try to provide for their own security. In most Anglo-American democracies the state encouraged investment in financial markets. 'Citizen capitalism' was further promoted by removing regulatory restrictions to provide more financial products and encourage competition between/among companies (Barry, Osborne and Rose 1996; Fudge and Cossman 2002; Pearce and Tombs 1998).

The Canadian government dismantled its 'four pillars' of economic regulation, the laws preventing any single financial sector from offering financial products in any other sector, in 1987. This deregulation enabled banks to sell mutual funds, insurance companies and security firms to offer banking services and so on. By the 1990s truly globalized trading markets facilitated further expansion: 'between 1980 and 2000, private capital flows ... increased more than six-fold to nearly US$4 trillion annually worldwide' (Phelps *et al.* 2003). Takeovers, friendly and unfriendly, built ever-larger oligopolies. In Canada in 2002, 777 companies accounted for 98 per cent of all market capitalization (worth more than $75m), but 60 companies controlled over half of this. Citizens became increasingly dependent on investment products. Forty-six per cent of adult Canadians owned publicly listed securities in 2003, up 23 per cent from 1990 figures.[3] Stock-holdings in 2003 accounted for 20 per cent of total household assets per family. And these percentages are small compared with countries such as the United States (Phelps *et al.* 2003: 6; Report on Business Magazine 2004).[4]

As public interest in the integrity of markets and public vulnerability to their ups and downs grew, calls for greater corporate transparency and financial accountability mounted. Mainstream newspapers such as the *New York Times* and the *Globe and Mail* began compiling charts rating company performance on a number of 'good governance' measures and publishing CSR 'scores'. While many 24-hour business channels acted as cheerleaders for the corporate world, some did not. With the maturing of the internet, pressure groups in the real and virtual worlds began to monitor and publicize corporate fraud, arrogance, lack of transparency and bloated executive salaries. Faulty products and corporate refusal to act on warranties have spawned numerous 'Corporation X sucks' type websites. Ever alert to new opportunities for profit, more and more commercial CSR packages came onto the market, offering management training courses, software packages, and more. All of this has increased pressure on business for more transparency, higher ethical standards and more responsible behaviour.

The business sector overall, and blue-ribbon corporations in particular, have responded by embracing the discourses and rhetorics of CSR. Many corporations have set up and funded umbrella organizations to promote CSR and established internal units to draw up agendas of reform (Andrews 2006; Christian Aid 2004). The Canadian Coalition for Good Governance (CCGG), established in June 2002, is the largest, best funded and arguably most influential of these. The CCGG, an alliance of 33 of the largest publicly-traded corporations in Canada (online: www.ccgg.ca, accessed January 12, 2010), issues CSR guidelines and commissions reports on a number of regulatory and political issues. Although the CCGG is a non-profit corporation, its ten Directors and governance bodies comprise a 'who's who' of corporate power in Canada: the CEOs of Canada's largest mutual funds, pension funds, and investment management corporations are all there. Established in response to Enron and Sarbanes–Oxley, the CCGG began by issuing a series of recommendations to 'provide more power, oversight and independence to boards of directors and audit committees' (*Globe and Mail,* January 27, 2004: B1, B5). Its guidelines reinforce the established 'best practices' of corporate governance: independent audits, independent Directors, transparency, regular reporting to shareholders, and regular monitoring of management and Boards (online: www.ccgg.ca/guidelines, accessed January 12, 2010).

A laudable response, some might say. However, the guidelines are not backed by non-negotiable penalties or sanctions for the non-compliant. The CCGG opposes government regulation – its stand on executive compensation: 'companies are already making strides to improve executive compensation practices … Regulations are not the answer', is typical (online: www.ccgg.ca/executive-compensation, accessed May 20, 2007). Professional groups promoting CSR are also keen to avoid state regulation or criminal statute: the Canadian Public Accountancy Board (CPAB), set up by accountants after Sarbanes–Oxley, established no mandatory standards for audits and auditors (*Globe and Mail,* January 27, 2004: B1, B5). New 'best practices' and conflict of interest rules from the Toronto Stock Exchange, the Broker Dealers Association (now the Investment Dealers Association) and the Canadian Venture Exchange (now the TSX Venture Exchange) all recommended non-binding self-regulatory regimes and 'good faith' partnerships (Shamir 2004; Kivenko 2010). Becoming a good corporate citizen, it appears, can be accomplished by consensus and peer pressure alone.

A number of other weaknesses have been identified in the corporate embrace of CSR (Christian Aid 2004; Corporate Watch 2006; Lubbers 2002). The language that underpins CSR initiatives is replete with vague, undefined terms such as 'transparency', 'trust' and 'learning' (Livesey and Kearins 2002: 245). Documents employ 'feel good' rhetoric exhorting 'stakeholders' to embed CSR in their corporate culture and 'embark on journeys' (Conley and Williams 2005: 15). Benchmarks or timelines holding corporations to account are rare. Oft-used terms such as 'caring' are undefined. Does 'caring' mean that member businesses must install scrubbers that threaten profits and stock prices? That the jobs and pensions of employees will be protected? That unions will be welcomed and risky investments avoided? Similar problems plague business promises to adopt a triple bottom line: are they committing themselves to consider constituencies outside the corporation in decision-making, to release more information and become more transparent, or not? Such vagueness means that those who wrote the rules – the corporations themselves – get to interpret where and how they apply. This creates 'the potential to reconstitute "reality" … in one-sided, arbitrary, and manipulative ways' (Livesey and Kearins 2002: 250).

Authorship of CSR rules is also problematic. CSR initiatives are generally drawn up by committees dominated by corporate employees. Not only do they have a vested interest in looking good to their employers, their 'common sense' assumptions and working definitions of 'practical' versus 'radical' CSR remedies will have been shaped by their personal biographies (typically upwardly mobile, white and privileged) and their corporate role. Their definitions of corporate responsibility, therefore, seldom question the limits of economic production and consumption, producing CSR statutes that assume the 'fundamental values of economic and management models, such as consumerism, growth, and efficiency' (Livesey 2002: 330). Such rules present CSR as a win-win proposition, reducing it to a risk-management process designed to assist companies in achieving their (economic) goals while providing them with a 'social licence' which guarantees public approval. Royal Dutch/Shell, for example, grounds its CSR proclamation in the unacknowledged assumption that creating wealth is always a 'good thing' (Livesey 2002: 332). What happens, then, if behaving responsibly conflicts with creating wealth? Can *any* limits on profitable activities be warranted?

This problem is exacerbated by the process that identifies the 'stakeholders' to be taken into account in corporate decisions. After observing seven CSR conferences and interviewing 40 CSR specialists in the United States and Europe, Conley and Williams (2005: 12) report that those designated as 'stakeholders' (the first step in making it into decision-making venues) are basically selected by the corporations setting up CSR committees. This does not necessarily mean critical voices are excluded – an NGO might be invited to the table because its members are particularly vocal on a particular issue. But it is unlikely to be selected if it is seen as 'unreasonable' or 'radical'. This exerts a subtle pressure on NGOs to cloak themselves in the language and rationales of commerce. Since languages constitute ideas (Foucault 1972), the adoption of business discourses sets boundaries (often narrow) on the process and gives business a key role in determining 'who participates, how things get said, and consequently, if indirectly, what gets said' (Conley and Williams 2005: 13).

Ambiguity and vagueness also pervade the reports companies produce on their CSR guidelines. A recent consultants' report on the best CSR reporting practices, commissioned and funded by the private sector and government,[5] rated 379 companies against ten sustainability categories: context and coverage; leadership and direction; polices, organization and managements systems; stakeholder relations; environmental performance; economic performance; integrated performance; extending influence upstream and downstream; and quality, credibility and communications (Stratos 2008: 3). But the report only looks at *how* the companies' reports are compiled and whether 'best practices' were employed – it does not consider whether the policies worked and sustainability actually improved (Stratos 2008: 3). Process, not substance, is emphasized throughout.

Overall, the form, priorities and goals of the corporate-driven CSR movement are consonant with those of the 'post-regulatory state' (Conley and Williams 2005: 31). Self-directed and self-regulated CSR movements are numerous, but their effectiveness as the third component of the disciplinary triangle is unknown (Christian Aid 2004; Corporate Watch 2006). However, since the ethic of 'shareholder value' – meaning demonstrated high quarterly profit levels – still occupies pride of place, ideologically, politically and legally, and the ongoing recession is threatening profits in many sectors and countries, it is difficult for even the best intentioned businesses to deliver on lofty CSR promises.

Again, this does not necessarily mean that CSR is a sham – the regulatory triangle is much more complicated. The process of negotiating with 'stakeholders', however limited and circumscribed, has at least the potential to bring different voices and perspectives into the corporate arena. Struggles over the meaning of discursive strategies never have a predetermined fate, negotiation is always a multi-faceted and unpredictable process (Livesey 2002: 338; also see Burchell and Cook 2006). No hegemonic project is ever complete, and once information about a corporation is made public, it serves as an opening gambit, a negotiating tool for state regulators, NGOs and other stakeholders (Livesey and Kearins 2002: 251). Indeed, forcing corporations to respond to voices outside financial arenas is in itself a noteworthy advance, 'a concession to advocates of sustainable development' which provides 'potential for ongoing transformation in the corporate world' (Livesey 2002: 338).

Conclusion

The ability of the regulated to shape the measures directed at them should be no surprise. Regulators typically come from and eventually return to regulated industries, and like most of their upper middle-class peers, their individual and collective 'common sense' on financial regulation is shaped by the perspectives of corporate Canada. Canada's foremost regulatory agency, the Ontario Securities Commission (OSC), holds regular meetings with those it designates as 'stakeholders' – major corporate actors, experienced executives from mainstream companies. They sit on Advisory Boards and meet regularly with senior Commissioners and the Executive Director. If this were done when disciplinary measures aimed at welfare mothers or the homeless were drawn up, if their opinions as stakeholders were solicited before new policies were written, how different policy would be!

There is little reason to expect that a national securities regulator in Canada will be any more effective at reining in the titans of Bay Street than the SEC has been in the USA. From all accounts, the culture of high-risk gambling with other peoples' money has not changed.

The verities accepted as 'common sense' principles of financial capitalism then and now equate progress and prosperity with a free and free-wheeling stock market exchange. Selling stocks to raise money for capital pursuits is intrinsically a 'good thing', an activity to be rewarded and encouraged. This is reflected in the contradictory goals – to promote and to sanction risk-taking – of every regulatory agency in the country. These culturally rooted and institutionally enshrined 'first principles' force agencies to justify every new statute and sanction, and authorize the business community – the very targets of the legislation – to shape laws to fit their needs and resist those they dislike. Indeed, the prosperity and success of the business sector as a whole is premised on generating continual, ever-increasing profits. This makes it 'sensible' and 'reasonable' for businesses and its senior executives to repeatedly seek out and reward profitable non-compliance,[6] and avoid, if possible, the disciplinary strategies represented by regulation, criminal law and CSR. As McBarnet (2006: 1104) found in her study of tax avoidance/ evasion: 'successful manipulation and circumvention of law not only provided "fraud insurance", it was a matter for business congratulations and professional pride. Creative compliance was something to be emulated rather than reviled. In business and in the legal and accounting professions, it was routine practice, deemed absolutely legitimate so long as the legal form … was technically accurate'.

What can we learn from this sorry history? For one thing it would appear that there is a 'mutually reinforcing' (Tombs and Whyte 2007: 69) character to the corporate disciplinary triangle of regulation, criminal law and CSR. On one hand, recent corporate scandals have exposed the limits of capital and the dominant neo-liberal model of corporate self-regulation. In response, new criminal laws were introduced and efforts were stepped-up to 'force' corporations to embrace their inner, good corporate citizen – a strategy Glasbeek (2002) notes is born from moments of desperation. At the same time, however, even if the disciplinary triangle has been pushed or pulled in certain directions, the ways in which the different corners are (re)constituted leaves little hope that any particular disciplinary element will produce a crackdown on corporate fraud or fundamentally change the ways in which corporations pursue the pot of gold at the end of the market rainbow. It would thus appear that the regulatory dance (Snider 1991) continues in a manner that favours the corporate capitalist status quo.

In the end, ratcheting up maximum penalties to make examples of a few – giving Bernie Madoff a 150-year prison sentence, for example – accomplishes nothing. It is symbolic excess that neither deters nor prevents the fraudsters of the future; it offers no restitution to the victims and no 'rehabilitation' to the offender. Most important of all, it does nothing to sanction or change the corporate institutions that facilitated and enabled the offences. The root of the issue is the high value dominant culture – business but also us – places on building financial castles in the sky and conferring multi-million rewards on those who do it. The prestige and the economic and political power Wall Street and its equivalents generate are the reason laws and regulations are weak. This is why regulators are regularly, systemically 'captured' by the targets of regulation. Remedies with the potential to challenge the assumptions underlying weak regulation never make it onto the political or regulatory agenda. The solutions that are being discussed – lessening the economic profit potential by levying a transaction tax on trades, setting limits on executive compensation, banning pay packages that reward certain kinds of risk-taking, restoring the building of the statutory firewalls of the past – can only be institutionalized *if* the cultural permission (which translates into the political will) to put them into effect can be sustained. And this, it appears, is fading fast.

References

Andrews, N. (2006) 'Corporatism and the Toronto Stock Exchange: A New Ontario Egg Board?' *Australian Journal of Corporate Law*, 19: 65–113.

Arvedlund, E. (2009) *Too Good to be True: The Rise and Fall of Bernie Madoff.* New York: Penguin Books.

Athanasiou, T. (1996) 'The Age of Greenwashing.' *Capitalism, Nature, Socialism*, vol. 7, pp. 1–36, Mar 1996.

Barry, A., T. Osborne and N. Rose (1996) *Foucault and Political Reason: Liberalism, Neo-liberalism and Rationalities of Government.* University of Chicago Press.

Braithwaite, J. (2005) *Markets in Vice, Markets in Virtue.* Annadale, Australia: Federation Press.

Burchell, J. and J. Cook (2006) 'Confronting the "Corporate Citizen": Shaping the Discourse of Corporate Social Responsibility.' *International Journal of Sociology and Social Policy*, Vol. 26, No. 3/4, 2006, pp. 121–137.

Carson, W.G. (1970) 'White Collar Crime and the Enforcement of Factory Legislation,' *British Journal of Criminology*, 10: 383–398.

Carson, W.G. (1980) 'The Institutionalization of Ambiguity: Early British Factory Acts,' in G. Geis and E. Stotland (eds), *White-Collar Crime Theory and Research.* Beverly Hills, CA: Sage.

Cernetig, M. (2002) 'Witch Hunt on Wall Street?' *The Globe and Mail,* June 1, 2002, p.F8.

Christian Aid (2004) *Behind the Mask: The Real Face of Corporate Social Responsibility.* Online: www.christianaid.org.uk, accessed November 24, 2008.

Condon, M. (1998) *Making Disclosure: Ideas and Interests in Ontario Securities Regulation.* Toronto: University of Toronto Press.

Conley, J.M. and C.A. Williams (2005) 'Engage, Embed and Embellish: Theory Versus Practice in the Corporate Social Responsibility Movement,' *Journal of Corporation Law*, 31, 1, 2005–2006, pp. 1–38.

Corporate Watch (2006) *What's Wrong with Corporate Social Responsibility*. Online: http://www.corporatewatch.org.uk/?lid=2670, accessed February 5, 2010.

Foster, J.B. (2010) 'The Age of Monopoly-Finance Capital', *Monthly Review, 61, 9*.

Foucault, M. (1972 [2001]) *The Archaeology of Knowledge*. Routledge, Taylor and Francis Group: London.

Fudge, J. and B. Cossman (2002) 'Introduction: Privatization, Law and the Challenge to Feminism' in Cossman, B. and J. Fudge, eds. *Privatization, Law, and the Challenge to Feminism*. Toronto: University of Toronto Press.

Garland, D. (2001) *The Culture of Control*. Oxford: Oxford University Press.

Glasbeek, H. (2002) *Wealth by Stealth*. Toronto: Between the Lines Press.

Gunningham, N., R.A. Kagan and D. Thornton (2003) *Shade of Green: Business, Regulation and Environment*. Stanford Law and Politics: Stanford University Press.

Haines, F. and A. Sutton (2003) 'The Engineer's Dilemma: A Sociological Perspective on Juridification and Regulation,' *Crime, Law and Social Change*, 39: 1–22.

Kirtzman, A. (2009) *Betrayal: The Life and Lies of Bernie Madoff*. Harper Collins.

Kivenko, K. (2010) *Investor Protection and the Investment Industry Regulatory Industry Organization of Canada*. Canada: The Fund Library. Online: www.fundlibrary.com (accessed: January 28 2010).

Livesey, S.M. (2002) 'The Discourse of the Middle Ground: Citizen Shell Commits to Sustainable Development,' *Management Communication Quarterly*, Vol. 15, No. 3, February 2002, 313–349.

Livesey, S.M. and K. Kearins (2002) 'Transparent and Caring Corporations? A Study of Sustainability Reports by The Body Shop and Royal Dutch/Shell,' *Organization & Environment*, Vol. 15 No. 3, September 2002, 233–258.

Lubbers, E. (ed.) (2002) *Battling Big Business: Countering Greenwash, Front Groups and Other Forms of Corporate Deception*. Common Courage Press.

McBarnet, D. (2006) 'After Enron: Will "Whiter Than White Collar Crime" Still Wash?', *British Journal of Criminology*, 46(6): 1091–1109.

McDonald, L.G. with P. Robinson (2009) *A Colossal Failure of Common Sense: The Inside Story of the Collapse of Lehman Brothers*. New York: Crown Business.

Oppenheimer, J. (2009) *Madoff with the Money*. Hoboken, NJ: Wiley.

Parker, Christine (2006) 'The Compliance Trap: The Moral Message in Responsive Regulatory Enforcement', *Law & Society Review*, 40(3).

Paulus, I. (1974) *The Search for Pure Food: A Sociology of Legislation in Britain*. London: Martin Robertson.

Pearce, F. and S. Tombs (1998) *Toxic Capitalism: Corporate Crime and the Chemical Industry*. Aldershot: Ashgate/Dartmouth.

Phelps, M., H. McKay, T. Allen, P. Brunet, W. Dobson, E. Harris and M. Tims (2003) *It's Time: Report of the Committee to Review the Structure of Securities Regulation in Canada*. Canada: Department of Finance, December.

Report on Business Magazine (2004) Advertising Supplement of the Toronto Stock Exchange, *Report on Business Magazine, Globe and Mail*, June 2004.

Rosoff, S., H. Pontell and R. Tillman (2006) *Profit Without Honor. White-Collar Crime and the Looting of America* (4th edn). New Jersey: Prentice Hall.

Royal Canadian Mounted Police (RCMP) (May 13, 2004) 'Former securities "Re-org" Administrator arrested.' Online: http://www.investorvoice.ca/PI/982A.htm (accessed February 27, 2011).

Shamir, R. (2004) 'The De-Radicalization of Corporate Social Responsibility,' *Critical Sociology*, Volume 30, Issue 3, pp. 669–689.

Shamir, R. (2005) 'Mind the Gap: The Commodification of Corporate Social Responsibility,' *Symbolic Interaction*, Vol. 28, Issue 2, pp. 229–253.

Shapiro, S. (1984) *Wayward Capitalists: Target of the Securities and Exchange Commission*. New Haven: Yale University Press.

Shearing, C. (1993) 'Towards a Constitutive Conception of Regulation', in J. Braithwaite and P. Grabosky, eds., *Business Regulation and Australia's Future*. Sydney: Australian Institute of Criminology: 67–79.

Slapper, G. and S. Tombs (1999) *Corporate Crime*. Essex, UK: Pearson Education.

Smith, A. (1994/1776) *An Inquiry into the Nature and Causes of the Wealth of Nations*. E. Cannan, ed., New York: Modern Library.

Snider, L. (1991) 'The Regulatory Dance: Understanding Reform Processes in Corporate Crime.' *International Journal of the Sociology of Law*, 1991, Vol. 19 Issue 2, pp. 209-236.

Snider, L. (1993) *Bad Business: Corporate Crime in Canada*. Scarborough: ITP Nelson.

Snider, L. (2004) 'Resisting Neo-Liberalism: The Poisoned Water Disaster in Walkerton, Ontario', *Social and Legal Studies*, V5 (2): 27–47, 2003.

Snider, L. (2009) 'Accommodating Power: The "Common Sense" of Regulators', *Social and Legal Studies* 18(2).

Stratos (2008) *Canadian Corporate Sustainability Reporting – Best Practices 2008*. Online: http://www.stratos-sts.com/publications/Best_Practice_Study_2008.pdf (accessed March 20, 2009).

Thompson, E.P. (1963) *The Making of the English Working Class*. New York: Pantheon.

Tillman, R.H. and M. Indergaard (2005) 'Introduction,' *Pump and Dump: The Rancid Rules of the New Economy*, Rutgers University Press.

Tombs, S. and D. Whyte (2007) *Safety Crimes*. Cullompton, Devon, UK: Willan Publishing.

Tucker, E. (1988) 'Making the Workplace Safe for Capitalism', *Labour/Le Travail*, 21, Spring: 45–85.

Wacquant, L. (2001) 'The penalization of poverty and the Rise of Neo-liberalism', *European Journal on Criminal Policy and Research*, 9, 401–412.

Newspaper articles cited

Grace Benn, K. (2010) 'Update: Bank Shares Up As Company Execs Testify At Hearing' Wall Street Journal, 2010. Online: http://online.wsj.com/article/BT-CO-20100113-710990.html?mod=rss_Hot_Stocks, accessed February 5, 2010.

Krugman, Paul (2010) 'Bankers Without a Clue', *New York Times*, January 14, 2010. Online: http://www.nytimes.com/2010/01/15/opinion/15krugman.html, accessed February 5, 2010.

McKenna, Barrie (2010) 'U.S. Headed for Another Bubble: TARP Watchdog.' *Globe and Mail*, February 3, 2010. Online: http://www.theglobeandmail.com/report-on-business/us-headed-for-another-bubble-tarp-watchdog/article1454235/, accessed February 5, 2010.

Statutes cited

Criminal Code of Canada, R.S.C., c. C-46.

Notes

1 Four former executives of Royal Group Technologies Limited were arraigned for a 'pump and dump' scheme that defrauded company shareholders of more than \$29 million; three former Nortel executives were accused of 'misstating' the company's financial results; and a senior executive in the financial sector was charged with fraud for his role in a mutual fund scam.

2 The 2008–2009 Integrated Market Enforcement Program Annual Report notes five convictions for capital market fraud between 2004 and 2009 (see Royal Canadian Mounted Police: http://www.rcmp-grc.gc.ca/pubs/imets-eipmf/2009-eng.htm#a4, date accessed: January 29, 2010). In October 2008, a senior executive of Betacom Corporation was found guilty for his role in recording false sales in the company's financial statements (see Royal Canadian Mounted Police, http://www.rcmp-grc. gc.ca/on/news-nouvelles/2008/08-10-01-imet-eipm-eng.htm, date accessed: January 29, 2010).

3 Control of companies is still concentrated within small corporate elites, and wealth distribution is wildly – and increasingly – unequal. In 1982 the average CEO in the US earned about 45 times as much as the average employee, by 2000 he (seldom she) earned 458 times as much (Cernetig 2002).

4 Despite heavy lobbying by the banking sector from 2003 on, Canada's federal government refused to allow banks to engage in many of the high risk trades that bankrupted many financial institutions in the rest of the world in the 2008–09 crisis.

5 The report notes that the sponsors had 'no input in the assessments or analysis' (Stratos 2008: 3).

6 McBarnet (2006) argues that the strictures of Sarbanes–Oxley combined with the US Sentencing Commission's 2004 Guidelines have successfully pressured corporations into adopting 'cultures of integrity which comply with the spirit, not just the letter of regulatory reform'. However recent events cast doubt on optimistic portrayals which fail to consider key structural and historical factors.

4 State complicity in the production of corporate crime

Steve Tombs

Introduction

There are a series of ways, some well recognised, others less so, in which states are complicit in the systematic, routine production of corporate crimes.

First, and most obviously, states are complicit in corporate crime production through their failures either to put into place more effective legal regimes, or to enforce adequately existing laws, or to respond effectively to violations of such laws, with respect to corporate activity. If all of this appears as complicity via omission, there is in fact a great deal of active work undertaken to maintain such omission – and this work will be explored.

Second, states are more actively complicit in their relationships with the corporate sector – as partners in economic activity, as out-sourcers and sub-contractors, as purchasers of corporate goods and services – and thus in the production of illegal activities.

Third, and perhaps least recognised, is that once one departs from a view of state–corporate relations as characterised by externality, then it becomes clear that 'the' state – at its various levels – is implicated in the production of corporate crime through the complex inter-dependence of these apparently separate sets of entities. Some aspects of these intimate relationships are captured by the emerging concept of 'state–corporate crime', and the usefulness, and limitations, of this concept will be explored.

This paper considers each of these forms of state complicity in turn. As it does so, its empirical reference point is safety crimes in the UK. On the basis of this exploration of the role of states in the production of corporate crime, we seek to indicate a more realistic view both of the extent to which illegal and harmful corporate activities can be more effectively controlled, and of the limits upon such control efforts.

State complicity through 'failure'

States are complicit in corporate crime production through a series of failures, specifically in terms of their failures to put into place more effective legal regimes; to enforce adequately existing laws; to respond effectively to violations of such laws. Such failings are well documented, and there is no need to enter into a detailed discussion of each of these aspects of complicity here. However, in order to emphasise the fact that 'failure' does not imply omission, it is useful to explore some aspects of this form of complicity.

One empirical indicator of the scale of non-enforcement of existing law – let alone the reluctance on the part of states to develop laws that might be more constraining of corporate activity – is to be found through an albeit brief overview of enforcement data in relation to occupational safety in the UK (see Tombs and Whyte, 2009, for more detailed considerations). There we find, over a recent five-year period, what we have elsewhere referred to as a 'crisis of enforcement' (Tombs and Whyte, 2008) which represents an effective institutionalisation of decriminalisation. Thus, for example:

- at 1 April 2002, the number of FTE HSE staff was 4,282; by 1 April 2008 there were 3,399 staff;
- of these, there were 1,238 'front-line inspectors' at 1 April 2008, compared with 1,625 in April 2002;
- in 2006/07, just 10.5 per cent of major injuries that were reported were actually investigated – compared with 18.3 per cent in 2001/02;
- enforcement authorities issued 7,715 enforcement notices in 2007/08, compared with 17,042 in 2001/02;
- there were 1,028 prosecutions in 2007/08, compared with 2,336 in 2001/02;
- the average penalty on conviction in 2007/08 was £12,896 – compared with £11,141 in 2001/02, an increase, but from an extremely low level.

Two observations need to be made here. First, that all of these absolute figures indicate very low levels of enforcement. Second, that on almost all of the above indicators – all save the level of fines, which are determined through the courts – we see a decline in HSE's enforcement activities. However, whether looking at the absolutely low level of enforcement or the trends which indicate a decline in these activities, we need to emphasise that while we can use the term 'failures', we should not confuse this with 'mere' complicity via omission. In fact, the trends in decline can only be understood within the context of *a great deal of work* – a long-term ideological softening up (Tombs, 2007, 2001) and much material effort – through and by the state in relation to corporate crime control in general, and safety law enforcement in particular. That is, a key context for the above data is the construction of what we can refer to, by way of shorthand, as the *Hampton Agenda*.

The emergence of this agenda can be traced back to the introduction of Regulatory impact assessments (RIAs) in 1998, with a newly formed Regulatory Impact Unit within the Cabinet Office given, a year later, the remit to ensure that RIAs were being implemented across government departments. RIAs aim to measure the costs and benefits of all proposed policy and legislative reforms affecting business, and contain structural biases towards less rather than more business regulation: first, their very rationale is the need to 'ensure any regulatory burden they add is kept to a minimum';[1] second, their economic form is likely to produce a financial argument for less rather than more regulation, since the business costs of meeting new regulatory requirements are more calculable than economic or social benefits of such regulation (Cutler and James, 1996). Thus a key function of RIAs in practice has been to pre-empt and minimise legislative and regulatory cost impacts upon business by formalising a business-sensitive cost benefit analysis in the legislative process.

More specifically in terms of health and safety policy, a key stage in regulatory 'reform' came with the publication of Revitalising Health and Safety (Health and Safety Commission and Department of the Environment, Transport and the Regions, 2000; henceforth RHS), a new regulatory strategy launched in June 2000. This prioritised the motivation of employers by explaining the benefits to industry of a good health and safety regime, while at the same time noting the need to 'legislate to make the punishment fit the crime' when 'health and safety standards are flagrantly ignored'. Such an approach was famously characterised by Braithwaite in terms of the need for regulators to speak 'softly' but carry 'big sticks' (Braithwaite, 2000a: 205–261), while in practice such strategic claims translate into much speaking softly, with big sticks far from apparent. Thus the *RHS* strategy, which observes that: 'while appropriate enforcement and deterrence is crucial, this must not be at the expense of promoting voluntary compliance and models of excellence' based upon 'partnership'. So while recognising that law enforcement has a place in the regulatory system, it is set against its notional opposite: 'partnership'. In practice, compliance styles of regulation pose a choice between walking softly *or* carrying a big stick, with the latter featuring always as a resort of the very last option.

With the election of a second Labour Government in 2001, the extent of New Labour's long-term plans for a reconstructed system of business regulation became fully apparent. After much ideological softening up through the proliferation of anti-regulatory discourse, the crucial moment came in March 2004; then, the Treasury, under Gordon Brown, established the Hampton Review, to 'consider the scope for reducing administrative burdens on business by promoting more efficient approaches to regulatory inspection and enforcement without reducing regulatory outcomes' (Hampton, 2005). Its report – *Reducing Administrative Burdens: Effective Inspection and Enforcement* – called for more focused inspections, greater emphasis on advice and education and, in general, for removing the 'burden' of inspection from most premises (specifically, for the reduction of inspections by up to a third which, across all regulatory agencies, would equate to one million fewer inspections). Then, in March 2005, the Cabinet Office's Better Regulation Task Force published its review of regulation, *Less is More: Reducing Burdens, Improving Outcomes* (2005); this proposed a crude mechanism for controlling the regulatory 'burden': a 'one in, one out' approach to regulation, whereby all new regulations were to be accompanied by the withdrawal of existing regulations. The recommendations of these reports came together in the Legislative and Regulatory Reform Act, which passed into law in November 2006. The aim of the law is to 'enable delivery of swift and efficient regulatory reform to cut red tape' (Cabinet Office, 2006). The Act itself therefore is framed by 'burdens on business' rhetoric, a rhetoric that juxtaposes economic health and success as a counter-balance to over-bearing investigation and enforcement. Thus, section 1 of the Act creates a remarkable new power for a Minister of the Crown to make an order that removes from government a 'regulatory burden', defined in the Act as a 'financial cost', an 'administrative inconvenience' or 'an obstacle to efficiency, productivity or profitability'.

The explicit pro-business rationale at the heart of the Hampton agenda reforms reached their high point in the new *Regulators Compliance Code*,[2] published in December 2007. Therein, regulators, including HSE, were advised that: 'By facilitating compliance through a positive and proactive approach, regulators can achieve higher compliance rates and reduce the need for reactive enforcement actions' (Para. 8); they should 'take account of the circumstances of small regulated entities, including any difficulties they may have in achieving compliance' (Para. 8.1); '[r]egulators should recognise that a key element of their activity will be to allow, or even encourage, economic progress and only to intervene when there is a clear case for protection' (Para. 3). Thus the Hampton Review and the reforms that followed have extended the scope and reach of the burdens on business agenda directly into the *day-to-day work* of inspectors, further marginalising the enforcement role of the HSE and giving renewed momentum to New Labour's pro-business trajectory.

State complicity through increasing interdependence with the corporate sector

A second way in which states are complicit in corporate crime production is through their increasingly formal and intimate relationships with the corporate sector. These relationships take various forms, such as in states' (local, regional, national) effective roles as joint partners with the private sector in various forms of economic activity, as out-sourcers and contractors of economic activity, and as purchasers of corporate goods and services.

Now, in one sense, states and private corporations have always existed in a relationship of dependence with capital. Certainly nation-states have been and remain engaged in a constant, 'competitive process of attraction-and-immobilization' (Holloway, 1994: 38) of capital – and importantly, one element of this is to provide the most 'favorable conditions for the reproduction of capital within [their] boundaries' (ibid. 1994: 34–35). More specifically, in any capitalist state, private corporations are key sources of providing goods, services, taxation and employment – all of which states are necessarily, politically, economically, and socially, for states.

However, we need also to be aware of the extent to which these relationships have been deepened and extended, through formal state policy and practice – and this makes state complicity in corporate crime arising out of these relationships empirically more likely. Thus, with the emergence in the UK, post-1979, of ideas and practices subsumed under the shorthand of 'neo-liberalism', we find an elevated ideological and material place for the private sector. There are numerous indices of this increasing status, including: private capital as an increasingly key provider of goods and services; private business increasingly represented as the model to be emulated (efficiency etc.); the increasing prevalence of business news, so that sectional interests are increasingly represented as national interests; the emergence of business-people as celebrities (see Snider, 2000; Tombs, 2001).

Thus, post-1979, if we confine our considerations to the UK, as neo-liberal ideas became powerful to the point of virtually uncontested dominance, then they also helped to produce that which they sought to describe and prescribe, notably in terms of increasing popular dependence upon the private sector. For as new markets were created by states for private capital through privatisation and deregulation, as states withdrew from providing a host of goods and services, many people really were made more dependent upon the private sector to provide basic goods and services: increasingly private sector organisations *must* provide goods and services which states have withdrawn from providing – and, having withdrawn from such provision, are less and less able to reassume such a role.

Across four Conservative governments between 1979 and 1997, literally hundreds of publicly owned companies were sold into private hands. British Aerospace, telecommunications, gas, electricity and water supply, shipbuilding, freight and ports, coal, railways, and atomic energy were all privatised during this period. In 1979, nationalised industries accounted for over 10 per cent of GDP; by 1993, this was less than 3 per cent, and public sector employment had fallen by 1.5 million. Little wonder, then, that by the time the first Labour Government was elected in 1997, under Blair, there was little left to privatise (Parker, 2004). And by then, with much of the economy now (again) in private hands, the ability of the state – in theory, at least, if having proven problematic in practice – either to manage, regulate, or even hold to account major economic actors had been all but relinquished. Thus, such shifts have created *new* and significant dependencies upon private capital, given the centrality of the goods and services at issue and which states have relinquished the monopoly to produce and/or provide.

The Labour Government did, of course, institute a series of major 'reforms' to the public sector and many to the nature of the welfare state, on the basis that, familiarly, there was 'no alternative'. These stopped short of further full-scale privatisation, but were generally couched in terms of greater 'choice' and 'efficiency'. There were also a series of measures rolled out to attract private capital into the 'public sector' – that is, through contracts, to further intertwine state and private corporate activities. The latter, under the guise of Private–Public Partnerships and the Private Finance Initiative, proved highly controversial; most crudely, each of these initiatives represented mechanisms for effectively privatising profits whilst socialising financial risks in areas previously untouched by private sector involvement.

Importantly however, it should be emphasised that almost all of these initiatives have been accompanied by the creation and re-creation of immensely complex – and many would argue highly inefficient – regulatory regimes. And this complexity is exaggerated when the regulation involves the provision of a basic service – such as gas, health, or rail travel. For some commentators, such changes in the role of the state have signalled the 'death of the Keynesian state', and the emergence of a 'regulatory' or 'advanced liberal' or 'post-social' state. Thus, 'Privatisation combined with new regulatory institutions is the classic instantiation of [the] prescription for governments to steer but not row' (Braithwaite, 2000b: 50). However sustainable such claims are, it certainly is the case that privatisation has increasingly seen Government shift from service provider to the chief architect in the construction, then regulation, of markets. We can also see in the emergence of the 'regulatory state' the resolution to an apparent paradox – a Government committed to privately owned, 'free' enterprise which has created a complex web of (re)regulation.

Thus we see here that regulation, following deregulation or privatisation of an area of economic activity, necessarily becomes more complex through reconstruction at arm's length. This itself is a stunning example of a key dissonance between the rhetoric and reality of the relationships between neo-liberalism and public policy – for while the former claims the supremacy of free markets, the latter in fact engages in an awful lot of work to construct and maintain markets so that they may appear to be free. Over half a century ago, Polanyi documented the 'embeddedness' of markets, and their construction through economic, social and public policy (Polanyi, 1971/1944). More recently, Sayer (1995) has argued that not only has a 'free' market never existed, but that an economy characterized by the term 'free market' simply could not exist. States help to constitute capital, commodity, commercial and residential property markets, help to produce different kinds of 'human capital', constitute labour markets, and regulate the employment contract; the state plays a role in constituting economic enterprises through specifying rules of liability, often specifying the rules of incorporation. In other words, regulation is a necessary function of a state even in the quintessential market economy, even while advocates of global neo-liberalism consistently deny such a role for the state and regulation. While 'the ideological notion of latent or implicit markets which only need freeing figures strongly in neo-liberal rhetoric' (Sayer, 1995: 104), this contrasts with the overwhelming empirical and theoretical evidence attesting to markets as social constructions.

Indeed, there is now a burgeoning literature which attests to the fact that states perform an ongoing role in the provision of an economic and legal infrastructure for the risk-taking activities of entrepreneurs. Paradigmatic here is the work of Vogel, who has documented the extent to which, and the ways in which, *freer* markets tend to be constructed through '*more* rules' (Vogel, 1996). Focusing upon Japan and the United Kingdom in general, and the regulation of telecommunications and financial service sectors – 'the most dynamic and the most global of industries' (ibid: 2) – Vogel presents a series of case studies which elaborate upon four ideal-typical forms of re-regulation: pro-competitive, juridical, strategic and expansionary re-regulation. While the first two of these ideal types 'undermine governmental control over industry', the latter two actually 'enhance government control' (Vogel, 1996: 18). He demonstrates the enormous amount of work that states perform in order to (re)construct markets, and also attempts to document empirically and then theorise the bases of the 'remarkably different ways' (Vogel,

1996: 3) in which states have reacted or indeed driven or exacerbated a seemingly universal logic of economic globalisation.

The link between these new state–corporate relationships and the production of crime is clearly, if gruesomely, illustrated in the killing of Simon Jones, a 24-year-old student, taking a year out of study, who signed on for casual work in 1998 with a local employment agency in Brighton, 'to get the dole off his back'.[3] Simon was required to register with the agency, Personnel Selection, whose role it was to find him work. Under the Job Seeker's Allowance scheme – part of New Labour's broader Welfare to Work strategy – claimants must continually demonstrate availability for and willingness to work; these conditions make refusing offers of work liable to lead to a withdrawal of state 'benefits'. Simon's first job with Personnel Selection was at Shoreham Docks, working for Euromin Ltd, a Dutch cargo company. He went to work in a ship's hold, unloading its cargo. Within an hour of arriving for his first day of work, he was dead; his head had been crushed and partially severed when a three tonne 'crane' grab closed around it. No prosecution was ever taken against Personnel Selection, though they are covered by the legal requirement to ensure the suitability of work which they assign or offer. Initially, the CPS also declined to prosecute Euromin, the firm for which the student was working (at just over £4 an hour) – though after a protracted, high-profile campaign by the Simon Jones Memorial Campaign, a judicial review led to Euromin being successfully prosecuted for two health and safety offences in November 2001, and fined £50,000.

The Simon Jones Memorial Campaign had based their fight around the issue of casualisation – a growing feature of working life in neo-liberal Britain. For the campaign, casualisation translates into people being 'forced into low-paid jobs with little or no training, no job security, no sick pay and no holiday pay means bigger profits for companies'. As one of the campaigners stated, 'Ten years ago, if you were going to work in a dock, you would have had to have some training and knowledge. Nowadays, with the growth of casualisation, the search for cheap and throwaway labour, you have people doing work on docks that they have no training to do.' Casualisation, short-term employment, and agency work are all common features of the re-regulated labour market. They are also furthered by a benefits system which forces claimants to take work – even work for which they are patently 'unfit' – on threat of withdrawal of financial support from the state. Finally, the role of Personnel Selection – acting as the 'middle-man' between the state and Euromin – is also symptomatic of a state contracting out its functions to the private sector. In short, Simon's death is only explicable in the context of neo-liberalism, and *a specifically constructed form of state–corporate complicity* (Tombs and Whyte, 2007: 21–24).

State–corporate crime and beyond

Some aspects of this increasingly complex relationship between states and the private sector, as well as a direct attempt to both theorise and document state complicity in the production of corporate crime, are captured by the emerging concept of 'state–corporate crime'. Developed by corporate crime scholars in the USA, the term state–corporate crime first appeared in 1990, when Kramer and Michalowski (2006a: 14) defined this phenomenon as: 'illegal or socially injurious actions that occur when one or more institutions of political governance pursue a goal in direct co-operation with one or more institutions of economic production and distribution' (ibid: 15).

Importantly, the concept of state–corporate crime directs our attention to deviance as the 'outcome of relationships between different social institutions' rather than as discrete acts; second, through focusing upon 'the relational character of the state', rather than viewing either business or government as closed systems, it locates potential for crimes and harms in 'the horizontal relationships between economic and political institutions' (Kramer and Michalowski, 2006a: 21). Thus what appear at first sight to be discrete events are in fact better understood as the products of processual, complex relationships between public and private actors.

The conceptual lens of state–corporate crime has been applied to a diverse range of events and processes, from the explosion of the space shuttle Challenger (Kramer, 2006), to the technological underpinnings of the Holocaust (Matthews, 2006), the contemporary seizure of natural resources in occupied Iraq (Kramer and Michalowski, 2006b; Rothe, 2006; Whyte, 2007) and diverse sectors such as the Latin American shrimp industry, the Nigerian oil sector, and the arms trade (Green and Ward, 2004: 28–51). A more recent, 'UK based', case of such crime has been revealed by the Haddon-Cave Report in October 2009 following his review of the crash of a Nimrod aircraft as it refuelled over Afghanistan in 2006. Haddon-Cave concluded that the Nimrod 'was lost because of … significant failures on the part of all those involved' (Haddon-Cave, 2009: 20), locating responsibility between the Ministry of Defence, BAE Systems and QinetiQ. Of particular interest is that the Report devoted a section to the 'lessons' of the Space Shuttle Challenger, drawing a close parallel between this and the crash of the Nimrod (Haddon-Cave, 2009: 447–454).

For Michalowski, Kramer and other scholars of state–corporate crime, such crime can be *initiated* and *facilitated* by states. Thus corporations engage in illegality at the prompt or with the approval of state institutions, and/or state actors fail to prevent, respond to or collude with such illegality. Yet we would argue that this perspective fails to capture the totality of the state–corporate relation. For it remains wedded to a tendency to think of corporations as autonomous entities which not only exist independently of, but often work in opposition to, states; we should bear in mind a rather important obviousness – namely that the corporation is a creation of the nation-state, and is maintained through an awful lot of state activity. As we have already indicated, corporations are institutions that are created for the mobilisation, utilisation and protection of capital within recent socio-historical state formations. As such, they are wholly artificial entities whose very existence is provided for, and maintained, through the state via legal institutions and instruments, which in turn are based upon material and ideological supports. Indeed, maintaining the conditions of existence of corporations, even, or perhaps especially, in 'free' markets, requires an enormous amount of state activity. The corporate form and the state are thus inextricably linked.

Thus the markets within which corporations act are themselves created and maintained by state activity – not least the re-emerged so-called 'free' market. These observations lead us to a key point in terms of thinking about state complicity in the production of corporate crime: for just as states create and sustain markets, so too can and do they create and sustain criminogenic markets, that is, markets that are conducive to, or facilitate, the production of harms and crimes.

How the creation and maintenance of a sector and a market can produce rather criminogenic outcomes can be illustrated through the case of UK construction, and safety crimes in construction in particular. The construction industry is one of the UK's most dangerous sectors. We need to be clear, however, that despite the fact that most fatalities and injuries in this industry – just as in every other industry – are likely to result from breaches of the law, few are ever processed as such (Tombs and Whyte, 2007). The sector has a fatal injury rate of over five times the all-industry average and accounts for 30 per cent of all worker deaths. In absolute terms, it has the highest absolute number of any sector, with the number of workers killed in the construction sector each year in Britain remaining in the region of around 70–80 since 1996/97 (Health and Safety Commission, 2007). And if we move beyond a specific focus upon safety, there appear to be very good reasons for thinking that the construction industry is criminogenic, that is, if we consider: the documented ill-health effects of working in an industry that has very high rates of asbestos-related disease; the tendency towards cartelisation that characterises the sector which generates price-fixing, bribery and corruption; the environmental damage associated with the industry, and the detrimental effects upon local human rights where its activities take place overseas.

The main causes of fatal injuries are relatively mundane and highly preventable. As the employers' body, the Federation of Master Builders, put it, 'there is nothing intrinsic about construction that suggests that somebody has to die … [yet the] culture has become so engrained that construction is dangerous, therefore someone is always going to get hurt' (cited in London Assembly Health and Public Services Committee, 2005: 9–10). Rather the source of risk for workers is located in the organisation of the sector and in work therein.

The construction industry is probably the last remaining heavy industry of any size in Britain. It employs 2.25 million people, and contributes up to 10 per cent of GDP, making it the single biggest industry in the UK and thus a key source of Treasury revenue. Government in general is the largest customer of construction industry services, while Defence Estates, responsible for the management of the MoD's land and property holdings at home and overseas is the 'single biggest customer of the UK construction industry'.[4] The industry is central to the myriad of local and regional regeneration schemes across the UK. If this has always been the case, it is a situation accentuated and further formalised through, first, the Public Finance Initiatives (PFI) and more latterly Public Private Partnerships, upon which the building of prisons, hospitals, schools, airports, and underground, rail and road networks, as well as flagship projects such as the London Olympics, the 'new' Wembley stadium and even the Millennium Dome are even thinkable. According to the Major Contractors Group, representing key UK players such as Carillion, Costain and Amec, construction companies engaged in the PFI expect to make 'between three and ten times as much money as they do on traditional contracts' (Corporate Watch, 2004). Industry sources estimated economic growth of the industry at 30 per cent between 1995 and 2005 (Lobban, 2005).

Our earlier observations regarding states establishing codes of rules, infrastructure and so on to bring corporations to life and to provide the conditions under which they are able to thrive, are clearly illustrated by the fortunes of the construction industry in recent years. For here is an industry whose success is largely down to state intervention in the economy, the creation of new regulatory mechanisms for public building programmes, the reform of planning regimes (Monbiot, 2001) and so on. The building trade has been given a major boost by the re-regulation of the industry.

Juxtaposed with the economic importance of the industry is the fact that HSE's enforcement record with respect to the sector is a poor one (Centre for Corporate Accountability, 2009; Donaghy 2009; UCATT, 2009), notwithstanding its own evidence of the scale of offending across the construction industry: the subject of frequent enforcement 'blitzes' by the HSE, these concentrated enforcement initiatives regularly lead to HSE ordering work to be halted on large numbers of construction sites (see Tombs and Whyte, 2007: 13–14), rather indicating a high level of safety crime across the sector. No doubt HSE would, all things being equal, prefer a safer (not to mention healthier) industry. *But all things are not equal.* In this context, HSE, as an agency of the Department of Work and Pensions, stands in opposition to other, much more powerful, branches of Government, including the Treasury, the Department for Business, Enterprise and Regulatory Reform, the Ministry of Defence, and the Foreign Office, to name but a few. Institutional inequality across those branches of the state is created by the outcome of competing political ideologies and practices. In an overwhelmingly pro-business climate, the economic success of business is always juxtaposed with the 'burden' of regulation – as summed up by the new Compliance Code for Regulators, discussed earlier. The parallel trends of growing economic importance and declining regulatory intervention, then, have to be first placed within the context of a complex and contradictory political sphere.

We can also note here how the state-constructed lines between legality and illegality are, at best, somewhat blurred. Thus the construction sector is based upon a large informal sector, with an estimated £4.5–£10 billion construction work nationally undertaken on a 'cash in hand' basis. Companies who do not pay their taxes are also likely to have a 'less safe working environment' for their workers; further, the informal economy creates market conditions that put 'pressure on legitimate builders to cut corners in order to compete for work' (London Assembly Health and Public Services Committee, 2005: 10). If it is indeed the case that this is a criminogenic industry (and see also Braithwaite, 1984, on pharmaceuticals and Carson, 1982, on the offshore oil industry, as further examples), it remains one that is established and maintained by, and central to, the national and local states.

In so far as its function is to support government-sponsored building programmes, generate export revenue and more generally contribute to economic growth, the construction industry can be said to have a symbiotic 'insider' relationship to the state. Meanwhile, HSE continues to go through the motions of regulation via inspections, blitzes, educative initiatives, and even the odd prosecution. In this sense, the construction industry can also be said to be external to the state. This dual relationship creates opportunities for and limits upon regulation, as the state is both dependent upon, but required to represent itself as regulator of, the sector.

Conclusion

It remains to emphasise why these differing views of state–corporate relations in general, and thus of state complicity in corporate crime production in particular, are of significance. Certainly, both empirically and theoretically it is useful to develop an understanding of the variety of ways in which states help to produce corporate crime. Not least, perhaps, because corporate crime research has often proceeded by way of a focus on case studies – thus, for example, raising questions of generaliseability – it was once described as an area characterised by theoretical under-development (Cressey, 1989). Albeit that the past twenty years has seen some significant theoretical contributions to this area of study, to the extent the sketches in this paper point to further lines of enquiry regarding the production of corporate crime, they may help to contribute further in this respect.

However, a further and more significant issue here is that viewing corporate crime through the lens of state complicity allows us a consideration of the most effective points of intervention in terms of control and prevention – and, indeed, of the limits upon such efforts.

In the context of state complicity through failure, clearly struggles for law reform can and do proceed – witness the long travails around the Corporate Manslaughter and Corporate Homicide Act which eventually reached the statute books in 2007 after the Law Commission had originally proposed reforms in 1996. Similarly, enforcement activities can be improved, notwithstanding the fact that current and recent trends indicate that this is unlikely (Tombs and Whyte, 2008, 2009). That said, given that this paper has argued that state failure in these respects hardly equates to state inactivity, then one must recognise that there are real limits upon, or at best obstacles in, reform efforts targeted at state institutions themselves.

In general, and as this paper has argued, state complicity becomes apparent once one moves from a view of state–corporate relations as characterised by externality, and recognises: a complex and necessary inter-dependence between apparently separate sets of entities; the corporation as both 'inside' and 'outside' of the state; the need to consider 'the state' at various levels. These observations point to even greater obstacles in controlling or preventing corporate crime, since each level of analysis herein indicates the extents to which states are intimately related to corporate activity and thus the production of crime and harm arising out of these activities.

However, this paper is not an argument for the impossibility of effective reforms, merely a demand that some of the targets and vehicles of reform need to be reconsidered or augmented. For example, states have classically and continue to represent themselves as protectors and guarantors of a general, often national, interest – so that exposing states' roles as in fact highly sectional in their complex relationships with the corporate sector is a useful tactic in itself. In the wake of the international economic crisis, critical attention has turned not just on the activities of financial institutions themselves, but also on the role of states in terms of regulation as well as their general dependence upon the wealth generated by the sector – especially in the UK. This is one example of an exposure of the imbrication of state and private business actors, and the political furore that can accompany it – though it is too early to say as we write whether there will be progressive outcomes to this. Beyond such forms of exposure and critique, it should also be recognised that states, *unlike corporations*, have duties to their citizens under human rights legislation – so that there may well be mileage in pursuing corporate harms and crimes via state activity or apparent inactivity through discursive and formal challenges to states under the rubric of human rights.

These are brief indications only of where the arguments contained in this paper leave those who would challenge corporate crime. Indeed, it is beyond the scope of a paper such as this to seek to generate answers. What it has sought to contribute to, however, is a consideration of where one might look for the most appropriate questions, and to where these might be best targeted.

Acknowledgements

Writing this paper has offered me the opportunity to draw upon work developed over a number of years. Thus whatever merits are here owe enormous debts to Frank Pearce and Dave Whyte, my friends and colleagues. The usual disclaimers apply.

References

Better Regulation Task Force (2005) *Regulation – Less is More: Reducing Burdens, Improving Outcomes*, London: Cabinet Office.
Braithwaite, J. (1984) *Corporate Crime in the Pharmaceutical Industry*, London: Routledge and Kegan Paul.
Braithwaite, J. (2000a) *Regulation, Crime, Freedom*, Aldershot: Ashgate.
Braithwaite, J. (2000b) The New Regulatory State and the Transformation of Criminology, in Garland, D. and Sparks, R., eds., *Criminology and Social Theory*, Oxford: Clarendon.
Cabinet Office (2006) *New Bill to Enable Delivery of Swift and Efficient Regulatory Reform to Cut Red Tape – Jim Murphy*, Cabinet Office News Release 12 January 2006, London: Cabinet Office Press Office, http://www.egovmonitor.com/node/4164
Carson, W.G. (1982) *The Other Price of Britain's Oil*, Oxford: Martin Robertson.
Centre for Corporate Accountability (2009) *Small Isn't Beautiful. Construction Worker Deaths 2007/2008: Employer Size and Circumstance*, London: UCATT, http://www.corporateaccountability.org/dl/foia/reports/cca_ucatt_deaths.pdf.

Corporate Watch (2004) UK Construction Industry Overview, http://www.corporatewatch.org/?lid=277.

Cressey, D. (1989) 'The Poverty of Theory in Corporate Crime Research', in Adler, F. and Laufer, W.S., eds., *Advances in Criminological Theory*, New Brunswick, NJ: Translation.

Cutler, T. and James, P. (1996) Does Safety Pay? A Critical Account of the Health and Safety Executive Document: 'The Costs of Accidents'. *Work, Employment & Society*, 10, (4), 755–765.

Donaghy, R. (2009) *One Death is Too Many. Inquiry Into the Underlying Causes of Construction Fatal Accidents. Cm 7657*, Norwich: The Stationery Office.

Green, P. and Ward, T. (2004) *State Crime. Governments, Violence and Corruption*, London: Pluto.

Haddon-Cave, C. (2009) *The Nimrod Review. An Independent Review into the Broader Issues Surrounding the Loss of the RAF Nimrod MR2 Aircraft XV230 in Afghanistan in 2006, HC 1025*, London: The Stationery Office.

Hampton, P. (2005) *Reducing Administrative Burdens: Effective Inspection and Enforcement*, London: HM Treasury/HMSO.

Health and Safety Commission (2007) *Statistics of Fatal Injuries 2006/07*, Health and Safety Commission/National Statistics, http://www.hse.gov.uk/statistics/overall/fatl0607.pdf

Health and Safety Commission and Department of the Environment, Transport and the Regions (2000) *Revitalising Health and Safety Strategy Statement*, Wetherby: Department of the Environment, Transport and the Regions.

Holloway, J. (1994) Global Capital and the Nation-State, *Capital & Class*, 52, Spring.

Kramer, R.C. (2006) 'The Space Shuttle *Challenger* Explosion', in Michalowski, R.J. and Kramer, R.C., eds., *State–corporate Crime*, New Jersey: Rutgers University Press.

Kramer, R. and Michalowski, R. (2006a) The Original Formulation, in Michalowski, R.J. and Kramer, R.C., eds., *State–corporate Crime*, New Jersey: Rutgers University Press.

Kramer, R. and Michalowski, R. (2006b) 'The Invasion of Iraq', in Michalowski, R.J. and Kramer, R.C., eds., *State–corporate Crime*, New Jersey: Rutgers University Press.

Lobban, P (2005) *Speech to the London Construction Awards*, 11 October, London: Construction Industry Training Board, at http://www.epolitix.com/Resources/epolitix/Forum%20Microsites/CITB/CITB_speech_111005.pdf

London Assembly Health and Public Services Committee (2005) *Building London, Saving Lives. Improving Health and Safety in Construction*, London: Greater London Authority.

Matthews, R.A. (2006) 'Ordinary Business in Nazi Germany', in Michalowski, R.J. and Kramer, R.C., eds., *State–corporate Crime*, New Jersey: Rutgers University Press.

Monbiot, G. (2001) *Captive State: The Corporate Takeover of Britain*, London: MacMillan.

Parker, D. (2004) *The UK's Privatisation Experiment: The Passage of Time Permits a Sober Assessment, CESifo Working Paper 1126*, at www.cesifo.de/pls/guestci/download/CESifo+Working+Papers+2004/CESifo+Working+Papers+February+2004/cesifo1_wp1126.pdf

Polanyi, K. (1971/1944) *The Great Transformation*, Boston, MA: Beacon Press.

Rothe, D. (2006) 'Iraq and Halliburton', in Michalowski, R.J. and Kramer, R.C., eds., *State–corporate Crime*, New Jersey: Rutgers University Press.

Sayer, A. (1995) *Radical Political Economy. A Critique*, Oxford: Blackwell.

Snider, L. (2000) The Sociology of Corporate Crime: An Obituary (Or: Whose Knowledge Claims Have Legs?), *Theoretical Criminology*, 4, (2), 169–206.

Tombs, S. (2001) 'Thinking About "White-Collar" Crime', in Lindgren, S-Å., ed., *White-Collar Crime Research. Old Views and Future Potentials. Lectures and Papers from a Scandinavian*

Seminar (With articles by James W. Coleman, Hazel Croall, Michael Levi and Steve Tombs), (BRÅ-Rapport 2001:1). Stockholm: Brottsförebyggande rådet/Fritzes, 13–34.

Tombs, S. (2007) 'Globalisation, Neoliberalism and the Trajectories of Public Policy: Closing (and Reopening?) Political Possibilities', *International Journal Management Concepts and Philosophy*, 2, (4), 299–316.

Tombs, S. and Whyte, D. (2007) *Safety Crimes*, Cullompton: Willan.

Tombs, S. and Whyte, D. (2008) *The Crisis in Enforcement: The Decriminalisation of Death and Injury at Work*, London: Crime and Society Foundation.

Tombs, S. and Whyte, D. (2009) 'A Deadly Consensus: Worker Safety and Regulatory Degradation under New Labour', *British Journal of Criminology*, 50, (1), 45–65.

UCATT (2009) *Health and Safety Dossier for the Department of Work and Pensions' Construction Inquiry into the Underlying Causes of Fatalities*, London: UCATT.

Vogel, S. (1996) *Freer Markets, More Rules: Regulatory Reform in Advanced Industrial Countries*, Ithaca, NY: Cornell University Press.

Whyte, D. (2007) 'The Crimes of Neo-Liberal Rule in Occupied Iraq', *British Journal of Criminology*, 47:177–195.

Notes

1 *Scrutinising New Regulations*, at http://www.berr.gov.uk/whatwedo/bre/policy/scrutinising-new-regulations/page44076.html.
2 See http://www.berr.gov.uk/files/file45019.pdf.
3 According to his friend, Emma Aynsley, cited at http://www.simonjones.org.uk/articles/bigissuesep98.htm.
4 http://www.bipsolutions.com/events/ctf_2007/speakers.html.

5 Penalising corporate 'culture'

The key to safer corporate activity?

Rick Sarre

Introduction

Using the criminal law to prevent and punish corporate wrongdoing has traditionally been fraught with difficulty. Indeed, the criminal law frequently plays at best a minor role in controlling and responding to corporate illegality.[1] This comes as no surprise to academic observers:

> Even when a formal criminal prosecution is undertaken, corporate defendants are well-positioned to defend themselves. Large companies are able to hire the best lawyers, secure 'professional' expert witnesses, and engage in delaying tactics that will outlast the political pressure that prompted the government to initiate a prosecution in the first place ... The lesson seems to be that the criminal justice system, as presently constituted, is simply not a viable forum for tackling corporate wrongdoing.[2]

Corporate manslaughter prosecutions in particular have rarely met with any level of success.[3] The most notable early case of a prosecution alleging corporate manslaughter in Australia was *The Queen v Denbo Pty Ltd.*[4] Denbo was prosecuted after one of its drivers was killed when his truck's brakes failed. Upon examination, prosecutors found that the company's vehicle service record was appalling. The company (through its directors) pleaded guilty and was fined £40,000. At the time of its conviction, however, Denbo Pty Ltd was in liquidation. The company was wound up six months before sentencing and never paid the fine. Later, like the Phoenix, it rose from its ashes, was reborn under a new name, and recommenced operations. The successor company did not pay the fine either.[5]

Internationally, the success rate (measured by guilty verdicts) in manslaughter prosecutions against corporations and individual officers is very poor indeed.[6] As Jim Gobert and Maurice Punch explain:

> [The] criminal law was not developed with companies in mind. Concepts such as mens rea and actus reus, which make perfectly good sense when applied to individuals, do not translate easily to an inanimate fictional entity

such as a corporation. Trying to apply these concepts to companies is a bit like trying to squeeze a square peg into a round hole.[7]

In the case of corporate officers and directors, with many individuals filling particular roles, it is rare indeed that a prosecutor will be able to establish a conjunction of the *actus reus* and *mens rea* of multiple individuals.[8]

That is not to say that manslaughter convictions are impossible. In July 2009, prosecutors secured the conviction of Alex Cittadini, an Australian boat-builder, based on a theory of manslaughter by omission. *The Excalibur*, a 15-metre racing vessel built by Mr Cittadini's company, Applied Alloy Yachts, overturned off Port Stephens, New South Wales, in September 2002 after its keel snapped in high winds. Four of the six crew drowned. When the yacht was salvaged, it was discovered that the keel had been cut and insufficiently re-welded during a reconstruction. The cut had then been covered up by polishing across the weld line. It was alleged at trial that Applied Alloy Yachts had not employed high-level quality assurance checks, partly because it would have required more paperwork and added time and cost to the project.

In April 2009, Mr Cittadini was found to have been criminally negligent in allowing the delivery of the yacht with a major fault. Judge Stephen Norrish concluded that there was an 'element of inexperience' in Mr Cittadini's employees when it came to making yachts. Four manslaughter convictions were returned against Mr Cittadini, notwithstanding the fact that Judge Norrish accepted his evidence that he was unaware of the cut, and that the employees' acts had been kept from him. Judge Norrish ruled that even if Mr Cittadini did not know about the cutting of the keel, he should have known and should have had in place a reasonable system to detect and prevent any variation to the design. The judge sentenced Mr Cittadini to three years jail.[9] However, the NSW Court of Criminal Appeal subsequently quashed the convictions and directed verdicts of acquittal, determining that the lower court verdict was 'unreasonable' and that the Crown Prosecutor's final address had caused 'a miscarriage of justice'.[10]

Prosecutions such as that of Mr Cittadini, however, are rare. This has led to persistent calls for reform of the law. The few egregious cases which are prosecuted will usually be well-covered by the media, with public outrage likely to follow if it appears that 'justice' has not been done, whether at the trial or, as in the *Cittadini* case, at the appellate level. The point was driven home in the aftermath of the *Cittadini* reversal when a survivor of the *Excalibur* tragedy, Brian McDermott, expressed his deep disappointment that no one had been held accountable for the deaths.[11] In fact, the *Cittadini* case was exceptional in that a prosecution for manslaughter had been brought in the first place; most industrial 'accidents' never make it into the criminal courts.

The death of Lydia Carter provides another tragic example. In October 2006, Ms Carter died after crashing her go-kart into a barrier while at a work function at the Auscarts track in Port Melbourne, Victoria.[12] She was wearing a seatbelt that did not fit properly, and safety barriers on the track had not been correctly installed. Judge Duncan Allen convicted and fined the parent company AAA

Auscarts Imports Pty Ltd a record £700,000 in May 2009, but the company had already gone into liquidation and would never pay the fine. Despite the finding that the company had showed a gross disregard for the safety of its employees and the public, neither the company nor any individual within it was ever held legally accountable for the death of Ms Carter.[13]

'Industrial manslaughter' and 'corporate culture'

To address criticism that too little was being done to prevent workplace deaths and accidents or to respond to them appropriately, many legislators have favoured simply raising the penalties prescribed by existing occupational health and safety laws. Under current Australian legislation there exists the possibility of a term of imprisonment for individuals who have personally engaged in gross negligence or other culpable behaviour leading to serious safety breaches.[14]

The fairness of imprisoning corporate officers, however, may be questioned. As a corporation's 'personality' is essentially a legal fiction, it is arguably unfair to make corporate directors and executives liable to incarceration solely by virtue of their status within a company where innocent victims have been seriously injured or killed. Imposing criminal liability on corporations for regulatory breaches by its senior officers is one thing; imposing personal criminal liability on senior officers simply because their company has committed an offence is quite another.[15] Even if personal liability of corporate officers were deemed to be desirable, it may be arbitrary to single out one or two such officers (the VPs in charge of Safety) to take the blame for the tragic consequences of a chain of errors that may involve many persons at many levels, even if the work environment as a whole can be characterised as insufficiently safety-minded.[16] Conversely, other critics have suggested that the law does not go far enough, pointing out that the imprisonment provisions do not necessarily apply to senior officers of non-corporations (such as partnerships and sole traders), transnational corporations or government-owned enterprises.[17]

Another method of controlling corporate misconduct, long advocated by commentators,[18] would be for the legislature to enact an offence of 'industrial manslaughter'[19] aimed at the company itself rather than at its directors and/or officers. Essentially, the idea is to treat corporations as if they were natural persons and to recognise that fault can lie with the organisation itself rather than with specific individuals who work for the organisation. However, corporate liability would not preclude individual liability; both the corporation and any individuals who may have been part of a 'web of decisions' that led to the eventual harm could be subject to prosecution.[20]

The naissance of the Australian developments can be found in the *Criminal Code Act 1995*, a Commonwealth of Australia Act,[21] which (specifically in Part 2) expands the notion of corporate criminal liability[22] by allowing for the attribution of recklessness and negligence to a corporation. Indeed, by virtue of the Act, corporations may be found guilty of any offence that is punishable by imprisonment if committed by a natural person. Harm caused by employees acting within the scope of their employment is considered to be harm caused by the body corporate.[23] This allows for the *physical* element of manslaughter to be attributed to a body corporate where the actions involved were engaged in by more than one person, who may or may not have met the requirement of being the 'guiding mind' of the corporation.

In respect of assigning the mental element of a crime to a body corporate, the Code provides several alternatives. The first is by creating an offence of manslaughter by gross negligence. While tort lawyers have long been aware of the difficulties in attributing negligence to corporations at common law, the Code overcomes this problem by attributing negligence to corporations through a theory of aggregation.[24] Negligence may be found on the part of the body corporate, according to the Code,[25] if the body corporate's conduct is negligent when *viewed as a whole*, that is, by adding together the conduct of any number of its employees, agents or officers. The rationale behind aggregation is explained by Gobert and Punch:

> A theory of aggregation arguably better captures the nature of corporate fault than a theory which imputes to the company a crime of a particular individual. There are times when, as a result of employee negligence, victims are seriously injured. Negligence, however, is generally not deemed sufficient to warrant imposing criminal liability on an individual and therefore also insufficient ... to hold a company liable for the agent's acts.[26]

A mental element other than negligence can be attributed to a body corporate under the Code if the corporation expressly, tacitly or impliedly authorised or permitted the commission of the offence.[27] Authorisation or permission may be established through proof of the actual state of mind of either the board of directors or other 'high managerial agents' of the body corporate.[28] In addition, and more innovatively, the Code allows authorisation or permission to be proved through reference to the body corporate's 'corporate culture'. 'Corporate culture' is defined as an 'attitude, policy, rule, course of conduct or practice existing within the body corporate generally'.[29] While this definition has not yet been judicially interpreted, there have been some attempts to put flesh on its bones. Jonathan Clough suggests:

> This 'corporate personality' or 'corporate culture' is seen both formally, in the company's policies and procedures, but also informally. It is a dynamic process with the corporate culture affecting the actions of individuals, and the actions of individuals affecting the corporate personality. Corporate culture may exist independently of individual employees or officers and may continue to exist despite changes in personnel. ... For example, while a corporation may outwardly claim to be concerned with occupational health and safety, if the pressure on individual managers is to meet unrealistic financial or time pressures, then there may be a temptation for corners to be cut and worker safety compromised.[30]

In other words, a body corporate can be deemed criminally liable for serious injury or a death in its workplace if it has a corporate culture that actively or passively permits or tolerates non-compliance with the law and this non-compliance leads to criminal harm.[31] This feature of the legislation is designed to cater to the situation where, despite the existence of documentation purporting to require employee compliance with the law, the reality is that non-compliance is not unusual, or is tacitly authorised by the company.[32]

The work of Peter Sandman is also apposite. He describes a not uncommon 'culture' situation thus:

> [W]e all become very skilled distinguishing the marching orders we are supposed to follow from the marching orders we are supposed to pay lip service to. Even though management are saying do this and do this and do this, the employees know that some of the things that management are saying they ought to do and some of the things that management are saying they ought to pretend to do. Management really meant it about safety, but the employees were assuming it didn't, were concluding that it didn't and were indeed perpetuating a culture that was unsafe and that they thought was the culture management wanted from them.[33]

In sum, then, the Code introduces new bases for liability, including attribution, aggregation and 'corporate culture'. Under the Code, and similarly under the UK *Corporate Manslaughter and Corporate Homicide Act* 2007,[34] both the mental and physical elements of manslaughter can be attributed to corporations *as entities*. While under the UK legislation prosecutions of corporate executives for complicity in their company's offence are specifically excluded[35] and the jury in a corporate manslaughter prosecution is only invited to 'consider' the extent to which the evidence shows that there were 'attitudes, policies, systems or accepted practices' that were likely to have encouraged a company's violation of a *health and safety* law leading to the offence,[36] the Australian Code goes much further. Corporate principals can be prosecuted and punished both individually and collectively by their association with the corporation *if the culture over which they preside* is one that encourages, tolerates or leads to non-compliance with the law.[37] Furthermore, a company with a poor 'corporate culture' will be considered as culpable for its intentional or reckless conduct as individual directors (or 'high managerial agents') were under the common law. Importantly, prosecutors can aggregate the requisite carelessness or 'risk denial', even though this may have the potential to scapegoat 'high managerial agents' regardless of their degree of involvement in the company's offence.

Industrial manslaughter prosecutions, then, are markedly different from those pursued under the common law and from those brought under traditional occupational health and safety legislation.[38] Corporations convicted of manslaughter under the Code can be subjected to heavier fines than apply under occupational health and safety laws.[39] Corporate officers are also subject to prosecution and sanctions.

Supporters of the revisions contained in the *Criminal Code Act 1995* may, however, be disappointed to learn that in practice the Code is not likely to be the panacea which they envisage. The Code only applies to Commonwealth of Australia offences, and manslaughter is not a Commonwealth offence.[40] As it stands, the primary function of the Code is to point the way forwards to individual States and Territories which wish to address workplace deaths in their jurisdictions. In order to give effect to the Code's lead, these States and Territories would need to adopt similar provisions in their criminal codes or, in the case of the common law States[41], to enact new criminal legislation. To date, the Australian Capital Territory is the only jurisdiction that has chosen to do so. All other States and Territories that have considered the issue have declined to follow the Code's example.[42] With no other new legislation on the horizon, therefore, it is to the Australian Capital Territory that we now turn.

Industrial manslaughter and 'corporate culture' in the Australian Capital Territory

In 2004, the Australian Capital Territory (ACT) became the first (and to date only) jurisdiction in Australia to introduce an offence of industrial manslaughter. The *Crimes (Industrial Manslaughter) Act 2003* added a new Part 2.5 (sections 49–55) to the existing Criminal Code. 'Industrial manslaughter' is defined as causing the death of a worker[43] while either being reckless about causing serious harm to that worker or any other worker, or being negligent about causing the death of that or any other worker.[44]

Section 49C *Crimes Act 1900 (ACT)* says:

An employer commits an offence if—

(a) a worker of the employer—
   (i) dies in the course of employment by, or providing services to, or in relation to, the employer; or
   (ii) is injured in the course of employment by, or providing services to, or in relation to, the employer and later dies; and
(b) the employer's conduct causes the death of the worker; and
(c) the employer is—
   (i) reckless about causing serious harm to the worker, or any other worker of the employer, by the conduct; or
   (ii) negligent about causing the death of the worker, or any other worker of the employer, by the conduct.

The ACT legislation provides for both employer and 'senior officer' liability[45] for industrial manslaughter, with maximum penalties being a combination of significant fines and terms of imprisonment.[46]

Chapter 2 of the Criminal Code incorporates the Commonwealth Criminal Code Act notions of 'corporate culture'. The key to the legislation is section 51:

51. (1) In deciding whether the fault element of intention, knowledge or recklessness exists for an offence in relation to a corporation, the fault element is taken to exist if the corporation expressly, tacitly or impliedly authorises or permits the commission of the offence.

    (2) The ways in which authorisation or permission may be established include–

        (a) proving that the corporation's board of directors intentionally, knowingly or recklessly engaged in the conduct or expressly, tacitly or impliedly authorised or permitted the commission of the offence; or

        (b) proving that a high managerial agent of the corporation intentionally, knowingly or recklessly engaged in the conduct or expressly, tacitly or impliedly authorised or permitted the commission of the offence; or

        (c) proving that a corporate culture existed within the corporation that directed, encouraged, tolerated or led to noncompliance with the contravened law; or

        (d) proving that the corporation failed to create and maintain a corporate culture requiring compliance with the contravened law.

    (3) Subsection (2) (b) does not apply if the corporation proves that it exercised appropriate diligence to prevent the conduct, or the authorisation or permission.

As under the Commonwealth Code, negligence of a corporation can be attributed by aggregation.[47] Similarly, the physical element of the offence (causing death either by an act or by omission) is not only attributable to a corporation by virtue of the conduct of the corporation's officers, but also by the conduct of its agents and employees.[48]

In practical terms, the new ACT legislation will have limited effect. The Australian Capital Territory is home to only 1.5 per cent of the Australian population, and has no heavy industry. Most of its employers and employees are government departments and public servants respectively. Moreover, the Australian government moved quickly to introduce (in 2004) a Commonwealth law that exempts ACT employers and employees from the provisions of the *Crimes (Industrial Manslaughter) Act (ACT) 2003*. This political response in effect represented a snub for the legislators of the Australian Capital Territory by their more conservative national masters. Its effect will be to exempt about 80 per cent of employers and companies in the Australian Capital Territory from the ambit of the industrial manslaughter legislation.

Despite the limited reach of the ACT legislation, its symbolic significance cannot be overstated. The possibility of a prosecution should concentrate corporate minds on workplace dangers that can lead to death. Both lawyers and academics eagerly await a test case to determine the effectiveness (or, indeed, workability) of these new provisions. To date there have been no such prosecutions.

Discussion

Given the persistence of deaths and injuries in Australian workplaces notwithstanding an increasingly punitive occupational health and safety regime, there is good reason to believe that occupational health and safety law is, on its own, an inadequate deterrent against workplace harm. There is growing support for the view that deterrence could be bolstered if directors and managers of companies were to be personally (and criminally) liable in circumstances where the potential harm is great, the risk obvious, the precautionary measures poor,[49] and corporate conduct 'conspicuously fail[s] to observe the standards laid down by law'.[50] There are many who believe, in addition, that deterrence would be enhanced if the penalties for a conviction were to include terms of imprisonment for senior managers even in the absence of *direct* culpability.[51]

Is this a safe assumption? Is there any evidence to suggest that the placing of these presumptively deterrent factors in legislation would make managers more likely to inculcate a culture of safety in their workplaces? Deterrence theory is in fact notoriously unreliable. The best that can be said about the threat of imprisonment may be that some people are deterred from some conduct some of the time by the threat of imprisonment.[52] The existing criminological evidence further suggests that the threat of being caught is a far stronger influence than the punishment which might follow if one were to be caught.[53] Moreover, an over-reliance upon prison as a crime-reduction strategy comes at a significant financial cost, and usually affects only those who cannot muster the resources, financial and personal, to aid in an acquittal or a plea in mitigation of penalty.

One might assume that the inclusion of the 'corporate culture' provisions, such as those found in the ACT legislation, will make prosecutions more likely as it may be easier to prove a poor culture than a manager's (or string of managers') direct culpability. At the very least, proof of a criminally deficient corporate culture will provide a second string to the prosecutor's bow.[54] And certainly the prospect of imprisonment sends a strong message to managers, as well as the business community, that culpable conduct will not be tolerated even if it means targeting individuals who may have been but one of a number of guilty parties.

Is there, however, any empirical evidence that introducing into the law of corporate criminal liability the notion of a criminogenic corporate culture will have a deterrent effect? Helpful for our purposes is a study by Andrew Hopkins arising out of the Gretley mine disaster. In November 1996, four miners drowned in a mining shaft 150 metres underground after they accidentally drilled into a flooded and disused shaft at Gretley, owned and operated by a Hunter Valley (NSW) colliery.[55] In August 2004 (almost eight years later), the Newcastle Wallsend Coal Company, its parent company Oakbridge, the mine's surveyor and two managers were found guilty of breaching the Occupational Health and Safety Act (NSW). Five other under-managers at the mine had charges against them dismissed.

Following this case, Hopkins interviewed the relevant managers of the companies involved. Based on these interviews, he concluded that there were a number of direct effects (including deterrence) that had occurred as a result of the prosecutions (and the obvious threat of future prosecutions) over and above the general moral censure that followed from the publicity about the case:

1   The threat of prosecution leads to thoughts of self-protection, and focuses managerial minds firmly on issues of safety;

2   the threat of prosecution gives rise to an increased tendency for managers to keep written records; and

3   the threat of prosecution leads managers to discipline employees who engage in violations of the rules.[56]

These conclusions are corroborated by the work of Dorothy Thornton, Neil Guningham and Robert Kagan. On the basis of their review of environmental law enforcement practices in eight jurisdictions in the USA they concluded that the threat of strong sanctions does have a deterrent effect, manifested in both a 'reminder' and a 'reassurance' function. The threat of prosecution reminds managers that they should review their compliance strategies regularly, and at the same time it reassures them that their competitors who violate the law are unlikely to get away with it.[57]

Important as these findings are, they would appear to relate to prosecutions in general, and not just those based on a deficient 'corporate culture'. The logic of those who support the addition of 'corporate culture' provisions to the law would seem to be that the deterrent effect of the law will be enhanced because prosecutions will be easier to mount, more likely therefore to be brought, and more likely to result in a conviction. In the absence of empirical evidence, however, these assumptions must remain in the realm of speculation.

More persuasive, perhaps, is the argument that the deterrent effect of a prosecution is bolstered if there is a likelihood of a prison sentence in the event of a conviction. Imprisonment, one assumes, is a far stronger deterrent than any sanction that does not involve imprisonment. This argument rests on the twin assumptions that the presence of 'corporate culture' provisions in the law will make a guilty verdict more likely and that, as a result of such a verdict, a corporate officer is more likely to face a jail term. Neither of these assumptions is necessarily sound. As noted previously, the likelihood of being caught may weigh more heavily in a corporate officer's decision-making than the prospect of imprisonment should he or she be caught – and prosecuted, and convicted. Moreover, as few corporate executives have a criminal record, while many can boast a distinguished history of public and community service, the likelihood of a court imposing a jail sentence even if there is a conviction may not be great.

If the new provisions (attribution, aggregation, culture and the threat of imprisonment) have their short-comings as deterrents, are there other options for the punishment of companies that have engaged in unacceptable practices? Commentators have suggested that the deterrent power of divestment of company equity, adverse publicity, corporate probation (with remedial and rehabilitative conditions), disqualifications from certain commercial activities, receiverships (or ordering someone else to run the company), and the threat of the loss of limited liability are, arguably, equally or more potent deterrents, and have thus encouraged their deployment.[58]

Even if no prosecutions are ever brought based on a company's deficient 'corporate culture', it does not follow that the 'corporate culture' initiatives can be judged a failure. The ACT and Code provisions have raised the profile of the importance of a company's culture. Directors and corporate executives who might not previously even have been aware of the concept now have to ask themselves what kind of culture exists within their company, what kind of culture do they want to exist, and how do they go about bringing such a culture into existence. Those managers who may have been only vaguely aware of the concept of a 'corporate culture' but had not given it serious thought will now need to give the matter greater attention.

Evidence, albeit preliminary, suggests that this is, in fact, happening. Corporations seem to be increasingly aware of their culture and eager to report good corporate practices.[59] Likewise, there is a growing appreciation that the right corporate culture will lessen the chances of an industrial death even absent the threat of prosecution. Indeed, one would think that an *ex ante* 'culture of safety' can, with the right incentives, be inculcated into the thinking of organisations without the need to prosecute (*ex post*) those who fail to create such a culture.

Evidence that companies are aware of the importance of 'corporate culture' might be gleaned from the so-called 'good corporate governance' reporting data published in the annual reviews of the Australian Stock Exchange (ASX).[60] Of particular significance in Table 5.1 is the rate of increase of reporting to the ASX's criteria for surveyed companies in Australia from 2007 to 2008 which shows a six-fold increase in occupational health and safety reporting over the relevant period.

Table 5.1 ASX Corporate Governance Council's Principles and Recommendations, 2009

Total companies reporting to ASX guidelines	*2008 top 300 companies*	*2008 companies generally*	*2007 companies generally*
Reviewed	*n*=244	*n*=1510	*n*=1291
Operational risk	54%	45%	9%
Environmental risk	32%	19%	8%
Sustainability	11%	3%	<1%
Climate change	4%	1%	n/a
Compliance	55%	42%	11%
Strategic	29%	20%	5%
Ethical conduct	7%	5%	2%
Reputation / brand	18%	9%	3%
Financial	57%	48%	10%
OH&S / legal	29%	25%	4%

One might safely assume that the focus of those reporting to these criteria is on the prevention of future harm as opposed to putting the pieces back together after damage has been done.[61] One might also read from these data that those who have responsibility for a company's safety record are seeing the positive contribution that an alignment of the interests of the corporation and its employees can have on profitability. Cultivating an appropriate culture can be an important goal in such an exercise.

Industrial manslaughter laws cannot, by themselves, lower workplace death rates unless they directly affect corporate or individual employees' perceptions of risk. That is where the importance of corporate culture enters the picture. An appreciation of risk needs to be embedded within a company's culture but beyond that, there also needs to be a variety of positive and negative control mechanisms, or, in other words, both 'carrots' and 'sticks'.[62] The challenge is to determine how to encourage such attitudes and behaviours even in the absence of the threat of legal sanction. For example, professional bodies, guilds and other business organisations might reward companies that display exemplary 'corporate cultures' and 'good governance'.[63] In the event of a prosecution and conviction, evidence that a company has taken steps to introduce a risk-aversive corporate culture should incline a court to impose a more lenient sentence, assuming that a variety of sentencing options are available to the court.[64] Whatever it takes, the development of good corporate culture is likely to be an effective regulatory tool regardless of what it adds to the industrial manslaughter deterrence debate.

Having said all that, is there not an argument for industrial manslaughter prosecutions on the basis of desert? The issue here is the symbolic function of the law in cases such as *Cittadini* and *Auscarts* referred to earlier. Is there not an important interest to be served in seeing that 'justice' is done when serious harm has been caused? Paul Almond puts the question as follows:

> High-profile work-related fatality cases, whether or not they result in prosecution, communicate messages about the risks arising from corporate activity. It is this *communicative* function that accounts for the degree of public concern provoked by fatality cases, which cannot simply be dismissed as a form of moral panic over an emotive issue, because it reflects the cognitive evaluation of socially grounded phenomena.[65]

Public perceptions are indeed important.[66] There is a perception amongst those who monitor 'law and order' politics that there is a latter-day preference for retributive sanctioning and a heightened intolerance of offending generally. However, Almond's research suggests that this does not necessarily translate into punitive attitudes to sentencing following corporate deaths. In a survey based upon readers responding to a series of vignettes, he found that:

> although personal decisions about liability and punishment were made on essentially moral grounds, this did not translate into the 'moral outrage' and demands for vengeance that characterize accounts of populist punitiveness.[67]

Indeed,

> the respondents' punishment preferences were rational and reasoned, and the emotive aspects of their attitudes were primarily regretful rather than vengeful ... there were signs that the desire to express condemnation and disapproval of offenders' conduct was counterbalanced by recognition of the need for humane and just penal policies.[68]

Almond's conclusions are important to the debate over the adoption of industrial manslaughter legislation. If, as he contends, the public is more concerned with controlling the underlying risks that lead to work-related deaths than the vilification of the offending company and its officers through condign punishment, then the argument for industrial manslaughter legislation (supported by provisions relating to 'corporate culture') is greatly diminished. If, on the other hand, the threat of an industrial manslaughter prosecution increases the deterrence by virtue of the ability of industrial manslaughter legislation to motivate corporate executives to take active measures to control serious risks, then such legislation may have more value than its detractors may be prepared to admit.

Conclusion

The debate over the value of industrial manslaughter laws will continue to feature strongly in corporate boardrooms, legislative committees, parliaments and academic (particularly criminal law) circles. The debate has been hampered by the multi-layered complexities and political tensions involved in drafting laws designed to bring responsible persons to account while remaining faithful to basic precepts of individual criminal responsibility and public policy. The concept of corporate culture may help to bridge this gap.

In the absence of persuasive evidence that attributing human offences to corporate entities, aggregating negligent minds and actions, locating criminal liability in poor 'corporate cultures', and allowing for the possibility of imprisonment in the most egregious of cases will reduce or eliminate deaths and injuries from the corporate workplace, changes to the *status quo* (outside of the Australian Capital Territory) are unlikely. Indeed, every other Australian State that has considered industrial manslaughter legislation has appeared reluctant to change its law, regarding any experimentation as an ineffective and potentially counterproductive means of addressing corporate killing.

All this is not to deny both the symbolic and practical importance of 'corporate culture' legislation and prosecutions. They serve to raise the visibility, priority and importance given to corporate risk management. They demonstrate to the public that the law does take corporate crime seriously and is prepared to act when appropriate. Without such legislation, cases like *Denbo*, *Cittadini* and *Auscarts* will continue to come before the courts without culpable defendants being held accountable or punished. Such a prospect is increasingly unacceptable, not only to victims and their families but also to members of the general public.

Notes

1   Sarre, R. (2001) 'Risk Management and Regulatory Weakness' in Ian Ramsay (ed) *Collapse Incorporated: Tales, Safeguards and Responsibilities of Corporate Australia*, Sydney: CCH, 291–323.
2   Gobert, J. and Punch, M. (2003) *Rethinking Corporate Crime*, London: LexisNexis Butterworths, 9.
3   See generally Celia Wells (2001) 'Corporate Criminal Liability: Developments in Europe and Beyond', 39(7) *Law Society Journal* 62.
4   (1994) 6 VIR 157.
5   Chesterton, S. (1994) 'The Corporate Veil, Crime and Punishment: *The Queen* v *Denbo Pty Ltd and Timothy Ian Nadenbousch*', *Melbourne University Law Review* 19, 1064.
6   Sarre, R. (2007) 'White Collar Crime and Prosecution for "Industrial Manslaughter" as a Means to Reduce Workplace Deaths' in Pontell, H. and Geis, G. (eds) *International Handbook on White Collar Crime*, New York: Springer, 648–662.
7   Gobert, J. and Punch, M. (2003) *Rethinking Corporate Crime*, 10.
8   Sarre, R. and Richards, J. (2005) 'Responding to Culpable Corporate Behaviour: Current Developments in the Industrial Manslaughter Debate', *Flinders Journal of Law Reform*, 8(1), 93–111.
9   'Boatbuiler Jailing May Spark New Case' *The Weekend Australian*, 11–12/7/2009, p 9.
10   'Appeal Win on Boat Deaths', *The Weekend Australian*, 18–19/12/2009, p 5.
11   Ibid.
12   Auscarts Convicted Over Gokart Death', Daniel Fogarty, www.news.com.au AAP, 6 May 2009.
13   A go-kart centre called Auscarts Racing still operates at the same venue, owned now by Port Melbourne Go-Karts Pty Ltd.
14   The existing and rising OH&S legislative penalties that apply in the various jurisdictions in Australia are reviewed in Catanzariti, J. (2004) 'Higher and Novel Penalties for Serious Safety Breaches', *Law Society Journal*, 48 (August). Refer also to *R v Clarke* (Unreported 2007) Queensland Court of Appeal. A supervisor failed to tie a woman's harness correctly as she was about to ride a flying fox. She was seriously injured when she fell off. At first instance, a jury in the District Court found the accused guilty and he was subsequently sentenced to two years and eight months imprisonment. He appealed on a number of grounds, including the severity of the penalty. The Court of Appeal unanimously rejected the grounds for appeal and refused leave to appeal against sentence.
15   But see Foster (this volume).
16   Moreover, there is the possibility that the mere mention of imprisonment will raise the likelihood that collaboration between employers and employees will break down, and that would be to the detriment of health and safety in the workplace generally. See former NSW Industrial Relations Minister John Della Bosca as cited by, and reported in, 'NSW: Govt to Introduce Tougher Laws for Negligent Employers' (AAP, 27 October 2004).
17   Discussed in Sarre, R. (2007) 'White Collar Crime'.
18   See, e.g., Fisse, B. and Braithwaite, J. (1988) 'The Allocation of Responsibility for Corporate Crime: Individualism, Collectivism and Accountability', *Sydney Law Review* 11, 468–513; also Polk, K., Haines, F. and Perrone, S. (1993) 'Homicide, Negligence and Work Death: The Need for Legal Change' ,in M. Quinlan (ed), *Work and Health: The Origins, Management and Regulation of Occupational Illness*, Melbourne: Macmillan.
19   Referred to in the UK and Europe as 'corporate manslaughter' or 'corporate homicide'. Industrial manslaughter is the term used in the Australian Capital Territory (ACT) for deaths in the workplace, not those caused by businesses that cause the deaths of non-workers.

20 Tomasic, R. (2005) 'From White-Collar to Corporate Crime and Beyond' in D. Chappell and P. Wilson (eds) *Issues in Australian Crime and Criminal Justice*, Chatswood NSW: LexisNexis Butterworths, 264.

21 This Act applies to all Australians. Most Australian criminal law is the responsibility of the States or Territories and these laws are only applicable within the relevant jurisdiction.

22 Part 2.5, Division 12. For a useful discussion of this Part, see Woolf, T. (1997) 'The Criminal Code Act 1995 (Cth) – Towards a Realist Vision of Corporate Criminal Liability', *Criminal Law Journal* 21(5), 257. For a discussion of the English equivalent, see Almond, P. (2007) 'Regulation Crisis: Evaluating the Potential Legitimizing Effects of "Corporate Manslaughter" Cases', *Law and Policy*, 29(3), 285–310 especially at 288.

23 Sections 12.1 and 12.2.

24 Section 12.4(2).

25 Section 12.4.2(b).

26 Gobert, J. and Punch, M. (2003) *Rethinking Corporate Crime*, 84.

27 Section 12.3(1).

28 Sections 12.3(2) (a) and (b).

29 Section 12.3(6).

30 Clough, J. (2005) 'Will the Punishment Fit the Crime? Corporate Manslaughter and the Problem of Sanctions', *Flinders Journal of Law Reform*, 8(1), 113–131 at 119.

31 Sections 12.3(2) (c) and (d).

32 Section 12.3(2) (d).

33 Sandman, P. (2001) 'Motivated intention and safety management', interview in *Safety at Work*, October 30, 1–8 at 2–3.

34 See generally Gobert, J. (2005) 'The Politics of Corporate Manslaughter – the British Experience', *Flinders Journal of Law Reform*, 8(1), 1–38.

35 CMCH 2007, Section 18.

36 CMCH 2007, Section 8(3).

37 The UK Act refers to the notion of corporate culture but does so only as an evidentiary factor, not as a basis for liability.

38 There is a philosophical issue alive here as well. Health and safety law may be regarded as a lesser form of proscription, as liability under OH&S attaches to a breach of duty (a guard rail was left open), rather than the outcome (a person died because the guard rail was open). The criminal law is thus more 'ends-driven' and less 'regulatory', and thus possesses greater legitimatory power than OH&S prosecutions which may be regarded as simply the end result of a routine enforcement activity. See Almond, P. (2007) 'Regulation Crisis' at 290 and 300.

39 This is not to say that the OH&S penalties are trifling; see Catanzariti, J. (2004) 'Higher and Novel Penalties for Serious Safety Breaches', *Law Society Journal*, 48 (August).

40 In August 2004, Greens Senator Kerry Nettle introduced into the Australian parliament the Criminal Code Amendment (Workplace Death and Serious Injury) Bill 2004, which was designed specifically to incorporate industrial manslaughter offences into the Commonwealth Criminal Code. The Bill has stalled.

41 There are, confusingly, different approaches taken to criminal laws amongst the States and Territories. Three States (Queensland, Western Australia and Tasmania, plus the Northern Territory and the Australian Capital Territory) have codified their criminal laws. South Australia, New South Wales and Victoria still use the common law.

42 Sarre, R. and Richards, J. (2004) 'Criminal Manslaughter in the Workplace: What Options for Legislators?' *Law Institute Journal*, 78, (1–2), 58–61.

43 And only a worker, for example, not a crew member aboard a yacht who is not a worker.

44 Crimes Act 1900 (ACT) ss 49C, 49D. Confusingly, the offence of manslaughter is proscribed in this Act while the requisites of criminal responsibility are found in

the Criminal Code (2002). The two pieces of legislation, therefore, need to be read together. The Crimes Act 1900 (ACT) s 7A specifically links the provisions.

45 Section 49D mirrors section 49C.

46 Maximum penalty: 2000 penalty units, imprisonment for 20 years or both.

47 Criminal Code 2002 (ACT) s 52.

48 Criminal Code 2002 (ACT) s 50.

49 Gobert, J. and Punch, M. (2003) *Rethinking Corporate Crime*, 96, referring to Ashworth, A. (1999) *Principles of Criminal Law*, (3rd edn) 199.

50 Per Cummins J., *DPP v Esso (Australia) Pty Ltd* [2001] VSC 296 (Unreported, Supreme Court of Victoria, Justice Cummins, 30 May 2001) [para 4]. For an insight into that prosecution, see Wheelwright, K. (2002) 'Corporate Liability for Workplace Deaths and Injuries – Reflecting on Victoria's Laws in the Light of the Esso Longford Explosion', *Deakin Law Review* 7(2), 323.

51 Anecdotally, it has been said that the sight of executives in handcuffs being led out of the building of failed US giant corporation Enron probably did more towards restoring public confidence in the justice system in the wake of that corporate malfeasance than anything else.

52 Tomaino J. and Kapardis, A. (2004) 'Sentencing Theory' in Sarre, R. and Tomaino, J. (eds) *Key Issues in Criminal Justice*, Adelaide: Australian Humanities Press, 86.

53 Tomaino J. and Kapardis, A. (2004) 'Sentencing Theory', 93.

54 We will be better able to make that judgement once there have been some judicial interpretations of the rather vague terms found in the legislation such as 'culture', 'attitude' and 'maintain'.

55 See also Phillips, K. (2006) *The Politics of a Tragedy: The Gretley Mine Disaster and the Dangerous State of Work Safety Laws in New South Wales*, Institute of Public Affairs, Work Reform Unit.

56 Hopkins, A. (2007) *Lessons from Gretley: Mindful Leadership and the Law*, Sydney: CCH, 134.

57 Thornton, D., Gunningham, N. and Kagan, R. (2005) 'General Deterrence and Corporate Environmental Behavior', *Law and Policy*, 27(2), 262–288.

58 See Sarre, R. (2002) 'Responding to Corporate Collapses: Is There a Role for Corporate Social Responsibility?' *Deakin Law Review*, 7(1), 1–19.

59 See, for example, the evidence provided in Sarre, R. and Doig, M. (2000) 'Preventing Disaster by Building a Risk-Prevention Ethic into Corporate Governance', *Australian Journal of Emergency Management*, 15, 54–57.

60 Australian Securities Exchange (ASX) report of reporting against the ASX Corporate Governance Council's Principles and Recommendations.

61 Clough, J. (2005) 'Will the Punishment Fit the Crime? Corporate Manslaughter and the Problem of Sanctions', *Flinders Journal of Law Reform*, 8(1), 113–131 at 120.

62 Fisse, B. (1990) 'Sentencing Options Against Corporations', *Criminal Law Forum*, 1(2) 211.

63 See this connection made in Hill, J. (2002) 'Corporate Criminal Liability in Australia: An Evolving Corporate Governance Technique?' in Low Chee Keong (ed), *Corporate Governance: An Asia-Pacific Critique*, Hong Kong: Sweet and Maxwell Asia, 519.

64 Tomasic, R. (2005) 'From White-Collar to Corporate Crime and Beyond' in D. Chappell and P. Wilson (eds) *Issues in Australian Crime and Criminal Justice*, Chatswood NSW: LexisNexis Butterworths, at 267.

65 Almond, P. (2007) 'Regulation Crisis', 293. (Emphasis in the original.)

66 Monterosso, S. (2009) 'Punitive Criminal Justice and Policy in Contemporary Society' *QUT Law and Justice Journal*, 9(1), 13–25.

67 Almond, P. (2008) 'Public Perceptions of Work-Related Fatality Cases: Reaching the Outer Limits of "Populist Punitiveness"?' *British Journal of Criminology*, 48, 448–467 at 463.

68 Almond, P. (2008) 'Public Perceptions of Work-Related Fatality Case', 464.

Part II

Organisational v. individual liability

6 The organizational component in corporate crime

Maurice Punch

The role of the organization

I write this paper as a sociologist/criminologist with an academic interest in business deviance and corporate crime and not as a lawyer or legal scholar.[1] The central thread in my work is that of deviance and crime in organizations or 'organizational crime'.[2] This assumes that in some way the firm`s institutional context and culture shape an environment that encourages, colludes or is culpably blind to law-breaking. This conceptual perspective does not sit easily with the law and with many lawyers, as both tend to be rooted in a rather narrow individualism; but also not with those social scientists and philosophers who would argue that organizations do not exist outside of the perceptions and actions of individuals. In a theoretical sense the latter are right but then they ignore the social nature of collective behaviour. When, for example, armies of millions of men sweep across countries, each individual soldier has at one level to comply in some way. Yet the military institution has proved remarkably successful at swiftly shaping individual citizens into large and obedient units that assault beaches, attack towns and jump out of aircraft into enemy territory. There is little evidence that before they assault the beach the soldiers dally to debate if the army they are fighting for really exists or if the shells exploding dangerously close to their vessel are being fired solely by individuals rather than by the armed forces of the enemy. It is equally short-sighted to think of decision-making at the top of a major corporation as that of 'individuals'; the executives have been groomed in the corporate culture and have been selected and shaped to function as a unit that works in the best interests of the company.

For it is in the nature of organizations – churches, schools, social movements, political parties and corporations – that they promote conformity and compliance with an asserted and assumed institutional reality. People assume the organization to be real; and it then operates as a real entity in their lives. If that were not so, and every individual had to ponder his or her own personal motives and conduct, then all the achievements of organized social life would be nigh impossible. But it simply is fact that the criminal law is highly conservative on this area and has very deep roots in individualism with a weak orientation to criminalizing and sanctioning organizational misbehaviour.[3] Wolf makes the point by rhetorically asking, 'How can a flow chart be guilty?'[4] It could even be said that the criminal law has never quite adapted to the rise of modern business corporations some two centuries ago and is still somewhat at a loss in coping with complex multinationals with dispersed subsidiaries in diverse jurisdictions within the contemporary global and post-Fordist economy.[5] This remains the case despite the fact that jurisprudence in Britain has for more than a century recognized that an organization can be held to have committed a criminal act.[6]

In my academic work, then, I assume both that people in organizations perceive the organization to be a real entity outside of themselves that influences their personal and collective conduct; and also that it is legally possible to take an organization to court for committing a crime.[7]

The institutionalized rather than the individual nature of some forms of corporate crime was discussed in the lapidary work of Edwin Sutherland in the 1940s.[8] Although he may have sown confusion by his use of the term 'white-collar crime',[9] which tends to convey highly placed corporate executives who break the law, a careful reading of his work makes clear that a central part of his thesis was that corporations too commit crimes. Sutherland shows that the offences by companies that he traces are not just individual, haphazard and random but that some industries offend more than others and that some companies are repeat offenders over time during which managers would have been replaced. It is, for instance, in the nature of price-fixing, industrial espionage, cartel-forming, insider trading, and market manipulation, that they are carefully constructed conspiracies, involving the highest levels of management, and requiring covert campaigns with sophisticated and creative camouflage. Sutherland was, then, the first academic to provide convincing evidence that executives in business organizations consciously and deliberately intend to break the law. Indeed it has become clear since his pioneering work that 'recidivist' corporations depend on a relay of executives who smoothly slot into the roles assigned to them and willingly do the company's bidding.

This phenomenon was well illustrated by Sutherland's disciple Geis in his classic article on price-fixing in the Heavy Electrical Equipment Industry.[10] He revealed that the crimes were strategic, long-term, systemic and industry-driven. Groups of executives would meet competitors at covert locations and negotiate the price-fixing; and this practice was maintained over time in accordance with fluctuating market conditions. This was collective conduct in that new managers were socialized into this strategic rule-bending to the extent that they saw it as 'normal' in the industry and felt it was justified in securing continuity and stability. As one of them explained, 'it had become so common and gone on for so many years that I think we lost sight of the fact that it was illegal'.[11] That this rigging of markets was against the principle of free enterprise to which they all subscribed, and against the criminal law in which they all purported to personally believe, had apparently escaped them. Indeed this law-breaking was seen as 'SOP', Standard Operating Procedure, and the individual executives fitted into this routine, widely accepted and standard way of conducting business which was conspiratorial and carefully camouflaged at the highest levels of the organization and hence fully intended. And they did it, they explained, not for any personal gain but for the corporation.

This organizational component in corporate crime is strongly reflected in some of the cases dealt with in my book *Dirty Business*.[12] Furthermore it runs through the work of a number of leading criminologists including Clinard and Yeager, Levi, Snider, and Slapper and Tombs.[13] It forms an important factor in the legally-oriented analysis of Gobert[14] which is more tuned than most legal scholarship to organizational as opposed to individual liability. This way of thinking and analysing argues that 'the organization did it' and hence liability should be sought not just at the individual level but also at the organizational level.

In short, I and others look not so much at the individual level – in terms of personal motivation, culpability and liability – but more at the organizational and institutional level. This takes us into an analysis drawing on the socio-political and regulatory environment of business, corporate culture, opportunity structures for business deviance, reward systems, recruitment and socialization, leadership, hierarchy, division of labour, decision making and how fiduciary responsibility and liability is structured within the corporation. These features shape a context in which individuals fit into collective behaviour and commit crimes for – or against – the organization while utilizing the organization as the criminal 'weapon' in the commission of their offence. It is of the essence that the *organizational component* is crucial to corporate crime – no organization, no crime.

Two main issues

Firstly, empirical analysis of corporate criminality is problematic because virtually every study of organizations reveals that, apart from the formal structure, there is an informal system or 'shadow' organization where, behind the glossy corporate front and the public relations rhetoric, there is an '*operational code*' about how the company really operates and how things really get done.[15] Under the surface there are practices which may enhance organizational aims – such as the price-fixing mentioned above or using bribery to ensure contracts in certain markets – or may, as in some forms of fraud or industrial enterprise, expose the organization to legal liability.

To illustrate, along with a group of consultants, I conducted a study into fraud within a major corporation that enjoys an excellent reputation as a 'good corporate citizen'. What we discovered was that management policies in fact stimulated the deviance which the company claimed it wanted to avoid; that the company's impressive-looking control apparatus was distinctly porous; and that a manager revealed to have engaged in 'creative' accounting was not ignominiously dismissed but rather sent off with a munificent farewell reception and a handsome golden parachute. In other words the 'organization' (the collective of senior management coupled to the organizational structure and culture) was stimulating the deviance; colluding in it by not tackling it adequately; effectively rewarding the deviant; and treating each case as an isolated incident so that there was no organizational learning. The senior executives were highly qualified managers in an institution with explicit ethical values but they found it almost impossible to accept that their policies in some way fostered deviant behaviour and that their organizational defences were inadequate to expose deviance. Indeed, to avoid reputational damage to the organization, they resist blaming the individual let alone the organization.

Secondly, and of perhaps great importance in the present context, is the evidence that the law typically focuses on individual liability and not organizational liability. For instance, I attended a conference in Amsterdam two years ago on 'systems crimes'.[16] Most of the participants were international lawyers and/or members of international war crimes and human rights tribunals of which there are several in the Netherlands. In terms of harm committed by collectives, the presentations focused on 'mega-harm' which were off the scale of harm caused by conventional, organized or corporate crime. Here the mass murder, genocide and systemic abuse of human rights – leading to death, mutilation, banishment, mass starvation and widespread sexual abuse – ran into the hundreds of thousands if not millions of victims. Many of the cases discussed involved states and state agencies which had consciously engaged in planned, systematic and prolonged execution of criminal offences or human rights abuses. These gross offences, like the Holocaust, could only be committed through organizational means.[17] And yet, as contributors uniformly pointed out, the prosecutions were typically of individuals, as was the case at the Nuremburg Tribunals after World War Two.

If one were to replace 'state' with 'corporation' in the above analysis, then the same arguments about collective liability would be discernible. The legal mind clearly has difficulty in determining mens rea and the actus reus when a crime is not committed by an individual but by an organization or other collective entity. It is the law itself, then, which forms part of the problem; it plainly is more comfortable in dealing with individuals than with institutions.[18] The criminal law in particular remains largely locked at the level of the individual. For instance, when the factories and mines of nineteenth-century Britain were held to account for deaths and injuries in the workplace, the legislators avoided the issue of intent – mens rea – by simply opting for strict liability offences. Yet in English jurisprudence, there are several cases reaching back almost a century and half which have held that a corporation, as a legal entity, can be held responsible for a crime.[19] This is also now true in a number of countries, including the Netherlands,[20] whereas those countries with a civil law tradition have more difficulty attributing a crime to an enterprise. Crimes can only be committed by humans, in this view, although business corporations can be prosecuted for 'administrative' or economic offences.[21]

In the literature on corporate crime there is a wealth of cases illustrating this theme of organizational culpability in corporate deviance. But for a range of reasons it has not always been possible to bring a criminal prosecution or obtain a conviction of the companies involved.[22] These much cited cases include:

- the fall of Barings Bank, which was bankrupted by the market manipulations of Nick Leeson with losses of over £800 million; only Leeson faced criminal prosecution and conviction although the evidence is replete with the organization's complicity;

- the capsizing of the *Herald of Free Enterprise* at Zeebrugge causing some 200 deaths: the ferry had sailed with the bow doors open which allowed water to enter the car deck and destabilize the boat. Despite a damning report on the culture of safety throughout the company and an inquest bringing in a verdict of unlawful death, a prosecution for corporate manslaughter failed;
- the scandal surrounding the drug Thalidomide, where some 8,000 children were born deformed in a number of countries because Thalidomide had been marketed as a tranquilliser that was 'harmless', even for pregnant women. Warning signals of a relationship between the drug and birth defects were ignored by the manufacturer. For a number of technical reasons both criminal and civil cases proved extremely difficult;
- there was a prosecution for homicide in the USA relating to the Ford Pinto car. The Ford Motor Company had produced an automobile with a design flaw that rendered the petrol tank vulnerable to rupture following a rear-end collision. After a series of 'accidents' in which people were severely burned, or burnt to death, a prosecution was brought against the company but failed;
- the explosion at the Union Carbide chemical plant in Bhopal, India, was the worst chemical 'accident' in history. Several thousand people (estimates vary between 3,000 and 5,000) were killed, 200,000 were injured, and many more victims still suffer twenty years later as a result of the incident. Union Carbide was held not to have kept to maintenance standards as the company was looking to sell off the plant, but there has never been a successful prosecution of the company.

From this corpus of failed prosecutions I shall focus more closely on four discrete areas and case studies.

Financial services

The field of white-collar and corporate crime has been in the spotlight in recent years by virtue of the revelations of overt risk-taking, excessive rewards and dubious business practices in financial services that have helped to foster a global economic crisis. At one level many individuals took decisions and behaved in ways that collectively led to dramatic and massive financial loss. But the collapse of once prestigious and seemingly unassailable banks and other financial institutions can be related to a web of institutional and organizational factors that shaped an environment that made these harms possible. In effect, this was a form of system failure.

A number of the interlocking variables included the globalization of the economy; the mergers in financial services that led to the creation of large, globally operating conglomerates; and the increasing domination of the centres of financial trade in New York, London, Frankfurt and Tokyo which became the drivers of modern economies. Their collective strength allowed them to lean on governments and influence if not intimidate regulators. The nature of the financial services industry changed with more and more complex instruments being brought to market. These often concealed that risk was being passed to the customer – and in a shareholder democracy the customers were schools, local authorities, universities, small businesses and charities as well as the usual large institutional investors. The intricacy of the instruments led to the key players within a company who dominated the acquisition of wealth receiving extravagant bonuses. But so too did their immediate superiors as well as others higher in the organizational hierarchy. The bonuses of the bosses, who did not always understand the nature of the new business world in which their employees were operating (this is clear, for example, from the Bank of England Report on Barings Bank)[23] were thus based on the inventiveness and productivity of their subordinates. The combination of ignorance and greed made the bosses loath to interfere with the 'golden goose' king-pins of the dealing rooms who could always threaten to decamp to a rival organization, taking their entire financial team with them.[24]

In short, in response to structural changes some highly dubious practices began to develop, especially in the USA, at an institutional and industry level, which went largely unchecked not just internally but also externally. Next to failures of first-line internal control, the crucial institution of external control should have been the accountancy firms. A few years ago these were dominated by the so-called 'Fat Five'. But to a large extent they had tied themselves closely to the major corporations which employed them. They supplied high-level staff, did much of the financial training and virtually ran the 'back-office' responsible for supervising transactions. They had also developed consultancy firms alongside their accountancy operations and through these became even more deeply imbedded in the corporations they were meant to be monitoring. Over time, a conflict of interest became built into the inter-institutional relations which led to indulgent supervision, massaging of financial records, and even the manipulation of their corporate employers.

Following the collapse of Enron it emerged that the formerly redoubtable Arthur Anderson had employed highly dubious practices, including destroying data, in order to cover up some of the discrepancies in the accounts of Enron and related companies. Anderson went out of business in the wake of a criminal prosecution (leaving what are now dubbed the 'Final Four' accountancy firms). To make matters worse, the Securities and Exchange Commission (SEC) proved to be wanting in its supervisory responsibilities, displaying all the symptoms of regulatory 'capture'. It had a revolving-door relationship with the industry, with senior personnel moving from one to the other, and it proved increasingly to be a toothless tiger under the pro-business regime of President G. W. Bush. Its enforcement strategy consisted largely of a form of plea-bargaining that avoided its having to pass on cases for prosecution, generated income to the government through fines, and offered corporations a let-off from further criminal or civil claims through pleas of *nolo contendere*. As has been aptly observed, such a plea is the rough equivalent of a statement that 'we didn't do it and we promise not to do it again'.

No doubt, individual greed and ambition played a large role in the global economic meltdown, but arguably even more significant were the system failures.

These revealed how systems were organized and functioned, and how they created new, structural opportunities for deviant practices with catastrophic consequences. In some respects the individuals slotted into the roles allocated to them and took advantage of the particular opportunities offered by this unique constellation of factors.

It is naïve to think that the actors in these major financial institutions, representing massive wealth and responsible for making high-stake decisions, are free-floating individuals who operate without being shaped by their own corporate environment. They are under internal pressures to achieve and are inevitably affected by the global context in which they function. In terms of legality and morality in western society it is possible to perceive those actors as individually responsible for their misdeeds, but at another level they can be viewed as mere puppets of larger institutional interests and intense corporate demands. Is it fair, then, that when a wheel comes off, the organization should escape without coming in for its share of the blame?

BCCI

Among the large financial services scandals and collapses in the literature, that of BCCI is particularly noteworthy. When BCCI went out of business in 1991 it was the seventh largest bank in the world. Its collapse revealed a complex tale of deception and manipulation on a grand scale with an unlikely cast of characters that included the CIA, Mossad, Hezbollah, presidents of narco-states and dons of international drugs cartels. But of key importance here is BCCI's institutional structure. It had its headquarters in London; was registered in Luxembourg as a holding company (which meant it did not fall under the banking regulations of Luxembourg); had a parallel company registered in the Cayman Islands which was ostensibly separate from BCCI but which was covertly tied to it; and utilized the latter shell company to purchase First Bank of America in the USA against all rules relating to the disclosure of ownership interests.[25]

In essence, then, the BCCI debacle is all about the use of organizational and apparently legal structural forms which, when combined with illicit 'shadow' organizations, allowed the bank to commit one of the largest financial frauds in history.[26] There is no doubt but that a group of individuals conspired to break the law but collectively they used the organization both as a sword to perpetrate their offences and a shield behind which to hide.

BCCI is also an instructive case in relation to sanctioning organizations. If a state's criminal justice system does decide to place more emphasis on corporate criminal liability then the question is raised of the appropriate punishment following a conviction. In such a case, central banks, along with some regulatory agencies in other industries, have the power to employ what might be called capital punishment by *executing* banks. When organizations are licensed you can kill them by closing them down through withdrawing their licence. This was the fate which befell BCCI.

Rail Industry (UK)

In the field of corporate crime there is considerable evidence that companies make policy decisions that lead to actions that can cause death and serious injury.[27] There has in fact been increasing scholarly interest in 'corporate violence' and workplace deaths and injuries. For example, there have been a number of train crashes in the UK leading to loss of life and serious injuries. It is almost certain that these casualties could have been avoided with a different safety policy. How did this situation arise?

The macro institutional environment forms the context. Following deregulation of the rail industry, there were some 100 companies of which 25 ran the rolling stock and two were responsible for track maintenance. Arguably the effect of this reorganization was to provide greater opportunities for short-term profit, low investment and 'milking' of the system. After all the restructuring, there remained the question of who is responsible for safety?[28] One critical decision that had previously been made by the rail industry was not to implement ATP (Automatic Train Protection) which is widely used on the European Continent and which stops a train automatically, without any intervention from the driver, when a train passes a warning signal which the driver has overlooked. The British industry favoured instead the retention of AWS (Automatic Warning Signal) which sounds a claxon when a train passes a warning signal and which requires the driver to manually intervene.

Installing ATP in British trains would almost certainly have saved lives but this was a strategic decision taken by the entire industry, principally on grounds of cost. The government could not interfere because having deregulated the industry it had in effect become a bystander. The point again is not that individuals were not involved but rather that they functioned in an institutional context that shaped specific opportunities which in turn led to 'accidents' involving many casualties including deaths.

Again the law proved a hindrance rather than a help in addressing the situation. Until passage of the Corporate Manslaughter and Corporate Homicide Act 2007 (whose long-term effect is still too early to determine), it was virtually impossible to gain a conviction for 'corporate manslaughter' against a major company in Britain.[29] This legal condition resembled what Reisman described as '*lex imperfecta*', or laws that were not really meant to work.[30] Thus, to a degree it could be maintained that the organization 'gets away with it' because of weaknesses in legislation, regulation and investigation.

This became apparent with the case of Great Western Railways (GWR) and the Southall train crash in 1997. An express train from London had arrived at Swansea and was preparing for its return journey to London. As mentioned, AWS is standard on all trains in Britain, but in fact the train in question was also fitted with ATP on an experimental basis. When the driver went to the original rear of the train, which was now the front, for the return journey he found that neither AWS nor ATP was functioning. He requested the station management at Swansea to switch the rear locomotive to the front so he could drive back with AWS, as he had never previously driven without AWS. However, company procedures allowed a train to be driven without AWS under certain circumstances, and local management refused the driver's request on the grounds that it would cause a delay which could incur a penalty for the company.

On the return journey to London the driver passed two warning lights and a red light. The train crashed into another one causing a major accident with seven deaths and many injuries. If the locomotive with AWS had been switched to the front, or if ATP had been standard in Britain or had been operating on this train, then the accident would almost certainly have not occurred and seven lives would have been saved.

There are two elements to note about the Southall train crash. First was the decision of the station management at Swansea not to switch the locomotives. This follows a pattern in transport and other industries where the pressure of deadlines, and the fixation on schedules, leads to means becoming ends in themselves so that participants lose sight of safety and stick to the immediate need to abide by the schedule or deadline. In this case there were government-imposed penalties for late arrival (as well as 'league' tables ranking rail companies for their ability to keep to published schedules) that may have been a decisive factor in the minds of the station management at Swansea.

The second and key issue is whether or not senior management within GWR in some way contributed to the crash by its decision-making. The crash led to a prosecution for corporate manslaughter against Great Western Railway. One could argue that, in effect, senior management had taken a decision at a strategic level in the interests of profitability, continuity and its shareholders which contributed to the deaths; although undoubtedly no director or corporate executive ever consciously contemplated causing such harm. Nonetheless, the Crown Prosecution Service was persuaded that there was legal blame and charged GWR with manslaughter. However, the case failed because of the legal difficulty of linking the risk taken at Swansea not to switch locomotives, and not to ensure a working AWS on the train, to the hierarchical chain of decision-making within the company.

It could be argued that both strategic decisions on safety at the industry level and the decision of the government to deregulate the rail industry had combined to breed a culture of corporate profit orientation and lack of investment in safety in which lower level functionaries felt pressured not to cause delays and to place adherence to timetables above passenger safety. But at no point was thought ever given to prosecuting either the industry or the government for its decision to deregulate the industry. Southall simply forms yet another unhappy chapter of corporate, industry and government decision-making that leads to deaths and injuries but escapes accountability.[31]

The Herald of Free Enterprise

When deaths occur in a corporate context and prosecutions are either not brought or fail, the victims, their families and the public can be left with a sense that justice has not been done. In England and Wales, there have been almost no successful prosecutions of large firms for corporate manslaughter. The problem can be traced to an interpretation of the law which virtually grants immunity to large companies against conviction, a state of affairs that has been described as a conspiracy of variables which permits companies to get off the legal hook through the 'decriminalization' of corporate crime.[32]

In order to secure a conviction against an English company for manslaughter under the common law, there had to be proof that a director or senior manager who was considered to be 'the directing mind' of the company had committed manslaughter. This was known as the 'identification principle'. The perpetrator of the offence had to be a person of sufficient status to be identified with the decision-making elite of the firm before the offence could be imputed to the company. Often this meant proving that the human offender was aware of the risk being taken, or the negligence being perpetrated, and had to have taken decisions which directly led to the resulting harm. In practice it was not only extremely difficult to determine who was part of the 'controlling mind and will' of the company but also to show that decisions taken at board level were directly responsible for harm caused at an operational level.

In the case of the *Herald of Free Enterprise*, a 'roll-on roll-off' ferry had left port with its bow doors open, which had the effect of leaving the entire car deck exposed if water were to enter through the open bow doors. The bosun responsible for closing the doors was not at his station on departure but asleep in his bunk and the first officer of the vessel, who was meant to be supervising him, had already gone to the bridge. The master of the vessel could not see if the bow doors were closed because there was no warning light installed on the bridge to alert him of the danger, despite repeated requests from the Master of the fleet to install such lights. These requests had been rejected by management on grounds of cost. Subsequently a court of inquiry on the accident brought out a damning report on the neglect of safety within the company,[33] and photos of the gaping bow doors on the capsized vessel lying half-submerged were their own evidence of the company's failure to adopt appropriate safety measures. And yet there was no conviction of the company in court. Furthermore, after the case against the company was dismissed, the Crown Prosecution Service withdrew the cases against the individual defendants, presumably to avoid the appearance of their being made scapegoats for the company's wrongdoing. In the end, then, no-one was ever convicted for the deaths of some 200 people.

Conclusion

In this paper, I have focused on both the role of the organization in corporate crime and the impotence of the law in tackling such crime. The organization can be both offender and victim – and both in the same case, as where an unsupervised bank official embezzles money from the bank. The organization often provides the motive, opportunity and means; it is the scene of crime; and the offences can be committed across time and in diverse locations depending on the structure of the company. These factors form difficulties for a legal system based on individual liability stemming from discrete offences at specific locations with direct causal relations. In a sense the law is a paper tiger, a statement of moral disapproval or intent (whether the offence is mala in se or male prohibita) or what is referred to as the 'law in the books'. In contrast, the 'law in action' revolves around legislation, enforcement, investigation, prosecution, conviction and deterrence through sanctions. In the arena of corporate crime many of these elements are weak and inadequate.

The legal mind has struggled with locating mens rea in an aggregate entity because, as I and others have argued, the criminal law has historically been focused on the individual. An 'aggregation theory of corporate liability', where aggregation represents 'a first step towards an approach to corporate criminal liability where a company's liability is not derivative, and where the company is liable in it own right for its own fault', would be an advance.[34] The ultimate advance would be the severance of corporate fault from individual fault.

The problem of weak laws is compounded when there are powerful and criminogenic organizations prepared to exploit the law and legal loopholes for their own profit. Some industries, such as transport and mineral extraction, are more criminogenic than others.[35] Companies can be recidivists and repeat offenders so we are not talking so much of isolated incidents as of recurring patterns; and of offences that take place over time. Crimes cannot simply be attributed to specific individuals when criminal patterns persist despite changes in personnel and fresh 'directing minds'. In a very real social sense there are no 'individuals' in organizations. In business, managers slot into the corporation, 'leave their conscience at home' and do what the collective demands of them.[36]

What I have tried to convey in this paper is that crimes by corporations suffer from the fact that the criminal law has considerable difficulty in recognizing collective guilt and in applying liability to an institution or organization. This leaves one with the feeling that the criminal law and criminal justice mechanisms (enforcement, investigation, prosecution, trial and sanctions) simply do not deliver justice. The law courts are no match for powerful, devious, wealthy and unscrupulous companies, with the result that all too often the 'real villains' get away with their crimes.

The scale of damage and harm created by corporate crime, particularly when it leads to avoidable death and injury, is of deep concern because the victims are often powerless citizens who suffer financially or physically. The image of companies concerned with the personal safety of their customers, which are competently run and which adhere fully to legal and regulatory standards, is a myth. As has become increasingly apparent in recent years, there are firms where management is able to disassociate itself from the consequences of its actions by underestimating risk and disclaiming responsibility whenever harm occurs, hiding behind the skirt of the law. In essence, executives employ the organization as an instrument to commit crime. Without the organization there could be no corporate crime. The thrust of my paper is that we should put the organization back into our academic work on corporate crime, and the organization firmly into the frame of criminal liability.

References

Bank of England Report (1991), *Inquiry into the Supervision of the Bank of Credit and Commerce International*. London: HMSO.

Bank of England Report (1995), *Report of the Board of Banking Supervision Inquiry into the Circumstances of the Collapse of Barings*. London: HMSO.

Bergman, D. (2000), *The Case for Corporate Responsibility*. London: CCA.

Braithwaite, J. (1985), 'White Collar Crime', *Annual Review of Sociology*. 11: 1–25.

Clinard, M. B. and Yeager, P. C. (1980), *Corporate Crime*. New York: Free Press.

Ermann, D. and Lundman, R., eds. (1978), *Corporate and Governmental Deviance*, 2nd edn. New York: Oxford University Press.

Ermann, D. and Lundman, R., eds. (1996), *Corporate and Governmental Deviance*, 3rd edn. New York: Oxford University Press.

Field, S. and Jörg, N. (1991), 'Corporate Liability and Manslaughter: Should We Go Dutch?', *Criminal Law Review*, February, 156–171.

Friedrichs, D. (2003), *Trusted Criminals: White Collar Crime in Contemporary Society*, 2nd edn. Belmont, MA: Wadsworth.

Geis, G. (1978), 'White Collar Crime: The Heavy Electrical Equipment Antitrust Cases of 1961', in M. Ermann and R. Lundman (eds), *Corporate and Governmental Deviance*. New York: Oxford University Press.

Geis, G. and Stotland, E. eds. (1980), *White-Collar Crime*. Beverly Hills, CA: Sage.

Gobert, J. (2008), 'The Evolving Legal Test of Corporate Criminal Liability' in J. Minkes and L. Minkes eds., *Corporate and White-Collar Crime*. London: Sage.

Gobert, J. and Punch, M. (2003), *Rethinking Corporate Crime*. Cambridge: Cambridge University Press.

Jack, I. (2002), *The Crash that Stopped Britain*. Cambridge: Granta Books.

Jackall, R. (1989), *Moral Mazes: The World of Corporate Managers*. New York/Oxford: Oxford University Press.

KPMG (2001), *Complianceprogramma`s, een brug tussen preventieve en repressieve rechtshandhaving*, Amstelveen: KPMG Forensic Accounting.

Levi, M. (2011), 'Political Autonomy, Accountability and Efficiency in the Prosecution of Serious White-Collar Crimes (this volume).

M. V. *Herald of Free Enterprise* (1987), *Report of Court No 8074*. London: HMSO.

Minkes, J. and Minkes, L. eds. (2008), *Corporate and White-Collar Crime*. London: Sage.

Mokhiber, R. (1988), *Corporate Crime and Violence*. San Francisco, CA: Sierra Club Books.

Nollkaemper, A. and van der Wilt, H. eds. (2009), *System Criminality in International Law*. Cambridge; Cambridge University Press.

Partnoy, F. (2003), *Infectious Greed*. New York: Holt.

Pearce, F. and Snider, L. eds. (1995), *Corporate Crime: Contemporary Debates*. Toronto, Canada: University of Toronto Press.

Punch, M. (1996), *Dirty Business*. London: Sage.

Punch, M. (2000), 'Suite Violence: Why Managers Murder and Corporations Kill', *Crime, Law and Social Change*, 33 (3): 243–280.

Reisman, M. W. (1979), *Folded Lies*. New York: Free Press.

Shover, N. and Wright, J. eds. (2001), *Crimes of Privilege: Readings in White-Collar Crime*. New York: Oxford University Press.

Slapper, G. and Tombs, S. (1999), *Corporate Crime*. London: Longman.

Snider, L. (2011), 'The Challenges of Regulating Powerful Economic Actors' (this volume).

Sutherland, E. H. (1949), *White-Collar Crime*. New York: Holt.

The Times (3 July 1999), 'Rail Crash Judge Says Faulty Law Forced Acquittal'.

van der Wilt, H. (2005), *Het kwaad in functie*. Inaugural lecture, Faculty of Law, University of Amsterdam.

Wells, C. (2001), *Corporations and Criminal Responsibility*, Oxford: Clarendon Press (2nd edn).

Wolf, S. (1985), 'The Legal and Moral Responsibility of Organizations', in J. Pennock and J. Chapman (eds.) *Criminal Justice*. New York: New York University Press.

Notes

1 Punch: 1996.
2 Ermann and Lundman: 1978.
3 Wells: 2001.
4 Wolf: 1985.
5 Gobert and Punch: 2003.
6 Slapper and Tombs: 1999.
7 ibid.
8 Sutherland : 1949.
9 cf. Braithwaite: 1985.
10 Geis: 1978.
11 Ibid: 68.
12 Punch: 1996; Clinard and Yeager: 1980; Slapper and Tombs: 1999.
13 Clinard and Yeager: 1980; Levi: 2009; Snider: 2009; Minkes and Minkes: 2008.
14 Gobert and Punch: 2003.
15 Reisman: 1979.
16 Nollkaemper and van der Wilt: 2009.
17 Ermann and Lundman: 1996.
18 Van der Wilt (2005) draws attention to this reluctance to prosecute collectives, from the view *societas delinquere non potest*; that it is 'second nature' in criminal law and prosecutions to look for the individual component; and that concepts such as conspiracy and 'joint criminal enterprise' are typically Anglo-Saxon in origin.
19 Slapper and Tombs: 1999.
20 Field and Jörg: 1991.
21 KPMG: 2001.
22 Mokhiber: 1988; Geis and Stotland: 1980; Friedrichs: 1996; Shover and Wright: 2001; Pearce and Snider: 1995.
23 Bank of England Report: 1995.
24 cf. Partnoy: 2004.
25 Punch: 1996.
26 cf. Bank of England Report: 1991.
27 Punch: 2000.
28 Jack: 2002.
29 Gobert and Punch: 2003.
30 Reisman: 1979.
31 GWR did, however, admit to breaches of health and safety regulations and was heavily fined.
32 Bergman: 2000.
33 M. V. *Herald of Free Enterprise*: 1987.
34 Gobert: 2008.
35 Gobert and Punch: 2003.
36 Jackall: 1988.

7 Individual liability of company officers

Neil Foster

Corporate or individual liability?

The use of the company structure has been a key feature of the way business has been conducted since the early part of the 20th century. The 'corporate veil', shielding shareholders from liability for corporate decisions, has been seen as a key feature of this structure. However, one of the problems with the 'corporate veil', excellent as it seems to have been for encouraging investment, is the shield that it can provide for incompetent or self-interested management decisions which harm others.

Company decisions, of course, are many and varied. Areas in which company officers may be held personally liable range from the 'traditional' issues of corporate governance (such as trading when insolvent, or obtaining a personal advantage from transactions without due disclosure) through to a range of other laws relating to the impact that the actions of the company have on other players in the marketplace, its own employees, or the general public through, for example, environmental laws. In Australia in recent years the personal liability of directors in relation to misleading statements made about a company's ability to fund a compensation scheme for injured workers has been a major topic of interest. Litigation involving the directors of companies related to James Hardie Industries Ltd has seen substantial fines and periods of disqualification imposed on those directors.[1]

My research has concentrated on the area of personal liability for workplace safety, and that will provide the focus for this paper. It provides a 'paradigm' example of a situation where the community as a whole would agree that there has been clear harm to someone (a worker is either injured or killed as a result of company decisions), and there is a strong sense that justice requires, not just the 'imaginary' corporate entity, but a real person, to bear responsibility for the harm. Principles developed in these cases may then be extrapolated to other areas where the general community perception of harm (anti-competitive behaviour, insider trading, and so on) is not so immediately apparent.

A number of serious workplace accidents in recent years have brought these issues to prominence. In the United Kingdom, incidents directing attention to workplace safety and company law issues include the sinking of the ferry *Herald of Free Enterprise* in 1987, the 1988 Piper Alpha oil rig disaster, and several fatal rail 'accidents'.[2] In Australia, explosions such as that at the Longford Gas plant in Victoria, have similarly brought to public attention the issue of directors' duties and liabilities. In many cases it is suggested, with good reason, that a board of directors and management have failed to set up proper procedures and systems for workplace safety. In his detailed review of the factors behind the Longford Gas explosion, Andrew Hopkins makes the point that 'if culture, understood as mindset, is to be the key to preventing major accidents, it is management culture rather than the culture of the workforce in general which is most relevant'.[3]

The Royal Commission into the Longford Gas explosion also identified a number of serious management failures which contributed directly to the accident, including a failure in training workers to deal with identified hazards, a decision to remove engineers from the plant to 'head office' which led to a lack of expert advice 'on site' when an emergency situation arose, and a failure to conduct a major hazard assessment of the plant involved which would have identified the danger of the 'accident' happening.[4]

Increasingly it is being recognised that injuries in the workplace are more often related to overall management decisions about safety procedures, and a corporate 'culture' that devalues safety, rather than individual employee acts of carelessness. If board members were made aware that by participating in management and failing to adequately address safety issues, they may be personally liable for the consequence of injuries or fatalities, then this could provide great incentive for change, reinforcing and supporting the current trend towards the introduction of 'systems-based' safety regimes.[5]

There are a number of existing *corporate* incentives for improving safety. Common law actions for workplace negligence and statutory workers compensation schemes can have a major financial impact on companies. Even where insurance fully covers liability, insurance premiums may rise in response to a poor industrial safety record. And criminal legislation in all Australian jurisdictions, as in many industrialised countries, provides for safety offences which, when committed by companies, now carry fairly hefty fines.[6]

But the nature of the company is that such financial burdens generally fall only upon *company* funds. Even given the strong incentives for directors to be seen to be conducting business profitably, in the end the worst that can happen in most cases is that the company may go insolvent. Suggestions have been growing over a number of years that directors and managers, who are making decisions that adversely affect safety, must be made to feel the impact of those decisions more personally.[7]

A number of converging lines of research suggest that focusing on the individual responsibility of corporate officers can be an effective way to alter corporate behaviour. Figure 7.1 is a 'pyramid' representing the strength of various factors influencing decision-making by corporate officers, taken from a paper presented by Bryan Horrigan, Director of the National Centre for Corporate Law and Policy Research.[8]

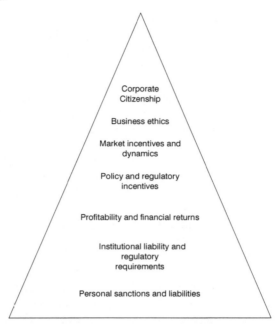

Figure 7.1 Factors influencing corporate decision-making (Horrigan, 2000)

In the well-known Maslow 'hierarchy of needs', until the lowest level of needs are met, others will be deferred. In this pyramid the lowest level represents the strongest incentive to change corporate behaviour. Horrigan suggests that the foundational, primary concerns for directors are the issues of 'personal sanctions and liabilities'. Managers will primarily be concerned with making decisions that will avoid imposition of personal sanctions, before they start to attend to issues of institutional liability.

Hopkins makes a similar point, both in his review of the causes of a mine disaster at Moura in Queensland:

> The financial costs of disasters such as at Moura do not appear to be sufficient to provide the necessary incentives. The threat of personal legal consequences is probably the best way of concentrating the minds of senior managers on questions of health and safety.[9]

and in his more recent study of the causes of the Texas City refinery explosion:

> Chief executive officers of companies like BP have a strong personal interest in cost cutting. Their remuneration consists (in part) of share options … So, all things being equal, a CEO can raise share prices by cutting costs. There is thus a powerful incentive for CEOs to drive cost cuts throughout an organisation. What is needed is some equally powerful incentive to ensure

that these cost cuts are not at the expense of safety. Perhaps the law should be holding CEOs personally accountable in this respect.[10]

In a study commissioned by the National Occupational Health and Safety Commission, Gunningham comments:

> In the literature review, regulation was identified by a large majority of studies as the single most important driver of corporations, and the threat of personal criminal liability (in particular of prosecutions brought against them as individuals) as the most powerful motivator of their CEOs to improve OHS ... Prosecution of individuals within the corporate structure has both specific and general deterrent effects, particularly if the prosecution is widely publicised.[11]

Gunningham and Johnstone cast doubt on penalties imposed on corporations because they can easily become a cost of doing business, and passed on to consumers, shareholders, or employees.[12] While serving as a member of the Federal Court of Australia, French J, in *Australian Securities and Investments Commission, in the matter of Chemeq v Chemeq Limited* [2006] FCA 936, commented:

> 98 ... Penalties imposed on officers of the corporation for their part in such contraventions affect those officers alone. Penalties imposed on the corporation may affect shareholders including those who have become shareholders on a set of assumptions induced by the very non-disclosure complained of. In some cases it is possible also that creditors may be affected. Who then is being deterred when only the corporation is penalised? I am not sure that there is a satisfactory answer to this concern within the present statutory scheme. One might imagine that if a penalty is to be significant to a corporation it will also be significant to its shareholders in its impact on the capital which backs their shares. In a company with capitalisation as high as that of Chemeq, the impact on individual shareholders may be insignificant. The penalties that count most are likely to be those imposed on the responsible individuals.[13]

Proposals for personal liability of company officers should not be viewed as a substitute for corporate liability, but rather as part of a multi-faceted strategy aimed at deterring business crimes. In their seminal 1993 treatise, Fisse and Braithwaite recommend that the law should:

> Seek to publicly identify all who are responsible and hold them responsible, whether the responsible actors are individuals, corporations, corporate subunits, gatekeepers, industry associations or regulatory agencies themselves.[14]

As Coffee, writing in 1981, explains:

[L]aw enforcement officials cannot afford to ignore either the individual or the firm in choosing their targets, but can realise important economies of scale by simultaneously pursuing both ... Thus, a dual focus on the firm and the individual is necessary. Neither can be safely ignored.[15]

In this context, Gunningham and Johnstone argue that, if 'individualism' (or, to be more accurate, individual managerial accountability) is not the sole prescription for the problem, it is at least a part, and a major part, of the overall solution.[16] They point out that the 'stigma' of a criminal conviction, and the possibility of a gaol sentence, are powerful deterrents which weigh heavily on the minds of company officers, and which cannot be 'externalised' and passed on to the company through indemnities.[17] Furthermore, in a detailed review of models for company liability, Lederman warns that, whatever the benefits of models which recognise 'corporate culture' and the like for imposing criminal liability on companies, ignoring the personal liability of company officers would undercut fundamental principles of individual autonomy and responsbility which underpin the criminal law.[18]

Smith, writing about prosecution for environmental crimes and comparing the situation in Australia with that in the United States, responds to some of the objections to individual liability. To the objection that corporations will nominate officials as 'scapegoats', she asserts that careful investigation will usually be able to establish where the true responsibility lies. To the oft-repeated assertion that corporations will appoint a 'vice-president for going to gaol', she contends that the existence of such a person is probably illusory, noting that she has never encountered a vice-president prepared to spend several years in a federal penitentiary.[19] Wise makes the point that 'being named in a pleading, put on trial, forced to make a public apology, required to pay a fine, or serve time in jail, are often expensive, professionally damning and personally humiliating consequences – results most individuals, including corporate officers, prefer to avoid'.[20]

From time to time the suggestion has been advanced that companies should be prosecuted for manslaughter rather than for offences under the specific workplace safety legislation.[21] One basis for the suggestion is that health and safety legislation is popularly viewed as 'regulatory' and not 'seriously criminal', and that a manslaughter conviction will carry a greater public stigma. But these proposals may have limited effect. The reason is simple: even a finding that a company is guilty of manslaughter will, as noted before, at worst result in insolvency for the company. It may leave individual directors still able to take advantage of the corporate veil, unless their personal liability is clarified. [22]

In any event, corporate liability for manslaughter should not be at the expense of individual liablity. One of the major weaknesses in the recently enacted *Corporate Manslaughter and Corporate Homicide Act* 2007 (UK) (CMCHA) is that it explicitly provides that: '[a]n individual cannot be guilty of aiding, abetting, counselling or procuring the commission of an offence of corporate manslaughter'.[23] Gobert comments:

The Act ... is disappointing in its failure to provide for the criminal liability of directors, corporate executives and senior managers who significantly contribute to their organisation's offence. To the contrary, these and other individuals are given immunity from accessorial liability.[24]

Models for individual officer liability

If personal officer liability for corporate OHS failings is to be adopted, there are a number of different models possible. This paper will not attempt to repeat the very helpful survey provided by the 2007 report commissioned for the UK Health and Safety Executive from the Centre for Corporate Accountability, *International Comparison of Health and Safety Responsibilities of Company Directors*.[25] A broad spectrum of approaches have been taken to individual liability, ranging from those jurisdictions such as Norway and the United States, which make no specific provision for individual liability at all,[26] to provisions which vary widely in the circumstances under which liability may be imposed. The CCA Report classifies legislation according to whether it imposes a 'clear and explicit positive duty' on directors, or whether it imposes a duty through the creation of offences which apply to directors indirectly (often as accessories in some way to commission of the offences by companies). Within these categories the legislation differs as to what duties are imposed, what defences are available to directors, and where the onus of proof lies in prosecutions. The UK legislation is characterised as imposing 'minimal or no duties' on directors.[27] As the subsequent analysis in this paper will attempt to show, this is an accurate description, in that while there is the possibility of prosecution, it is made difficult by the need to show specific elements of personal involvement by the relevant officer.

Which model is placed at the 'harsh' end of the spectrum (or the 'effective' end, depending on one's perspective!) will depend on the criteria that are adopted for placement, of course. It is suggested, however, that many business commentators (at least in the Australian context) would place the Queensland and NSW versions of personal liability towards that end.[28] Elements of these provisions that are seen as being 'tough' on company officers include the fact that once there has been shown to be a company contravention of the law, the officer bears the onus of proving that one of the relevant defences applies. Presumably one could put at the very end of the spectrum a notional law which simply made every director of a company automatically liable to the full force of the law whenever their company had offended, with no defences available at all. There are no such laws in fact, to my knowledge.

My aim in this paper is not to undertake an exhaustive review of all the various options but rather to review two of the options, however, which may be seen to lie at least in the general vicinity of the different ends of the spectrum. At one end is the UK model, and at the other, the NSW model. It is hoped that a comparison of these models will provide a general insight into the issues which will inform any future model of individual liability in the safety area (and indeed, in most other areas as well).

The UK model

Section 37 of the *Health and Safety at Work etc. Act* 1974 (UK) (*HSWA*) provides:

> s 37 Offences by bodies corporate.(1) Where an offence under any of the relevant statutory provisions committed by a body corporate is proved to have been committed with the consent or connivance of, or to have been attributable to any neglect on the part of, any director, manager, secretary or other similar officer of the body corporate or a person who was purporting to act in any such capacity, he as well as the body corporate shall be guilty of that offence and shall be liable to be proceeded against and punished accordingly.

Until recently there had been few decisions illuminating the interpretation of s 37.[29] But there is now some recent important guidance from cases in the Court of Appeal and the House of Lords.

R v P

The ruling of the Court of Appeal in *R v P* [30] came by way of an appeal on a preliminary point of law decided by the trial judge. The case involved the death of a six-year-old boy who was thrown from a forklift on which he was riding as a passenger when it collided with another forklift which was unsafely loaded. The company 'P Ltd' was charged with breaches of the *HSW Act* and a 'Mr G', the managing director of the company, was charged under s 37.

The narrow issue raised on appeal related to what the prosecution needed to establish to show 'neglect' under s 37. The trial judge had ruled that in order to show 'neglect' it had to be shown that not only did Mr G have 'a duty to inform himself of the facts' concerning the safety risk, but also that he knew of the 'material facts'.[31] In so ruling the judge was apparently following an (unreported) ruling of MacKay J in a prosecution following a railway accident at Hatfield,[32] which equated 'neglect' with 'turning a blind eye' to circumstances which the officer really knew about, and called it explicitly a 'subjective test and not equivalent to inadvertence, laziness or even gross negligence'.[33]

The Criminal Division of the Court of Appeal rejected this view of s 37. Latham LJ, for the Court, noted at [12] that it placed the burden of proof on the prosecution at too high a level. 'Neglect' did not require showing a subjective awareness (otherwise there would have been no need to add the other elements of 'consent' and 'connivance'). The Court added at [13] that the question will always be:

> whether ... , where there is no actual knowledge of the state of facts, [that] nonetheless the officer in question of the company should have, by reason of the surrounding circumstances, been put on enquiry so as to require him to have taken steps to determine whether or not the appropriate safety procedures were in place.

In adopting this more 'objective' standard the Court at [8]–[9] approved the comments of Emslie, LJG in *Wotherspoon v HM Advocate*[34] on the proper interpretation of the word 'neglect' in s 37:

1   The word presupposes some duty which the person concerned has failed to carry out
2   'The section as a whole is concerned primarily to provide a penal sanction against those persons charged with functions of management who can be shown to have been responsible for the commission of a relevant offence by ... a body corporate'
3   Accordingly, a finding of 'neglect' cannot be made without identification of a failure to take steps which the accused's position within the company required him or her to take.
4   Issues of the knowledge of the accused of the need for action, or whether the accused should have been aware of the need, will be relevant.
5   Where the Act refers to the need for the company offence to be 'attributable to' the officer's neglect, this does not mean that the neglect must be the sole cause of the offence: 'in our opinion any degree of attributability will suffice'.

In applying the decision in *Wotherspoon*, the Court of Appeal in *R v. P* affirmed the need for a court to pay attention to the 'objective' question of what a director 'ought to have known', rather than the subjective question of what the director actually knew. As the Court said at [14], 'if there were circumstances which ought to have put him on enquiry' as to dangerous practices being adopted by the forklift drivers, Mr G might still be found guilty of 'neglect'. The problem however with provisions like s 37, which require proof of 'neglect' as a threshold issue, is that they require evidence to be produced as to the role of the specific officer at the particular time.

R v Chargot Ltd

The second major decision giving guidance on s 37 was that of the House of Lords in *R v Chargot Limited (t/a Contract Services)*.[35] In that case an employee of Chargot, who had been assisting in works being carried out on a farm, was killed when a dump truck he was driving overturned. Mr Ruttle, who was apparently the managing director of a group of companies including Chargot, and on the board of a contracting company which was also charged in relation to the incident, was charged under s 37 of the *HSWA*. The trial judge entered convictions against both companies and Mr Ruttle. An appeal to the Court of Appeal failed[36] and the House of Lords affirmed the convictions of all the defendants.

A key issue in the judgment concerned the interaction of the duty to do what was 'reasonably practicable' under ss 2 and 3 of the *HSWA*, and the reversal of onus of proof provisions in s 40 of the Act. The House affirmed that once a risk to safety is proved, the onus falls on the company to show that it was not reasonably practicable to do more. It is not necessary for the prosecutor to prove the precise particulars of the alleged risk.[37] Their Lordships also confirmed the view that had been taken by the Court of Appeal in *R v Davies*,[38] that this reversal of onus was not in breach of the obligations of the UK under article 6(1) of the *European Convention on Human Rights*, as it was a 'proportionate' response to the social, legal and economic purposes of the law relating to workplace safety.[39]

With respect to *individual* liability under s 37, Lord Hope stated at [32] that the liability of the company must first be established, and then whether the offence involved the individual defendant's 'consent, connivance or neglect'. His Lordship at [33] approved the statement in *R v P*[40] that the relevant question is what the officer 'ought to have known' and not simply his or her actual knowledge.

The distinction between 'consent' and 'neglect' was brought out by noting that in *Attorney-General's Reference (No 1 of 1995)*[41] Lord Taylor in the Court of Appeal had ruled that where 'consent' is alleged, a defendant has to be shown to have known the material facts which constituted the offence by the company and to have agreed to its conduct of the business on the basis of those facts (at 980). In *Chargot*, Lord Hope agreed and added that consent could be established by inference as well as by proof of an express agreement.

'Neglect', on the other hand, does not imply 'agreement' but rather a lack of attention to some duty that should have been performed. Lord Hope commented at [33] that what was necessary to show in relation to these respective mental elements of the offence will vary with the circumstances, but implied that it will usually be easier to show that they existed where the officer concerned was 'in day to day contact with what was done', than in circumstances where 'the officer's place of activity was remote from the work place or what was done there was not under his immediate direction and control'.

In *Chargot*, Mr Ruttle was a 'hands on' director. Once the breach by the company had been demonstrated, the prosecution needed to show that the breach was due to his consent, connivance or neglect. For whatever reason, at the end of the prosecution case he chose not to give evidence. But, as Lord Hope commented at [37], the jury was then entitled to act on the evidence that had been introduced by the prosecution – 'that he was directly involved in the works and that the way they were carried on was subject to his specific instructions and control' – and then to further conclude that the relevant mental state had been made out.

There is another issue arising under the *HSWA* which may need further scrutiny in the future. It relates to the defence of 'reasonable practicability' which is available to the company. If a director is charged under s 37, does the Act operate to allow an individual defendant to make out a defence that it was not 'reasonably practicable' for him or her to have done more? Or must the prosecution show that compliance was not 'reasonably practicable'? Or is this issue irrelevant by the time that s 37 comes to be considered?

On its face s 37 would not appear to require a separate re-consideration of the issue of 'reasonable practicability' in a prosecution under that provision as the issue will have already been addressed when the tribunal of fact considered the preliminary question of whether or not the company has committed an *HSWA* offence. By the time s 37 falls to be considered there is no further need (or opportunity) to consider the 'reasonably practicable' defence. Nor is s 37 subject to the 'reversal of onus' provision of s 40, which is confined on its terms to sections 2–6.[42] The Court of Appeal in *Chargot*[43] had also addressed the issue:

> 16 The second respect in which it is said that the judge erred in the third appellant's case was in his direction to the jury … that if they were satisfied that he had caused the second appellant to commit the offence through his neglect, connivance or consent, they should then go on to consider whether he had proved that it was not reasonably practicable to do more than he did. In other words he imported section 40 of the Act into the consideration of the charge under section 37. This was clearly wrong: see *R -v- Davies* [2003] ICR 586. But it cannot affect the safety of the conviction. The judge directed the jury, albeit wrongly, to consider the reverse burden issue, but only after they had been satisfied that the elements of the offence under section 3 had been proved against the second appellant and that it had not discharged its burden under section 40, and that he had caused that breach by his connivance, consent and neglect. Once the jury had reached that conclusion, the third appellant's guilt had been established. The further direction was pure surplussage, and if anything favourable to the third appellant.

Thus, the only issues that a jury ought to consider are: (1) was the company guilty of an offence? and (2) had the defendant caused this by his 'consent, connivance or neglect'? In deciding the first question the jury will have to consider the question of 'reasonable practicability', but in doing so the issue will be considered in the context of either s 2 or s 3, which are subject to the s 40 reversal of onus. Once the jury has reached a decision on the guilt of the company, the question of 'reasonable practicability' becomes irrelevant to s 37.

While the House of Lords in *Chargot* did not directly comment on the reasoning of the Court of Appeal, their careful analysis of the elements of the s 37 offence signified that there was no need to consider 'reasonable practicability' in respect of the corporate director or officer's liability. Lord Hope's analysis at [35]–[36] outlines the steps in determining the company's failure to ensure safety, the need for the company at that stage to prove that they had done what was reasonably practicable, and then if it failed at that point the limited burden on the prosecution to prove 'consent, connivance or neglect'.

In short, the only sensible way of interpreting the provisions seems to be that in consideration of an s 37 offence, there need be no 'reconsideration' of the 'reasonably practicable' defence, as this defence should already have been taken into account when dealing with the preliminary question of the company's guilt. This, as will be shown below, is the same position that the NSW courts have reached on the analogous question of whether, in an offence charged under s 26, the general s 28 defences should again be available.[44]

Experience under the NSW model

As the terms of the NSW legislation are likely to be less familiar to a European audience, it is perhaps worth a slightly more detailed summary of their operation.[45] The NSW legislation in question is the *Occupational Health and Safety Act* 2000 (NSW) (*OHS Act* 2000), which, like most other Australian legislation on the topic, finds its roots in the Robens Report, the same report that in the UK led to the *HSWA*. The legislation which operates in NSW at the moment is s 26 of the *OHS Act* 2000 (NSW):

> 26 Offences by corporations – liability of directors and managers
>
> (1) If a corporation contravenes, whether by act or omission, any provision of this Act or the regulations, each director of the corporation, and each person concerned in the management of the corporation, is taken to have contravened the same provision unless the director or person satisfies the court that:
>
>   (a) he or she was not in a position to influence the conduct of the corporation in relation to its contravention of the provision, or
>
>   (b) he or she, being in such a position, used all due diligence to prevent the contravention by the corporation.
>
> (2) A person may be proceeded against and convicted under a provision pursuant to subsection (1) whether or not the corporation has been proceeded against or been convicted under that provision.

Features of s 26 which are worth highlighting include:

- Before there can be personal liability, the company concerned must itself have been found guilty of a contravention of the legislation;
- The provision applies to both formal 'directors' who are members of the Board, and also those 'concerned in management';
- The essence of s 26 is that the officer is 'deemed' to be guilty of a breach of the provision that the company breached, simply by virtue of their position, unless they can make out one of the two statutory defences, 'unable to influence' or 'due diligence';
- The onus of proof of these defences rests on the accused officer.

It is also worth noting that in recent years NSW, like some other Australian States, has introduced something like a 'corporate manslaughter' provision, which may be breached by an individual officer. In NSW the relevant provision can be found in s 32A of the *OHS Act* 2000, the main parts of which are:

> 32A Reckless conduct causing death at workplace by person with OHS duties
>
> (1) In this section: 'conduct' includes acts or omissions.

(2) A person:

   (a) whose conduct causes the death of another person at any place of work, and

   (b) who owes a duty under Part 2 with respect to the health or safety of that person when engaging in that conduct, and

   (c) who is reckless as to the danger of death or serious injury to any person to whom that duty is owed that arises from that conduct, is guilty of an offence.

   ...

(5) If a corporation owes a duty under Part 2 with respect to the health or safety of any person, any director or other person concerned in the management of the corporation is taken also to owe that duty for the purposes of subsection (2).

(6) Section 26 (Offences by corporations – liability of directors and managers) does not apply to an offence against this section. However, this does not prevent a director or other person concerned in the management of a corporation from being prosecuted under this section for an offence committed by the director or other person.

Under s 32A, the essence of the contravention is 'recklessness' causing death. Unlike other provisions under the 'general duties' part of the Act, the s 32A offence cannot be 'deemed' to be committed, but it can be made out if an officer is personally reckless. So far there have been no reported decisions on the scope of s 32A, but it does provide an example of a powerful personal liability provision.

On the other hand there have been a number of decisions on the meaning and scope of s 26, which will now be reviewed.

The Gretley appeal

The Full Bench appeal in *Newcastle Wallsend Coal Company Pty Ltd & Ors v McMartin* (the *Gretley appeal*)[46] provided clarification of the extent and meaning of s 26. Since the appeal decision was discussed in some detail in an article published in 2008,[47] only brief comments will be provided here.

The case involved an inrush of water into an underground coal mine, which killed four miners. The water came from abandoned workings that had been thought to be some distance away from where the digging at the time was going on. One reason for the error by management about the location of the previous workings was an ambiguous plan of the area that had been provided by the relevant government department. Prosecutions were instituted, not just against the relevant companies, but also against a number of senior and middle managers.

The *Gretley* case was one of the first to use the general provisions of the *OHS Act 2000* (or indeed the mine-specific legislation which was in force for many years) in a formal court prosecution against a mining company.[48] It was also one of the first cases where a prosecution was undertaken of managers who were (literally) not 'at the coal-face', but instead were making decisions at a place which was removed from the circumstances which directly led to the specific incident.[49]

'Concerned in management'

The *Gretley* court first had to consider the scope of the phrase 'concerned in management', as none of the officers charged were formally members of the board of the relevant companies. Staunton J at first instance had given detailed consideration to this issue, and had concluded that someone who was not on the board could still be caught by s 26 where they had:

1   decision-making power and authority,
2   going beyond the mere carrying out of directions as an employee,
3   such as to affect the whole or a substantial part of the corporation,
4   which powers relate to the matters which constituted the offence under the Act.[50]

This interpretation of the phrase 'concerned in management', was adopted by the Full Bench, which referred both to the judgment of Staunton J, and the decision of the NSW Court of Appeal in *Morrison v Powercoal Pty Ltd v IRC of NSW.*[51]

Interaction of defences in ss 26 and 28

Another important issue in *Gretley* was whether an officer, charged under s 26 or its former equivalent, can rely not only on the 'internal' s 26 defences of 'unable to influence' and 'due diligence', but also on the general s 28 defence of 'reasonable practicability'.[52] By way of background, the structure of the NSW legislation is to provide for *prima facie* offences of 'absolute liability' in the 'general duties' area of the Act, but to provide in s 28 for some general defences, of which the most important one is 'reasonable practicability'. (This may be contrasted with the structure of the UK *HSWA*, where the company offences themselves include an element of 'reasonably practicable'. The resulting legal position, however, is the same, as under s 40 of the *HSWA*, where an element of an offence includes 'reasonably practicable', the onus lies on the accused to show that it was not 'reasonably practicable' to have done more.)

In the *Gretley Appeal* at [498]–[499] the Full Bench confirmed the comments of a previous Full Bench in *Morrison v Powercoal Pty Ltd*[53] denying the availability of s 28-type defences to an s 26-type prosecution, and noted that this view was supported by the tenor of the judgments in both the Court of Appeal in *Powercoal,*[54] and the High Court in dismissing a special leave application in *Daly Smith Corporation (Aust) Pty Ltd & Anor v WorkCover Authority (NSW).*[55]

The consequence is that an officer will be able to rely on the two specific s 26 defences, but will not be able to 'relitigate' the general issues of 'reasonable practicability'. In the end this should not be important, as before personal liability can arise, the court will need to have been satisfied that the company had contravened the Act, and in doing so it will need to have considered the application of the s 28 'practicability' defence in relation to the company.[56]

Prosecutorial discretion and s 26

A final point worth noting in respect of the *Gretley Appeal* is that the controversial nature of the proceedings in the public press were reflected in an unusually sharp exchange of views within the Industrial Court itself, some of which related to the decision to prosecute the officers. In his judgement in the case, Marks J at [746] made a pointed criticism of the decision of the prosecutors to proceed with the s 50 prosecution against the company officers, where the company at a very early stage of the actual trial had offered to plead guilty if the personal charges were dropped. It is submitted that this criticism was unfounded; that for reasons already noted, it was well worthwhile pursuing the prosecution of officers who were not involved directly on the spot, not only for the sake of justice being done in these proceedings, but also by way of a message being sent to other company officers. It is worth noting that in later proceedings related to costs, the other members of the Full Bench were in turn quite bluntly critical of the previous remarks of Marks J, calling them 'unfair' and 'immoderate', and reinforcing the established view that the decision on who to prosecute is very much one that the courts must leave to the prosecution authorities.[57]

Powercoal (Foster)

The *Powercoal* litigation has a complex history, but most relevant to this paper is the decision to prosecute Mr Peter Foster,[58] who was the manager of Awaba colliery on 17 July 1998 when a portion of the roof in the underground area collapsed, killing a worker. After an initial acquittal of the company (which automatically meant an acquittal of Mr Foster),[59] the Full Bench of the IRC in Court Session overturned both acquittals and entered guilty verdicts[60] and sentences.[61] The company and Mr Foster then attempted to seek review of the decision in the NSW Court of Appeal. In *Powercoal Pty Ltd & Foster v Industrial Relations Commission of NSW & Morrison*[62] the attempted review was refused.

Mr Foster argued that as mine manager at Awaba he was not of sufficient seniority to be caught by the provisions of s 50 of the *OHS Act* 1983 (equivalent of the present s 26). His contention was that the phrase 'concerned in the management' in relation to a corporation meant that he would have to be involved in the overall management of the company as a whole, rather than simply as a local manager.

In dismissing the application for review, Spigelman CJ made the following points:

• The question of what 'concerned in the management' means cannot be resolved simply by consideration of cases dealing with the phrase as used in legislation governing companies; it must take its meaning from the context in which it is used. The relevant issue in considering the meaning of the phrase in the *OHS Act* 2000 is 'any aspect of the operations of the company insofar as it raises safety considerations' – para [102].

- The fact that the same person might be both an employee (and hence liable under s 20 of the *OHS Act* 2000) and also a person 'concerned in management' for the purposes of s 26, does not mean that s 26 should be 'read down' to exclude employees. 'The scope, purpose and object of the legislation is not such that one should read down the language of one section by reason of the possibility of an overlap' – para [105].
- The broad purposes of the Act, to encourage safety and apply to a range of possible defendants, lead to a conclusion that the phrase should not be interpreted narrowly or technically. Rather, a purposive approach to interpretation [required at common law, and now by s 33 of the *Interpretation Act* 1987] suggested that the words 'management of the corporation' should not be read so as to apply only to central management.

The judgement provides a valuable foundation for a proper understanding of the reach of s 26 of the current Act. The decision, however, is less clear on the question whether the general s 53 (now s 28) defences can be relied on by an officer charged under s 50 (now s 26). While the failure of the Full Bench of the IRC to apply the s 53 defences was a ground on which Mr Foster had sought review of the decision, in the end the tenor of the judgment of Spigelman CJ in the Court of Appeal is that this ground could not succeed, simply because the Full Bench had in any event gone on to consider the s 53 defences and found against Mr Foster on that point.[63] But, as also noted previously, the consistent view of the Industrial Court as expressed in the *Gretley Appeal*, is against applying the general defences to the s 26 offence, and there seems no reason to suppose that the Court of Appeal would not support that view were it directly presented for decision.

Ritchie

Rivalling *Gretley* in its impact, the decision in *Inspector Kumar v David Aylmer Ritchie*[64] illustrates the far-reaching nature of the safety obligations imposed on senior managers.[65] The case involved an explosion which occurred when a tank was being chemically cleaned in a workshop in Sydney. Mr Ritchie was the Chief Executive Officer of the company involved, Owens Container Services Australia Pty Ltd, a part of the multinational Owens Group which operated in a number of locations in Australia, New Zealand and around the Pacific.[66] However, he accepted at the beginning of the trial that the company had committed the relevant offence (indeed, it had pleaded guilty to an s 8 offence).

The case required consideration of the two defences in s 26: 'unable to influence' and 'due diligence'. Haylen J first considered the defence of 'unable to influence', under para 26(1)(a). Counsel for Mr Ritchie conceded that in formal terms anyone who is a director has the legal ability to 'influence' a company's decision-making. But he argued that, if this limb of s 26 were to apply at all to directors (as opposed to those 'concerned in management'), then it must be interpreted to allow a director who was not 'hands on', and who only visited the site occasionally, to argue that in practical terms he had little opportunity to influence safety on the ground.

This interpretation was rejected. Haylen J commented that in legislation which imposed 'strict or absolute' liability on employers, it was not surprising to find a high standard of care expected from directors. In normal circumstances the simple fact of being a member of the Board will amount to sufficient influence. His Honour accepted that there might be some rare cases where a formally appointed director could succeed in a defence of 'unable to influence' – the examples he offered were where the director might be in a minority and be continually out-voted, or where the director was absent from board meetings due to illness for a long period, and uninformed of the relevant decision.[67]

With respect to his Honour, it seems arguable that even the acceptance of these limited exceptions to the 'influence' of a formally appointed director could be said to be too generous. These two examples would both be prime candidates for a defence of 'due diligence'; in each case the legal power to influence is still there, but the defendant would be able to claim that, while having legal authority, in practice he or she had 'done the best that they could'. It is submitted that a simpler and more obvious interpretation of the defence is that para (a) is not intended to be operative in relation to formally appointed directors, unless they can show that the instrument of their appointment somehow limits their legal power to influence decision-making.

Whether or not this is correct, in the circumstances of the case Mr Ritchie could not demonstrate any obstacle to his ability to influence the company's decisions.[68] In fact, in addressing the question of 'due diligence', he gave extensive evidence of his overall control over company policy. The irony is that a director who attempts to demonstrate a 'due diligence' defence under para 26(1)(b) will usually find it hard to argue in the alternative that under para (a) he or she had insufficient influence over the company.[69] Haylen J concluded his rejection of Mr Ritchie's para (a) defence by noting at [176]:

> In the present case, Mr Ritchie submits that regard should be had to the 'real world' where directors of a number of companies with various operations, living and working remotely from the worksite, have no effective control or ability to influence the conduct of the corporation in relation to its contravention of the Act … [T]hat argument should be rejected and recognition given to the actual authority and control of Mr Ritchie to influence the conduct of the company in relation to the company's contravention of the Act … , Mr Ritchie could actually influence the conduct of the company in relation to the breach but elected not to do so because he wished to concentrate on other matters. Mr Ritchie has therefore not made out a defence under s 26(1)(a).

The defence of 'due diligence' was next considered. Haylen J stated at para [177] that 'the hallmark of this defence is that the defendant would need to show that he had laid down a proper system to provide against contravention of the Act and had provided adequate supervision to ensure that the system was properly carried out'. His Honour then found that, while Mr Ritchie could not have been expected to be familiar with the finer details of every process used by the company, more could have been done to ensure that systems were in place for safety, and that those systems were put into practice.

This analysis of the para (b) defence may have been overly cursory, but the prosecutor had presented a very powerful case, and at [178] his Honour indicated that he accepted 'the general thrust of the prosecutor's submissions'. On this basis it seems worthwhile to set out here two paragraphs from the prosecutor's detailed submissions on the question of 'due diligence', recorded earlier in the judgment:

> 153 Having regard to these authorities, the prosecutor submitted that the statutory defence under s 26(1)(b) required the Court to be satisfied that:
>
> (a) there was in place a systematic approach designed to achieve compliance with a regulatory scheme established by the Act and to prevent its contravention;
> (b) that the system so established was both proper and appropriate so as to achieve the regulatory requirements of the Act and, in particular, was not merely some paper scheme that paid lip service to the Act or merely exaggerated the reality of the system that was in place; and
> (c) that the system was properly enforced and policed to achieve the regulatory outcome of preventing contraventions of the Act.
>   It was submitted that, for the defendant to make out the defence, each of these elements had to be established.
>
> 154 The defence was not advanced by the defendant emphasising how busy he was in the work of the Group, his geographical remoteness and his lack of daily involvement in the day-to-day operations of the business; precisely those factors made it imperative that the system he put in place or oversaw was proper and adequate to ensure compliance with the Act and that the means of ensuring the system was in force. The evidence showed a number of systems but the reality of the Race site was that there was no qualified or proper auditing, there was no appropriate training in occupational health and safety generally or in risk assessment specifically, and reliance was placed on a system of assumptions. Those administering the system had no means of effectively enforcing it and there was no evidence as to how the enforcement was achieved.

Emphasis was thus placed on the fact that, while there were paper systems in place, the actual auditing of compliance was not properly supervised, and there was no evidence that those who had been appointed to supervise safety in the company had appropriate qualifications and experience. Mr Ritchie on a number of occasions had said that he 'assumed' that the people he had appointed were doing their jobs. The court obviously found that more was required. He received a personal penalty of $22,500.[70]

With respect, this seems an unsatisfactory decision in a number of ways. Not only was Mr Ritchie's conviction fairly harsh, he was unlucky not to have received the benefit of s 10 of the *Crimes (Sentencing Procedures) Act* 1999 (which allows for no conviction to be recorded).[71] The prosecutor here gave a good summary of matters that a court ought to take into account in considering 'due diligence', but on reading the facts it is hard to say why Mr Ritchie ought not to have been found to have exercised such diligence. Evidence was accepted that he received regular reports on safety matters from company officers, had given directions to his Divisional Managers to monitor safety, made personal inquiries about safety matters when conducting site visits, and appointed people to positions whose job descriptions included the need to monitor safety. There was no evidence, for example, that he was aware of regular problems in the Container Division, or failed to respond when issues were brought to his attention. Frankly this is a conviction that seems to be at the very limit of what is acceptable.

On the other hand, it has certainly sparked interest in professional circles,[72] and perhaps it will serve as a genuine reminder to senior executives of their responsibilities. But the courts do need to be careful not to apply the legislation to such an impossibly high standard that a reaction will set in, where those who are duty-holders simply 'give up' trying to comply. Furthermore, even when directors and officers may be liable, their degree of involvement in the events which have caused a risk may merit their receiving different sentences.[73]

Smith

A series of proceedings involving Mr Tom Smith illustrates a number of aspects of the operation of s 26. In *WorkCover Authority v Daly Smith Corporation (Aust) Pty Ltd and anor*[74] the company Daly Smith (DSCA) and its owner and managing director, Mr Smith, were prosecuted over an incident which saw a labour hire worker employed by DSCA lose four fingers of one hand. Consistently with other decisions involving labour hire firms, DSCA were found to have been liable, despite the fact that the victim was working for a 'host employer' at the time. DSCA were liable because they had not put in place steps to ensure that adequate training was provided (see paras [67]–[69], which rely in part on DSCA's own policy documents referring to relevant training to be given to labour hire employees), nor had they arranged for a proper risk assessment to be undertaken [97]. The court found that there were 'reasonably practicable' steps that could have been taken to rectify these problems, and hence the s 53 defence did not apply.

In addressing the personal charge against Mr Smith, Staunton J at [124] began by issuing what amounted to a judicial rebuke to the prosecutor in the case, who had apparently assured Mr Smith at an initial interview that he (as opposed to the company) would not be prosecuted. Nonetheless, a prosecution against Mr Smith had been instituted and needed to be dealt with. Her Honour found that Mr Smith as a director was *prima facie* guilty of the same offence as the company. She ruled that the defences under s 53 of the Act were not applicable to the s 50 charge.[75] She also ruled that Mr Smith was not able to establish the defence of 'due diligence' because, while there was a paper policy on safety, he did not 'ensure that the policy became the basis for an entrenched systemic process' within the company, and 'took no proactive steps to "adequately supervise compliance" with the company's policy' – paras [131]–[132].

Following his conviction, Mr Smith received a penalty of $5,000.[76] The fact that he had consistently denied that the company should have done any more than it had actually done seemed to have weighed against him in sentencing. In the sentencing proceedings Staunton J commented at [57], [59]:

> Mr Smith clearly formed, and still holds, the opinion that his obligations arising under s 15(1) and s 50 of the Act were and are properly satisfied by the delegation of his authority to Mr Teahan …[77] In addressing the principle of specific deterrence in relation to DSC, I drew attention to the lack of remedial steps taken since the incident as indicated in the evidence of Mr Smith. That evidence suggested a complete misapprehension of the obligations imposed by s 15(1) of the Act in order to ensure a safe system of work, not merely a comprehensive policy structure. The failure of Mr Smith, on his evidence, to acknowledge his obligation to compel a systemic adoption of DSC's policy into overall safe systems of work renders specific deterrence particularly relevant in my considerations.

An appeal to the Full Bench in *Daly Smith Corporation (Aust) Pty Ltd and anor v WorkCover*[78] was taken but was not successful. Among the grounds of appeal were that the s 53 defences were applicable to offence charged by means of s 50. In rejecting this argument, the Full Bench referred to its own previous judgments in *Powercoal (Foster)*[79] and *Inspector Jorgenson v Daoud*[80] and implicitly accepted at [66] that Staunton J's reference, in considering 'due diligence', to the Canadian decision of *R v Bata Industries Ltd (No 2)*[81] was correct.

Conclusions

What lessons can be learned from a comparison of the UK and NSW personal liability provisions? One feature that will immediately impress any researcher is the far greater number of reported court decisions in NSW than in the UK. In part this may be an artefact of the different databases that are available for research. In NSW all decisions of the Industrial Relations Commission, the 'court arm' of which hears OHS prosecutions, are available on the AUSTLII database (www. austlii.edu.au). But other factors may also be in operation. The NSW regulator, WorkCover NSW, appears to have adopted a far more proactive role in instituting prosecutions against individual officers than has been taken in the UK. This may be due to a number of factors, but it is at least worth asking whether the different forms of legal liability have had a role to play.

One clear difference between the UK and NSW law is that under s 26 of the NSW *OHS Act* 2000, once the guilt of the company is established, and likewise the position of the officer (as either a formal director, or otherwise 'concerned in management'), the onus of proof shifts to the individual charged to make out the relevant defences – either 'no influence' or 'due diligence'. In contrast, establishing an offence under s 37 of the *HSAW* requires further proof by the prosecution of the defendant's 'consent', 'connivance' or 'neglect'. The prosecution, moreover, has to show 'consent', 'connivance' or 'neglect' by proof beyond reasonable doubt. Typically this will require evidence of what the duties of the relevant officer ought to have been, or what he or she ought to have been aware of. The decision in *R v P* [82] at least clarifies now that there is no need to introduce evidence of the actual, subjective knowledge of the officer.

The difference between the UK and NSW approaches to individual liability can be illustrated by an Australian example. A recent press report highlights a Victoria OHS prosecution undertaken of a company which ran a 'go-kart' centre, which was fined a record amount of $1.4 million for an incident leading to the death of a patron.[83] However, the fine could not be paid, as the company had gone into liquidation, a fact lamented by the trial judge. But what about a prosecution of the company's directors? The press report goes on to say that: 'Worksafe Victoria executive director John Merritt said there was not enough evidence to charge the individual ... directors for their roles in the incident.'

It should be noted that the above case arose in the State of Victoria [84] where s 144 of the *Occupational Health and Safety Act* 2004 provides that:

> (1) If a body corporate ... contravenes a provision of this Act or the regulations and the contravention is attributable to an officer of the body corporate failing to take reasonable care, the officer is guilty of an offence ...

The Victoria provision resembles UK s 37 in requiring that the prosecution bears the onus of presenting evidence that demonstrates fault on the part of the company officer. In contrast, numerous decisions in NSW suggest that a charge against the directors of the company would have had a better chance of succeeding, for the burden would have been on the directors to come forward with evidence (which they should have easy access to, if it existed) of how they had taken due care to provide for the safety of customers.

In sum, the law on the operation of s 26 of the *OHS Act* 2000 (NSW) has been clarified in recent years by a series of judicial decisions of the NSW courts. It now seems apparent that:

- The term 'concerned in management' is not restricted to those in the 'central' management of a large firm, but extends to a wider group of managers who have decision-making power and authority, going beyond the mere carrying out of directions as an employee, such as to affect the whole or a substantial part of the corporation, which powers relate to the matters which constituted the offence under the Act.[85]
- The general defences under s 28 of the Act are not applicable to the specific charge under s 26, which contains its own defences of 'unable to influence' or 'due diligence'.[86]

- The 'unable to influence' defence will be narrowly construed, possibly so that where a formally appointed board member is involved it can only apply where the articles of association of the company impose some unusual limitation on the member's powers.[87]
- The 'due diligence' defence requires consideration of a range of 'proactive' activities whereby safety systems are not only established on paper, but also implemented on the ground, their operation regularly monitored, and specific issues responded to when they are drawn to attention.[88]
- It is perfectly possible for a senior manager who only visits a workplace occasionally to be held not to have exercised 'due diligence' and to receive a personal fine.[89]
- Where more than one manager is convicted under s 26, differential fines may be imposed depending on the culpability of the individual.[90] In some (though by no means all) cases, no conviction might be entered where a manager, while technically guilty, had little involvement in decisions which led to the incident, and had made a genuine effort to introduce and monitor safety systems.[91]

It is submitted that the NSW provisions provide an example of a workable personal liability scheme in an important area of company operations – the health and safety of workers. Even if one might disagree with individual decisions under the legislation, the information available from the cases provides a rich database of material highlighting important issues that policy-makers should take into account when framing laws as to individual liability of company officers.

Notes

1 See *Australian Securities and Investments Commission v Macdonald (No 11)* [2009] NSWSC 287 (23 April 2009) for the findings of liability against the directors, and *Australian Securities and Investments Commission v Macdonald (No 12)* [2009] NSWSC 714 (20 August 2009) for the imposition of penalties.
2 These are discussed in a number of articles dealing with corporate criminal responsibility. See, e.g., Clarkson, CMV 'Kicking Corporate Bodies and Damning Their Souls' (1996) 59 *Modern Law Rev* 557–572.
3 A. Hopkins, *Lessons from Longford: The Esso Gas Plant Explosion* (Sydney: CCH, 2000), at 76; see also his earlier book *Managing Major Hazards: The Lessons of the Moura Mine Disaster* (Sydney: Allen & Unwin, 1999). Hopkins has also provided insightful and highly readable analyses of issues of risk and 'safety culture' in relation to other incidents in his later books, see *Safety, Culture and Risk: The Organisational Causes of Disasters* (Sydney: CCH, 2005); *Lessons from Gretley: Mindful Leadership and the law* (Sydney: CCH, 2007); *Failure to Learn: the BP Texas City Refinery disaster* (Sydney: CCH, 2008).
4 See generally *The Esso Longford Gas Plant Accident: Report of the Longford Royal Commission* (Commissioners, the Hon Sir D.M. Dawson & Mr B.J. Brooks), June 1999 esp paras 13.7 (training deficiencies), 13.54 (failure to conduct a 'HAZOP' [hazardous operations] risk assessment of the plant where the accident occurred, despite this being acknowledged as necessary by Esso's own guidelines), 13.83 (removal of experienced engineers off-site to Melbourne). The Royal Commission at para 15.7 concluded that

there had been a breach of the *Occupational Health and Safety Act* 1985 (Vic), a conclusion that was re-affirmed by the subsequent conviction of Esso and fine of $2 million, see *DPP v Esso Australia Pty Ltd* (2001) 107 IR 285, [2001] VSC 263.

5   See, for example, the approaches discussed in N. Gunningham & R. Johnstone, *Regulating Workplace Safety: System and Sanctions* (Oxford: OUP, 1999).

6   See, for example, s 12 of the *Occupational Health and Safety Act* 2000 (NSW), which provides for a maximum penalty of 5,000 penalty units in the case of a corporation. On the current 'exchange rate' this amounts to $550,000, see s 17 *Crimes (Sentencing Procedure) Act* 1999 (NSW).

7   This of course is not the only solution to the problem of encouraging responsible corporate behaviour. Many writers have put forward creative models which aim at improving 'corporate citizenship'. See, for example, Fiona Haines, *Corporate Regulation: Beyond 'Punish or Persuade'* (Oxford: Clarendon, 1997) and Christine Parker, *The Open Corporation: Self-Regulation and Corporate Citizenship* (Cambridge: CUP, 2002).

8   B. Horrigan, 'Dynamic Interaction and Tension for Government and Non-Government Corporations Between Profit-Making, Corporate Governance, Corporate Citizenship, Corporate Regulation, Business Ethics, Human Rights and a Civil Society in the Era of the Internet, Globalisation and Interconnectedness', Attachment 4; paper presented to the Australasian Law Teachers' Association Conference, University of Canberra, July 2–5, 2000.

9   A. Hopkins 'Repeat Disasters: The Lessons of the Moura Coal Mine' in C. Mayhew & C.L. Peterson *Occupational Health and Safety in Australia* (St Leonards: Allen & Unwin, 1999) 140–157, at 157.

10 Hopkins, *Failure to Learn* (2008), above n 3 at 82.

11 N. Gunningham, *CEO and Supervisor Drivers: Review of Literature and Current Practice* (Report prepared for the NOHSC, October 1999), at 39–40.

12 N. Gunningham & R. Johnstone, *Regulating Workplace Safety: System and Sanctions* (Oxford: OUP, 1999).

13 I am grateful for the citation to this comment in P. Herzfeld, 'Still a Troublesome Area: Legislative and Common Law Restrictions on Indemnity and Insurance Arrangements Effected by Companies on Behalf of Officers and Employees' (2009) 27 *Company and Securities Law Jnl* 267–298, at 292 n 173.

14 Fisse and Braithwaite, *Corporations, Crime and Accountability* (Cambridge University Press: Cambridge (1993), at 134. Their 'desiderata' 1 and 7 which deal specifically with individual accountability reflect the same principle: see pp.135–136.

15 J.C. Coffee, Jr ' "No Soul to Damn: No Body to Kick": An Unscandalized Inquiry into the Problem of Corporate Punishment' (1981) 79 *Michigan L Rev* 386–459, at 387, 410.

16 Gunningham & Johnstone (1999), above, n 13 at 218. See also F. Haines, *Corporate Regulation: Beyond 'Punish or Persuade'* (Oxford Socio-Legal Studies; Oxford: Clarendon Press, 1997).

17 Discussion of the extent to which indemnities against fines in this area may be offered by companies is another topic, dealt with to some extent by Herzfeld (above n 13). Whatever the resolution of this issue, though, imprisonment where available and the 'stigma' of conviction will be borne by the individual officer.

18 E. Lederman, 'Models for Imposing Corporate Criminal Liability: From Adaptation and Imitation toward Aggregation and the Search for Self-Identity' (2000) 4 *Buffalo Criminal Law Review* 641, at 703. See also S.L. Smith, 'An Iron Fist in the Velvet Glove: Redefining the Role of Criminal Prosecution in Creating an Effective Environmental Enforcement System' (1995) 19 *Criminal Law Jnl* 12–20.

19 Smith (1995) above, n 19 at 16.

20 N. Wise, 'Personal Liability Promotes Responsible Conduct: Extending the Responsible Corporate Officer Doctrine to Federal Civil Environmental Enforcement Cases' (2002) 21 *Stanford Environmental Law Jnl* 283, at 285–286.

21 In the UK, of course, this has now become a reality. See *Corporate Manslaughter and Corporate Homicide Act* 2007, discussed below.

22 See C. Wells, 'Corporate Killing' (1997) 147 *New Law Jnl* 1467.

23 CMCHA s. 18.

24 J. Gobert, 'The Corporate Manslaughter and Corporate Homicide Act 2007 – Thirteen Years in the Making But Was It Worth the Wait?' (2008) 71 *Modern Law Rev* 413 at 414.

25 D. Bergman, C. Davis & B. Rigby, HSE Research Report 535 (HMSO, 2007), http://www.hse.gov.uk/research/rrhtm/rr535.htm.

26 See above, n 26, ch 7. Of course there are circumstances which might create liability, such as where a director is also an employee, or as noted in the Report, at 98 n 14, the rare case where a sole director has in effect been held to 'be' the employer by piercing the corporate veil. But there are no specific provisons in the health and safety legislation creating individual liability.

27 Above, n 25 at 99.

28 Section 167 of the *Workplace Health and Safety Act* 1995 (Qld); s 26 of the *Occupational Health and Safety Act* 2000 (NSW).

29 See N. Foster 'Personal Liability of Company Officers for Corporate Occupational Health and Safety Breaches: section 26 of the *Occupational Health and Safety Act* 2000 (NSW)' (2005) 18 *Australian Journal of Labour Law* 107–135, at 122 n 62. There is however a 'Guidance Note' issued by the Health and Safety Executive in relation to s 37, see http://www.hse.gov.uk/enforce/enforcementguide/investigation/identifying/directors.htm.

30 [2007] EWCA Crim 1937, [2008] ICR 96.

31 Above n 31, quoting from the trial judge.

32 *R v Balfour Beatty Infrastructure Services Ltd, Network Rail and ors* (Central Criminal Court, 7 Oct 2005). The citation is provided in B. Barrett, 'Liability for Safety Offences: Is the Law Still Fatally Flawed?' (2008) 37 *Industrial Law Jnl* 100–118, at 102 n 7.

33 See above n 31 at [11] for this quote from MacKay, J.

34 1978 JC 74; 19 May 1978 (Emslie LJG, Cameron, J. & Johnston LJJ).

35 [2008] UKHL 73 (10 Dec 2008); [2009] 2 All E.R. 645.

36 *R v Chargot Ltd* [2007] EWCA Crim 3032; [2008] ICR 517.

37 See Lord Hope, above n 36 at [21].

38 [2003] ICR 586.

39 See Lord Hope, above n 36, at [28]–[30].

40 Above, n 30.

41 [1996] 1 WLR 970.

42 See *R v Davies*, n 39.

43 Above, n 36.

44 See the discussion below near n 53.

45 For a detailed summary of the operation of the legislation up to 2004–2005, see Foster, 'Personal Liability' (2005), above n 30. A more recent review of the operation of the personal liability provisions around Australia can also be found in P. Harpur, 'Occupational Health and Safety Issues and the Boardroom: Criminal Penalties for Directors for Company's Lack of Safety' (2008) *Bond University Corporate Governance eJournal* (see http://epublications.bond.edu.au/cgej/10).

46 (2006) 159 IR 121, [2006] NSWIRComm 339.

47 N. Foster, 'Mining, Maps and Mindfulness: the Gretley Appeal to the Full Bench of the Industrial Court of NSW' (2008) 24 *Journal of Occupational Health and Safety, Australia and New Zealand* 113–129.

48 Since Gretley, however, there have been so many such prosecutions that some commentators now suggest that prosecutions are too commonly used in the mining sector in NSW. See, for example, N. Gunningham 'Prosecution for OHS Offences:

Deterrent or Disincentive?' (2007) 29 *Sydney Law Review* 359–390; and *Mine Safety: Law Regulation Policy* (Sydney: Federation, 2007) esp ch 7.

49 For some time prosecutions under the former s 50 of the 1983 Act had mostly been limited to officers who were 'directly involved in the incident', but as I noted in 2005, more recently there have been signs that prosecution of higher officers were starting to take place. See N. Foster, above n 30 at 114–116.

50 *McMartin v Newcastle Wallsend Coal Company Pty Ltd* [2004] NSWIRComm 202.

51 (2005) 145 IR 327, [2005] NSWCA 345 (discussed below).

52 See N. Foster, above n 30 at 130.

53 (2004) 137 IR 253, [2004] NSWIRComm 297 at [163]–[167].

54 Above, n 51.

55 [2006] HCA Trans 475. See the discussion of the *Smith* proceedings below.

56 It will be recalled that a similar issue was resolved in a similar way in respect of s 37 *HSWA* in the *Chargot* case, see above n 36 and accompanying text.

57 See *Newcastle Wallsend Coal Company Pty Ltd and Ors v McMartin (No 2)* (2007) 164 IR 326, [2007] NSWIRComm 125 at 126–127.

58 Just to be clear, no relation to the present author, as far as I know!

59 *Morrison v Powercoal Pty Ltd and anor* [2003] NSWIRComm 342 (Peterson J).

60 *Morrison v Powercoal Pty Ltd and anor* (2004) 137 IR 253; [2004] NSWIRComm 297.

61 *Morrison v Powercoal Pty Ltd and anor (No 3)* [2005] NSWIRComm 61 (7 March 2005); in fact on sentencing Mr Foster received the benefit of s 10 of the *Crimes (Sentencing Procedure) Act* 1999, which allowed the court to enter no conviction in 'extenuating circumstances', see [143]. But the application for review to the Court of Appeal still went ahead.

62 (2005) 145 IR 327, [2005] NSWCA 345.

63 See Spigelman CJ, above.

64 [2006] NSWIRComm 323.

65 The question of who qualifies as a senior manager may in itself be difficult to determine. See, e.g. *WorkCover Authority v Anywhere Tower Cranes Pty Ltd and ors* [2007] NSWIRComm 44 (secretary's claim that she was only a nominal director did not absolve her of responsibility for safety).

66 The defendant was in fact a resident of New Zealand at the time of the incident.

67 Another situation, also rarely encountered, is where the defendant was not in a position to influence the conduct of the corporation in relation to its contravention of the provision in question because of a formal provision in the company rules limiting their power: see *Inspector James v Sunny Ngai and ors* [2007] NSWIRComm 203.

68 See also *Inspector Aldred v Herbert* [2007] NSWIRC Comm 170.

69 See the comment by Haylen J, in *Ritchie* at [179]: 'In a sense the more evidence that the defendant calls to make out the s 26(1)(b) defence, the likelihood is that such evidence will diminish the case attempting to be established under s 26(1)(a).'

70 See [2006] NSWIRComm 384 for sentencing proceedings. It is perhaps worth noting that proceedings flowing from the same incident against another company officer, the Division General Manager, *Inspector Kumar v Rose* [2006] NSWIRComm 325, resulted in a fine of $18,500 after a guilty plea at an early stage of the proceedings.

71 Compare *Morrison v Barry John Cahill* [2007] NSWIRComm 114.

72 See, commenting on the decision, J. Catanzariti, 'Danger at Work: Directors Face Strict OHS liability' (Dec 2006) *Law Society Journal* 52–54; S. Nicol, 'Directors Beware: Personal Liability for Occupational Health And Safety Breaches' (March 2007) *Keeping Good Companies* 98–100; S. Nettleton 'OHS Due Diligence – A Guide for Directors and CEOs' (March 2007) *Company Law & Governance Update* 5–8, available at http://www.blakedawson.com/ in the 'Publications' area.

73 Compare *WorkCover v Steel* [2005] NSWIRComm 215 with *WorkCover v Burn* [2005] NSWIRComm 206. See also *Inspector Reynolds v Ocean Parade Pty Ltd and ors* [2006] NSWIRComm 400 (Schmidt J.).

74 [2004] NSWIRComm 349 (Staunton J).

75 At [126], following her Honour's own previous decision in *McMartin v Newcastle Wallsend Coal Co* [2004] NSWIRComm 202.

76 [2005] NSWIRComm 101.

77 See also *WorkCover v Akerman-Apache (Joint Venture) Pty Ltd and ors* [2006] NSWIRComm 370 (directors cannot delegate their responsibility to ensure safety).

78 [2006] NSWIRComm 111.

79 Above, n 603.

80 (2005) 143 IR 170, [2005] NSWIRComm 135 (FB).

81 (1992) 7 CELR (NS) 245, noted N. Foster, n 30 at 130.

82 Above, n 30.

83 http://news.ninemsn.com.au/national/812760/1-4m-fine-for-death-of-go-kart-patron.

84 One unresolved issue is whether Australia's 7 or 8 different jurisdictions should 'harmonise' their differing occupational health and safety laws. This issue has been the subject of two recent Reports by a panel commissioned by the incoming Rudd Labour government. See the Reports of the National Review into Model Occupational Health and Safety Laws (the *First Report* of October 2008, and the *Second Report* of January 2009), available at http://www.nationalohsreview.gov.au/ohs/Reports/ discussed in N. Foster, 'The National Review into Model OHS Laws: A Paper Examining the Duties of Officers and Due Diligence' (Paper presented to a *Symposium on the National Review into Model OHS Laws*, Canberra, 5 May 2009; published on the NRCOHSR website as Working Paper No 66), available at http://ohs.anu.edu.au/publications/pdf/wp%2066%20-%20Foster%20symposium%20paper.pdf. Draft model legislation for possible introduction by the various jurisdictions in 2011 has now been made available, see http://www.safeworkaustralia.gov.au/swa/ModelLegislation/Model+OHS+Legislation/.

85 *McMartin v Newcastle Wallsend Coal Company Pty Ltd* [2004] NSWIRComm 202; see also the *Powercoal* decision in the Court of Appeal, above n 62 and accompanying text.

86 See *Gretley Appeal*, above n 47 and accompanying text.

87 See the discussion in *Ritchie*, above n 65 and accompanying text.

88 See for example *Herbert (Salamander Shores)* [2007] NSWIRComm 170.

89 See *Ritchie*, above n 65; and *Smith*, n 74.

90 See *Sayhoun* and *Burn and Steel*, n 74.

91 See *Cahill*, n 72.

8   Squaring the circle

The relationship between individual and organizational fault

James Gobert

Introduction

When harm that would seem to call for criminal liability occurs in a business setting, the question arises of how to allocate blame between the individual whose acts are the most immediate cause of the harm, the corporate executives whose policies led to the acts which caused the harm, and the company itself. Historically, prosecutions, both in the UK and elsewhere, have typically been brought against the employee whose wrongful acts were most directly linked in terms of time and space to the harm. Prosecutions of the directors and corporate officers who formulated the harm-causing policy were more infrequent, and more infrequent still were prosecutions of the company itself.[1]

In part, corporate criminal liability was long ignored because a legal basis for prosecuting a company was lacking. Few jurisdictions had statutes specifically directed to corporate criminality. Often, even when enacted, such statutes had lain dormant on the statute books.

The situation was seemingly different in common law countries such as England where the absence of legislation should not have proved fatal. Relevant offences had been developed by the courts with respect to natural persons, and general statutes governing statutory interpretation allowed criminal laws relating to natural persons to be applied to legal persons.[2] So, for example, extending the law of theft or manslaughter to companies should have been viable in theory. However, in practice the jurisprudential development foundered on the inability of the courts to transpose traditional common law concepts such as *actus reus* and *mens rea* to inanimate fictional entities such as companies. How does a company 'act' and where was its 'mind' to be located?

The problem with ignoring the role of companies and corporate executives in the commission of criminal offences is that it produced an incomplete and flawed picture as to why crimes occurred in a business setting. As a result, institutional reform that could have avoided recurrence of the offence often was not undertaken. Meanwhile, ordinary employees, who may have simply been carrying out work assignments ordered by their superiors, became the scapegoats for harm more properly attributable to their company and its managers.

Recent years have witnessed an increasing trend among states to enact laws imposing criminal liability on companies that wilfully, recklessly or through gross negligence cause harm in the course of their business operation. In some instances liability is strict or 'absolute' (the causing of the harm alone being sufficient to justify criminal liability without proof of fault), most notably in the regulatory field,[3] or based on negligence.[4]

The emergence of statutes imposing corporate criminal liability raises the question of the continuing status of criminal liability for individuals for harms that occur in a business context. Has such liability survived the shift to corporate liability; and, if so, what is the relationship between the liability of the company and the liability of its directors, officers and senior managers?[5]

Two examples may serve to illustrate the complexity of the relationship between individual and organizational fault. In *R v. Adomako*[6] an anaesthetist was convicted of gross negligence manslaughter when his patient died after he had failed to take appropriate responsive measures following a disconnection of the endotracheal tube that supplied oxygen to the patient. Dr. Adomako had sole responsibility for monitoring the patient, even though prior to his taking on this task it had been carried out by two persons – a registrar and an assistant. Dr. Adomako had never previously acted as the sole anaesthetist in such a situation. On the morning in question he had worked at the hospital until 3.30am, and then had to be back on the wards at 7.00am. That he was tired – probably overtired – seems indisputable. However, his overtiredness, his stressful work schedule, and the absence of back-up assistance were all irrelevant to the charge of gross negligence manslaughter.

The point on which I wish to focus is not whether Dr. Adomako was grossly negligent. The very fact that he had attempted to work while overtired demonstrated poor, if not criminally negligent, judgement. More intriguing, however, was the disinclination of the criminal justice system to probe the contributory role of the hospital and the NHS in bringing about the patient's death. Neither was prosecuted.[7] Yet it seems clear that NHS policies, which (at the time) tolerated if not required junior doctors and interns to work 90+ hour weeks, inevitably were destined to produce overtired physicians who would be unduly prone to error.

A not dissimilar situation occurred in respect of the 1997 Southall rail crash. The crash occurred after the driver's concentration had lapsed and the train passed two warning signals and a stop signal before crashing into a freight train. Seven passengers were killed and many were severely injured. Although at first blush the cause of the crash seemed to be the driver's negligence, subsequent investigation revealed that (a) there was no backup driver in the cab, and (b) neither the Automatic Warning System (AWS), which would have sounded an alarm when the train passed the signals in question, nor the Automatic Protection System (ATP), which would have brought the train automatically to a stop in this situation, were operational. Although experienced, the driver had never previously driven without AWS.

Part of the reason why ATP was not installed on the train rested with the rail industry, which had lobbied the government against the recommendation of Mr. Justice Hidden, following a public inquiry into the cause of the Clapham rail crash a decade earlier,[8] that all trains be equipped with ATP. Although standard in continental European states, the industry managed to persuade the government that to require ATP on UK trains would be both unnecessary and prohibitively expensive. Ironically, the Great Western train involved in the Southall crash was fitted with ATP on an experimental basis, although, as indicated, it was not operative at the critical time.[9]

Unlike in *Adomako*, the employer, Great Western Railways, was prosecuted for manslaughter with respect to the deaths resulting from the Southall crash. Charges were dismissed, however, because the court could not find the necessary link between individual and corporate liability which had to be established under the then prevailing 'identification' test of corporate criminal liability,[10] which brings us back to the question of the proper relationship between corporate and individual liability.

Vicarious corporate liability

In the modern era, a consensus appears to be emerging, slowly and perhaps grudgingly,[11] that companies can and should be subject to criminal prosecution in their own right,[12] regardless of whether an individual can also be prosecuted. What remains unsettled is the appropriate test of criminal liability. Many countries impute criminal liability to a company based on proof of an individual's offence. In the United States, for example, corporations can be criminally liable when a crime has been perpetrated by any employee, officer, or agent of the company who at the time was engaged in the company's business with intent to benefit the company.[13] The status of the offender within the company is immaterial.

While such 'vicarious' liability may exert pressure on companies to supervise their staff more carefully to avert illegality, it may also unfairly penalize companies who have conscientiously tried to avert offences. That a disgruntled employee or mischief maker is able to circumvent controls imposed by the company may not be a fair reflection on how the company carries out its business. Vicarious liability also is conceptually troubling for offences that have a *mens rea* element. It is one thing to hold that an employee's acts are the company's acts (for how else but through its employees can a company 'act'), but it is quite another to attribute the employee's idiosyncratic state of mind to the company.

The English courts were disinclined to hold companies potentially liable for every offence committed by any employee and also to impute an ordinary employee's state of mind to the company.[14] Instead, they adopted a test of corporate criminal liability that has come to be known as the 'identification' doctrine. Under this doctrine a company is liable only for crimes committed by persons who can be characterized as part of the 'controlling mind and will' of the company,[15] or who at least have organizational authority to carry out the harm-causing transaction at issue on behalf of the company.[16]

The advantage of the 'identification' doctrine is that it locates the 'mind' of the company in persons who have the power to change corporate policy. The disadvantage is that the doctrine will often allow corporate executives (and derivatively, their companies) to escape criminal liability because they will not have committed the *actus reus* of the offence or because a *novus actus interveniens* (intervening act) – the independent acts by employees carrying out the flawed policies – may be found to have broken the chain of causation between corporate policy and resulting harm.

The distinction between persons who represent the mind of a company and those who constitute its 'hands', as Lord Denning famously expressed it,[17] is both simplistic and misleading. The image of the worker robotically carrying out company orders may do a disservice to employees generally. Granted that employees may not be allowed to substitute a personal preference as to how to carry out their job for company policy, there will inevitably be many grey areas where they have to exercise discretion. What arguably is critical is what guidance and training they have received in exercising discretion.

As a practical matter, authority in large companies often must perforce be delegated, as directors and senior management are not in a position to oversee every aspect of the company's business operation. While a company can be liable for crimes committed by persons to whom decision-making authority has been delegated, the delegation must come from a person 'identified' with the company, which of course brings the inquiry full circle. The issue is more complicated when delegation has been partial, as there then arises the question of *how much* authority needs to be delegated in order to effect a transfer of 'identification'.

Another problem with the identification doctrine arises when a corporate executive acts contrary to the company's best interests.[18] Unlike under the American doctrine of vicarious corporate liability, where a corporation will not be held liable for an offence that was not committed to benefit the company, a UK company can, pursuant to the identification doctrine, be liable when its chief executive loots the company for personal gain[19].

Nonetheless, despite the distinctive nomenclature, the identification test is in reality a species of vicarious liability. It is a restrictive species in that not everyone who is employed by the company or associated with it has sufficient status to lead to the company's being held vicariously liable for their crimes. Nonetheless, the company is liable for the offences of individuals. Corporate criminal liability remains derivative, and the company can be convicted despite the fact that it has conducted its business without fault and in an impeccable manner.

Vicarious individual liability

While it is not uncommon for a corporation to be held vicariously liable for an offence committed by an individual, the converse of holding an individual vicariously liable for a company's offence is rarer. For one thing, there is not the same conceptual need for a 'constructed' theory of liability, as individuals who commit a criminal offence can be prosecuted in their own right. Furthermore, in jurisdictions adhering to a vicarious theory of corporate criminal liability, there is an undeniable circularity in imputing an individual's offence to the company and then imputing the company's offence to the individual.

There will, however, be situations where a prosecutor will want to be able to prosecute a company's directors and officers for the company's offence. One such situation is where the company has gone into liquidation and no meaningful penalty can be imposed against it. In most jurisdictions, the main – if not the only – sanction against a convicted company is a fine,[20] but a company in bankruptcy may not have the assets to pay a fine.

The Scottish case of *Balmer*[21] is illustrative. Here a partnership could not be prosecuted for a fire that had broken out in its nursing home because the partnership had been dissolved and the partners could not be prosecuted individually because the partnership – and not the partners – was legally responsible for the nursing home. Yet, particularly in jurisdictions where criminal fines can be used to compensate victims,[22] allowing financial redress to be obtained from a company's directors and officers for the company's offence will enable persons injured as a result of the offence to receive much-needed compensation.

Another instance where a prosecution of a company's directors and officers may be deemed highly desirable is where the company is merely the vehicle for executing the individual's offence. Often a corrupt corporate official is not in a position to carry out a criminal scheme as an individual. For example, an individual may not be able to extort money from a foreign government. However, in the capacity as the chief executive of a multi-national company (MNC), the individual may demand a bribe for locating the MNC's subsidiary within the jurisdiction in question.[23]

Prosecutions of corporate executives may also be sought where imposing a fine on the company may not be deemed adequate to assuage the outrage felt by either the public or the victims. Corporate executives, their salaries secure, may not be personally affected if a fine is imposed on their company. The fine often can be passed on to consumers of the company's products (through price increases), or else be recouped by making ordinary workers redundant. In neither case will the corporate executive be disadvantaged. The prospect of a jail term has a far more realistic likelihood of exerting a deterrent effect on such executives than a financial penalty imposed on their company.

While, as noted, derivative liability of directors and corporate officers for their company's offence is far less common than derivative liability of a company for offences of its directors and corporate officers, it is not unknown, particularly in respect of regulatory offences. In Europe derivative individual liability can be found under Spanish law[24] and in Luxembourg.[25] Often, the seemingly paradoxical result is that a director can be liable for the company's offence even though the law of the state does not recognize corporate criminal liability.

Beyond Europe, one finds the following provision in New South Wales, Australia (discussed in Neil Foster's chapter in this volume):

26 Offences by corporations-liability of directors and managers
(1) If a corporation contravenes, whether by act or omission, any provision of this Act or the regulations, each director of the corporation, and each person concerned in the management of the corporation, is taken

to have contravened the same provision unless the director or person satisfies the court that:

(a)   he or she was not in a position to influence the conduct of the corporation in relation to its contravention of the provision, or

(b)   he or she, being in such a position, used all due diligence to prevent the contravention by the corporation.

(2)   A person may be proceeded against and convicted under a provision pursuant to subsection (1) whether or not the corporation has been proceeded against or been convicted under that provision.

The troubling aspect of these statutes is the same as we saw in holding companies derivatively liable for offences of their directors and managers. The danger is that of imposing criminal liability in the absence of fault – or more accurately, as under both the NSW statute and most statutes imposing derivative liability, the defendant is afforded a defence of 'due diligence' – liability without the prosecution having to prove guilt beyond reasonable doubt. Although reverse burden of proof provisions have been upheld by the courts,[26] they are clearly in tension with the generally accepted proposition that a defendant is presumed innocent until the state establishes guilt beyond reasonable doubt.

Non-derivative theories of corporate liability

To avoid the circularity of holding companies criminally liable for offences committed by their employees/officers/directors, and then holding the officers and directors of the company liable for their company's offence, there needs to be a legal basis of corporate liability which is grounded in the independent fault of the company and not the derivative attribution of the crime of a third party to the company.

Although the 'identification' doctrine may have solved the problem of where to locate a company's *mens rea*, it failed to address the objection that any form of vicarious liability risks holding a company criminally liable when it has not been at fault. Under the 'identification' doctrine, and under the American version of vicarious corporate criminal liability as well, a company's efforts to avert illegality by its personnel – no matter how well-conceived, well-intentioned, and generally effective – are in the final analysis irrelevant.

The way to address the issue of principle, and perhaps also the objection of the English judges that the American test of vicarious liability is too broad, is to require a showing of fault as a prerequisite to a company's conviction. But in what way can a company be said to be at fault when a crime has been committed by one of its employees, agents or officers?

It is submitted that a company is at fault when the following four conditions are present:

1   The company is, or should have been, aware of the risk;
2   The company has a legal duty to prevent the offence;

3   The company has the capacity to prevent the offence; and
4   The company fails to prevent the offences.

While it might be contended that the duty of prevention lies with the company managers, this would be to draw.
While it might seem that this responsibility lies with individuals, that would be to draw the lines of responsibility too narrowly. The responsibility is a collective one owed by the organization.

The failure to prevent a criminal offence is often not so much a function of incompetent management but of a more pervasive corporate ethos or culture that tolerates negligent working practices and illegal shortcuts. The company, for example, may turn a blind eye to misleading selling practices by its sales force, the offering of bribes by its official representatives, and the disregard of legally mandated safety practices by its workforce.

A company's ethos or culture often cannot be tied to a particular individual or individuals. It may have evolved over time, it may never have been set down in writing, and its roots may lie in policies and practices established by the long-deceased founders of the company. While it can be argued that the individuals who perpetuate the criminogenic culture should be legally responsible for it,[27] these individuals may not even be aware of deeply ingrained, long-established but illegal practices passed from one generation of workers to the next, and any attempt to reform such 'folkways' may be met with employee resistance.

Although it would be an overstatement to say that criminal liability based on a company's failure to prevent an offence has become the norm, one can see green shoots throughout Europe.[28] While many of these statutes also recognize vicarious corporate criminal liability, they provide an alternative basis of liability grounded in the company's failure to have prevented an offence.

Australia is singularly notable for having attempted to capture the concept of a criminogenic corporate culture in statute. The Federal Criminal Code Act (1995), a model statute which admittedly has only been adopted in one Australian state (the Australian Capital Territories[29]) provides:

(1) If intention, knowledge or recklessness is a fault element in relation to a physical element of an offence that may be committed by a company, that fault element must be attributed to a body corporate that expressly, tacitly or impliedly authorized or permitted the commission of the offence.

(2) The means by which such an authorization or permission may be established include …

(c) proving that a corporate culture existed within the body corporate that directed, encouraged, tolerated or led to non-compliance with the relevant provision; or

(d) proving that the body corporate failed to create and maintain a corporate culture that required compliance with the relevant provision …[30]

The Australian legislation creates no new offences, but rather applies the concept of 'corporate culture' to existing offences which have intention, knowledge or recklessness as a fault element. It allows a company's criminal liability to be based on a 'corporate culture' that directs, encourages, tolerates or leads to non-compliance with the law and imposes on companies an affirmative duty to create and maintain a law-compliant culture.[31]

The above statutes are visionary in conceiving of a model of corporate fault that is not linked to the commission of an offence by a corporate agent. They also pave the way for examining the nature of the relationship between individual and corporate liability.

Complicity

The key to unraveling the relationship between individual and corporate liability lies in the law of criminal complicity. Not invariably but frequently directors, corporate officers and senior managers aid and abet their company's offences, and similarly companies aid and abet the offences of their directors, officers and senior managers.

The complicity of corporate executives

Methodological individualists maintain that all events can be traced to human agency and human agency alone.[32] However, one does not have to be a methodological individualist to appreciate the role that individuals play in respect of the corporation. A company is an inanimate entity, a legal fiction. It needs the input of human beings[33] to function, and to set its goals and priorities.

Corporate management is responsible for conceiving, formulating, approving and implementing policies that will allow the company to achieve its objectives. Corporate executives and managers will receive the credit – and the bonuses – when these policies succeed. By the same token, they must accept responsibility when they fail, at least when the policies have not been fully analysed.

Ignorance is no defence. For a corporate executive to claim unawareness of a seriously misguided policy is tantamount to admitting a dereliction of duty. The job of the corporate executive is to be aware of such policies. Further, to claim not to have personally appreciated the risks associated with a given policy ignores the executive's ability to seek out the advice of others, including outside consultants, who have the requisite expertise.

If, as suggested in the previous section, corporate fault lies in the failure to prevent criminal offences within a company's business operation, the key to prevention is devising an effective system of risk management and supervision. This is the responsibility of corporate management.

The process begins with the hiring and training of employees. If, for instance, a death or serious injury were to occur as a result of the improper operation of equipment, those who hired a clearly unsuitable person to be in control of the equipment or who failed to provide adequate training for the employee may be as, if not more, responsible for the resulting harm than the employee. In a sales context, the sales staff need to be informed in advance of the permissible limits of 'puffing' and when they are on slippery ground in not volunteering relevant but unrequested information (as occurred in respect of the 'Equitable' Life policyholders).

Corporate officers and senior managers will also be charged with devising a system of supervision for those engaged in the day-to-day carrying out of corporate policies. Effective supervision probably represents the 'last clear chance' to avert illegality. Traditionally, supervision consisted of oversight by another human being, but in the modern age, it is increasingly technological, as the proliferation of CCTV cameras attests. Even if inadequate to prevent an offence, effective supervision will help to ensure its prompt discovery and damage limitation.

Unions frequently assert that managers place profits ahead of safety. A delicate balance obviously needs to be struck, but frequently that balance seems to be struck too much in favour of profitability. For instance, it is typically senior managers who decide what funds to allocate to a company's research and development (R&D) programme. In times of fiscal exigency, the R&D budget is often the first to be cut. Yet by not taking R&D sufficiently seriously, a company may wind up exposing users of its services or products to an inordinate risk of injury or death.

The link between a death and an underfunded R&D department may be difficult to appreciate in practice. There are no guidelines as to how much should be spent on R&D. Costs need to be balanced against benefits. Spending millions to produce a marginally safer product that would have to be priced beyond the ordinary consumer's budget may be satisfying to the soul but fatal to the financial viability of the company.

On the other hand, when the expense of R&D is minimal and the failure to expend the necessary moneys may cost human lives, most persons would support the expenditure, even if it means paying slightly more. Take the case of the *Herald of Free Enterprise*. The *Herald* capsized when it sailed with its bow doors open and water entered the car deck, destabilizing the ferry.[34] Nearly 200 passengers and crew lost their lives. Prior to the disaster, ships masters had lobbied for warning lights to be placed on the bridge to alert them when the bow doors had not been shut.[35] This eminently reasonable proposal was dismissed (indeed, ridiculed) by company directors as unnecessary because employees were already being paid to close the doors. Yet immediately following the disaster the requested warning lights were installed without fanfare. What this unhappy tale seems to have shown is that the problem lay not with the technological feasibility or the cost of installing the bridge lights but rather with misguided risk management policies and a distorted sense of priorities on the part of the directors.

A similar pattern occurred after the Southall train crash, which was described in the introduction. It was noted that had ATP been installed, the train would automatically have been brought to a halt after it passed the warning signals without the need for human intervention. At the public inquiry into the crash, the managing director of Great Western testified that the company had not been able to make ATP work effectively (although this did not seem to be an obstacle to the many European train operators who had fitted their trains with functioning ATP systems). Be that as it may, GWR had no problem installing ATP on all of its trains following the crash, a response which served to underline the disingenuousness of the managing director's testimony.

To recap, corporate directors, officers, and senior managers who knowingly or negligently ignore criminogenic risks inherent in the formulation or implementation of company policies, or wilfully blind themselves to the risks, are complicit in any resulting corporate illegality. These decision-makers are engaged in such grossly negligent risk management that the law should have no qualms in recognizing their role as aiders and abettors of their company's offence.

The idea that persons in positions of responsibility can be complicit in offences committed by their organization has been recognized in the military context. Under the International Criminal Court Act 2001:

> (2) A military commander, or a person effectively acting as a military commander, is responsible for offences committed by forces under his effective command and control, or (as the case may be) his effective authority and control, as a result of his failure to exercise control properly over such forces where—
>
> (a) he either knew, or owing to the circumstances at the time, should have known that the forces were committing or about to commit such offences, and
>
> (b) he failed to take all necessary and reasonable measures within his power to prevent or repress their commission or to submit the matter to the competent authorities for investigation and prosecution.
>
> (3) With respect to superior and subordinate relationships not described in subsection (2), a superior is responsible for offences committed by subordinates under his effective authority and control, as a result of his failure to exercise control properly over such subordinates where—
>
> (a) he either knew, or consciously disregarded information which clearly indicated, that the subordinates were committing or about to commit such offences,
>
> (b) the offences concerned activities that were within his effective responsibility and control, and
>
> (c) he failed to take all necessary and reasonable measures within his power to prevent or repress their commission or to submit the matter to the competent authorities for investigation and prosecution.
>
> (4) A person responsible under this section for an offence is regarded as aiding, abetting, counselling or procuring the commission of the offence.[56]

One might note that under s.4 of the statute, the liability accruing to human defendants is that of an accessory.

While the recognition of accessorial liability was thus accepted by the UK Parliament in the military command context, six years later it was to be rejected by Parliament in respect of corporate manslaughter. Section 18 of the CMCHA 2007 expressly excludes individual liability for aiding, abetting, counselling or procuring corporate manslaughter.[37]

The CMCHA creates an anomaly within the legal structure governing business-related deaths. The drafters of the CMCHA had stressed the link between the law pertaining to corporate manslaughter and violations of the relevant Health and Safety at Work etc. Act 1974, going so far as to assure companies that they had nothing to fear from the CMCHA as long as they complied with health and safety laws. Yet when a company is successfully prosecuted for a health and safety violation, its officers can be held liable (in effect) as an accessory to the company's offence. Section 37 of the Health and Safety at Work etc. Act 1974 provides:

> 37. (1) Where an offence under any of the relevant statutory provisions committed by a body corporate is proved to have been committed with the consent or connivance of, or to have been attributable to any neglect on the part of, any director, manager, secretary or other similar officer of the body corporate or a person who was purporting to act in any such capacity, he as well as the body corporate shall be guilty of that offence and shall be liable to be proceeded against and punished accordingly.[38]

The complicity of the company

Methodological individualists were right to recognize the role of human agency in producing a crime, but this is only part of the picture. Without incentives offered by the company, without the provision of the means by which the offence is committed, without a supportive corporate culture and without the post-crime camouflage provided by the organization, the crime may never have been committed.

The Accessories and Abettors Act 1861 provides:

> Whosoever shall aid, abet, counsel, or procure the commission of an offence shall be liable to be tried ... and punished as a principal offender.

How does this Act, drafted with natural persons in mind, apply to companies? There are two key issues to be addressed: the *actus reus* of being an accessory and the *mens rea*.

Actus reus

In what ways can a company 'aid, abet, counsel, or procure' the offence of an individual? Often aiding and abetting will consist of assigning an unsuitable individual to a post where he can commit an offence. The case of Nick Leeson and Barings Bank is instructive. The bank collapsed following unauthorized trading by Leeson in its Singapore office. Leeson had been assigned to the Singapore office by the bank despite the fact that he had been denied a trading licence in London, a fact which the bank did not disclose to the Singapore authorities. Leeson also had very limited experience as a trader before being placed in charge of the Singapore office.

Leeson's case also illustrates how a company can 'counsel' an offence. While counselling often takes the form of commanding, exhorting, urging or even bribing the principal to commit the offence, more indirect and subtle forms of counselling can also occur. In Leeson's case corporate policies encouraged (another recognized form of counselling) his offences. Extravagant bonuses, far exceeding an individual's salary, were paid to traders based on the amount of profit they generated. These bonuses encouraged high-risk gambles rather than more prudent investment strategies. Leeson departed from the safe arbitrage strategy in which he was supposed to be engaged (where trades in one stock market are set off against identical trades in another market, the profit being produced by the differential of the value of the shares in the two markets) in favour of win–loss trades destined to produce either substantial profits or massive losses. Unfortunately for Barings, they produced the latter.

Another common way that companies facilitate illegality is by providing the means or instruments that enable an offence to be committed. In *R v Robert Millar (Contractors) Ltd and Robert Millar*[39] a lorry driver was convicted of causing death by dangerous driving when a defective tyre on the heavily-weighted lorry that he was assigned burst. The lorry then crashed into a car, killing its six occupants. The company was charged and convicted as an accessory to the driver's offence. The Court of Appeal upheld the company's conviction, reasoning that the company, through its managing director, was aware of the serious risks to other road-users that were posed. The court saw this as a case of 'counselling' and 'procuring', although 'aiding and abetting' may have been an equally apt description of the company's fault.

In law an accessory may be more culpable than a principal and incur a more severe penalty as a consequence. This apparent juxtaposition may be especially appropriate in cases involving corporate complicity. In *Robert Millar*, the driver was dealt with more leniently at sentencing than the company. The Court of Appeal approved, stating that the more severe sentence given the company was justified because it bore primary responsibility for the deaths.

A company is almost invariably better placed to rectify criminogenic and dangerous working conditions than are its staff. Employees may be afraid to object for fear that they may lose their jobs if they refuse to accept the company's working conditions. In any event, employees may be powerless if the corporate employer chooses to ignore their protestations, as it did in *Millar*.

A company has both the power to control and the right to control the acts of its employees while they are engaged in the company's business. William Wilson asserts that the right of control becomes a duty to control in three situations:

1   where the secondary party has ownership or control of property used by the principal;

2   where the secondary party stands in the relationship of employer and the principal is an employee or independent contractor;
3   where the secondary party has ownership or control of premises used by the principal.[40]

All three situations are commonplace in the corporate context. A company will typically own or control the property, equipment and tools used by its workforce. The relationship of a corporate enterprise with those who work for it or represent it will almost always be one of employer–employee or that of an independent contractor paid by the company. And not infrequently injuries, particularly those to workers, occur on premises owned or controlled by the company. Wilson argues that in these situations the failure to satisfy a duty of control constitutes unlawful encouragement or assistance.

Companies 'procure' (another basis of accessorial liability recognized in the 1861 Act) a criminal offence by creating or allowing to be perpetuated a corporate culture that blinks at illegality. How a company responds to an employee's offence may be highly revealing. Is, for example, the executive who bribes an overseas government official to secure a lucrative contract disciplined or awarded a substantial bonus for securing the contract? If the latter, can comparable officials be left in any doubt as to where the company's priorities lie? In contrast, dismissal or suspension would send the opposite message. In business, however, bonuses are far more likely to be awarded for generating profits than for law-abiding behaviour.

The tolerance of a corporate culture in which profitable but illegal ways of conducting the company's business are deemed acceptable presents one of the strongest cases for holding a company liable as an accessory. Maintaining such a culture should arguably override factors that would otherwise count in a company's favour. The company may hire qualified employees, provide appropriate staff training, put on seminars in business ethics, and adopt policies strictly forbidding all violations of the law, but it is for naught if the prevailing corporate ethos accepts that 'all is fair in love, war and business' as long as it leads to increased profits.

A company's culture also often provides a ready rationalization and camouflage for the corporate executive's offence. Legions of white collar criminals, when caught, pointedly assert that they were not pursuing individual gain but rather seeking to advance the best interests of their company.[41] This indeed may not be untrue – one of the key differences between ordinary crimes and business crimes is that the latter often conform to the accepted norms of the offender's company.[42] Of course, the offenders conveniently ignore in their calculus the bonuses and promotions that they will receive if their crimes succeed and go undetected or are ignored. In law, moreover, the motive why a crime is committed – whether selfish or altruistic – is generally deemed irrelevant to the offender's liability.

Mens rea

One of the thorniest issues in the law of complicity relates to the *mens rea* required for criminal liability. Where an accessory 'aids, abets, counsels or procures' an offence *intentionally*, there is relatively little quarrel that the accessory should be liable. The controversy arises when the offender does not intend or desire the crime, but rather is ambivalent as to whether it occurs. This is not uncommon, as companies tend to be preoccupied with profit and unconcerned with whether that profit will be at the expense of the commission of a criminal offence. The seller of rifles, for instance, is generally not interested in whether the rifle will be used to hunt bears or assassinate world leaders.

The critical legal issue is whether a company can be convicted as an accessory to a crime that it does not have the purpose or interest in promoting. In *National Coal Board* v *Gamble*[43], a weighbridge operator employed by the Coal Board issued a ticket to a lorry driver that allowed the driver to take his vehicle on to the road even though his load exceeded the permissible weight limit. Neither the weighbridge operator nor the Coal Board had any interest in whether the driver committed the offence. Indeed, the weighbridge operator warned the driver that he would be violating the law by driving an overweight vehicle. In these circumstances the Coal Board was nevertheless charged and convicted of being an accessory to the driver's offence.

On appeal, Devlin J. held that knowledge that one's acts would assist the commission of an offence constituted *prima facie* evidence of an intent to assist. It would seem more accurate to state that the company, through its representative (the weighbridge operator), *knew* that the assistance provided would lead to the offence, just as surely as a weapons manufacturer who sells to a known 'hit man' knows that its guns will be used to kill human beings, even if it is ambivalent as to whether any killing takes place or, indeed, fervently hopes that it won't.

Just as companies will rarely *intend* to cause a serious crime, they rarely will 'know' – unless they make inquiries – that their assistance will give rise to a criminal offence. But do companies have a duty to make such inquiries? Are they obligated to question their customers as to what use they will make of their products? For instance, what if a weapons manufacturer suspects but does not 'know' that the government to which it is selling tanks and submachine guns will use them to kill peaceful protesters?

Under section 45 of the Serious Crime Act 2007, a person commits an offence if:

a. he does an act capable of encouraging or assisting the commission of an offence; and
b. he believes—
   (i)   that the offence will be committed; and
   (ii) that his act will encourage or assist its commission.

The *mens rea* of this section is a *belief* that an offence will be committed. This should be contrasted to the section that immediately precedes it which makes it an offence to *intentionally* encourage or assist the commission of a crime but specifically states that foresight of an offence is not the equivalent of 'intent.' Read together, the two sections raise the question of whether 'foresight' can constitute a 'belief' under s. 45; and if so, whether the test of belief should be what the particular defendant believed or what would have been believed by a reasonable person in the defendant's position. When does a suspicion become a belief?

In *Roper v Taylor's Central Garage (Exeter) Ltd* [43] Devlin, J discussed the nature of 'knowledge':

> There are, I think, three degrees of knowledge ... The first is actual knowledge, which the justices may find because they infer it from the nature of the act done, for no man can prove the state of another man's mind; and they may find it even if the defendant gives evidence to the contrary. They may... feel that the evidence falls short of that, and if they do they have then to consider what might be described as knowledge of the second degree; whether the defendant was, as it has been called, shutting his eyes to an obvious means of knowledge ...
>
> The third kind of knowledge is what is generally known in the law as constructive knowledge: it is what is encompassed by the words 'ought to have known' in the phrase 'knew or ought to have known.' It does not mean actual knowledge at all; it means that the defendant had in effect the means of knowledge ... The case of shutting the eyes is actual knowledge in the eyes of the law; the case of merely neglecting to make inquiries is not knowledge at all – it comes within the legal conception of constructive knowledge, a conception which, generally speaking, has no place in the criminal law.

The concept of 'shutting one's eyes' or 'wilful blindness' is particularly apt in a corporate context. Although at first blush it might seem that a company has no 'eyes' to shut, the opposite is true. Just like a company's 'acts' arguably consist of the sum total of the acts of its employees, so too are the company's eyes the collective eyes of its employees. Companies, unlike individuals, are able to take advantage of these eyes. Suggestion boxes, for example, can direct employees to report (anonymously) any illegality that they observe being perpetrated in the company's name.

On the other hand, one might take issue with Devlin's rejection of constructive knowledge, based on a duty to make inquiries, in the field of corporate crime. A company's potential to cause far greater harm than an individual by aiding and abetting a criminal offence should lead to a higher duty to investigate than might be appropriate for the individual.

Illustrative is *Doe I v Unocal Corporation*. [44] In this case the United States Ninth Circuit Court of Appeals declined to dismiss a case seeking to hold Unocal liable for international human rights abuses committed by the Myanmar government in connection with the construction of a natural gas pipeline funded in part by Unocal. Based on Myanmar's past record of human rights violations, the Ninth Circuit concluded that the company had reason to know that the Myanmar government might well commit similar violations in connection with the natural gas project. Thus the Court reasoned that Unocal could be found liable for aiding and abetting the Myanmar military's illegal policing operations in connection with the construction of the pipeline. The case, however, was eventually settled after Unocal's motion for summary judgment failed.

The duty to make inquiries will depend on the nature of the company's products as well as the reputation of the end-user. In the Nuremburg trials after World War II, the court in the *Zyclon B* case[45] held that a manufacturer of poison gas used in the concentration camps could be liable as an accessory to the genocide of the Nazi government, whereas a corporation that simply made loans to the Nazi government could not.

Conclusion: Translating theory into practice

This chapter has sought to identify the relationship between corporate and individual fault. As a preliminary matter, this required an examination of the nature of corporate fault. The traditional criminal law concept of *mens rea*, so valuable in determining the moral culpability of a natural person, becomes a hindrance when the issue is the 'mind' of an inanimate fictional entity such as a company. Natural persons who commit proscribed acts accompanied by a wrongful state of mind can properly be said to be blameworthy, but those who cause the same harm but without fault cannot. Once this cipher function of *mens rea* is recognized, it can be dispensed with and the primary question of when a company can be said to have behaved in a blameworthy manner addressed directly.

It was submitted that a company behaves in a blameworthy manner when it fails to prevent a crime which it has a legal duty to prevent; when it was, *or should have been*, aware of the risks presented; when it had the capacity to prevent the violation; and when it was not unreasonable for the law to expect it to do so. The corollary is that companies should not be subject to criminal liability when they conduct their business operation in a non-culpable manner. To advocate 'corporate fault' as the basis of corporate criminal liability is to accept defences based on the absence of fault. Lack of fault can be demonstrated by a company's taking reasonable precautions, exercising 'due diligence', putting in place supervisory systems that will detect and prevent illegality, and establishing a law-compliant corporate culture.

Having identified the nature of corporate fault, we were in a position to examine the nature of the relationship between the liability of legal persons and that of natural persons. It was argued that each can be, and often is, complicit in the other's offence. When offences by individuals occur in a corporate context, it may be because the company's policies, culture and ethos authorize, encourage, condone or tolerate the illegal behaviour. Institutional rewards, bonuses, salary increases and promotions can encourage criminality. That the individual was committing the offence on behalf of a company provides a handy rationalization for the crime.

At the same time it would be naive not to recognize the role of individuals in contributing to corporate offences. Without natural persons to give a company direction and to devise its aims, priorities and policies to allow it to achieve its goals, the company is not only a fictional but an inert entity. Management has the day-to-day responsibility for ensuring that the company is properly run. While the company may provide the setting, the means, and the incentives for criminal activity, it is the responsibility of corporate directors, officers and senior managers to ensure that such misconduct does not occur.

Although not formally described in terms of complicity, the Bribery Act 2010 illustrates the relationship involved. Section 7 of the Act, entitled 'Failure of commercial organizations to prevent bribery' recognizes and criminalizes a company's role in failing to prevent bribery:

(1) A relevant commercial organization ('C') is guilty of an offence under this section if a person ('A') associated with C bribes another person intending—
   (a) to obtain or retain business for C, or
   (b) to obtain or retain an advantage in the conduct of business for C.

while Section 14 recognizes the accessorial role of corporate officials:

(1) This section applies if an offence under section 1, 2 or 6 is committed by a body corporate....
(2) If the offence is proved to have been committed with the consent or connivance of—
   (a) a senior officer of the body corporate..., or
   (b) a person purporting to act in such a capacity,
   the senior officer or person (as well as the body corporate or partnership) is guilty of the offence and liable to be proceeded against and punished accordingly.

In the corporate context, organizational and individual criminal liability is often linked. Each may be complicit in the offences of the other, neither should be made a scapegoat for the offences of the other, and an identification and understanding of the relevant principles is essential to advance legal analysis.

Notes

1 The same emphasis on individual as opposed to organizational liability can be seen in international law where the International Criminal Court (ICC) claims jurisdiction only over individuals.
2 See Interpretation Act 1978 s.5.
3 Laws regulating pollution are often of this character.
4 See, e.g., the Austrian, Danish and Italian country reports (this volume).
5 The reference to individual liability in the text is to the liability of directors, corporate officers and senior managers, and not the liability of ordinary workers. While it is frequently the acts of the latter which are most closely linked to the harm in question, the employee may simply be carrying out corporate policies formulated by corporate management, policies which they could only ignore or disobey at the risk of losing

their job. If, on the other hand, an employee acts in violation of company policy or on a 'frolic of his own', then legal liability can be assessed under the ordinary rules of criminal law.

6   [1995] 1 AC 171.

7   Whether such a prosecution against the NHS could have been brought at the time is itself questionable.

8   Hidden Report, Investigation into the Clapham Junction Railway Accident (1988).

9   Officials from GWR testified at the HSE inquiry into the causes of the crash that they had been unable to make ATP work effectively and that their drivers had therefore not received training in its use.

10 *Attorney General's Reference (No. 2 of 1999)* [2000] 2 Cr. App R. 207. Subsequently the criminal prosecution against the driver was dismissed, perhaps, one might speculate, because the CPS decided it would be unseemly to prosecute the driver and not the company.

11 See James Gobert 'The Corporate Manslaughter and Corporate Homicide Act 2007 – Thirteen years in the making but was it worth the wait?' (2008) 71 *Modern Law Review* 413.

12 See James Gobert 'The Evolving Test of Corporate Criminal Liability' in John Minkes and Leonard Minkes *Corporate and White Collar Crime* (2008) London: Sage.

13 See *New York Central & Hudson River Railroad Co. v United States*, 212 US 481 (1909). Although this was a federal court case, many states subsequently followed the federal lead and adopted a vicarious liability test of corporate criminality.

14 In the regulatory field, the courts are more willing to employ a test of vicarious liability.

15 See *Tesco Supermarkets Ltd. v Nattrass* [1972] AC 153.

16 See *Meridian Global Funds Management Asia Ltd. v. Securities Commission* [1995] 3 All ER 918.

17 *H. L. Bolton Engineering v T.J.Graham and Sons Ltd.* [1957] 1 QB 159, 172.

18 See, e.g., *Moore v. Bresler Ltd* [1944] 2 All ER 515.

19 As arguably occurred in the case of Robert Maxwell and the Mirror Group.

20 See James Gobert 'Controlling Corporate Criminality: Penal Sanctions and Beyond' *Web Journal on Current legal Issues* (April 1998).

21 *Balmer v HM Advocate* [2008] HCJA 44, discussed in High Court Justiciary 20 May 2009, discussed in Celia Wells, 'Containing Corporate Crime: Civil or CRIMINAL CONTRols?' (this volume).

22 E.g., Finland. See Country Report: Finland (this volume).

23 See generally Bribery Act 2010.

24 See Country Report: Spain (this volume).

25 See Country Report: Luxembourg (this volume).

26 See, e.g., *R v Chargot Ltd* [2008] UKHL73; *R v Director of Public Prosecutions, ex parte Kebeline* [2000] 2 AC 326.

27 See Bob Sullivan (1996) 'The Attribution of Culpability to Limited Companies' *Cambridge Law Journal* 15.

28 See, e.g., the Austrian, Finnish and Italian country reports (this volume).

29 See Rick Sarre, 'Penalising Corporate "Culture": The Key to Safer Corporate Activity?' (this volume).

30 Criminal Code Act (1995) s. 12.3.

31 Under the CMCHA 2007 (UK), a jury may consider a company's 'corporate culture' but this is (a) permissive rather than mandatory, (b) of evidentiary rather than substantive significance, and (c) only is allowed when a death is attributable to a health and safety violation.

32 See, e.g., F. Hayek *Individualism and the Economic Order* (1949) Chicago: University of Chicago Press; K. Popper *The Poverty of Historicism* (2002/1957) London: Routledge.

33 Or perhaps, in the twenty-first century, computers designed, built and programmed by human beings. London: HMSO.

34 Dept of Transport, The Merchant Shipping Act. mv *Herald of Free Enterprise*: Report of Court No. 8074 (1987).

35 *Ibid.*, para 18.5.

36 International Criminal Court Act 2001, s. 65.

37 Corporate Manslaughter and Corporate Homicide Act 2007, s.18. To re-emphasize the point, section 62 of the Serious Crime Act 2007 repeats the admonition against prosecuting an individual for encouraging or assisting corporate manslaughter.

38 The concept of accessorial liability of directors and corporate officers is also contained in the more recently enacted Fraud Act 2006 s 12.

39 [1970] QB 233.

40 William Wilson, *Doctrine and Theory* (3rd Ed., 2008), London: Longman.

41 In a BBC interview with David Frost, this was a point made by Nick Leeson in his defence.

42 See generally A. Nollkaemper and H. van der Wilt (eds.) *System Criminality in International Law* (2009) Cambridge University Press.

43 [1951] 2 TLR 284.

44 395 F.3d 932 (9th Cir. 2002).

45 Trial of Bruno Tesch and two others ('the *Zyklon B* case'), in 1 Law Reports of trials of War Criminals 92–103 (1947).'

Part III
Particular offences

9   Environmental offending, regulation and 'the legislative balancing act'

Nigel South

Introduction: setting the scene

One consistent theme in political and economic concerns regarding the environment is the search for a reasonable balance between environmental protection and the costs of providing this.[1] This is particularly evident in legal and regulatory considerations. Whether in global, national or local contexts, Du Rees (2001: 115) argues that what is reflected here is:

> ... a question of the way environmental criminal law has been constructed as a form of *legislative balancing act*, which involves making compromises between different interests, i.e. economic factors and environmental considerations. [emphasis added]

Some mechanisms of oversight such as that applying to the pharmaceutical industry (Abraham and Lawton-Smith, 2003) have been characterised as victims of 'regulatory capture', as they develop over time, becoming populated by personnel crossing between industry and regulator. This control dilemma is well known internationally and can also apply in the case of influencing environmental legislation (Simon, 2000: 640–642). A regulatory system can also be manipulated from the very early stages of its inception (Szasz, 1986) as the case of the relationship between the biotech company Monsanto and successive US governments has shown (Eichenwald *et al.*, 2001). In this example, Monsanto supported regulation of new genetic modification of food crops with the aim of pre-empting potentially hostile and restrictive legislation and also as a means by which to reassure an uncertain public. Monsanto got 'the regulations it wanted. ... an outcome that would be repeated ... through three administrations' but also got flexibility in the regulatory system: 'If the company's strategy demanded regulations, rules favored by the industry were adopted. And when the company abruptly decided that it needed to throw off the regulations and speed its food to market, the White House quickly ushered through an unusually generous policy of self-policing' (Eichenwald *et al.*, 2001: 1).

However, Du Rees (2001: 115) also points out that environmental oversight bodies frequently fall victim to a different kind of anomaly – one that is built into their very structure:

agencies whose task is to apply the law and report suspected offences have a dual role whose two sides are in competition with one another. … both helping companies to follow the environmental laws, and prosecuting their breaches of the law. This unclear role gives rise to an uneven application of the law …

Mindful of difficulties in pursuing regulation, this essay will provide examples of particularly troubling environmental or 'green' crimes and then consider some issues and problems regarding regulation, prosecution and punishment.

A green perspective for criminology and socio-legal studies

A growing field within criminology and socio-legal studies now focuses on these issues and has been variously termed a green, environmental, conservation or eco criminology (Lynch, 1990; South, 1998a; White, 2008; Herbig and Joubert, 2006; Walters, 2010). The term 'green criminology' was first used by Lynch (1990: 3) who brought together the radical agenda of critical criminology with an awareness of environmental issues and activism. However, Lynch acknowledged that environmental hazards, harms and crimes had been previously examined by criminologists with an interest in the 'crimes of the powerful' such as corporate and white-collar offending[2] and hence there is continuity as well as the promise of something new in this developing field of 'green criminology'.

The following two sections provide illustration and discussion of harms and crimes relating to (i) pollution and waste disposal/dispersal, and (ii) deforestation, species decline and resource depletion.

Harms and crimes relating to pollution and waste disposal/dispersal

Simon (2000: 634) comments that 'most large American environmental polluters are transnational in scope', engaging in 'international environmental wrongdoing'. Exploring the idea of 'institutionalised insensitivity to right and wrong' (ibid: 635) as an underpinning of environmental injustice, Simon lists a long record of violations of environmental and white-collar crime laws. Importantly, the scale of such insensitivity and injustice is largely unrecorded and unacknowledged in the public arena as media coverage can be 'censored' and stories massaged by the expensive public relations companies employed by corporations.[3] By such means can corporate messages manipulate opinion and employ techniques of neutralisation (Sykes and Matza, 1957), the public receive reassurance, and critics be marginalised. At the global level, Simon indicts the waste industry as chronically open to corruption, all the more devastating when 'most of its victims include the least powerful people on the face of the earth, poverty-stricken people of color, most of whom are powerless to resist the environmental deviance of multinational firms' (ibid: 639).

Many studies have drawn attention to the environmental victimisation of communities of the poor and powerless due to the frequency with which their locations may be the sites of, for example, polluting industry, waste processing plants or other environmentally hazardous facilities (Bullard, 1994). In the aftermath of the famous Love Canal case in the USA it was assumed lessons had been learned and such short-sighted and irresponsible behaviour would be avoided in a future that would benefit from greater awareness of both the health and financial costs of toxic waste dumping. This has not proved the case and in the period of nearly forty years between the events around Love Canal, near Niagara, USA and the coming to court of a case in Corby in England, little seems to have been learned, awareness has not been sharpened and regulatory bodies still do not manage to act to prevent victimisation.

In the 1940s, Love Canal was an abandoned navigation channel used by a company called Hooker Chemical as a convenient disposal dump for thousands of drums of toxic chemical waste (Szasz, 1994: 42). In 1952 the canal was covered up and one year later Hooker sold the land to the Niagara Falls Board of Education. A school was built. Developers built homes and 'unsuspecting families' moved in. In the 1970s, after heavy rains, chemical wastes began to seep to the surface, both on the school grounds and into people's yards and basements. Federal and state officials confirmed the presence of 88 chemicals, some in concentrations 250 to 5,000 times higher than acceptable safety levels. Eleven of these chemicals were suspected or known carcinogens; others were said to cause liver and kidney ailments (ibid.).

Also dating from the 1940s was the operation of the massive steel works at Corby in the county of Northamptonshire, England. During its 46-year history, this '680 acre site had produced a dizzying array of dangerous waste – nickel, chromium, zinc, arsenic, boron and cadmium' (Gordon, 2009) but when the time came to close and dismantle the plant through the 1980s and 1990s, it was as if Love Canal and numerous developments in public health awareness and waste management had never happened. The local authority had taken control of the site and now needed to dispose of the waste from the old steel works and this they proceeded to do, 'in the back of open lorries, sludge spilling onto the public roads of the town' with one local remembering 'the smell and the metallic taste of it, and how if you drove behind one of the lorries, your car always ended up covered in a light film' (ibid.). Reporting as the High Court heard a group litigation case against Corby Borough Council at the end of July 2009, Gordon (31 July, 2009) records that the court heard how

> waste was dumped all over Corby by staff that Mr Justice Akenhead described ... as being 'unqualified and insufficiently experienced'; a waste management expert who saw how the materials were disposed of, was said to have been 'appalled'. Even at the time that the land was being 'reclaimed', an auditor described the operation as 'naïve, cavalier and incompetent.' ... after a ten year battle, the Judge ruled that Corby Borough Council had

been negligent and that the dumping of toxic material may have caused birth defects in children.

This was a case described by lawyers acting for the affected families as 'the biggest child poisoning case since Thalidomide' (Gammell, 2009) yet at the end of the day, not only did watchdog bodies dismally fail but justice could still have been denied the families if they were unable to prove causation between the toxic materials disturbed and distributed during decommissioning of the works and the instances of birth defects in individual children (Semple Fraser, 2009). However nearly one year later, in April 2010, Corby council withdrew its legal challenge and reached an agreement to pay compensation to the affected children, albeit without accepting liability in the case.

Such 'toxic tragedies' (Cass, 1996) are commonplace internationally, frequently exhibiting characteristics such as: difficulty of prosecution due to problems in drawing together evidence that can tie commercial operations to specific illegal offences; cases of corruption; and strong industry 'profit-at-all-costs' motivations (Cass, 1996: 110–112). In the latter case, the rationality of a business enterprise may lead to deliberate choice of criminal activity due to the low chance of detection, difficulty of finding proof of guilt and options for 'fixing' cases should they come to the attention of rule- or law-enforcers or even the courts (Cass, 1996: 112 drawing on Sutherland, 1949). Within this general pattern may be found what Gobert and Punch (2003: 27) refer to as 'crime facilitative industries in which one can discern a recurring and disproportionate pattern of criminal activity. Persons with a criminal record may be attracted by the opportunities provided by these industries, seeing in them the potential for remunerative illicit business'. Gobert and Punch draw on the work of Huisman and Niemeijer (1998) to identify some of the features that may make elements of the Netherlands waste disposal business prone to rule-bending and criminal opportunism. It seems highly likely that the same features will be found more broadly across Western Europe.

> Companies are paid prior to delivery and, as a result, are easily tempted to take on contracts they cannot possibly fulfil. They then will turn to illegal methods for satisfying their obligations. The firms involved are typically small and run by managers with a dominant managerial style but few qualifications. By providing high rewards and/or by establishing dependency relationships, managers who are averse to regulation and unions are nonetheless able to create a loyal workforce. At the same time these managers will strive to forge good contacts with government officials, employing professional consultants to advise them on how to portray an image of being environmentally friendly ... Behind this façade the companies will consciously and systematically violate the law.

Certainly, rule-bending and possibly criminal opportunism are features of the following case. In 2009, a major waste disposal multinational, Trafigura, was being sued in London's High Court by thousands of Africans reporting injuries which they attributed to toxic waste that was landed and disposed of on 19 August 2006, in and around Ivory Coast's largest population centre, the city of Abidjan (Jones and MacKean, 2009). According to the BBC news programme Newsnight (13 May 2009), this was 'the biggest toxic dumping scandal of the 21st century' (at least so far) and 'the type of environmental vandalism that international treaties are supposed to prevent'. The toxicity of this waste was confirmed by a toxicology expert consulted by the BBC who observed that such a combination (which included 'tons of phenols which can cause death by contact, tons of hydrogen sulphide, lethal if inhaled in high concentrations, and vast quantities of corrosive caustic soda and mercaptans') could 'bring a major city to its knees'(Newsnight report, 13 May 2009). In addition to the London case. Trafigura were sued in the Netherlands by Greenpeace resulting in a fine against the company of €1 million for operating in and leaving Amsterdam with this cargo. There is one further legal development of note that followed from this episode. This is of some significance for this area of environmental crime and law enforcement, although sadly but predictably, this is for what was not achieved rather than what was.

Responding to this case in the year it occurred, the EU Commissioner for the Environment, Stavros Dimas, reported that this was unfortunately only one of many such incidents and that '51% of EU waste shipments in 2005 were found to be illegal', a staggering proportion (and not including, of course, those shipments not detected as illegal). In response, in 2007 the European Commission proposed that an EU-wide framework of criminal penalties should be established to address the problem of companies that manage to avoid serious punishment by identifying and operating from those jurisdictions with the least stringent or punitive laws: '"Member states have very different ways of punishing environmental pollution" said the commission official, so things are done in the country "where there are least sanctions" ' (Mahony, 2007). Regrettably, this attempt to unify and standardise penalties across the EU was rejected by the European Court of Justice in October that year, arguing that while the EU could oblige member states to introduce penalties for pollution, it could not determine 'the type and level of the criminal penalties to be applied'. As has occurred with much environmental legislation this potentially dilutes protectionary measures and enforceable penalties and leaves open opportunities to take advantage of jurisdiction in the most lenient and facilitating host country available.

Harms and crimes relating to deforestation, species decline and resource depletion

It is now recognised that the future well-being and security of humanity is dependent on the health and sustainability of our planet and the other species with which we share it.

Whether environmental goods come to have market value as luxuries, for example in response to demand in the fashion and food retail industries, or in more mundane ways as necessary for their contribution to the manufacture of other products, resource conservation and management are increasingly important.

Here the equation of balance between 'economic factors and environmental considerations' is important because livelihoods, industries and even national economies can be dependent on meeting demand without destroying future supply. Yet in both legal and illegal trans-national trades in environmental goods, even clear indications and evidence of increasing scarcity (consequences of excessive hunting, fishing, mining etc.) can still be ignored as demand and profit overwhelm deferral and stewardship. Serious ecological damage can be carried out with official licence, especially where underpinned by corruption and suppression of criticism. The consequences for populations and habitats now and into the future can be deeply worrying. One example is the clearing of forests of old growth trees in Tasmania, a rapacious process involving cutting down the trees, burning the land, introducing pesticide into water sources and polluting the atmosphere, all to provide a product for the transnational trade in woodchip for the Asian paper manufacturing industry and for other materials (Flanagan, 2007). A further example of a legal trade in timber that in this case was linked to crime, the arms trade and also fuelled civil war, was the case of 'conflict timber' from Liberia. Here 'a unique west African forest was halved in size in five years' and despite the calls of international NGOs for boycotts, the trade in such conflict timber, similar to the trade in 'conflict diamonds' from Sierra Leone, continued until 2003 (Boekhout van Solinge, 2008: 14).

In instances of illegal trade, the scope is diverse and enormously profitable including trading in and transportation of illegally harvested fish, rare wildlife species or body parts (e.g. ivory, animal organs for certain traditional medicines), as well as precious stones, and plants for legal and illegal drug manufacturing (Hauck, 2007; Putt and Nelson, 2008; Boekhout van Solinge, 2008; Naylor, 2005; Lemieux and Clarke, 2009). Such exploitation is injurious not only to environmental well-being and security but also to civil society and, in the developing world, to indigenous peoples who see the resources of their natural economy disappearing with no profitable return or investment reverting to them (South, 2007). As Boekhout van Solinge (2008: 24) observes, deforestation threatens the human rights of millions of indigenous people who are increasingly 'fighting and competing with multinationals over natural resources'.

Where once the idea of illegal trans-national trades in environmental goods was barely remarked upon, there is now a growing acknowledgement of the corruption and damage related to such trade and also of its contiguity and occasional merger with other global markets for drugs, arms and humans. Elliott (2009: 65) notes that:

> Organised crime groups … have become actively involved in the most lucrative areas of transnational environmental crime. The trade in endangered species, for example, is reported to constitute part of what Williams refers to as the 'diverse portfolio of criminal activities' (2001a: 70) in which Russian and Chinese crime groups, African-based smuggling rings, and even South American drug cartels are now involved. Asian crime groups are central to the trade in rhinoceros horn and tiger parts, the Cali

drug cartel is thought to be trafficking drugs and wildlife together into the US, and the Neapolitan Carmorra is reported to be 'deeply involved in the trafficking of animals' (Williams, 2001b: 78–9; UN Commission on Crime Prevention and Criminal Justice 2002: 6).

Smuggling of the rare and the scarce has always been profitable and the exercise of controls and protection over certain species of wildlife and plants has stimulated the international illegal wildlife trade (Wyatt, 2009). This has now been widely recognised not only by conservation organisations but also by international policing agencies, with the size of the trade estimated to lie between $10 and $20 billion (National Zoo, 2008). Whichever limit is correct, these are significant figures, with the large variation reflecting the hidden dimensions of the market and the fact that there is as yet no set standard to judge the value of wildlife, meaning that such estimates will vary widely across the globe (Cook *et al.*, 2002). As this value is exclusively monetary, generated 'by existing data and other sources, (which) provide only one dimension of the value of wildlife for human well-being', it 'should be taken only as an indication of the minimum value of wildlife for consumptive purposes' (Fernandez and Luxmoore, 1997: 1–2; South and Wyatt, in press), i.e. it does not reflect the damage done to ecological systems through capture, harvesting and removal of species from their natural habitats.

Environmental legislation and regulation

In most industrialised countries, early legislators sought to deal with environmental matters through public health or resource statutes, in some cases through civil codes and in others through the criminal law. The latter has typically been targeted against industrial polluters who pollute water or land, causing – in legal terms – public health dangers or public nuisance problems (Alvazzi del Frate and Norberry, 1993: 6). As described by the deputy chief prosecutor for the UK Environment Agency (Brosnan, 2002: 298), the growth in new environmental legislation passed since 1974 reflects:

> growing awareness of the serious threat environmental crimes potentially pose to human health and the damage that can threaten sensitive ecosystems. Contaminated land, for example, may easily pollute aquifers that will take decades to recover. The costs of remedying the situation can be millions of pounds. Successful criminal prosecutions are important as a punishment, a deterrent and for the wider publicity they generate. The established principle is that the polluter should pay.

The question is whether the principle is or can be applied in practice.

Legislation in various forms has gained pace since the mid-twentieth century, and the 1972 United Nations Conference on the Human Environment is generally credited with giving rise to greater awareness of the need for environmental regulation. It led to a Declaration and an Action Plan with 109 recommendations in six broad areas (including human settlements, natural resource management, pollution, educational and social aspects of the environment, development, and international organisations) as well as a programme to manage the 'global commons' and the establishment of a UN environment programme. Since 1990, conferences such as the Rio Earth Summit in 1992, Earth Summit 2 in New York in 1997, the Bali Climate Change Conference in December 2007, and most recently the Copenhagen Conference 2009, have produced agreements and commitments of various kinds and degree. However the prospects for translating such commitments into real actions are frequently queried and the outcome of the Copenhagen Summit was greeted with disappointment.

Mechanisms of uncertain regulation and enforcement

The two 'models' that regulatory laws and mechanisms of enforcement may follow are generally referred to as the compliance and deterrence models (Hawkins, 1983; Pearce and Tombs, 1990, 1991; Webb, 1995: 339–344). The compliance approach seeks conformity with law or regulations without need for resort to policing and punishment of infringements. Instead behaviour is influenced by offering inducements and incentives, or by establishing administrative procedures designed to avoid non-compliance opportunities. Deterrence strategies work by aiming to enforce the law, detecting violation and prosecuting and penalising offenders. Punishment serves as a warning to others. In practice, elements of the two approaches may be combined.

Compliance systems are criticised by some because they only impose penalties after an offence has been committed. Such penalties may be quite limited in scope, usually economic measures in the form of a fine. Others argue that more punitive measures should be taken and that where deterrent punishments have been used in the past these have had an impact – especially where imprisonment and negative publicity follow (Pearce and Tombs, 1990, 1991). However, a further view supports the mixing of the voluntarism assumed in the 'pure' compliance model with tougher enforcement and shaming interventions (Braithwaite, 1989) as an effective strategy. This does indeed sound sensible and potentially powerful, yet a common complaint, in the UK at least, is that such flexibility and imagination is lacking.

'Tougher but more flexible sentencing needed'

The quote above was a key conclusion of the UK Parliament Environmental Audit Committee in its 2004 report on Environmental Crime and the Courts (2003–04 Session, May). The report paints a picture of an 'unsatisfactory' sentencing system which despite some changes and improvements remains inflexible, with fines frequently verging on the 'derisory'. According to the Committee,

The current sentencing system is just not flexible and imaginative enough adequately to punish corporate bodies ... It is disgraceful that some companies openly boast about their crimes as though they manifested some sort of commercial talent ... The Government must adopt a much tougher stance with businesses – regardless of their size and nationality – which flagrantly flout the law. (para 26)

The Committee urged a coordinated approach to curbing offences against the environment by ensuring better use of sentencing, and in the same Parliamentary Session also published its report on Wildlife Crime (7 October 2004). Government subsequently reported on progress regarding its recommendations following the latter and indicated how a joined-up system was emerging with the formalisation of a National Harm Reduction Strategy, bringing together Prevention, Intelligence and Enforcement, national recording of wildlife crime incidents and the launch in October 2006 of a national Wildlife Crime Unit (www.Parliament.uk, Appendix on Updated Government Response, Environmental Audit Tenth Special Report, Session 2007–08, 25 November 2008).

In the UK, the Government Environment Agency publishes statements affirming a commitment to policies and practices aiming to limit climate change, noting that 'Emissions from major sources of pollution, such as transport, are tackled through various measures at European, national and local level. Local authorities control air pollution from smaller industrial processes' (Environment Agency, 2009). However there have always been problems of inadequacy of resources for enforcement of such rules and laws (Hutter, 1986; du Rees, 2001) and this applies across the breadth of corporate or economic crimes involving 'breaches of health, safety, environmental, consumer or food legislation committed by both large multi-national corporations and local businesses' (Croall, 2009: 167). Many such offences may seem trivial yet on an accumulating scale can lead to 'modest to devastating changes in people's experience of the environment and conditions of life' (South, 1998b: 444). Yet 'trivialisation' is often the process applied to treatment of both small but also larger-scale offences and is an outcome of the legislative balancing act and weaknesses in the models of regulation and enforcement in play. De Prez (2000) reports a study of the handling of prosecutions brought by the Environment Agency in magistrates' and crown courts and concludes that the trivialisation of environmental offences, whether due to the way that either the prosecution case is presented or the defence responds, can only 'serve as an impediment to enforcement as a whole, for if the implications of criminalisation are neutralised, then for the large scale operators, so is the threat of prosecution' (De Prez, 2000: 76).

Outside the court and on the wider political stage, support for sanctions can wax and wane illustrating how vulnerable to political values and the social construction of public agendas environmental regulations and law actually are. This is so in parts of Europe but has been particularly notable in the USA, well illustrated by just one example produced in the transition from the Clinton to Bush administrations. Clinton had supported the Environmental Protection Agency in mounting legal action against more than fifty power plants for various offences and seeking to exploit loopholes in the 1990 Clean Air Act. However following assumption of office by President Bush in January 2001, the new administration suspended or diluted legal enforcement and various lawsuits in progress at the time (Borger, 2001: 12).

Looking to the future, global enforcement models will need to be developed and tried out but will also need to be based on legitimate expectations of support for their effectiveness across borders. At present, enforcement agencies are not only hampered by the internal contradictions of their mission (as 'regulatory friend') and weak sentencing procedures or penalties but also face barriers such as differing definitions of offences and differences of approach between jurisdictions. Thus not only is enforcement neutered but also data gathering and comparison are very difficult. An internationally 'joined-up' approach will need comparative research based on practical example and evaluation, and some degree of harmonisation of understanding and approach in areas of law and enforcement (South, 2009).

Conclusions

While recent years have seen a proliferation of treaties and prohibitions relating to environmental crime, a well-known pattern has also seen these mirrored by the formulation of rationales for non-compliance, the opening up of loopholes and the emergence of new commercial (legal or illegal) opportunities for people to evade, break and ignore them. Current concerns regarding climate change place emphasis upon the prospects and problems of a more resource-hungry world. The implications of this may be the intensification of competition and hence potential for conflict within and between states. This will lead to 'haves and have-nots', those 'within the gates' and those 'outside'. New questions of regulation and of management of resources relative to 'rights' will emerge.

In this respect, the maintenance of the 'legislative balancing act' is, of course, not the only way of proceeding into the future. As Boekhout van Solinge (2008: 26) has noted, Gray (1996) proposed a civil law liability of 'ecocide', defined as 'causing or permitting harm to the natural environment on a massive scale' which would 'breach a duty of care owed to humanity in general'. For Gray this would be an approach derivable from international law and commitments to human rights to life and to health. In similar terms, Berat (1993) argued for adoption of the concept of 'geocide' as a means of framing violations of health and environmental rights that follow from intentional destruction of species and habitats (Boekhout van Solinge, 2008: 26).

In all probability, at least in the immediate future, the positions outlined by Berat and Gray may be somewhat utopian, but somewhere between these and the current overly-pragmatic and deeply un-ambitious systems characterised by 'regulatory capture' and 'legislative balance' must lie something more appropriate and effective for the 21st century. If regulatory reform requires 'regulatory crisis' (Snider, 1991) and a 'shift in social mood' (Tombs and Whyte, 2006), then to paraphrase and add to Croall's (2009: 180) conclusions, it is to be hoped that recent financial crises, growing global awareness of climate change, and failures of international negotiation, may herald a move away from models of deregulation and legislative balancing acts toward greater recognition and stronger regulation of activities that are so harmful to humanity and the environment that they threaten the planet.

References

Abraham, J. and Lawton-Smith, H. (eds) (2003) *Regulation of the Pharmaceutical Industry*, Houndmills: Palgrave.

Alvazzi del Frate, A. and Norberry, J. (eds) (1993) *Environmental Crime, Sanctioning Strategies and Sustainable Development*, Rome: UNICRI and Canberra: Australian Institute of Criminology. Publication No 50.

Berat, L. (1993), 'Defending the Right to a Healthy Environment: Towards a Crime of Geocide in International Law', *Boston University International Law Journal* 11: 327–348.

Boekhout van Solinge, T. (2008) 'Crime, Conflicts and Ecology in Africa.' pp. 13–34 in *Global Harms: Ecological Crime and Speciesism*, edited by Raghnild Sollund. New York: Nova Science Publishers.

Borger, J. (2001) 'U.S. Lets Fight Against Smog Disappear into Thin Air'. *The Guardian*, August 9. p. 12.

Braithwaite, J. (1989) *Crime, Shame and Reintegration*, Cambridge: Cambridge University Press.

Brosnan, A. (2002) 'Prosecuting environmental Crime – The Role of the Environment Agency', *Magistrate* 58, 10, 298–299.

Bullard, R. (1994) *Unequal Protection: Environmental Justice and Communities of Color*. San Francisco: Sierra Club Books.

Cass, V. (1996) 'Toxic Tragedy: Illegal Hazardous Waste Dumping in Mexico' in *Environmental Crime and Criminality: Theoretical and Practical Issues*, edited by S. Edwards, T. Edwards, and C.Fields, New York: Garland.

Cook, D., M. Roberts, and J. Lowther (2002) *The International Wildlife Trade and Organised Crime: A Review of the Evidence and Role of the United Kingdom*. http://www.wwf.org.uk/filelibrary/pdf/organisedCrime.pdf. Accessed 8 October 2005.

Croall, H. (2009) 'Community Safety and Economic Crime', *Criminology and Criminal Justice* 9, 2: 165–185.

de Prez, P. (2000) 'Excuses, Excuses: The Ritual Trivialisation of Environmental Prosecutions', *Journal of Environmental Law* 12: 65–77.

Du Rees, H. (2001) 'Can Criminal Law Protect the Environment?', *Journal of Scandinavian Studies* 2: 109–126.

Eichenwald, K., Kolata, G. and Petersen, M. (2001) 'Biotechnology Food: From the Lab to a Debacle', *The New York Times on the Web*, January.

Elliott, L. (2009) 'Combating Transnational Environmental Crime: "Joined Up" Thinking About Transnational Networks.' in *Eco-Crime and Justice: Essays on Environmental Crime*, Kristiina Kangaspunta and Ineke Haen Marshal (eds). Turin: UNICRI.

Environment Agency (2009) 'Air Quality', UK Environment Agency web site, http://www.environment-agency.gov.uk/business/regulation/38787.aspx. (Accessed 7 February 2010).

Fernandez, C. and R. Luxmoore (1997) 'The Value of the Wildlife Trade', *Industrial Reliance on Biodiversity – WCMC Biodiversity Series 7*. Cambridge, UK: World Conservation Press.

Flanagan, R. (2007) 'Paradise razed', *Telegraph.co.uk*, 28 June. http://www.telegraph.co.uk/earth/environment/conservation/3298789/Paradise-razed.html

Gammell, C. (2009) 'Corby Birth Defects: Worst Child Poisoning Case since Thalidomide', 29 July, *Telegraph.co.uk*, accessed 6 January 2010.

Gobert, J. and Punch, M. (2003) *Rethinking Corporate Crime*, London: Butterworths.

Gordon, B. (2009) 'Corby's Toxic Waste: The Families Speak Out', 31 July, *Telegraph.co.uk*, accessed 6 January 2010.

Gray, M. A. (1996) 'The International Crime of Ecocide', *California Western International Law Journal* 26: 215–271.

Hauck, M. (2007) 'Non-compliance in Small-Scale Fisheries: A Threat to Security?' in P. Beirne and N. South (eds) *Issues in Green Criminology*, Cullompton: Willan.

Hawkins, K. (1983) 'Bargain and Bluff: Compliance and Deterrence in the Enforcement of Regulation', *Law and Policy Quarterly* 5: 35–73.

Herbig, F. J. W. and Joubert, S. J. (2006) 'Criminological Semantics: Conservation Criminology – Vision or Vagary?', *Acta Criminologica* 19, 3: 88–103.

Huisman, W. and Niemeijer, E. (1998) *Zicht op Organisatiecriminaliteit: Een Literatuuronderzoek.*, The Hague: SDU uitgevers.

Hutter, B. (1986) 'An Inspector Calls: The Importance of Proactive Enforcement in the Regulatory Context', *British Journal of Criminology* 26, 2: 114–128.

Jones, M. and MacKean, L. (2009) 'Dirty Tricks and Toxic Waste in Ivory Coast', *BBC news online*, 13 May, http://news.bbc.co.uk/go/pr/fr/-/1/hi/programmes/newsnight/8048626.stm.

Lemieux, A. and R. Clarke (2009) 'The International Ban on Ivory Sales and its Effects on Elephant Poaching in Africa', *British Journal of Criminology* 49, 4: 451–471.

Lynch, M. (1990) 'The Greening of Criminology: A Perspective On the 1990s', *Critical Criminologist* 2: 3–4, 11–12.

Mahony, H. (2007) 'EU Court Delivers Blow on Environment Sanctions', *EUObserver.com*. Accessed 23 October 2009.

National Zoo, Lectures and Symposia (2008) http://nationalzoo.si.edu/ActivitiesAndEvents/Lectures/. Accessed 4 March 2008.

Naylor, R. T. (2005) 'The Underworld of Ivory', *Crime, Law and Social Change* 42: 261–295.

Pearce, F. and Tombs, S. (1990) 'Ideology, Hegemony and Empiricism: Compliance Theories of Regulation', *British Journal of Criminology* 30, 4: 423–443.

Pearce, F. and Tombs, S. (1991) 'Policing Corporate Skid-rows: A Reply to Keith Hawkins'. *British Journal of Criminology* 31, 4, 415–426.

Putt, J. and Nelson, D. (2008) 'Crime in the Australian Fishing Industry', *Trends and Issues in the Crime and Criminal Justice* 366: 1–10.

Rowell, A. (1996) *Green Backlash: Global Subversion of the Environment Movement*, London: Routledge.

Semple Fraser (2009) *Environmental Update August 2009*, Semple Fraser Commercial Law website: http://www.semplefraser.co.uk/index.php?s=81.

Simon, D. R. (2000) 'Corporate Environmental Crimes and Social Inequality', *American Behavioural Scientist*, 43: 633–645.

Snider, L. (1991) 'The Regulatory Dance: Understanding Reform Processes in Corporate Crime', *International Journal of the Sociology of Law* 19, 209–236.

South, N. (1998a) 'A Green Field for Criminology: A Proposal for a Perspective' *Theoretical Criminology* 2, 2: 211–233.

South, N. (1998b) 'Corporate and State Crimes against the Environment: Foundations for a Green Perspective in European Criminology' in V. Ruggiero, N. South and I. Taylor (eds) *The New European Criminology*, London: Routledge.

South, N. (2007) 'The "Corporate Colonisation of Nature": Bio-prospecting, Bio-piracy and the Development of Green Criminology' pp. 230–247 in *Issues in Green Criminology: Confronting Harms against Environments, Humanity and other Animals*, Piers Beirne and Nigel South (eds) Cullompton: Willan.

South, N. (2009) 'Ecocide, Conflict and Climate Change: Challenges for Criminology and the Research Agenda in the 21st Century' in K. Kangaspunta and I. Marshall (eds) *EcoCrime and Justice*, Rome: UNICRI.

South, N. and P. Beirne, eds. (2006) *Green Criminology* (International Library of Criminology, Criminal Justice and Penology) Dartmouth: Aldershot and Brookfield.

South, N. and Wyatt, T. (in press) 'Comparing Illicit Trades in Wildlife and Drugs: An Exploratory Exercise'. *Deviant Behavior.*

Sutherland, E. (1949) *White-Collar Crime: the Uncut Version*, New York: Dryden Press.

Sykes, G. and Matza, D. (1957) 'Techniques of Neutralization: A Theory of Delinquency', *American Sociological Review* 22: 664–670.

Szasz, A. (1986) 'Corporations, Organized Crime, and the Disposal of Hazardous Waste: An Examination of the Making of a Criminogenic Regulatory Structure', *Criminology* 24: 1–27.

Szasz, A. (1994) *EcoPopulism: Toxic Waste and the Movement for Environmental Justice*, Minneapolis: University of Minnesota Press.

Tombs, S. and Whyte, D. (2006) 'Community Safety and Corporate Crime' in P. Squires (ed.) *Community Safety: Critical Perspectives on Policy and Practice*, Bristol: Policy Press.

U.N. Commission on Crime Prevention and Criminal Justice (2002) *Progress Made in the Implementation of Economic and Social Council Resolution 2001/12 on Illicit Trafficking in Protected Species of Wild Flora and Fauna: Report of the Secretary General*, E/CN. 15/2002/7.

Walters, R. (2010) 'Eco crime' in J. Muncie, D. Talbot and R. Walters (eds). *Crime: Local and Global*, Cullompton: Willan.

Webb, K. (1995) 'Controlling Corporate Misconduct Through Regulatory Offences: The Canadian Experience', pp. 339–351 in F. Pearce and L. Snider (eds) *Corporate Crime: Contemporary Debates*, Toronto: Toronto University Press.

White, R. (2008) *Crimes Against Nature: Environmental Criminology and Ecological Justice*, Cullompton: Willan.

Williams, P. (2001a) 'Transnational Criminal Networks' in J. Arquilla and D. Ronfeldt (eds) *Networks and Netwars: The Future of Terror, Crime and Militancy*, Santa Monica: Rand.

Williams, P. (2001b) 'Organising Transnational Crime: Networks, Markets and Hierarchies' in P. Williams and D. Vlassis (eds) *Combating Transnational Crime: Concepts, Activities and Responses*, London: Frank Cass.

Wyatt, T. (2009) Personal communication; see also Wyatt, T. (2008) *The Illegal Wildlife Trade and Deep Green Criminology: Two Case Studies of Fur and Falcon Trades in the Russian Federation*, PhD Thesis, University of Kent.

Notes

1 In the recent past this was seen as a key issue by the US Bush administration, underpinning opposition to the Kyoto agreement, viewed by anti-environmental 'hawks' as a European conspiracy to damage America's competitiveness and 'reduce' its standard of living to European levels.
2 See e.g. essays reprinted in South and Beirne (eds) 2006.
3 Sometimes referred to as 'greenwashing' as corporations likely to be criticised for activities harmful to the environment seek to promote their pro-environment credentials (Rowell, 1996; Simon, 2000: 642).

10 Investigating safety crimes in Finland

Anne Alvesalo-Kuusi

Introduction

This article introduces the results of an empirical research project on the police investigation of harms caused by occupational safety crimes in Finland, a jurisdiction in which such crimes are – somewhat unusually – the responsibility of mainstream policing agencies. It begins with an account of the location – and absence – of these harms in crime control strategies and action plans against economic crime. This is the case even though safety crimes are included in the penal code, and in the concept of economic crime as it is defined by the police. The empirical evidence upon which this paper is based is an analysis of data gathered as part of a survey of police in Finland which focuses on their perceptions about and approaches to occupational safety incidents, the investigation of safety crimes, and the perceived place of such offences within the criminal justice system.[1]

Safety crimes in criminal justice policy and the law

The Finnish Government made a decision of principle to fight economic crime. The decision included an action plan which initially involved a three-year programme of reform in the control of economic crime and the grey economy. The first action plan began in 1998 and extended through 2001. It was followed by successive action plans lasting from 2002 until 2005, and then from 2006 to 2009. The 2010–2011 action plan is currently being implemented.

According to the official definition of the Finnish police, economic crime is 'a criminalised act or neglect which is committed in the framework of, or using, a corporation or other organisation'. Safety crimes are included on the list of 'economic crimes'. Despite the broad definition of economic crimes, the types of offences that have primarily been subject to scrutiny – both in the action plans and in practice – have been crimes where the victim has been the tax-authority, 'markets' or other enterprises; crimes such as book-keeping offences, tax evasion, crimes committed by debtors, and certain forms of other financial crimes such as insider trading. In terms of these types of offences, the programmes have been relatively successful. Financial crime has effectively been recognised as a legitimate target for mainstream criminal justice agencies and has risen up the law and order agenda both politically and within popular consciousness. Police in particular, but also other agencies of or working alongside the criminal justice system, have begun routinely to seek to control economic crime, while among officers such work has begun to be recognised as 'real' police work.[2] Of course, these initiatives have not been without their problems, and have been subject to some criticism.[3] But the social impact of criminalising economic crime has been hugely significant. In so far as economic offending is now labelled using the language of crime, has secured sustained government commitment to resources, is the subject of state-funded research activity, features in consolidated crime statistics and is subject to renewed enforcement efforts across and beyond the criminal justice system, the Finnish initiative speaks persuasively to the often disputed ability of states and criminal justice systems to address economic crime.[4]

Some forms of economic crime are more likely to be subject to demands for effective regulation than others.[5] It has been argued that financial crimes often attract more punitive responses than, for example, health and safety or environmental offences. The reason why is said to be that such crimes threaten the effective functioning of capitalism.[6] Although relatively few cases reach the courts, when they do, courts will tend to treat economic crimes that subvert the normal functioning of markets with more gravity, and serious violations will often attract a prison sentence.[7] Having said this, it is important to recognise that the mainstreaming of policing and punitive responses to financial crimes are rarely sustained and rarely apply to all forms of financial crime.[8]

In the relatively rare instances that regulation and enforcement does proceed against business offences, the emphasis is on 'financial' as opposed to 'social' offending.[9] Safety crimes, although formally included in the category of economic crime, tend to receive a lower priority within the context of national crime prevention strategies. For example, the national programme against violence[10] deals with 'workplace violence' but this concept does not include safety crimes. In the National Crime Prevention programme 'particular attention is to be directed against offences that cause feelings of insecurity and that may occur in the every-day environment'.[11] Yet here too there is no explicit reference to safety crimes. The recent national programme on internal security,[12] which 'includes a concrete description of those matters regarding inland security which touch all people in one way or another and are a part of every-day well-being', mentions safety at work in a chapter titled 'diminishing accidents and disasters'. Crime prevention issues are dealt with in another chapter, and safety crimes are briefly referred to in the section dealing with economic crime. However, no specific measures against safety offences are mentioned in the list of recommendations regarding crime prevention. Despite the extensive social, physical, psychological and financial harm caused by safety offences, such crimes seem to have fallen between the stools of 'violent' crime on the one hand and 'economic' crimes on the other.

In Finland, although the occupational safety and health (OSH) administration has a duty to regulate safety at work,[13] the police are generally responsible for the prevention and investigation of crime, including safety offences. If there is reason to believe that a crime has taken place, the police must conduct an investigation.

Safety crimes are included in the penal code and are defined by the police within the category of economic crime. Yet, they remain absent from national crime prevention strategies and are not incorporated into the tasks of economic crime units. Despite the fact that the Finnish legislator expressed its disapproval of procedures that violate safety at work laws by including safety crimes in the penal code in 1995, such crimes seem to have been ignored or 'forgotten' in national crime prevention strategies.

In Finnish law, safety crimes or 'work safety offences' are demarcated as a discrete set of offences. According to the Finnish penal code 47:1 § 'An employer, or a representative thereof, who intentionally or negligently violates work safety regulations or causes a defect or fault that is contrary to work safety regulations or makes a situation contrary to work safety regulations by failing to monitor compliance with them in the work he/she supervises, or by failing to provide for the financial, organisational or other prerequisites for work safety shall be sentenced for a work safety offence to a fine or to imprisonment for at most one year.' The elements of a safety offence can be fulfilled even when there is no injury or death.[14] In addition, a crime is committed even if there is no danger: the violation of work safety regulations is enough to constitute a crime. Behind this is the idea of presumed danger. This is not the same as what is termed 'endangerment' in many jurisdictions, since no concrete or even abstract endangerment is required. The violation of safety regulations is punishable *per se*.

Under Finnish law, only individuals – not corporations – can be prosecuted as offenders, apparently because the formulation of a viable notion of corporate fault proved impossible in the legislative process. But the law does possess a degree of flexibility: even if corporations cannot be deemed to have a 'guilty mind', criminal sanctions can be imposed on them even where no individual offender is found. In other words, if a safety crime is committed in the framework of a corporation, while it may not be possible to find the corporation guilty of a crime, it is possible to impose a fine on it. This is an interesting and original approach that avoids the complications which arise in other jurisdictions when concepts such as *mens rea* are sought to be applied to companies.[15]

Hence, the formulation of liability for safety crime is relatively flexible, both in terms of its inchoate mode and in terms of its application to individuals and corporations – at least in theory – and is easily applied to a range of circumstances. The letter of the law, in this case, is not an obstacle in the processes of determining work safety violations as crimes.

Policing safety crime

Three forms of data are used to inform this paper. First, a questionnaire was sent to all local police districts (90) in Finland to understand how safety crime investigation is organised across police districts. In addition, a total of 13 police officers, some more and some less experienced in safety crime investigation, were interviewed thematically. Finally, data were also derived from an analysis of 910 case reports of safety incidents reported to the police in 2003.

The data provides a picture of both the 'structural readiness' of the state to deal with safety crimes (the degree to which we can observe the commitment of the state's formal political, legal and policing mechanisms to the criminalisation of safety crimes) and the 'conceptual readiness' of police officers to investigate safety crimes (the degree to which police officers themselves indicate an ability to move beyond their conventional role of maintaining inter-personal disorder). The analysis of the thematic interviews and case reports also provides a picture of police investigative practices.

Organisation of investigation

At the time of the study, there were 90 local police departments in Finland, a country with a population of just under 5½ million people. In the vast majority of cases, the investigation of safety crimes is not allocated to specialised units or individuals. Rather, safety crimes tend to be investigated by whoever happens to be on duty or by non-specialised, general crime investigators. A minority are allocated to specialists within Finnish police departments. In 10 per cent of departments, safety crimes are investigated by violent crime squads; in a smaller number of departments, by specialist economic crime squads. Only one unit has full-time investigators who are dedicated to safety crime investigation. In this sense, safety crimes are 'anybody's property' and therefore 'nobody's property'.

Approximately 70 per cent of the units included in the survey reported that there were no investigators in their unit who had gone through any kind of vocational training or had taken any courses in investigating safety crimes. Vocational training provided by the police organisation on the investigation of safety crimes is scarce compared with other forms of investigation. Interviewees also perceived this as a problem; their knowledge of how to investigate safety crimes is learned 'on the job' and is therefore highly dependant on the number and types of cases they investigate.

Most commonly, the police become aware of potential safety crimes from calls to the emergency centre. Following those calls, a patrol will typically visit the crime scene to gather forensic evidence (normally restricted to taking photographs) and interview witnesses. At this point, the case does not yet have the status of a criminal investigation. Investigators will rarely go to the crime scene immediately unless there has been a death or very serious injury.

The police do not always inform the OSH about the incident. In 2003, 63.1% of the case reports mentioned that the OSH was informed, and usually this happened on the same day as the incident. OSH inspectors may go to the scene immediately, but most commonly, the inspection and investigation is conducted afterwards, the former usually a couple of weeks and the latter a couple of months after the incident. The police will commonly await the regulators' report before deciding whether or not to proceed with a criminal investigation, and will usually only do so if asked by the regulators. Thus in practice the regulators' assessment will greatly influence whether a safety incident is dealt with as a crime. Though legally possible, only rarely will the police begin a criminal investigation without the support of OSH inspectors. Thus, although police officers may formally take the lead in the decision to proceed with a criminal investigation, the view of OSH inspectors – when it is sought or provided – is pivotal to this decision.

Of the 910 cases that were brought to the attention of the police in 2003, 24.5 per cent (223 cases) were defined as possible crimes worthy of criminal investigation and 17.1 per cent (156 cases) were sent to the prosecutor. Although there are no figures available to indicate how many of those were prosecuted and/or led to a conviction, the ratio is likely to be comparatively high due to the demanding threshold that needs to be met to warrant bringing cases to the public prosecutor. Approximately 140 people are found guilty of safety crimes in Finland each year.[16]

Safety crimes as rubbish

Many interviewees spoke quite openly of their difficulties in conceptualising safety incidents at work as crimes. This was due, on the one hand, to the limitations of their knowledge regarding the law and related technical matters; and, on the other, to the fact that safety incidents as such were not thought of as being 'awfully criminal'. Even though some of the interviewees worked in violent crime squads, they didn't regard safety crimes as belonging within their remit; safety crimes simply did not fit into their conceptual map of violent incidents. Some interviewees regarded safety cases on a par with offences such as infringements of restraining orders or cases such as libel; others viewed them as not worthy of police intervention (in the words of one, 'worthless shit'); and still others described safety incidents as too 'odd' to fall within the realm of legitimate police work. What these responses indicate is that how safety cases are defined directly affects the way they are processed:

> It is such an odd thing. The Finnish police are good in investigating traditional crimes. It has to be a murder!! It has to be a murder!! Yes. No, no, no, this is such an odd area. That's how it always goes, when things are odd, you file them.

Quantitatively, the reluctance of police investigators to define safety incidents as 'real crime' is indicated by the finding that only one out of four incidents in 2003 was registered with a 'report of an offence' form. The rest were registered using the 'miscellaneous' form, with the most common title for the incident being 'investigation of an accident at work'. The fact that this title is a ready-made option in the crime registration system indicates a separate point: that the registration process as such furthers the characterisation of work safety incidents as 'accidents'. In the course of the interviews, the police officers were asked to describe a typical case. The idea of safety incidents as accidents or resulting from bad luck permeates the typical description of a 'typical' case:

> It seems that we investigate quite clear accidents sometimes … These are not real [violent crimes], these are accidents. A typical case is probably such an incident where people have worked with a certain routine for years and then someone takes one accidental sidestep and falls from somewhere. Yes, they are incidents which involve a lot of bad luck.

In conjunction with the perception that safety violations were unforeseeable, the interviewees revealed a tendency to consider such incidents as isolated events happening at a certain time and in a certain place. Related to this perception, the interviewees' discussion of particular incidents rarely recognised that such incidents might have a historical context; in other words, there was no recognition that what occurred before or after the incident was in any way connected to the incident.

The conceptualising of safety crime as 'worthless' related to a reluctance to accept their distinct legal construction as a reason warranting police intervention. The fact that the *actus reus* of safety crimes, rather than involving a criminal 'act', often involves an 'omission' such as a failure to provide protective measures for employees, or a failure to ensure safe working, was cited as a reason why police investigators were less interested in them. Some interviews reported that it was difficult to understand how negligence can be defined as criminal, or why safety crimes are considered important when 'it's only a matter of omission'.

> There [where safety crimes are investigated] is no action. There are no active crimes, except the touching up of young girls [at the workplace].
>
> These are not [perceived as crimes in the police]. Because crimes are only those where someone does [something]. It takes a while to piece together the omission aspect.

Some interviewees reported that it took time and a lot of reading of law texts before one could understand the nature of these crimes. The difficulty of understanding the different basis for liability, and the issue of knowing who might be criminally responsible, were common themes mentioned by interviewed officers.

Not all officers interviewed looked at safety incidents in this way, however. Some were critical about the way most police officers in their view tended to think. Those who were more experienced in investigating safety cases than those who investigated such cases sporadically were more prone to perceive safety incidents as involving criminality. As one interviewee said, 'it took me three years before I understood these are crimes, not accidents'.

Not real police work

All of the interviewees reported that the investigation of occupational safety crimes is not valued by the police and is not seen as 'real' police work. However, some did concede that the investigative expertise of the police provided a justification (perhaps the only justification) for police involvement. It was noted that the police had specialist skills and experience of attending crime scenes where there is a corpse, and that this was a good reason for involving police investigators in such cases.

At the same time, some interviewees reported that many of their colleagues would actively avoid being allotted such 'UFO cases'. As one interviewee observed:

> No-one wants the climax of their career to be the investigation of safety crimes. That is totally obvious. It can't be made media-sexy ever. ... it is somehow so ordinary; there is no glamour in it.

Safety cases are viewed by many police as less dynamic or exciting, or involving a 'lack of action'. Several described such casework as mundane or 'as puttering around for old gramps-type of work'. One interviewee summed this point up as follows:

> I think the middle age for those who want to investigate is 45 or so. It is probably a good place for police officers who want to slacken their pace and prepare for pension.

The comments above are very similar to those made about economic (financial) crime before it was regularised into the work of the Finnish police. Economic crime investigators said that they had been given nicknames such as 'cardigan soldiers' or 'sandal men' who work with silk gloves and white shirts and ties. However, largely because of the implementation of the action plans, the attitudes towards economic crime investigation changed, and economic crime is now to a large extent perceived as 'normal' police work.[17]

A few of the interviewees either stated explicitly or implied that the investigation of safety crimes – whether undertaken by the police or OSH inspectors – is, or had been, somehow political or politically loaded. Two interviewees said that, albeit probably less so today than in the 1970s and 80s, there was attached to safety crime investigation the risk of being labelled as some sort of leftist or 'campaigner of stuff that begin with the word labour'.

> ... one has to be careful, when one talks about these [cases], that one doesn't get, you see, one is labelled so easily. One is labelled so easily then.
> ... Let me put it this way; there are a lot of those [in the OSH] who used to march on the 1st of May.

Many of the interviewees either stated explicitly or implied that these attitudes – their view that safety crime investigation was peripheral to 'real' police work, or was 'leftist' police work – produce a reluctance on the part of many officers to engage in the investigation of safety crimes.

The policing of safety crimes as a legitimate activity is therefore questioned by police who view it as either worthless or intrinsically political work. There are strong echoes of a longstanding body of research on the policing of domestic violence which at one time was also referred to by police as 'rubbish work'. Police officers themselves see safety crimes at best as 'abnormal' work in the scope of their duties, and at worst as 'deviant' policing.

Safety criminals as legitimate targets

Interviewees expressed difficulties in conceptualising suspects in safety crimes as potentially 'criminals'. One of the more experienced and committed investigators of safety crimes, noted:

> ... but then when we ask these foremen or CEOs to be interrogated and they arrive with their ties around their necks and when you say that listen, this is a crime we are talking about, and then they look at you and [say] 'you're kidding'. And they don't even look like criminals. This was a matter of adjustment, that [without experience] it was weird to interrogate ordinary people about a crime that kind of felt like an accident, was no-one's fault ...

Another interviewee, with less experience and commitment to policing safety crimes, stated that there was only one positive thing about safety crime investigation:

> You deal with other types of people. Usually you deal with the victim and the pile of shit [suspect] in a normal way. When investigating accidents at work, you are dealing with normal people with whom there is a possibility to have a discussion.

The preceding quotes illustrate a common perception that persons who commit safety violations are 'normal' people, as opposed to criminals who engage in 'street' crime who are constructed as 'abnormal', with reference to a notion of a criminal sub-culture or stereotype. To treat 'normal' people as criminals was considered by police investigators as abnormal or odd.

In particular, many police appeared to sympathise with foremen and displayed a marked reluctance to view them as criminals or pursue their potential criminal liability. Foremen were seen to be overloaded with work such that they 'did not have time to supervise all those five construction sites ... and then someone fell down there'. Interestingly, the liability of more senior managers to ensure a safe working environment was not mentioned in accounts that were sympathetic with middle management and foremen. There was no mention in the interviews, for example, that in such cases management should be liable for failing to employ sufficient staff to ensure safe working conditions. Accompanying this blind spot could be discerned a pessimism that it would even be possible to hold senior management responsible for a safety crime:

Of course it's the closest bosses who bear the responsibility. Even though the others [upper management] so to speak, bear the responsibility.

Interviews were therefore dominated by a bipolar perspective that, on the one hand, found it difficult to conceptualise senior management culpability – either because of stereotypic assumptions about criminal types or because of an inability to escape commonly applied concepts of intent in the crimes they were used to working with – and, on the other, a pessimism about the willingness of the courts and the criminal justice system to hold the most senior managers to account.

The evidence gained from the interviews is supported by quantitative analysis. In the crime reports involving safety offences, only 28.8 per cent of the suspects represented senior management; the rest came from the ranks of middle and lower level management. In court over half of the convicted defendants fell in the category of low level management.[18] Unfortunately, the data do not allow us to know if the tendency to investigate and convict lower levels of management is correlated with police attitudes towards safety crimes and criminals. Whatever the reason, it is clear that there is a bias that many police officers are not happy with, but most appear to be resigned to. This bias is certainly not discouraged by the inability of police officers to conceptualise culpability at a senior management level.

Despite the inability to conceptualise culpability at senior levels in the corporate hierarchy and of the pressures created by the corporate structure, a small minority of officers appear to have developed a deeper understanding of the financial motivations that may lie at the heart of safety offences. Three interviewed police officers defined safety crimes as 'economic crimes', and explicitly identified the financial benefits of this type of offending. In contrast, the majority of the interviewees did not regard safety crimes as belonging to the category of economic crimes. They did not perceive – or had never thought about – the possibility that there could be some economic interest in cases of occupational safety incidents

P: Well yes, if a railing at some construction site has not been built, what is the economic angle in that some worker falls and hurts his hand?

I: I guess it has been thought that the costs that have been saved would be it.

P: Seems a bit far-fetched.

From the quotation above, one can discern how narrow time-frames and the tendency to focus on isolated incidents buttress the traditionally asserted 'intentionalism' of the criminal justice system.

Some interviewees denied, when directly asked, that not taking care of safety at work might be of benefit to the employer. These denials were often accompanied by explanations more or less explicitly making the point that the failures of employers to provide for the financial, organisational or other prerequisites for work safety were located in something other than financial benefit:

> Yes but, I say that it is more about negligence if someone doesn't build railings, they don't get any economic benefit from that, you know. It is always the hurry …

There are two important points that can be extracted from this understanding of the role of the employer. First is the perception that economic benefit is not attainable by negligent omission, only by intended acts. Second is the fact that omissions that result in a crime are disconnected from the more general, profit-maximising, objective of firms. Thus, while offences may be attributed to a tendency to 'hurry', the reasons for having to 'hurry' remain unseen, or are considered to be an inevitability, part of the inherent dangers of some forms of work. What officers appear not to grasp is that failing to employ a sufficient number of workers to reduce 'hurry' can lead to safety incidents while saving money for the employer, and may be a motive for the 'hurry'. What the interviews reveal then, is an approach on the part of police officers to understanding the relationship between motive, intent and criminality that deliberately obscures the possibility that profit may be involved in the crime.

Victim-blaming

Just as safety offenders are not deemed to be 'normal' criminals, neither are the victims of safety crimes deemed to be 'normal' victims. Linked often to the construction of safety incidents as 'accidents', the theme of victim-blaming was discernible in many of the interviews, where the contributory role of the victim was prominent in one way or another:

> … it is not the responsibility of the employer if some idiot blunders by oneself, does something stupid. There cannot be someone looking over every Tom, Dick and Harry.

> Let's say now really, there are normal people there, and someone has been fooling about at their work.

The idea of the accident-prone worker did not appear to be linked by interviewees to certain personality types. Rather, qualities such as stupidity or foolishness were associated with the victims. Being intoxicated at the workplace was also mentioned in some of the interviews; 'there are those, where you see a bottle dropping from their back pocket'. In 60 case reports (6.6 per cent) there was a reference to the fact that the victim had been breathalysed. One interviewee felt that it was typical for the police to presume that intoxication was the cause of safety incidents, but was extremely critical about this bias:

> My colleagues, almost all of them, think that when an accident at work happens, the first question to make is 'how drunk were you'. I say to them: 'a

construction site has to be so safe, that even if someone is totally wasted, they shouldn't fall from there'.

In addition to focusing on the behaviour of the victim, sometimes co-workers were blamed:

It may be that things [regarding work safety] are quite ok. But then someone has done something and moved it. Some cleaner or someone has lifted some board and has left it in a bad place. And someone else comes and steps there. There are a lot of cases where the employee doesn't take care.

A contributory role of the victim or a statement given by the victim that nobody should be blamed was mentioned in 10 per cent of case reports. In a few of those reports the description of the incidents implies that the employee has not only been negligent, but actively had 'sawed' or 'pushed' and had been injured because of that action:

The employee had sawed his own finger.

X had pushed his hand in the dough machine.

Several interviews noted that not uncommonly victims blamed themselves. Self-blaming by employees was also documented in case reports. Even though safety offences are not complainant offences (i.e. they are offences that do not require the victim or a member of the public to initiate investigation), a victim's inability or unwillingness to implicate others was used as a justification for not proceeding with an investigation:

The employee thought that it was his own fault and there was no need for further investigations.

About the incident, X [the victim] tells that it was just an accident, which just happens even if one is careful … he has no claims, and he doesn't even know who to blame.

The quantitative analysis in the case reports indicates that an assumption of the victim's contributory role is not insignificant to the progress of the case. Only 5.5 per cent of the cases where the fault of the victim was mentioned proceeded to the prosecutor. This compares with a figure of 17.1 per cent in all cases.

Conclusion

Although safety crimes are inscribed in the penal code, they remain – in comparison to financial crimes – relatively low on the political agenda. Finnish law can be said to display a relatively high degree of structural readiness to allow the criminalisation of safety offences. The Finnish Penal Code adopts a relatively flexible approach to the definition of safety crimes, which leaves a high degree of discretion in the hands of police investigators and prosecutors.

The interviews and quantitative data analysed here reveal that this zone of police discretion allows officers to interpret safety crimes in a particular way. Typically, this translates into a reluctance to criminalise events that are seen as accidents on the one hand, or 'worthless' in terms of police work on the other; the perception that policing safety crimes is a highly political or 'deviant' police activity; the reluctance to recognise safety criminals as legitimate targets of police intervention, or to recognise the viability of criminalising senior managers; and the predominance of victim blaming and victim precipitation in police reports of safety crimes.

Some of those attitudes and practices can undoubtedly be improved with training. The interviews reveal major gaps in the police knowledge of this area of law. Most interviewees were not even aware of the concept and extent of corporate liability in Finnish law. If so, they can hardly be expected to gather the evidence of a 'crime' that the court would need to convict and punish the offender. Interviews also revealed how officers regularly used the term 'accident' loosely to justify their reluctance to become involved in this type of police work. This betrays a lack of understanding of law in the sense that the penal code draws a clear distinction between 'negligent' acts and omissions (which can constitute an offence) and 'accidents' (which are not punishable). Educating the police in the law relating to safety crimes, and particularly the distinctive legal construction of individual and corporate liability and the concept of negligence as it applies to safety crimes, could influence the attitude and approach of the police to the investigation of safety offences. At the moment, the rudimentary and often erroneous knowledge possessed by police officers means that they are seldom able to act appropriately in such cases, even if they were willing.

However, the data shows that even where it is clear that police officers know the law, they rarely accept that their intervention is justified, necessary or worthwhile. Some police thought that all safety offences should be investigated by the OSH. Other officers found it difficult to work with a concept of crime based on negligence and 'omissions'. Whether improved training would be enough to precipitate a cultural change that would cause police to take safety crimes more seriously is an open question. However, it is instructive that experienced investigators were less likely to have a blind spot to safety crimes or an obvious distaste for this type of police work, and were more likely to express a commitment to the role of the police in investigating such offences. One interviewee argued that the problem cannot be dealt with by piecemeal procedural change because the 'typical' police officer may never understand these cases: 'You need a particular mindset to be a good safety crime investigator.'

The above quotation suggests that one possible way forwards would be to consider ways of making the investigation of safety crimes more attractive to the 'typical' police officer. This might entail changes in investigative practices. Research on the work of reformed economic crime investigation in Finland has revealed how new investigative initiatives such as home searches of businesses and the tracing and recovery of the proceeds of crime have elevated the status of economic crime investigation from that of paperwork to 'real' police work. The perceptions of what constitutes 'real' police work are powerful, and it seems that economic crime investigation became more 'real' once it more closely imitated dominant representations of what the police do. Largely as a result of action plans and their implementation, attitudes changed and economic (financial) crime investigation came to be perceived somewhat more as normal police work than was the case before the action plans. Changes in investigative practices are therefore justifiable not only for the sake of making the investigation of safety crimes more 'sexy' for the average constable but also because the effective discovery and exposure of such crimes may require the use of more pro-active methods.

Another practical reform would be for the investigation of workplace crimes to be allocated to economic crime units. This change could affect positively police investigators', prosecutors' and courts' readiness to link underlying formulations of liability and economic interests. It could bring out a wider perspective on investigation, so that economic interests, indirect causes, liability formulations and the fact that criminal sanctions can be imposed on corporations would be paid greater attention.

History has demonstrated that cultural or 'canteen' attitudes to crime can be changed over time, especially when there is the political will to enforce such changes. Transformations in the conception and attitudes to safety offences within the police culture may hold the promise for reform of an area that has long been misunderstood, undervalued and neglected.

Notes

1 See also Anne Alvesalo and Dave Whyte: 'Eyes Wide Shut: The Police Investigation of Safety Crimes' *Crime, Law and Social Change* 2007 (48), 57–72.
2 Anne Alvesalo, 'Economic Crime Investigators at Work', *Policing and Society*, 2003 (Vol. 13, No. 2), 115–138.
3 Anne Alvesalo, 'A Sitting Duck or a Trojan Horse? Critical Criminology, Control and White-collar Crime', *The Critical Criminologist*, 1999 (9), 5–7 and Anne Alvesalo and Steve Tombs, 'Can Economic Crime Control Be Sustained?', *Innovation: the European Journal of Social Science Research*, 2001 (14:1), 35–53.
4 Anne Alvesalo and Steve Tombs, 'The Emergence of a "War" on Economic Crime: The Case of Finland,' *Business and Politics*, 2001 (3:3), 239–267.
5 Gary Slapper and Steve Tombs, *Corporate Crime* (Dorset: Longman Criminology Series, 1999).
6 Maurice Punch, *Dirty Business: Exploring Corporate Misconduct. Analyses and Cases.* (London: Sage Publications, 1996) and Michael Levi, 'The Investigation, Prosecution and Trial of Serious Fraud', *The Royal Commission on Criminal Justice, Research Study No. 14* (London: HMSO, 1993).
7 David Kirk and Anthony Woodcock, *Serious Fraud: Investigation and Trial*, 2nd edn (London: Butterworths, 1997).
8 Gary Fooks, 'Contrasts in Tolerance: The Peculiar Case of Financial Regulation'. *Contemporary Politics*, 2003 (Vol. 9, No. 2) 127–142.
9 Laureen Snider, 'The Sociology of Corporate Crime: An Obituary (Or: Whose Knowledge Claims Have Legs?)', *Theoretical Criminology*, 2000 (4: 2), 169–206.

10 Finnish Ministry of Justice, *Kansallinen ohjelma väkivallan vähentämiseksi* (National programme for reducing violence) (Helsinki: Oikeusministeriön julkaisuja, 2005:2).

11 *Working together for a safe society.* The National Crime Prevention Program, Ministry of Justice, The National Council for Crime Prevention, Finland (3.3.1999). Retrieved 24.5.2007 from http://www.rikoksentorjunta.fi/uploads/b5qs9pt42ny.rtf, p2.

12 Finnish Government, *Valtioneuvoston periaatepäätös 23.9.2004 sisäisen turvallisuuden ohjelmasta* (2004). (National programme on inland security) (Sisäasiainministeriö).

13 The ministry of social affairs and health defines the role of the OSH in the following way 'the occupational safety and health (OSH) administration seeks to influence the operations of working communities and the working environment in order to improve the employees' safety, health and working conditions and the results of the operations. The OSH administration works in close cooperation with the labour market organisations. Besides the traditional inspection and monitoring services, the OSH administration focuses on the development of multi-faceted instruction, guidance and information services. The European context and international cooperation require that the administration must assume new levels and standpoints in its work'. Retrieved 13.6.2007 from http://www.stm.fi/Resource.phx/eng/subjt/safet/index.htx.

14 Negligent homicide, negligent bodily injury and imperilment are criminalised elsewhere (chapter 21) in the Penal Code. If someone is injured or dies at work, the culprit can be found guilty to work safety offence and negligent bodily injury/ homicide.

15 Steve Tombs and Dave Whyte, *Safety Crimes* (Collumpton: Willan, 2007).

16 Since cases often involve several suspects, this figure cannot be used to indicate the likely proportion of investigations that result in conviction.

17 Anne Alvesalo, 'Economic Crime Investigators at Work', *Policing and Society*, 2003 (Vol. 13, No.2), 115–138.

18 The statistics on convictions were produced from separate data which consist of cases adjudged in the Uusimaa region in 2003–2004. See Anne Alvesalo and Kirsi Jauhiainen, 'Työturvallisuustapaukset poliisissa', in A. Alvesalo and A.-M. Nuutila (ed.), *Rangaistava työn turvattomuus*. Poliisiammattikorkeakoulun oppikirjat 13. (p.17). (Helsinki: Edita Prima Oy 2006).

11 Political autonomy, accountability and efficiency in the prosecution of serious white-collar crimes

Michael Levi

Introduction

The level of present and future trust in law enforcement agencies is a powerful influence on views about the legitimacy of crime control. This article focuses upon a particular sub-set of 'the trust issues', the prosecution of serious fraud and allied financial crimes, which episodically comes to the political fore. In some countries, mostly but not exclusively poor ones, in which economic and social power are highly concentrated, anger at fraud and corruption can manifest itself in demands for prosecution of elites as well as recovery of the proceeds of their frauds and bribes. This is not a new phenomenon. In the aftermath of the South Sea Bubble, Viscount Molesworth called for the directors of the South Sea Company to be declared guilty by Parliamentary fiat and to suffer the Roman punishment for parricide – being sewn into a sack with a snake, cockerel and monkey and thrown into the river to drown (Carswell, 1960: 174). A look at some African, Asian and South American countries – where senior politicians, almost invariably *former* leaders, go to jail – illustrates this. (Sceptics might note the frequency with which, in time, similar allegations of kleptocracy are made against the incoming administrations, demonstrating the weakness of criminal law alone as an instrument of prevention.) Even in the USA, post-banking bail-out, this public rage has been directed at Wall Street elites (and, after the Gulf of Mexico disaster, at BP). We normally blame the people perceived as causing the problem: this locus of blame is influenced by both socially constructed values and media campaigns, etc., and can focus on 'criminals', crime non-preventers, investigators, prosecutors, judges and/or juries.

Feeley and Simon (2007) and Garland (2008) suggest a difference in *general* social construction of crime since the 1960s, according to which the cultural temperature has been raised frequently at fear of different crimes and criminal groups. Yet even at times of economic crisis such as that experienced in many countries in the late 'noughties', Western governments have regularly sought to defuse the risk of a social movement against white-collar crimes (broadly defined to include both elite and non-elite commercial crimes), preferring to deal with them more softly by regulation and occasional symbolic prosecution. The USA has historically had a more vigorous approach to the prosecution and regulatory sanctioning of elites and, assisted by easier rules for founding corporate criminal liability, corporations than has had the UK. Moreover, US prosecutors have been able to base political careers around white-collar crime fighting, even if, as former New York Attorney General Eliot Spitzer found, they can come crashing down again later, due to his attempt to hide his interstate electronic payments for high class call girls.[1] By contrast, UK prosecutors have not sought political careers, and none of those who have 'rocked the boat' by suggesting an aggressive approach to prosecution have been appointed to top positions in fraud prosecution agencies.

Given (a) the relative unresponsiveness of British police and prosecutors to public sentiments, especially those not expressed via the media and/or by their departmental heads, and (b) the length of time taken to deal with complex frauds through the criminal process, it would not be surprising to see little change. However, it is interesting to explore the aspects of change and continuity through the lens of transformations (and non-transformations) in the elements that make up the prosecution of serious fraud, and it is this to which we now turn.

First, some background. One of the problems that surrounds terms like 'serious fraud', 'white-collar crime', 'economic crime' and 'financial crime' is that they misleadingly aggregate a set of quite disparate phenomena, which are more meaningfully analysed in terms of variations in victim and offender status and interests. We should review not just the social composition of prosecuted offenders but also the status of their victims in order to assess the social meaning of prosecutions for corruption and fraud. It is helpful to see fraud and corruption prosecutions as an attrition process that passes or does not pass through the successive filters of awareness, reporting, recording, investigation, prosecution and trial. Unless a 'case' passes through all of these filters, criminal justice sanctions cannot be applied, though there remain important alternatives such as regulatory fines, occupational disqualification and bad publicity that may be imposed if the actor is subjectable to those sorts of penalties. This review will not examine the merits and demerits of criminal versus regulatory modes of control – important though that debate is – but will focus on the criminal route.

The more complex a case is, the more it needs resources and competence at all of these stages. Thus resource starvation can indirectly destroy the willingness to take on major cases, since the opportunity cost of doing so is high. On the other hand, as alleged in the prosecution of Putin's opponent Mikhail Khodorkovski, former CEO of Yukos oil, and some other Russian émigré 'oligarchs', resource abundance can be directed in a politically partisan way, to prosecute (or to extort funds from) the regime's opponents and to let off the regime's supporters, and this is especially easy if there is no *de facto* independence. However, prosecuting elite cases also needs a mindset of seeing 'what happened' as criminal and a willingness to tackle it via the criminal law, and it is this mindset that is often far from natural. We are used to seeing criminals as 'not like us' so if someone is (or appears to be) 'like us', it is difficult for us to treat them as a 'real' criminal. So the composition of 'the fraud problem' depends partly on the flow of complaints/investigations and partly on the pragmatic assessment of 'political' (with a small or large 'p') difficulties within the resources available.

A short history of the prosecution of serious white-collar crimes in England and Wales

Resources act as an upper limit on prosecutions. In the early 1970s, for example, a third of the entire Fraud Division of the DPP's Office were working full-time on the Poulson local government corruption case that caught the then Home Secretary, Reggie Maudling, within its ambit (Gillard, 1974). In the late 1970s, the Department of Trade – the main vehicle for the prosecution of misconduct by company directors rather than of fraud by outsiders – had only eight lawyers working on company fraud. Three particular periods of prosecutorial crisis in the UK suggest themselves. The first was in the early 1980s; the second in the early–mid 1990s; and the third in the aftermath of the BAE transnational bribery investigations and global financial crisis.

Police–prosecutor joint working was first piloted in 1981 as a means of putting into practice the recommendation of closer co-operation between the main parties responsible for commercial fraud control (Jardine Working Party, 1979). Nevertheless, a series of unsuccessful prosecutions and scandals in the early 1980s culminated in the appointment in 1983 of Lord Roskill – a Law Lord with a known lack of enthusiasm for juries – to chair the Fraud Trials Committee (1986). This was partly envisaged as a mechanism for increasing the conviction rate by eliminating costs and 'inefficiencies' in the prosecution process and getting rid of juries in complex cases, but broadened out into a more radical and wide-ranging review of the investigation and trial of 'serious fraud' (a term that was never clarified then or subsequently). Meanwhile, pressure from the financial services sector for more competent and faster prosecution of commercial fraud led in January 1985 to the creation of a permanent Fraud Investigation Group (FIG) within the Office of the DPP. In 1986, when Roskill reported, the FIG had a total of 60 staff, of which only 18 were professionals, with a budget of £1.5 million. In terms of external professional expertise, it had access principally to a budget-price accountancy panel, which was used quite sparingly. Some questioned why FIG could not have been given more resources, obviating the need for a new body with its own infrastructure costs. However, as part of a push for the international credibility of London as the premier global financial services centre, it was felt that a higher profile was needed to show the international community that the British[2] were serious about tackling fraud, and thus, the Serious Fraud Office was created. As the Home Secretary Douglas Hurd expressed it in the Parliamentary debate on the Roskill report:[3]

> We intend to create and seize every opportunity for stern action against fraud. We think this is crucial for the City and for the country so that private enterprise can flourish in a clean environment. It is crucial for public confidence, and our competitive position in international markets that the probity of our financial institutions, especially in the City, should be beyond doubt. Those who save and invest, whether grand or small, should be well protected by our law from dishonest practices, however complicated the transaction. We are

> determined that the pursuit and the bringing to justice of fraudsters should be carried out with commitment and skill. If our present instruments for cutting our fraud are blunt we must manufacture a new carefully directed scalpel … Early detection of irregularities can often prevent serious fraud and as with all crime, prevention is our first aim. If prevention fails then the machinery for dealing with fraud must be effective.

The latter was intended to include *all* major fraud cases, but organisational wrangling led to the exclusion of insider dealing, tax and social security fraud cases (author interviews with Lord Roskill, 1987, 1991). Although no-one at the time raised questions about prosecutor independence from government, the police ensured that they retained discretion over resource allocation for fear that they might have to give too many officers to fraud investigations, and this remained a source of tension. The Criminal Justice Act 1987 did create a separate body with vague accountability to Parliament via the Attorney General parallel to the Director of Public Prosecutions, who retained the discretion to prosecute (or not) police-investigated fraud cases and *all* corruption cases. At that time, transnational bribery cases were not contemplated, and the OECD transnational bribery convention – which later was to generate such problems for the Serious Fraud Office (hereafter, SFO and for the UK government) – was not even a glimmer in the eye. It also inaugurated for the first time in England and Wales (though not Scotland) lawyer-headed investigations, aiming to reduce the cost and time wasted on police investigations on lines that the prosecution counsel later considered inappropriate, or not investigating things that counsel later considered essential.

The SFO led to an increase in major fraud prosecutions generally and an upsurge in cases involving otherwise legitimate company executives. In the first seven years of its operation, the SFO had a very real effect on increasing the throughput of prosecutions involving otherwise legitimate company officers: an average of only sixteen cases *per annum* involved organisational frauds committed through otherwise legitimate companies; fewer still, an average of only four cases *per annum*, involved chief executive officers working for financial institutions situated in London's financial markets or public limited companies (Fooks, 2003). Fooks appears to assume that this is *disproportionately* small, whereas this judgement depends on abstract arguments about what is the 'true level' of frauds of different types, about which what counts as evidence is disputable.

The first few major SFO prosecutions gave little reason to suspect lack of prosecutorial nerve. Compared with the sorts of prosecutions into marginal figures that had gone before, the prosecution of the chief executive of Guinness, a partner in a major brokerage firm, a lawyer (and some more 'entrepreneurial' City of London figures) looked like a serious attempt to deal with elite crime (though in the event, the elite professionals were not convicted – see Levi, 1991). This was followed by a prosecution of County NatWest Bank, brokers Phillips & Drew (by then bought by UBS), and a range of fairly elite lawyers and investment advisers, in relation to the hiding of problems in a corporate takeover. This generated concern in some financial services circles about the non-accountability (to them) of the SFO, even though most defendants were acquitted, and then the remaining defendants had their convictions quashed by the Court of Appeal, alongside comments that the judge had failed to see the wood for the trees in his conduct of the trial and summing up.

November 1992 and early 1993 witnessed two extraordinary events. The first was the prosecution by HM Customs & Excise of three directors of a company called Matrix-Churchill for allegedly violating prohibitions on the export of arms components to Iraq by *deceiving* the Department of Trade and Industry into granting export licences. The second was the sending of a watch inscribed 'Don't let the buggers get you down' by Michael Mates MP – then Conservative Minister of State for Northern Ireland – to Asil Nadir, after the latter had been charged by the SFO with defrauding Polly Peck International of over £30 million (in specimen charges).[4] Mates had to resign following the revelation that he had sent the watch to Nadir,[5] who fled bail to the non-extraditable, diplomatically unrecognised Republic of North Cyprus (his home and site of many of his business operations) – from which he returned in 2010 to face long delayed criminal charges, having been assured by the Serious Fraud Office that they would not oppose bail.[6] The problem is, as always, 'accountable to whom for what'? *Inter alia*, these and some other fraud cases involving powerful defendants and potential defendants have opened up interesting issues such as the relative autonomy of the *prosecution* as well as the *policing*[7] process from 'the government': the arms-for-Iraq enquiry conducted by Lord Justice Scott (1996) highlighted the enormous amount of intra-governmental 'politicking' that can occur in some high profile cases, as well as the ambivalent role of the Attorney General as both party politician and senior law officer with 'accountability' to Parliament for prosecutions and the constitutional power of stopping them by entering a *nolle prosequi*.[8] This tension over the ambivalent political and judicial roles was to re-emerge over the dropping of the bribery charges against (and the legality of the invasion of Iraq) BAE.

Especially before the Human Rights Act, legislation on powers to investigate white-collar crime seemed often to diverge from that of 'ordinary' crime, largely because it is seen as analytically separable from it and does not attract significant civil rights lobbying: businesspeople's rights do not interest many on the political left, and because of their social status and articulate familiarity with verbal combat, they are not seen to be at risk of miscarriages of justice in the UK (Levi, 1987, 1993).[9] They are, in a sense, the most unappealing group among those who might lay claim to 'victim status'. For these reasons, paradoxically, there have been relatively few challenges from the civil libertarian left to the unalloyed use of the 'crime control' (as opposed to the 'due process') model to combat 'white-collar crime'.

Roskill had broadly intended a fully fledged inquisitorial regime in which, as in Department of Trade and Industry Investigations, self-incriminating answers obtained under compulsion would be admissible unless specifically oppressive. Committal proceedings were to be replaced by preparatory hearings at which the accused would be required to present their detailed defence to the prosecution's allegations, to iron out most areas of dispute before the trial began. However, under pressure from Jeremy Hutchinson – a leading QC in the House of Lords – *inter alia*,[10] a Home Office Minister watered down the proposal and although it became a specific offence to lie to the SFO, statements made under compulsion under s.2 of the Criminal Justice Act 1987 could be admitted in evidence only if the defendant made statements in the witness box which were inconsistent with his earlier remarks. Since few defendants give evidence (and few would be advised by their lawyers to give evidence whatever the powers of the SFO), this is mainly irrelevant in practice (Levi, 1993).[11] One intriguing issue that has remained undiscussed outside of the Guinness and Nadir cases, however, is what jurisprudentially is required before these powers can be triggered: the legislation requires that the case be 'serious' *or* 'complex', but does not define these terms, and the guidelines issued by the Director of the SFO to indicate what sort of cases he will consider taking on state vaguely that cases would normally involve over £1 million *and/or* be of significant 'public interest'.[12] However, apart from their line management, and the mechanism of loose accountability to (while preserving independence from) the Attorney General, this means that the only accountability of these criminal investigators, armed with considerable powers, is to the courts (in evidence admissibility decisions and verdicts). Police who work on the cases (but who have fewer powers) are subject to the police discipline code, but others are subject only to the managerial and general civil service discipline code.[13]

Fairness in serious fraud prosecutions

In *The Case for the Prosecution*, McConville *et al.* (1991) make the argument that cases are constructed by the prosecutor on the basis of police reports and perceptions of 'what happened', in which the police re-form witnesses' statements into their own reified amalgam of conviction-supporting material. Hypothetically, serious fraud cases – to which they make no reference – would not be expected to look like this, for their density and the elite status of suspects should protect them from the strong arm of the law, while prosecutors are involved in the supervision of the police fraud investigations in a way that seldom happens elsewhere, even in murders (Maguire and Norris, 1993). Serious fraud cases – of which cases dealt with by the Serious Fraud Office are only a sub-set, since insolvency cases are dealt with by the Department of Business Innovation and Skills, some market abuse cases by the Financial Services Authority, and tax fraud cases are prosecuted by the Crown Prosecution Service, who also process many equally serious police investigations conducted under PACE powers – would be expected to involve lengthy negotiation over access to documents, over interpretations of what happened, and over the decision to prosecute itself rather than to impose administrative penalties. (For very dated but still relevant American illustrations of this filtering, see Mann, 1985.)

Police influence over witness statements can transform the complexity of the real world into a reified one in which witness culpability is minimised while the suspect(s)'s culpability is maximised.[14] It is also an article of faith rather than evidence that professional status will immunise interviewers against taken-for-granted 'frames' within which the evidence and their interviews are viewed. What the SFO regime does is to ensure that interviews with key professional witnesses (under s.2) are taped and are conducted by lawyers and accountants, removing one layer of such unsupervised steering. However, it remains deeply problematic to know which witnesses are telling the truth and, more especially, how 'blameworthiness' is distributed. For example, accountants may find it convenient for their position in being sued later for professional negligence if it is believed that they were told lies by the directors than if they failed to check things without being told lies or even suggested various 'dodgy' manoeuvres; it is also less damaging professionally to their reputations for competence. What is anyone who was not actually there at the time to make of conflicting interpretations of what was said (given that, unlike ordinary police cases, the SFO can make them have to say *something* unless they have a – tightly circumscribed – 'reasonable excuse' not to answer)?[15] Simply because fraud has a lot more documentation than other crimes does not mean that the interpretation of roles and who knew (or was told) what is unproblematical. One of the most public illustrations of this is the undercurrents about the drafting of witness statements by civil servants and ministers that emerged from that portion of the Tribunal of Enquiry by Lord Justice Scott (1996) that dealt with the Matrix-Churchill export licences.

Whatever the disputes about Lord Justice Scott's interpretation of 'what happened', it cannot reasonably be denied that prosecution witnesses radically re-framed events in order to fit the prosecution's theory to enable conviction to take place. Had the background documentation that the ministers' Public Interest Immunity certificates covered (and sought to hide) not been made available to the defence, as it eventually was, there is every probability that the Matrix-Churchill directors would have been wrongly convicted for deceiving the Department of Trade and Industry export licence department into believing that the arms components were made for civil use.[16]

The second crisis for the SFO arrived in 1992–5, when the Serious Fraud Office came under increasing attack from defence lawyers and in the media both for 'over-prosecution' and for failing to obtain convictions in high profile cases, culminating in the acquittal of the public 'folk devils' Kevin and Ian Maxwell (Corker and Levi, 1996; Levi, 2009). One basis (or pretext) for these attacks was that the SFO levy 'scattergun' charges (though in Blue Arrow, the reverse complaint was that they made only one compendious charge). Research at the time suggested that the number of charges reflected an initial 'maximum bid' designed to give flexibility at a relatively early stage in the process, to see what the defence line would be in response, and it was expected that these would be whittled down at the preparatory hearings (Levi, 1993). Indeed, it was the *appearance* of ruthless pruning by the judge of the prosecution's initial charges in the Nadir case that gave rise to some surface plausibility in the allegation that the SFO was trying to get the judge removed and was using the accusations that Nadir's associates had tried to bribe the judge as a pretext for so doing.[17] (In reality, what happened was that a large number of charges were dismissed by the trial judge on technical grounds, subject to a then pending House of Lords ruling on the meaning of 'appropriation'. Following their

Lordships' decision, the charges were reinstated and the prosecution then selected a sample of those original charges to continue with.)

Throughout, the revenue departments have continued with their focus on financial settlements as an alternative to prosecution except where they regard it as strategically important for deterrent (and long-run revenue-maximising) purposes (Levi, 2010). In cases where their targets were (offshore) donors to the Conservative Party such as Mr Octav Botnar, then Chairman of Nissan UK and in 1994 and 1995 a fugitive in Switzerland from later UK tax evasion charges, this preference for money recovered over criminal convictions is obviously 'sensitive'. Despite various actual and anticipated pressures, however, the prosecution of Botnar (and a co-director and auditors, who were convicted, by the Inland Revenue), Nadir (by the Serious Fraud Office), and the Matrix-Churchill directors (by HM Customs & Excise), lends support to those who argue that law enforcement officials enjoy relative autonomy from the government, at least under most circumstances, despite the complex liaison between heads of prosecution departments and the Attorney General. Indeed, there is a sense in which the determination of HM Customs & Excise (now HMRC or, for prosecutions, the CPS) to go ahead with its prosecution of the Matrix-Churchill directors may be read as a reflection of that political and institutional independence: it appears that unlike the 1990 case in which allegations of supplying components to Iraq for a 'supergun' were dropped on the advice of the Attorney General, no such formal advice was given by the Attorney General over Matrix-Churchill, though he was active in seeking to promote Public Interest Immunity certificates which would have denied important information to the defence.

No fraudsters are targets of police/populist retributive sentiments to the extent of terrorists or drugs traffickers, but who would argue that the Maxwell brothers or Peter Clowes (of investment fraud Barlow Clowes) were viewed more favourably than 'ordinary decent criminals'? Anyone observing the public and presidential excoriation of BP over the Gulf of Mexico oil spillage might wonder how the company or its chief executive could get a fair trial (for jury prejudice in a UK context, see Corker and Levi, 1996; Honess *et al.*, 2002). In the Barlow Clowes, Blue Arrow, Guinness, Polly Peck, and Maxwell cases, there were very high profile arrests in the glare of publicity, accompanied by allegations that 'the SFO' *deliberately* used what the Americans call 'the perp walk' as a prejudicial PR stunt. (Since his alleged victims were 'only' shareholders – many of them institutional ones – Nadir, unlike Clowes or the Maxwells, was unlikely to have been a populist hate figure before his dramatic flight, and perhaps – despite the consequential publicity – even after it.)

In every realm of criminal justice, even where there is undercover infiltration or covert surveillance (particularly without video-recording), imperfect approximations are made regarding 'what happened'. The police and regulators have their interpretations, which may reflect their cynical lack of empathy with the 'commercial community'; the jury have theirs, which may reflect dislike of rich Jews, Muslims or foreigners generally, or excessive respect for their social superiors as much as the evidence.[18] There is more pressure from police authorities and the

Home Secretary to deal with crime on the streets than crime in the suites, but the place of Britain in a global economy, as well as the security of retirement pensions and redundancy payments, depends also on Britain's reputation for dealing with financial misconduct. That, of course, creates its own pressures to get convictions, to show other countries that 'we' deal with our fraudsters effectively, as well as to demonstrate the 'effectiveness' of individual and agency decisions to prosecute.

Reasonable people can disagree over whether or not they have discovered a 'smoking prosecutorial gun' in overt political motivation for white-collar prosecutions. Asil Nadir failed to come up with the tapes or records that would have substantiated his claim that 'they' (i.e. the UK and US governments) wanted him out of the way to promote a peace settlement regarding the Turkish Republic of North Cyprus. Likewise, how did the interests of the Conservatives in cracking down on City crime (and in forestalling commercially competitive US leaks about 'untouchable' British City crooks, arising out of US Securities and Exchange Commission and US Department of Justice interviews with insider trader Ivan Boesky) lead senior officers in the Metropolitan Police Fraud Squad to arrest Guinness Chairman Ernest Saunders, but not to arrest other 'City criminals' who presumably could equally have been selected to satisfy the Conservatives' alleged pre-1987 election political white-collar blood-lust? These functionalist 'explanations' of prosecution decision-making in white-collar crime cases do not appear to work at the level of agency.

This brings us to the third crisis for the prosecution of white-collar crimes, the BAE case and its aftermath. The history of the case is elegantly set out in *R (on the application of Corner House Research and others) v Director of the Serious Fraud Office* [2008] UKHL 60, and there is little need to rehearse it in detail here. Suffice it to state that when the SFO investigation got close to obtaining information it needed from Switzerland to mount a prosecution of BAE for transnational bribery in relation to the Saudi Al Yamamah contract, the Saudis threatened to withdraw counter-terrorist assistance, which – doubtless fortuitously – placed it beyond the 'national economic benefit' issues outlawed by s.5 of the OECD Convention as a reason for not prosecuting. On the face of it, the Law Officers behaved wholly properly in requiring representations by BAE and by the Saudis to be referred first to the SFO Director, and the Attorney General examining the issues *qua* the most senior lawyer, even if the SFO Director disagreed with his judgment on the strength of the case. The SFO Director eventually agreed that the threat to UK national security overrode the benefit of continuing that particular case against BAE. Lord Bingham added (para 32) that:

> the discretions conferred on the Director are not unfettered. He must seek to exercise his powers so as to promote the statutory purpose for which he is given them. He must direct himself correctly in law. He must act lawfully. He must do his best to exercise an objective judgement on the relevant material available to him. He must exercise his powers in good faith, uninfluenced by any ulterior motive, predilection or prejudice.

Notwithstanding the legal arguments, this produced an international outcry, stimulated by Cornerhouse and other NGOs, and by the OECD itself which continued to question the UK government's sincerity in its commitment to the OECD Convention and its slowness in passing modern anti-bribery laws. Questions continued to be raised about the role of the Attorney General as a Cabinet member and supervisor of the DPP and SFO Director, though the SFO Director insisted that he had taken the decision personally to allow national security considerations to override the desirability of a prosecution, preserving constitutional propriety. The new Labour Attorney General, Baroness Scotland, insisted that Labour reject the proposal not to allow her to overrule the DPP or SFO Director. This was an issue that did not excite the public but continues to raise important questions about the objectivity of decisions to prosecute and not to prosecute (as also in the USA, though the Federal authorities have a Congress-approved Special Prosecutor arrangement that seeks – not always successfully as in Clinton and 'Whitewatergate' – to depoliticise prosecution decisions about political elites).

The closest fit for the paranoid conspiracy theorists of prosecution decisions might appear to be Matrix-Churchill, at least in terms of reflecting the desire to show the public that Britain had *not* willingly provided the weapons used to kill its own soldiers in the Gulf War.[19] Some support for this explicitly political 'reading' is that in an earlier case, Margaret Thatcher sent her best wishes for the success of their 'sting' operation to Customs & Excise, which were conveyed to the undercover agents nine months *before* they arrested Daghir and Speckman, who were successfully prosecuted for allegedly supplying arms components to Iraq.[20] Yet even the determination to go ahead with the prosecution of Matrix-Churchill directors seems to have more to do with the resentment of Customs & Excise at what they viewed as political interference with their earlier planned prosecution over the supply of 'Supergun' components to Iraq[21] than with national politics: in this sense – and somewhat ironically, in view of its miscarriage potential – it represents the triumph of legal over political values. But how can we properly decide on whether or not a prosecution or non-prosecution decision is affected by explicit political factors (or, for that matter, by the cultural attitude more common in Britain than in the USA or Australia – the desire not to 'rock the boat')? 'Methodic suspicion' often leads to the ignoring of counter-evidence, but 'insider researchers' are confronted with the classic Cicourel (1968) problem of being torn between our personal judgement that X would never have conspired to do Y, and the risk that we too have 'gone native' and have been misled by excessive familiarity with our research subjects. If John Le Carré had written up the Matrix-Churchill affair in the form of a novel, many might have found it to be an unrealistic portrait of shiftiness and ineptitude on the part of some civil servants and Ministers.

But to demonstrate that state institutions sometime behave like that does not mean that *all* paranoid or self-serving allegations of political conspiracies are true. Though far less is involved in the specimen charges in the indictment, the amount of money missing from Polly Peck, fraudulently taken or not, was equivalent to the total net losses from car crime in England and Wales that year. Granted that people thought by the prosecutors and by the civil investigating accountants to be Nadir's nominees may not actually have been such, it is unsurprising that prosecutors and investigators at the SFO should have come up with the hypothesis that a man who transferred so many millions to an offshore company acting on lawful authority but allegedly without any apparently good business reason might have been intending to steal it! Since Nadir returned from North Cyprus in 2010, the public have the opportunity of holding the SFO to 'proper' account for the fairness of the decision to prosecute, though this judgement will be based on very stale evidence. Besides, it was long ago …

Even when there is no explicitly political 'spin' to a case, what does seem highly plausible is that once the team of lawyers, accountants, and police focus upon a case, a momentum builds up in which it becomes hard to call off a prosecution. There are no statistics on how many cases initially accepted after 'case vetting' by the SFO staff are subsequently not prosecuted, but Case Controllers possess low status compared with external counsel, and some tend to be deferential towards their recommendations when they advise on prosecution. Although the case vetting officer is not normally the Case Controller, unlike some other cases (except, from a police perspective, major enquiries), so much money is poured into the investigation of an SFO case that it can look like incompetence and a vast waste of money, or even a 'cover-up'[22] if no prosecution results. If – as happened up to a point over the manipulation of the stock market in the Blue Arrow and Guinness cases – independent counsel acting for the Crown appear to be waging a cultural war against what they view as corrupt accepted practice within 'the Establishment', the momentum of the prosecution is carried along in a wave of enthusiasm, and one arrives at the prosecution of large numbers of defendants. The current policy and practice of the SFO is far removed from this, and the Director is well aware not only of the financial limitations of pursuing investigations to prosecution but also of the need to leverage its efforts via a more general 'fraud and corruption reduction' strategy. This shift away from reliance on the criminal justice process has generated much criticism, and difficulties in the courts over plea negotiations.

The emotional contradiction many people experience when reviewing the prosecution of white-collar crime is that convicting 'the suits' may be seen as a necessary prerequisite of 'equal justice'. This is brilliantly captured in *Bonfire of the Vanities*, where the prosecutors long to put some rich white guys in jail, instead of the poor blacks whom they feel deep down have little real alternative to crime (Wolfe, 1987). Serious fraud and corruption prosecutors might get it wrong either in imagining possible lines of defence or in imputing culpability.[23] On the other hand, the depth of prejudicial publicity which follows a corporate collapse is a powerful impetus to carry people forward to prosecution, fuelled by media suspicions of 'cover up' if they do not do so. The prosecution of white-collar crime, as much as any other, entails the perpetual refrains of 'was he behaving dishonestly?' and 'what did he know and what was he told about this transaction?' The criminal law bifurcates people into the crude binary division of 'guilty' *or* 'innocent', and in the complex world of corporate actions where there are so many people who are potentially indictable, this yields strange and bitter fruit, in which many of the prosecution witnesses are as unattractive and prone to generate disinformation as are the defendants.

Even before the current SFO Director announced the policy of seeking to get corporate bribers to volunteer confessions in return for more lenient treatment (which he is unable to guarantee),[24] there was debate about the role of informants in the criminal justice process. But it is a very rare case where, as in the first Guinness trial in 1990, the judge has to give a massively complex set of jury instructions which revolve around whether the Finance Director, Olivier Roux, was really an unindicted accomplice or was merely a key witness (source: trial transcript). Likewise, it is a curious system in which, because the Serious Fraud Office – which determines its own workload – considers itself to be 'full up' with large cases, a vast fraud is dealt with by the police under ordinary police powers, going on to the CPS, which the week before or after might have attracted the extra powers (and financial resources) of the SFO. Even if the government had decided to merge the SFO with the CPS Central Fraud Group (created in April 2010, after the merger with the Revenue and Customs Prosecution Office), this line-drawing problem of seriousness and complexity would not disappear. The business plan stresses independence and accountability for performance (http:// www.cps.gov.uk/your_cps/our_organisation/cfg/publications/interim_business_ plan_1_jan_2010.html),[25] but how these declarations will generate legitimacy is unclear. How the diminishing number of prosecutorial bodies will fit with the Economic Crime Agency, announced in June 2010, which plausibly will deal with cases currently investigated by the SFO, the Office of Fair Trading, and, to a lesser degree, by the Serious and Organised Crime Agency, remains to be seen. The Chancellor of the Exchequer observed (16 June 2010, http://www.hm-treasury. gov.uk/press_12_10.htm): 'We take white-collar crime as seriously as other crime and we are determined to simplify the confusing and overlapping responsibilities in this area in order to improve detection and enforcement.' But perceptions that elites are dealt with on different criteria than ordinary people are not shifted by declarations alone.

Conclusions

Compared with the voluminous literature on police accountability (Reiner, 2000), prosecutorial accountability has been largely neglected, at least prior to BAE. This is not true in France, Italy, Spain or even Switzerland, where high profile investigating magistrates have gone after political elites at home and abroad, and where there have been highly politicised attempts to restrain this vigour by bringing them under more central governmental control. The important issues of accountability raised by serious fraud and corruption prosecutions – and, perhaps even more importantly, by *non-prosecutions* and (in the USA) *deferred prosecutions* (used against business and professional elites to avoid the collateral damage from felony convictions) – are unlike most faced in other arenas, and arise principally because of the political (with a small or large 'p') ramifications of particular cases, exaggerated by the potential for asset recovery. These controversies include party political donations (including alleged 'cash for honours') from businesspeople – on which political parties became highly dependent from the 1980s onwards – who sought favours such as well-photographed dinners with the Prime Minister and other leading figures, used by them for subsequent PR purposes to impress people overseas as well as in the UK. They also include broader conceptions of 'public interest' which are difficult to unpack. In theory, prosecution decisions are made by the Directors of Public Prosecutions and of the Serious Fraud Office, autonomously from their political heads. However, they are also answerable to the Attorney General who in turn is answerable to Parliament. In practice, it is rare for answers to be given to current cases, but concern from MPs (including Ministers) can transmit across to those dealing with the case, and prosecutors are dependent on the government for funding. My research for the Royal Commission on Criminal Justice – and longer observations and interviews over the past three decades – did not enable me to disentangle whether the non-prosecution of senior industry or governmental persons in some cases was due to 'influence' or merely to the well-attested fact that remoteness from actual decisions makes it hard to convict people for corporate crime and therefore, consistent with the Code for Crown Prosecutors, arguably improper to prosecute them. A good illustration is the problem of ascertaining the role played by former Home Secretary Reginald Maudling in the corrupt building scandals of architect John Poulson and in the investment 'scams' of American Jerome Hoffman (Gillard, 1974), where a 'professional' judgement of the probability of conviction is hard to separate from a 'political' (and bureaucratic survival) judgement of the downside risks of acquittal (or, for that matter, of conviction).

Though their overall conviction rate (including guilty pleas) varies between two thirds and over 90 per cent, the low conviction rate in 'famous name' SFO prosecutions makes the Law Officers of the Crown as well as the case lawyers look bad, and this is something they normally seek to avoid. Bureaucracies need the support of politicians (including the Attorney General) for resources, and there have been major campaigns against the Serious Fraud Office under the rubric of insufficient courage and cost-effectiveness, whose deeper motivation may lie in the ambivalent feelings of politicians and businesspeople about the *desirability* of the effective prosecution of fraud. Finding what sort of system would plausibly provide the kind of transparency of decision-making that might reassure people that decisions were *not* influenced directly or indirectly by 'political' considerations is too major a task for our existing knowledge, but it seems unlikely that any system, even in theory, would meet all the necessary and sufficient conditions for 'true independence'. My object here has been to try to integrate some themes in 'white-collar crime control' with the mainstream of literature on police and prosecutorial accountability, and, in an arena unfamiliar to many criminologists, to raise some issues of major practical as well as ideological importance about the methodology of equal justice and impartiality. How to ensure high levels of motivation, skill and courage among prosecutors while giving them the independence that can mean freedom not to do enough remains an elusive task.

Acknowledgement

This chapter was written under the auspices of Economic and Social Research Council Professorial Fellowship (RES-051-27-0208).

References

Audit Commission (1993) *Helping with their Enquiries*, London: HMSO.

Braithwaite, J. (1984) *Corporate Crime in the Pharmaceutical Industry*, London: Routledge.

Carswell, J. (1960) *The South Sea Bubble*, London: Cresset Press.

Cicourel, A. (1968) *The Social Organisation of Juvenile Justice*, New York: John Wiley.

Corker, D. and Levi, M. (1996) Pre-trial publicity and its treatment in the English courts, *Criminal Law Review*, September: 622–632.

Feeley, M. and Simon, J. (2007) Folk devils and moral panics: an appreciation from North America, in D. Downes, P. Rock, C. Chinkin and C. Gearty (eds.), *Crime, Social Control and Human Rights*, Cullompton: Willan.

Fisse, B. and Braithwaite, J. (1993) *Corporations, Crime, and Accountability*, Cambridge: Cambridge University Press.

Fooks, G. (2003) Contrasts in tolerance: the curious politics of financial regulation, *Contemporary Politics*, 9(2): 127–142.

Fraud Trials Committee (1986) *Report*, London: HMSO.

Garland, D. (2008) On the concept of moral panic, *Crime, Media, Culture*, 4: 9–30.

Gillard, M. (1974) *A Little Pot of Money*, London: Private Eye and Andre Deutsch.

Honess, T., Barker, S., Charman, E. and Levi, M. (2002) Empirical and legal perspectives in the impact of pre-trial publicity, *Criminal Law Review*, September: 719–727.

Levi, M. (1987) *Regulating Fraud: White-Collar Crime and the Criminal Process*, London: Routledge.

Levi, M. (1991) Sentencing white-collar crime in the dark? The case of the Guinness Four, *The Howard Journal of Criminal Justice*, 30 (4) 257–279.

Levi, M. (1993) *The Investigation, Prosecution and Trial of Serious Fraud*, Royal Commission on Criminal Justice Research Study No.14, London: HMSO.

Levi, M. (2009) Suite revenge? The shaping of folk devils and moral panics about white-collar crimes, *British Journal of Criminology*, 49 (1): 48–67.

Levi, M. (2010) Serious tax fraud and noncompliance: a review of evidence on the differential impact of criminal and noncriminal proceedings, *Criminology and Public Policy*, 9(2): 449–469.

Maguire, M. and Norris, C. (1993) *The Conduct and Supervision of Criminal Investigations*, Royal Commission on Criminal Justice Research Study No.13, London: HMSO.

Mann, K. (1985) *Defending White-Collar Crime*, New Haven: Yale University Press.

McConville, M., Sanders, A. and Leng, R. (1991) *The Case for the Prosecution*, London: Routledge.

Reiner, R. (2000) *The Politics of the Police*, 3rd edn., Oxford: Oxford University Press.

Scott Report (1996) *Report of the Inquiry into the Export of Defence Equipment and Dual-Use Goods to Iraq and Related Prosecutions*, London: HMSO.

Thomas, C. (2010) *Are juries fair?* Research Series 1/10, London: Ministry of Justice.

Wolfe, T. (1987) *Bonfire of the Vanities*, London: Paladin.

Notes

1 It was doubtless a pleasant irony for the bank involved that its Suspicious Activity Report alerted the authorities to the misconduct of this former anti-white-collar crime crusader who had zealously pursued many banks with financial penalties for misconduct.

2 Technically, even in pre-devolution days, Scotland developed more FIG-like separate arrangements under the Crown Office with some enhanced powers, so this applied mainly to England and Wales, but was intended to cast a halo also over the financial services community in Edinburgh (author interviews).

3 *HC Deb* 13 February 1986 vol 91 cc1148.

4 The 'buggers' referred to were the solicitors acting for the liquidators of Polly Peck, who had seized his expensive watch rather than, as popularly believed, the Serious Fraud Office, though the latter may have been included in the term.

5 The revelation that, subsequent to the exposé about the watch, he had accepted a free loan of a car for his wife from Nadir's Public Relations advisers was a further accelerant of his departure.

6 He has announced his desire to return several times, most recently in June 2010. http://www.timesonline.co.uk/tol/news/uk/crime/article7145186.ece

7 When used in this article, the term 'policing' includes non-police agencies.

8 This power was used to stop what would have been 'Guinness 3' when, to the consternation of the police, it was decided that following a confidential submission by the defence, there was insufficient evidence to support a prosecution against a senior partner in the major stockbroking firm Cazenove. One interpretation of this decision to drop charges is that it was a 'political' decision to avoid prosecuting the most elite of those charged in Guinness; another, which I find more plausible, is that the submission made it likely that key prosecution witnesses would be discredited in the subsequent trial, leading it to collapse.

9 Contentious issues have arisen mainly in the context of extradition of white-collar defendants to the USA where, it has been alleged in the well-funded PR campaigns of 'the NatWest Three' and later cases such as alleged price-fixer Ian Norris (http://www.supremecourt.gov.uk/decided-cases/docs/UKSC_2009_0052_Judgement.pdf) and the computer hacker Gary McKinnon, they are unfairly disadvantaged.

10 Walter Merricks, a dissenting member of the Roskill Committee, lobbied hard with the media on behalf of the Law Society to suggest that the proposals were too Draconian.

11 Indeed in some respects, it may act to the defendant's *advantage*, since it creates a pressure not to give evidence which otherwise s/he might be tempted to give!

12 There is currently no case law on what constitutes reasonable suspicion by the SFO on which their powers may be triggered. The conceptual latitude here is considerable, though in practice, the use of powers is limited because the SFO restricts itself to a modest number of cases under investigation at any one time. It seems extraordinary, however, that the powers of the state to require the suspect's co-operation should depend on the existing caseload of the SFO rather than on any inherent qualities of the case to be investigated. Current (2010) guidelines for case acceptance are:

The key factors we consider before taking on a case are:
- Does the value of the alleged fraud exceed £1 million? Is there a significant international dimension?
- Is the case likely to be of widespread public concern? Does the case require highly specialised knowledge, e.g. of financial markets? Is there a need to use the SFO's special powers, such as Section 2 of the Criminal Justice Act?

Serious or complex: what do we look for?
In addition to the above criteria we look for factors such as:

Seriousness

Whether the case involves or is linked to organised crime; whether the fraud will impact on the integrity of the financial market; whether there is a wider group than shareholders or creditors who have lost money as a result of the alleged fraud; whether the fraudsters have targeted financial institutions and government (local or central) or other public serving authorities

Compexity

Whether the case involves multiple countries; whether the evidence to be obtained during the course of the investigation will be found in multiple locations (within the UK or in other countries); whether the case involves multiple and complex financial transactions – e.g. involving many companies, accounts, Trusts and countries; whether the investigation will need to involve a large accountancy analysis.

13   One prosecutor was disciplined for failing to ensure that documents which were ordered to be sealed pending a court ruling on legal professional privilege were not tampered with.

14   As the Scott enquiry showed, the careful 'manufacture' and harmonisation of civil servants' witness statements was a crucial part of what plainly would have been a miscarriage of justice had they been convicted. However, the 'negotiation' of statements was carried out by civil servants themselves rather than by police or even by the investigations division of Customs & Excise.

15   I am not arguing here for the sort of libertarian 'freeze' that (by inference) McConville *et al.* (1991) get into, where because one cannot be certain that X did Y, we should prosecute or convict almost no-one. That might simply lead to mass vigilantism, with even less respect for due process and evidence.

16   The vendors of arms to Iraq, whether encouraged by the security services or not, make unlikely heroes for civil libertarians!

17   I have no evidence that would enable me to test the accusations, but the assertion by Nadir's counsel that no High Court judge is bribable because none has been accused in the past is unimpressive logic. Those who initially made the allegations to the police have now fled to Nadir's hideaway in the Turkish Republic of North Cyprus, alleging now that the police put them up to it (which unsurprisingly is strongly denied); it seems reasonable to question what the motivation of the police would be for such action. However, the possibility of such allegations – and the conviction of several county judges in a long-running undercover investigation in Chicago – was one reason why I recommended that defendants should be able to opt for trial without jury subject to the consent of both judge and prosecution. (This route away from possible jury prejudice was ignored by the Royal Commission.) The DPP's Office – the DPP having herself been Director of the SFO at the time of the main investigation – has subsequently decided that there should be no prosecution of those alleged to have been involved in the plot.

18   Although on balance, Thomas's (2010) research gave the jury system a clean bill of health, her study did not focus on what happens in accusations against elites.

19   It is hard to believe that this prosecution decision, taken by HM Customs & Excise, was undertaken with top-level governmental approval, since many outside that department appreciated the risk that 'the wheel would come off' (as it did), and would have judged it not worth that symbolic gain. Once taken, it may have seemed too hard to work out how to stop the prosecution. However, what is crucial is that the charges involved *deception* of the DTI officials, and it is devastatingly obvious that they were not deceived about the export licence applications.

20   The convictions were later quashed by the Court of Appeal: *R v Daghir*, *The Guardian*, May 25 and 26, 1994.

21   The overlap between political interference and 'legal advice' arises from the dual role of the Attorney General.

22 During 1994, after a preliminary investigation and review of extensive evidence provided by a private investigator on behalf of (formerly) wealthy Lloyd's 'names', the SFO controversially decided that there was insufficient evidence to justify their proceeding against those involved in managing the Gouda Walker syndicate. This was viewed by some as 'the Establishment' closing ranks, and some of those allegedly defrauded who had seen the original report remained dissatisfied by the SFO decision. How can we tell who was right? Transnational bribery cases raise similar issues.

23 As Braithwaite (1984) and Fisse and Braithwaite (1993) demonstrate, it is astonishing how lines of accountability that are clear for managerial purposes suddenly become opaque when interrogated critically by outsiders. The apparent ignorance displayed by all senior Cabinet ministers except Michael Heseltine of the change in policy over the supply of arms to Iraq is another case in point.

24 See the important cases of *R v Dougall* [2010] EWCA Crim 1048; and *R v Innospec* [2010] EW Misc 7 (EWCC), which represent the determination of the judiciary not to allow the SFO Director to agree specific sentences with the accused in return for their cooperation.

25 RCPO measures until 31 March 2010 included:

- A conviction rate of 85%.
- No more than 2.5% of cases in which a jury is empanelled result in a judge-directed acquittal.
- The number of closed cases at 31 March is equal to or greater than the number of cases received during the previous 12 months.
- Where a trial is ineffective, this will be due to prosecutorial error in no more than 2.5% of instances.

Part IVa

Country reports

Countries with criminal liability

12 Country report: Austria

Ingrid Mitgutsch

Introduction

Under the 'Second Protocol to the Convention on the Protection of the European Communities' Financial Interests', Austria had been obliged to establish 'effective, proportionate and dissuasive sanctions' against corporations which commit offences.[1] Having been granted a transitional period of five years, Austria had to comply with this obligation by 19 June 2002. It was nonetheless one of the last member states to fulfil the requirements. It was only on 1 January 2006 that a new 'Act on the Liability of Corporations for Criminal Offences'[2] (Corporate Liability Act; CLA) entered into force in Austria. Like any individual perpetrator, corporations can now be prosecuted and convicted, i.e. held criminally responsible for various offences. The CLA consists of 30 articles which determine the substantive responsibility of corporations as well as sanctions (§§ 1–12), special provisions on criminal procedure (§§ 13–27) and concluding formal provisions (§§ 28–30). Thus the CLA complements the already existing codes of criminal law and criminal procedure[3] which now apply also to corporations unless their scope is restricted exclusively to natural persons (§ 12 sect CLA).

The scope and test of corporate criminal liability

With regard to the offences referred to by the CLA, the Austrian legislation takes a rather broad approach.[4] By referring to 'Straftaten', i.e. to offences, in general and without further restrictions, the new act applies to any kind of criminal offence which is contained either in Austria's penal code or in any other Austrian statute (§ 1 sect 1 CLA). Thus, the CLA applies not only to the offences which had been the initial target of the obligations under European law, such as fraud, money laundering or other offences against the communities' financial interests, but also to offences which are traditionally committed by natural persons, like negligent killing or bodily injury.[5]

Organisations covered

In this respect, the CLA's approach to the question is similarly broad: in principle, any kind of corporation, even the state, municipalities and churches or other religious groups, no matter if they have legal personality or not,[6] can now commit offences which will entail the corporation's criminal liability. The only exceptions the CLA provides for are the inheritance after the death of a decedent, the state or a municipality when acting by sovereign power and churches or other religious groups when providing pastoral counselling (§ 1 sect 2 and 3 no 3 CLA).

Test of corporate criminal liability

According to § 3 sect 1 CLA, the offence in question must be either committed for the (direct)[7] benefit of the corporation or constitute an infringement of the corporation's duties (which may derive from the whole legal system, especially from civil and/or labour law, and which include the duties as an employer as well as the duties according to health and safety regulations etc.).[8]

In addition, it is necessary to show that an individual has engaged in wrongful conduct which may then be imputed to the corporation. In this connection, two alternatives may be distinguished, depending on whether or not the individual is a decision-maker within the corporation. According to § 2 CLA, decision-makers are persons who have the power to represent the corporation, who have internal supervisory power or who exert essential influence over the corporation in any other way.

Whenever a decision-maker commits a criminal offence, the offence can be imputed to the corporation. The corporation's criminal liability thus depends on the fact that the decision-maker has acted unlawfully, i.e. without a defence, and with individual fault (§ 3 sect 2 CLA).

According to the second (and more innovative) alternative basis of corporate liability, provided for in § 3 sect 3 CLA, a corporation may be held criminally liable whenever a criminal offence has been committed by a staff member which has been facilitated by a decision-maker neglecting his or her reasonable and necessary diligence in supervising the staff member. In this connection, it has to be noted that the responsibility of the corporation also varies according to the *mens rea* of the staff member: if the staff member acts intentionally, the corporation will also be responsible for an intentional offence, even if the decision-maker who has failed to control the staff only acted negligently; on the other hand, if the staff member acts negligently, then the corporation will only be liable for an offence of negligence even if the decision-maker acted intentionally. As to individual fault, however, corporate criminal liability does not depend on the fault of the staff member but on the fault of the decision-maker failing to exert due diligence.[9]

Liability of directors and corporate officers

In this connection it has to be noted that, according to § 3 sect 4 CLA, corporate criminal liability is neither subsidiary to individual liability nor does it prevail. Neither kind of criminal liability excludes the other, so that in principle, cumulative proceedings and sanctions against an individual, in many cases an employee (decision-makers as well as staff members) of the corporation in question, and the corporation itself are possible.[10]

Sanctions and sentencing

Under the CLA, only fines may be imposed on a convicted corporation (§ 4 sect 1 CLA). Other forms of sanctions which were discussed prior to the implementation of the CLA[11] but were not adopted included (limited or unlimited) supervision of the corporation, various restraints of its competences and even the liquidation of the corporation. The calculation of the fine which can be imposed on the delinquent corporation follows the traditional Austrian daily rate system which combines the gravity of the offence on the one hand with the economic situation of the convicted defendant (in case of corporations with their financial return) on the other.[12] Fines are not measured in absolute numbers but instead in daily rates, the number of which increases according to the gravity of the offence. The minimum number of daily rates is 40, whereas the maximum number is 180 (§ 4 sect 3 CLA). Daily rates have to be fixed according to the corporation's daily financial return and vary from €50 to €10,000. Thus the maximum daily fine a convicted corporation may be obliged to pay is €1,800,000. When the convicted corporation is a non-profit organisation, i.e. a humanitarian or religious organisation, the daily rate varies from €2 to €500 (§ 4 sect 4 CLA).

As is the case with sanctions against natural persons, the fines which are imposed on the corporations are subject to aggravating or mitigating factors (§ 5 CLA) and to (full or partial) suspension which may be combined with certain obligations, such as the obligation to pay for the damages caused by the corporation's offence. The suspension may also be withdrawn if the corporation does not comply with the obligations described above or is convicted anew during the period of probation (§§ 6 ff CLA).

It should be noted that in cases where, for some reason, the corporation is not able to pay the respective fine, recourse to decision-makers or other staff members is explicitly prohibited under § 11 CLA.

Investigation, prosecution and proceedings

In proceedings against corporations, general rules of criminal procedure such as the Austrian Criminal Procedure Code (§ 14 sect 1 CLA) apply. The proceedings may be combined with those against an individual person. If this is the case, then the proceedings against the corporation fall under the jurisdiction of the court which has jurisdiction over the natural person's offences (§ 15 sect 1 CLA).

If the proceedings are conducted separately, then jurisdiction for the trial of the corporation is determined by the location of the corporation's head office (§ 15 sect 2 CLA). The latter test applies also to cases where there are no proceedings against an individual (proceedings against corporations not being dependent on a prosecution of an individual).

In criminal proceedings against a corporation, the corporation has not only the position, but also the rights of an accused (§ 15 sect 1 CLA). Nevertheless, its decision-makers have to be summoned and questioned as persons accused, whereas this applies to other staff members only if they are also individually charged with the offence in question (§ 17 sect 1 CLA).

In cases of combined proceedings, evidence at the trial will be given jointly with respect to both proceedings. The closing speech, however, will first be given only with respect to the individual. Only after a conviction of the individual will the proceedings continue with respect to the criminal liability of the corporation (§ 22 sect 1 and 2 CLA). When the natural person is acquitted, the prosecutor has three days to declare whether the charges against the corporation will be continued in a separate proceeding (§ 22 sect 3 CLA). A verdict by which a corporation is held criminally responsible may be appealed against according to general principles of criminal procedure (§ 24 CLA).

Prosecution of corporations lies in the hands of the public prosecutor (or the private prosecutor with regard to certain offences; § 13 sect 2 CLA and § 71 CPC), as is generally the case in Austrian criminal procedure (§ 20 CPC). The legislation of 2006, however, has brought a shift from the hitherto strict obligation of the prosecutor to take legal action whenever a conviction is deemed likely, towards a more relaxed attitude which gives the prosecutor the discretion to refrain from a prosecution which seems dispensable with respect to the gravity of the offence, the expected (and disproportionate) costs of the proceedings, etc.[13]

Waiver of prosecution is not permitted (§ 18 CLA) in cases where prosecution is necessary in order to fulfil the requirements of (individual or general) deterrence or where there is a particular public interest in the proceedings. There are, however, circumstances in which a waiver of prosecution according to § 18 CLA is not appropriate even though the offence in question is not a grave one. The CLA provides in § 19 that under certain conditions, 'diversion', i.e. an alternative way of ending (or of not even starting) criminal proceedings may be allowed. The prosecutor may also suspend a prosecution if the corporation proves it has paid all damages caused by its offence and fulfils certain tasks under § 19 sect 1 no 1 to 3 CLA, e.g. the performance of a certain amount of non-profit charitable work or the alteration of its organisational, personal or technical structures in order to prevent further offences.[14] Only after those requirements are successfully fulfilled, may the prosecutor definitely abandon all further proceedings.

Conclusion

The Corporate Liability Act of 2006 has been implemented in order to provide for adequate criminal prosecution and sanctioning of corporate misconduct in various areas, such as business life, protection of the environment or product liability. It is a comprehensive and well-balanced piece of legislation which fulfils only very few international standards.[15] However, so far, no cases of corporate criminal liability have been brought before the courts, and it remains to be seen whether the idea of corporations being held criminally liable will become an active part of Austrian legal life or if it will remain merely a means of fulfilling Austria's obligation under EU law, which does not mirror the cultural situation in the respective member states.

References

Boller, Die strafrechtliche Verantwortlichkeit von Verbänden nach dem VbVG (2007).
Frank-Thomasser/Punz, Das neue Unternehmensstrafrecht (2006).
Hilf, Kriminalpolitische Hintergründe und ausgewählte Fragen des materiellrechtlichen Teils, in Landesgruppe Österreich der Internationalen Strafrechtsgesellschaft (AIDP), Die strafrechtliche Verantwortlichkeit von Verbänden (2009) 25.
Hilf, VbVG (2006).
S.Seiler, Strafrecht Allgemeiner Teil II (2008).
Schmoller, Criminal Responsibility of Corporations. A New Regulation in Austria, in: The Operation of the Serbian Legal System (2006).
Stärker, Verbandsverantwortlichkeitsgesetz (2007).
Steininger, Verbandsverantwortlichkeitsgesetz (2006).
Steininger, Verbandsverantwortlichkeitsgesetz Kommentar (2006).
Zeder, Ein Strafrecht juristischer Personen: Grundzüge einer Regelung in Österreich, ÖJZ (2001) 630 ff.
Zeder, VbVG (2006).
Zirn, Die Normadressaten des VbVG, in *Hilf/Pateter/Schick/Soyer* (Eds), Unternehmensverteidigung und Prävention im Strafrecht (2007) 55.

Notes

1 See *Zeder,* VbVG 9 ff.
2 BGBl I 2005/151.
3 *Steininger,* Verbandsverantwortlichkeitsgesetz Kap 1 Rz 2 ff.
4 *Schmoller,* Responsibility 187.
5 EBRV 994 BlgNR 22. GP 16.
6 *Zirn,* Normadressaten 55 ff; *Steininger,* Verbandsverantwortlichkeitsgesetz Kommentar § 1 Rz 14 ff; *Stärker,* Verbandsverantwortlichkeitsgesetz § 1 Anm 5.
7 *Steininger,* Verbandsverantwortlichkeitsgesetz Kommentar § 3 Rz 9 f; vs *Boller,* Verantwortlichkeit 159.
8 See *Steininger,* Verbandsverantwortlichkeitsgesetz Kommentar § 3 Rz 15.
9 *Steininger,* Verbandsverantwortlichkeitsgesetz Kommentar § 3 Rz 50; *Schmoller,* Responsibility 189; *Frank-Thomasser/Punz,* Unternehmensstrafrecht 10.
10 EBRV 994 BlgNR 22. GP 23 f.
11 See *Hilf,* Hintergründe 45 ff; *Zeder,* ÖJZ 2001, 630 ff.
12 *S.Seiler,* Strafrecht Allgemeiner Teil II Rz 42 ff.
13 *Schmoller,* Responsibility 193.
14 *Boller,* Verantwortlichkeit 245 ff; *Schmoller,* Responsibility 193.
15 *Hilf,* VbVG, Einführung 11 and 27 f.

13 Country report: Belgium

Melanie Ramkissoon

Introduction

Business entities may be criminally prosecuted in Belgium for violation of the Penal Code. The criminal liability of legal persons was established under the Belgian legal system with the introduction of the Act of 4 May 1999, which amends the Criminal Code. Of particular relevance are Article 5 defining liability, and Articles 7*bis*, 35–37*bis*, and 41*bis* on the applicable penalties. The same Act also amends other legal provisions, such as the Code of Criminal Procedure and the Code of Criminal Investigation.[1]

Article 2 of the Act of 4 May 1999 re-introduced a new article 5 in the Criminal Code. Ever since 1934, there had not been any type of corporate criminal liability under Belgian law; since 1999, *societas delinquere non potest* has been transformed into *societas puniri potest*.

Scope and test of corporate criminal liability

Offences that legal persons can be held criminally liable for

In principle, legal persons which are subject to criminal liability can be held liable for any criminal offence under Belgian law. The latter distinguishes three types of criminal offences, defined by reference to their corresponding penalties:[2] (i) **crimes** (*misdaden* or *crimes*) which carry with them criminal penalties; (ii) **misdemeanours** (*wanbedrijven* or *délits*) which carry with them correctional penalties; and (iii) **contraventions** (*overtredingen* or *contraventions*) which carry with them police penalties.

While the principle remains that a legal person can be held liable for all three types of criminal offences, article 5.1 of the Belgian Criminal Code provides that it can only be held liable for 'criminal offences which have an intrinsic link with the legal person's goal or with guarding its interests', or for 'criminal offences which, according to the specific circumstances, have been committed on its behalf'.

The Cassation Court has interpreted the criterion of 'intrinsic link with the legal person's goal' as not requiring that the legal person's statutory goal needs to be directed towards the offence, but only that the offence needs to have been committed during the realisation of the said statutory goal.[3]

The implication of article 5.1 is that the organisation will not have to answer for acts of employees or agents having taken advantage of it and having acted for their own interests.

Legal entities subject to criminal liability

The scope of corporate criminal liability under the Belgian legal system is a broad one. Article 5 of the Criminal Code applies to both public and private legal persons, including partnerships. Furthermore, it expressly stipulates that the following economic actors are to be considered legal persons even though domestic law does not necessarily accord them legal personality:[4] temporary associations and joint ventures; companies referred to in Article 2.3 of the co-ordinated Acts on commercial companies;[5] companies which are in the process of being established; and civil partnerships which have not been constituted as a commercial company. Therefore, many types of economic actors can be held criminally liable. A 'legal personality' is not necessarily a prerequisite to criminal liability.

However, the same article expressly excludes a number of legal persons belonging to the public law/political sphere, which thus in effect receive criminal immunity:[6] the federal State, the regions, the communities, the provinces, Brussels and its suburbs, communes, intra-communal territorial bodies, the French Community Commission, the Flemish Community Commission, the Joint Community Commission, and public welfare centres (one for each commune). As is evident from this listing, virtually all public authorities are immune from criminal prosecution, and only a civil law suit could potentially be brought against such a defendant.

Subsidiaries

Under Belgian law, parent companies are not liable for the acts of their subsidiaries. However, if the parent company takes part in the dealings of its subsidiaries (or any third party), traditional rules of participation in a crime apply. According to one author, the Belgian parent company could be liable where the order to commit the offence, or acts necessary to it, were given or undertaken by the parent company in the furtherance of its own objectives or in defence of its interests, or where these acts were undertaken on its behalf.[7]

The test of liability

Under Belgian law, the criminal liability of legal persons is not a derived liability. For there to be proceedings and a conviction against a legal person, there is no need for evidence that an offence has been perpetrated by an individual who works for, or is otherwise associated with, the legal person.

Curiously, the law does not specify how responsibility for acts is to be attributed to legal persons. This is considered to be a factual matter that is best left to the assessment of the judge. The liability of a legal person may be based on the attitude of the legal or statutory bodies, or it may be established as a result of material acts committed by certain of its employees or representatives.

The general principle of criminal law which requires intent to be an element of an offence also applies to legal persons. The law makes it clear that, for a legal person to be held criminally liable, 'it must be established that the offence was the result of an intentional decision taken within the legal person, or, through a specific relationship of cause and effect, of negligence by the legal person'.[8] Since the legal definition of an offence requires intent, the decision will probably have been made at a higher level, although the law does not exclude the possibility that a legal person may be held liable for the action of a person at a lower level.[9]

Belgian law does not provide for multiple responsibility except in cases where it is clear that the offence can be attributed to a natural person who acted intentionally. Article 5.2 provides that: 'When the liability of a legal person is invoked only because of the action of a known natural person, only the person who committed the more serious offence can be convicted. If the known natural person committed the offence knowingly and willingly, he can be convicted at the same time as the legal person liable.'

Two situations may thus arise, depending on whether the known natural person committed an offence or whether he/she committed the offence knowingly and wilfully. In the former situation, the judge will have to choose to convict either the natural person or the legal person. In the latter, both the natural and legal persons can be convicted.

Liability of directors and corporate officers

In situations where a legal person is liable solely because of the intervention of an identified natural person, only the person who committed the more serious fault may be convicted. If the natural person committed the fault knowingly and wilfully, he/she may be convicted at the same time as the legal person.[10]

The scope (in the sense of *rationae materiae*) of corporate criminal liability in Belgium covers all offences, whether or not they require intention. For offences requiring intent, like bribery,[11] both an individual and a legal person might be liable, or either one of them could be liable while the other is not.[12] The scope (in the sense of *ratione personae*) of corporate criminal liability is equally broad, including both public and private legal persons, such as commercial companies and associations, as well as certain entities that do not have legal personality but are assimilated to legal persons.

In Belgium, article 61 of the Companies Code allows a corporate body to be a manager or a member of the Board of Directors of a company. Therefore, a natural person must be assigned to oversee the activities of the corporate person, and to act on its behalf. The assigned natural person will assume the same criminal and civil liability as if he/she was performing the same activity on his/

her own behalf. Provisions on criminal liability of managers, administrators and members of the Board of Directors are thus directly applicable to the assigned natural person.[13]

Sanctions and sentencing

Under Belgian law, companies and other legal persons are liable to fines of up to €10 million or more, depending on the nature of the offence and, in the case of bribery, on the public official bribed.[14]

Elements taken into consideration by the judge in applying penalties

Penalties are determined by the judge based on the circumstances surrounding the crime and the personal characteristics of the perpetrators. The Criminal Code includes special provisions for extenuating and aggravating circumstances, according to which the judge may take various factors into account, when he determines the penalty. Under Belgian law, these rules are applicable to legal persons too. Furthermore, under the probation law of 29 June 1964 (art. 18), a legal person may also obtain a suspended or deferred sentence.

In cases of foreign bribery, there are four essential factors in determining the penalty: the gravity of the offence, the offender's legal history, the length of proceedings, and the pressure exerted on the offender. The first two may constitute aggravating circumstances, while the last two may be seen as extenuating circumstances.[15]

Insofar as fines are concerned, art. 41*bis* of the Criminal Code provides for a specific conversion mechanism for converting the duration of prison sentences for natural persons into a monetary penalty for legal persons.[16] If the offence committed is a crime or a misdemeanour, the mechanism is that: where the law provides for a life-long prison sentence, the corresponding fine ranges between 240,000 and 720,000 Belgian Francs;[17] where the law provides for both imprisonment and a fine, the corresponding fine is between 500 Belgian Francs (to be multiplied by the number of months of the minimum prison sentence) and 2,000 Belgian Francs (to be multiplied by the number of months of the maximum prison sentence); where the offence only carries a fine, the correspondent fine for the legal person will be the same. A similar mechanism, with lower amounts, has been provided for contraventions. In practice, however, in order to find out the real level of the fine (one that reflects inflation), the amounts mentioned above should be multiplied by 45.[18]

Other sentences available

Penalties are not limited to fines; accessory penalties are also available. According to article 7*bis* of the Criminal Code, a judge may order the dissolution of the company, prohibition on the conduct of its corporate business, the closure of one or more of its establishments, or the publication/dissemination of the judgment.

The judge may also order the confiscation of assets which were the object of the criminal offence, were used for committing the offence, were the result of the offence, or were acquired directly from the offence (pursuant to articles 42 seq. of the Criminal Code).

Articles 42–43 provide the substantive and procedural details of the penalty of confiscation, which applies to both legal and natural persons. Article 43 stipulates that, if the offence constitutes a crime or a misdemeanour, the sanction of special confiscation will always apply. In cases involving a trans-national company, the sanction of special confiscation can be imposed even if the assets to be confiscated are situated outside Belgian territory.[19]

Finally, under the legislation governing public procurement and the contractual clauses for the granting of public export guarantees, the company that perpetrated the offence may also have its export privileges suspended, and be barred from public procurement in Belgium.

Criminal remedies

Article 7*bis* of the Belgian Criminal Code provides details of the statutory criminal penalties applicable to corporate bodies. For crimes, misdemeanours and contraventions, a fine or a special forfeiture can be imposed. Additional penalties for crimes and misdemeanours include dissolution (not applicable to public organisations), prohibition of activities linked with the company's object (except for public service activities), closure of one or more establishments (except those where public services are performed), and publication of the Court decision.

Article 41*bis* of the Belgian Penal Code provides a conversion mechanism between the prison sentence applicable to natural persons (in criminal cases) and corresponding fines applicable to corporate bodies. Corresponding to a sentence of life imprisonment is a fine between €240,000 and €700,000. Where the law provides imprisonment and/or a fine for the natural person, the corresponding sentence for a legal person is a fine ranging from €500 (to be multiplied by the number of months for minimum imprisonment) to €2,000 (to be multiplied by the number of months for maximum imprisonment). Where the sentence for an individual is a fine, the corresponding sentence for a legal person is the same.

Non-criminal remedies

A number of non-criminal penalties may be imposed on legal persons. These are *sui generis* penalties created at European level for violations such as non-compliance with the principle of free competition, as well as administrative penalties and fines.[20]

Conclusion

Since the law of 4 May 1999 was introduced, Belgian judges have used it to a significant extent. Research undertaken by the criminal police[21] shows that, by the end of April 2004, 381 judgments had been passed (in all areas of law), using various provisions of the 1999 law.

The most frequent convictions were for violations of labour laws (47 per cent of the judgments), environmental law (9 per cent), customs regulations (9 per cent), and company law (8 per cent). Fewer than 6 per cent of the convictions were for economic and financial offences, and they were mainly related to articles 196 and 197 of the Criminal Code (forgery and use of forgeries) and article 193 (falsifying accounts). Apart from a ruling in a minor case involving corruption of police officers in a small Belgian town, no legal person has been convicted for bribery of a public official. The great majority of convictions involved unintentional crimes, which is not surprising, given the lack of clarity in article 5 of the Criminal Code about how to determine the mental element of the offence.

Also according to this research, the convictions that took place through April 2004 covered a wide range of legal entities: business corporations (almost 40 per cent) and private companies (50 per cent), but also not-for-profit organisations, partnerships, joint stock companies, cooperatives, and public law companies. Insofar as sanctions are concerned, Belgian judges resort to a wide range of principal and accessory penalties: fines (64.3 per cent of convicted companies), confiscation (in nearly 10 per cent of cases) and accessory penalties (8 per cent of cases).

It is interesting to note that, despite the existing Belgian principle of '*décumulation*' between the criminal liabilities of legal persons and individuals, the research shows that, in 346 out of the 381 recorded cases, individuals were prosecuted together with the company.

Notes

1 See generally P. Waeterinck, *De strafrechtelijke verantwoordelijkheid van de rechtspersoon, een kritische analyse van enkele capita selecta uit de eerste rechtspraak*, in A. De Nauw (ed.), *Strafrecht van nu en straks*, Brugge, die Keure, 2003; A. Masset, *La loi du 4 mai 1999 instaurant la responsabilité pénale des personnes morales: une extension du filet pénal modalisé*, J.T. 1999; H. Van Bavel, *De wet van 4 mei 1999 tot invoering van de strafrechtelijke verantwoordelijkheid van rechtspersonen*, A.J.T. 1999–2000. Cf. OECD report 'Belgium: Review of Implementation of the Convention and 1997 Recommendation', available at: http://www.oecd.org/dataoecd/13/7/2385130.pdf

2 Cf. a survey conducted as part of *Commerce, Crime, and Conflict: A Comparative Survey of Legal Remedies for Private Sector Liability for Grave Breaches of International Law and Related Illicit Economic Activities: Belgium*, FAFO, pp. 6–7, available at: http://www.fafo.no/liabilities/CCCSurveyBelgium06Sep2006.pdf

3 Ibid., pp. 8–10.

4 S. Van Dyck, *De (privaatrechtelijke) rechtspersoon als strafbare dader van een misdrijf. Het toepassingsgebied rationel societatis privati iuris van de wet van 4 mei 1999*, T. Strafr. 2001, pp. 227–260.

5   This is the agricultural company, which is governed by Book XIII of the Belgian Company Code (articles 789–838).

6   S. Van Garsse, *De strafrechtelijke verantwoordelijkheid van publiekrechtelijke rechtspersonen*, C.D.P.K. 2000, pp. 347–359.

7   Damien Vandermeersch, *La loi du 4 mai 1999 instaurant la responsabilité pénale des personnes morales*, p. 4 (study submitted to the OECD examining team during the Phase 2 on-site visit to Belgium). See OECD phase 2 Report, p. 39.

8   *Proposition de loi instaurant la responsabilité pénale des personnes morales*, Vandenberghe, *Doc. Parl.*, 1-1217/1, 23 December 1998, p. 2. It covers, for example, the case in which defective internal organisation of the legal person, inadequate safety measures or unreasonable budget restrictions created conditions that made it possible to commit the offence.

9   Cf. OECD Report, p. 8.

10   Allens Arthur Robinson, Corporate Culture, p. 48, http://198.170.85.29/Allens-Arthur-Robinson-Corporate-Culture-paper-for-Ruggie-Feb-2008.pdf

11   Corruption in Belgium is an intentional offence; the act must have been committed knowingly and wilfully.

12   For non-intentional offences, concurrent liability is a complex matter that can require a comparison of the degrees of fault of the individual and the legal person.

13   Cf. 'Corporate Criminal Liability in Belgium' in *Belgium Iustica Newsletter*, February 2009, p. 2, http://www.legalink.ch/xms/files/Newsletter/Belgium_Iustica_newsletter_3.pdf

14   Article 41*bis* of the Criminal Code provides a mechanism for converting prison sentences to fines in the case of a legal person (cf. OECD Phase 2 Report, p. 40).

15   OECD Phase 2 Report, p. 40.

16   For the many difficulties raised by this article and its conversion mechanism, see R. Verstraeten and B. Spriet, *De rechtspersoon en zijn geldboete*, in *Liber Amicorum Jean Dujardin*, Kluwer, 2001, p. 321.

17   One euro is approximately 40 Belgian Francs.

18   See the Law of 5 March 1952 on 'opdecimes' on monetary penalties in criminal cases, plus an annual Royal Decree implementing this law.

19   For details about the trans-nationality issue, see G. Vermeulen, *Internationale strafrechtelijke aspecten bij beslag en inverbeurdverklaring*, in D. Vandermeersch and others, *Beslag en verbeurdverklaring van criminele voordelen*, Maklu, 2004. Cf. the FAFO Survey, pp. 8–10.

20   See *Corporate Criminal Liability in Belgium*, p. 2.

21   *L'application de la loi du 4 mai 1999 instaurant la responsabilité pénale des personnes morales sous forme de statistiques*, Brussels: SPF Justice, Criminal Police Office, 30 April 2004.

14 Country report: Denmark

Ana-Maria Pascal

Introduction

Corporate criminal liability was introduced in Denmark in 1996, when a new chapter was added to the Danish Criminal Code – Chapter 5, 'Liability of Legal Entities'. Key sections are articles 25–27, dealing with the scope and test of liability. According to Robinson,[1] Denmark has created the widest basis of criminal liability for legal entities. Because the wording of the Code allows for multiple interpretations, the court has wide discretion in assessing culpability and sentencing.

Article 25 of the Code provides that 'legal persons may be punished by a fine, if such punishment is authorised by law or by rules pursuant thereto'. This covers any offence included in the Code. The only limitations stated in the section on corporate criminal liability refer to the liability of municipalities and state authorities (see below).

The scope and test of corporate criminal liability

Scope of liability

Article 26 of the Danish Criminal Code provides that

(1) Unless otherwise stated, provisions on criminal responsibility for legal persons etc. apply to any legal person, including joint-stock companies, co-operative societies, partnerships, associations, foundations, estates, municipalities and state authorities.

(2) Furthermore, such provisions apply to one-person businesses if, considering their size and organisation, these are comparable to the companies referred to in subsection (1) above.

The last provision is generally understood to refer to sole proprietorships with at least 10 employees. Other considerations such as the volume of sales and profits would also be relevant.

State authorities

Article 27(2) of the Danish Criminal Code states that

> Agencies of the state and of municipalities may only be punished for acts committed in the course of the performance of functions comparable to functions exercised by natural or legal persons.

Unless otherwise stated, the provisions on corporate liability laid down in Article 26(1) apply to municipal and state authorities. However, such entities may only be punished for violations committed while carrying out activities corresponding to those carried out by private individuals or companies, therefore in their entrepreneurial activity only. This includes functions such as telecommunications, public transport etc. State institutions and municipalities cannot be held liable for offences committed in connection to the exercise of official powers.[2]

Parent companies and subsidiaries

Under the section on 'special rules for parent companies and subsidiaries', the DPP guidelines provide that a parent company is not liable for offences committed by its subsidiaries. Conversely, subsidiaries are not criminally liable for offences committed by parent companies. International bodies like the OECD[3] have expressed concerns about this provision, which places outside of Danish jurisdiction foreign bribery acts committed by Danish companies abroad and could discourage Danish law enforcement agencies from investigating such acts.

Although the general rule is that only the subsidiary can be prosecuted for offences committed within the subsidiary, a parent company may still be held liable, dependent on the circumstances and the type of offence. The parent company may, for instance, be prosecuted for lack of control or insufficient instructions, or if the basis for the offence committed within a subsidiary is in fact a decision taken by the parent company.[4]

Test of liability

Identification (and, even less, conviction) of individual offender(s) is not a *sine qua non* requirement for holding the legal person criminally accountable under Danish law. During the trial of the legal person, however, it must be proved that 'someone' within the company committed the crime either intentionally or by negligence (dependent on the offence in question).

Under article 27(1) of the Danish Criminal Code,

> Criminal liability of a legal person is conditional upon a transgression having been committed within the establishment of this person by one or more persons connected to this legal person or by the legal person himself.

This provision does not, according to the Danish authorities,[5] restrict the application of the offence to high level employees and persons with managerial responsibilities. The person responsible for the offence does not have to be formally employed by the legal person; instead, a contractual relationship is sufficient. In terms of intent, it must be shown that the person in issue had the relevant mental state, whether negligence or intent.[6] If the corporate management or an executive employee acted with intent or gross negligence, not only the company but also the individual personally responsible must be prosecuted.

Under article 27(1), in order to hold a legal person criminally liable, it must be shown that (a) the offence has been committed in the course of its business, and (b) that the offence is attributable to one or more persons connected with (or contracted by) the company. Thus, offences committed in connection with purely private acts will not give rise to criminal corporate liability.

Indeed, acts or omissions are attributable to the company only if they relate to the carrying out of assignments for the company. That is why the phrase 'within the establishment' from article 27(2) should be read as meaning 'in the course of business', so as to exclude offences committed by employees while undertaking purely private acts. The rationale behind this is that such offences don't have the prerequisite functional link with the activity of the company, and therefore the latter should not be held liable.

However, acts which are contrary to corporate policy may still be attributed to the company, but not where such acts are 'totally abnormal'. It is less than clear what exactly counts as abnormal. Gorm Nielsen gives the example of an employee who used the fork on a fork lift truck to lift himself, even though there was a basket specifically for the purpose. The High Court acquitted, but the Supreme Court convicted, noting the act was not aberrant enough to warrant dismissal. Nielsen comments:

> The question of guilt is typically satisfied by an employee having negligently broken the rules. This is enough. Whether or not any blame attaches to management is irrelevant under Danish law. The company will also be found guilty in cases where management has been very active in ensuring observance of the law. The fact that it is irrelevant whether management has been active or passive is probably the question attracting most debate. But, if in order to obtain judgement against the company, the prosecutor has to prove the manager is personally liable, he may as well bring the charges against him personally. If managerial negligence must be proved, company liability will lose much of its meaning.[7]

If the corporate management or an executive employee of the company is found to have acted with intent or gross negligence, not only the company but also the individual(s) personally responsible must be prosecuted. Generally, the legal person and the natural person are tried together in the same proceeding, but it is possible to prosecute the legal person independently.

Liability of directors and company officials

Under Danish law, each director or company official will be judged individually, so there is, in principle, no risk of being liable for offences committed by other directors or employees.[8] However, since the general rule of complicity (article 23 of the Criminal Code) also applies to directors, in cases where an employee is found guilty of a criminal offence a director may be held liable for negligent complicity if he/she had an obligation to have issued orders and guidelines pertinent to the behaviour of the employee, and didn't.

According to the explanatory notes to the new act,[9] corporate liability is often considered to be the principle liability – especially if the negligence is not grave, or if the offence is committed by subordinate staff rather than executive management.[10] If, however, company management or an executive director is found to have acted with intent or gross negligence, they will also be prosecuted alongside the company.

If the company is wholly controlled by an individual (who is both the day-to-day manager and the main shareholder), prosecution is generally instituted against the individual.[11] It would be very unusual for the company to be prosecuted as well.

Investigation and prosecution

The Administration of Justice Act (AJA) sets out the rules on investigation and prosecution, which are the same in all criminal offences. There are no offence-specific rules. Section 742(2) of the AJA provides that the police must launch an investigation upon the laying of information (by a victim, competitor or any other source) or on its own initiative, where it may reasonably be presumed that a criminal offence has been committed. The police may decide to terminate the investigation in cases where no preliminary charge has been made during the investigation.

Danish criminal procedure is based on the principle of discretionary, rather than mandatory, prosecution. However, prosecutors will almost always take action when so warranted by the evidence. The prosecution service includes two specialised units: the Office of the Public Prosecutor for Serious Economic Crimes (SØK) and the Special International Crimes handling war crimes and crimes against humanity. The former includes 53 investigators and 23 prosecutors. It investigates and prosecutes serious cases of economic and financial crimes (e.g. fraud, embezzlement, breach of trust, tax offences, corruption, extortion, usury and insider trading). When deciding whether or not to investigate, the SØK looks at the complexity of the case, whether there is a link to organised crime, and whether special business methods were involved.[12]

A national Serious Fraud Office (SFO) led by a senior prosecutor handles investigations and prosecutions of the most serious economic crimes, including bribery. The SFO is comprised of expert investigators and prosecutors, who work in close cooperation with legal specialists during the investigative stage.

Upon completion of an investigation, the prosecutor determines whether or not to bring formal charges. The test in support of this decision is whether, considering the evidence available, a conviction is more probable than an acquittal. The prosecution may, in rare circumstances, decide to withdraw a charge despite the necessary evidence being in principle available. Such withdrawal may be affected in cases where the efforts and costs required to prosecute are not justified by the importance of the case and the expected punishment (section 721 of AJA).[13] Detailed rules governing the prosecuting authority are laid down in Part 10 of the AJA.

Sanctions and sentencing

Under the Danish Criminal Code, the imposition of fines for corporate crimes is governed by the same rules as those applying to natural persons. The fine will be fixed as a lump sum for offences laid down in special criminal laws (as opposed to the Criminal Code, which is generally applicable). The size of the fine is left to the discretion of the court. Thus there are no minimum or maximum limits applicable.[14]

Special consideration must be given to the nature of the offence (article 80), the perpetrator's capacity to pay, and the level of gain or amount saved following the perpetration of the offence (article 51(3)). These criteria should make it possible to impose substantially larger fines on a legal person than on a natural person. However, no statistical data could be obtained on the level of fines imposed on companies by Danish courts.

Other available sanctions include seizure and confiscation of assets and proceeds (e.g. profits or other benefits derived by the perpetrator from the unlawful act or other improper advantage obtained or retained through the offence), exclusion from participation in public tenders, and cancellation of export credit guarantees.

Conclusion and future directions

International agencies have expressed concern about the low level of sanctions imposed for serious economic and financial crimes in Denmark, as well as about the Danish provisions regarding jurisdiction (in particular, for parent companies and their foreign subsidiaries) and how these may have a negative impact on the level of investigation and prosecution of foreign bribery offences.

Given the latter concern, a bill proposing changes to the Criminal Code with respect to Danish jurisdiction was introduced to Parliament in November 2007.[15] The suggested amendments would have provided for more precise rules on criminal jurisdiction, including for crimes committed by legal persons. The bill was adopted the following year (act no. 490 of 17 June 2008). It achieves a comprehensive revision of the general provisions of the Criminal Code concerning Danish criminal jurisdiction.[16]

Measures have also been taken during the last three years addressed to the prevention and detection of foreign bribery through auditing and taxation. Since

2007, the Danish Central Tax Administration (SKAT) and the Public Prosecutor for Serious Economic Crime (SØK) have developed a special training course for Tax Officers in the Anti-Tax Fraud Units and the Tax Control Units in the Local Compliance Departments. The training consists of the following main components: how to detect and report corruption, bribery, money laundering and financing of terrorism; cooperation with the relevant law enforcement authorities; guidelines for companies to prevent them from becoming involved in such situations.[17]

With respect to improving the investigation and prosecution process, the Danish National Police College has intensified its training of police officers and prosecutors, by developing and delivering a special training programme on investigating financial crimes, including fraud and corruption.[18] This programme has been implemented since 2005.

In 2006, a reform of the police force was presented by a Danish Member of Parliament as a 'new way of fighting crimes in Denmark'. It envisaged an overall re-organisation of police units at district level with a strengthening of the role of the chief constables in fixing priorities and resources and the possibility of employing experts to assist investigators and prosecutors in complex cases.[19] The Danish police reform took effect on 1 January 2007 and 12 new police districts were established as a result. They are headed by commissioners, who report to the chief executive officer of the police, the National Commissioner. The Minister of Justice is the chief police authority.[20]

Given Denmark's relationship with Greenland and the Faroe Islands, the Minister of Justice introduced a bill regarding a new Greenlandic Criminal Code and a new Greenlandic Administration of Justice Act for the Danish Parliament, which were adopted in April 2008 and came into force on 1 January 2010. With the new laws in place, Greenland meets the requirements of the OECD Convention on Combating Bribery of Foreign Public Officials in International Business Transactions. With respect to the Faroe Islands, the Ministry of Justice prepared a decree setting out changes to the Criminal Code in the Islands. Based on these changes the Ministry of Justice will contact the Faroese authorities about bringing the Convention into force in the Faroe Islands.[21]

According to a 2008 Transparency International report on anti-corruption activities, Denmark is among sixteen countries that have a significant enforcement system in place. Problems reported include insufficient access to information about cases, deficient whistleblower protection, and lack of transparency in the internal processes of the Serious Economic Crime Squad and the Ministry of Justice. In 2008, there were 17 pending investigations into companies involved in the UN Oil-for-Food programme in Iraq (including Novo Nordisk), but no current investigations (as a formal decision of the Minister of Justice to proceed is needed).[22]

Last year, European officials noted that, given the generally low number of corruption cases in Denmark, it is difficult to foresee all consequences of the current legislation. They also criticised the low level of criminal sanctions in respect of bribery offences.[23]

Notes

1 Allens Arthur Robinson, *'Corporate Culture' as a Basis for the Criminal Liability of Corporations*, United Nations, February 2008, p. 58.
2 Dana Rone, *Legal Scientific Research on Institute of Criminal Liability of Legal Entities in Eight Countries – Nordic Countries (Finland, Sweden, Norway, Iceland and Denmark) and Baltic Countries (Latvia, Lithuania and Estonia)*, report prepared for the Ministry of Justice of the Republic of Latvia, March 2006, www.tm.gov.lv, p. 29.
3 Cf. OECD Phase 2 Report on Denmark, 2006, http://www.oecd.org/dataoecd/14/21/36994434.pdf, p. 54.
4 Kromann Reumert, Criminal Liability of Companies Survey: Denmark, Lex Mundi Publications, http://www.lexmundi.com/images/lexmundi/PDF/Business_Crimes/Crim_Liability_Denmark.pdf, 2008, p. 4.
5 Cf. OECD Phase 1 Report on Denmark, 2001, http://www.oecd.org/dataoecd/39/57/2018413.pdf, p. 9.
6 See Allens Arthur Robinson, supra, note 1.
7 Gorm Nielsen, 'Criminal Liability of Collective Entities – the Danish Model' in Eser, Heine and Huber (eds), *Criminal Responsibility of Legal and Collective Entities* (1999) 189, n 6, 192–193, cit. in Allens Arthur Robinson, supra, note 1.
8 Cf. Kromann Reumert, supra, note 4, p. 8.
9 The Director of Public Prosecutions has issued guidelines on the choice of liable persons in cases involving corporate liability. The guidelines are found in Notice No. 5/1999, which states that the general rule is to prosecute the company as such. See OECD Follow-up Report on Denmark (2008), http://www.oecd.org/dataoecd/4/56/41073747.pdf, p. 18.
10 See Rone, supra, note 1, p. 26.
11 Ibid., p. 27.
12 Ibid., p. 41.
13 Kromann Reumert, supra, note 4, p. 5.
14 Ibid., p. 2.
15 Cf. OECD Follow-up Report on Denmark, supra, note 9, p. 19.
16 See the *Fifth Periodic Report of Denmark Concerning the International Covenant on Economic, Social and Cultural Rights*, published by the Royal Danish Ministry of Foreign Affairs, December 2009, http://www.ft.dk/samling/20091/almdel/reu/bilag/259/789757/index.htm, p. 31.
17 Ibid., p. 10.
18 Ibid., p. 16.
19 OECD Phase 2 Report on Denmark, cf. supra, note 3, p. 39.
20 Cf. *Report on the Danish Police Reform*, published by Rigsrevisionen in August 2009, and available at http://www.rigsrevisionen.dk/media(1376,1033)/16-2008.pdf, p. 1.
21 Ibid., p. 17.
22 Fritz Heimann and Gillian Dell, *Progress Report 2008: Enforcement of the OECD Convention on Combating Bribery of Foreign Public Officials*, Transparency International, 24 June 2008, http://sup.kathimerini.gr/xtra/media/files/meletes/econ/offic240608.pdf
23 *Evaluation Report on Denmark on Incriminations*, Third Round, published by the Council of Europe's Group of States Against Corruption (GRECO), 2 July 2009, and available at http://www.coe.int/t/dghl/monitoring/greco/evaluations/round3/GrecoEval3(2008)9_Denmark_One_EN.pdf, p. 16.

15 Country report: Estonia

Ana-Maria Pascal

Introduction

Estonian law subjects legal persons to criminal liability. The Penal Code (PC), adopted in June 2001 and entered into force on 1 September 2002, provides for both criminal offences and administrative breaches. Similar to the situation in Lithuania, 'norms of the Penal Code of Estonia regarding legal entities contain features of formal offences, where importance of guilt is minimal'.[1]

According to the Estonian Penal Code, offences can be divided in two categories: criminal offences and misdemeanours. Section 3 of the Penal Code describes the former as offences 'provided for in this Code and the principal punishment prescribed for which in the case of natural persons is a pecuniary punishment or imprisonment and in the case of legal persons, a pecuniary punishment or compulsory dissolution'. A misdemeanour is 'an offence provided for in this Code or another Act and the principal punishment prescribed for which is a fine or detention'.[2]

The scope and test of liability

Scope of liability

Legal persons include general partnerships, limited partnerships, private limited companies, public limited companies, commercial associations, foundations and non-profit associations. Section 14(3) of the Estonian Penal Code expressly excludes the state, local governments and legal persons in public law from criminal liability. In the case of an infringement of the law by these organisations (considered to be acting in the public interest), a natural person may still be prosecuted and punished.

Legal persons are subject to criminal liability for four kinds of offences: environmental offences, copyright offences, crimes against order in the state, and offences related to inadequate fulfilment of various terms.

Test of liability

The grounds for holding legal persons criminally liable are given in Section 14 of the Penal Code, titled *Liability of Legal Persons*, which states that:

(1) In the cases provided by law, a legal person shall be held responsible for an act which is committed by a body or senior official thereof in the interest of the legal person.

(2) Prosecution of a legal person does not preclude prosecution of the natural person who committed the offence.

(3) The provisions of this Act do not apply to the state, local governments or to legal persons in public law.[3]

There is no precondition of identification or conviction of a natural person. The two main criteria stated in the first paragraph are the involvement of a senior official in the offence and the interest of the legal person. These are not defined in the Penal Code but in jurisprudence materials and other laws. Indeed, 'the Estonian penal law is based on the principle that when there is no definition of a legal concept in the penal law, the definition has to be derived from other laws (uniformity of legal order principle)'.[4] Sometimes, the particulars and the limits of applicability of the two elements have to be determined on a case-by-case basis.

Regarding the first criterion – that the offence be committed by a 'body or a senior official of the legal person' – the key question here is to establish the scope of these terms, as the higher the threshold (for 'senior official'), the more difficult it is to establish the liability of the legal person. The individual in question must have either acted directly or through an intermediary, or indeed instigated the perpetration of the offence.

If the offence was not committed by the 'general meeting' or the 'management board' (which are the main *bodies* of a legal person) but by one of its sections, departments, or offices, then a senior person must be identified in order to trigger the liability of the legal person. That individual can be, for instance, the chief executive responsible for the particular section or department in which the offence was committed.

Whether a natural person is a senior official depends on his/her authority and position within the organisation. The natural person must have decision-making power that identifies him/her with the legal person and its course of action. This includes, for example, executive directors, accountants, etc.[5]

The rationale behind the second criterion – that the crime be committed in the interests of the legal person – is to separate acts of individuals committed for personal gain from those committed to benefit the legal person. Benefit is interpreted broadly to include both pecuniary and non-pecuniary advantage. The benefit to the legal person needs to be immediately identifiable and any monetary benefit need not show up in the book-keeping.[6] The main point of this requirement is, therefore, to ensure that offences committed when individuals act on their own behalf and for their own personal interest (rather than in the interest of the legal person) do not trigger corporate liability.

Investigation and prosecution

The rules regulating the investigation and prosecution process in Estonia can be found in the Code of Criminal Procedure (CCP).[7] The rules are based on a principle of mandatory criminal proceedings:[8] once the elements of a criminal offence have been reported, investigative bodies and Prosecutors' Offices must initiate criminal proceedings and take all measures prescribed by law to establish whether a criminal act has taken place and, if so, to identify the person(s) who committed it (section 6).

Section 32 of the CCP provides that the acts of criminal procedure will be performed independently by investigative bodies, unless the permission of a court or a Prosecutor's Office is necessary.

The main investigative bodies are enumerated in Section 212 of the CCP: the Police Board, the agencies administered thereby, and the Security Police Board. In addition, there are a number of specialised agencies that conduct pre-trial proceedings in specific cases: the Border Guard Administration (for criminal offences relating to illegal crossing of the state border or illegal conveyance of persons across the state border), the Tax and Customs Board (for tax fraud and criminal offences involving violation of customs rules), the Competition Board, the Environmental Inspectorate, the Rescue Board (for criminal offences involving violation of the fire safety requirements), the Technical Inspectorate (for violations of the rules for industrial, construction and mining operations, the rules for driving or operation of machinery or safety rules for machinery), the Labour Inspectorate (for violations of occupational health and safety rules), and the Prisons Department of the Ministry of Justice.

For money laundering offences, there is a special independent unit in the Central Criminal Police, called the Financial Intelligence Unit, which can request information about suspicious transactions if there is sufficient reason to suspect that money laundering activities are taking place. The unit may also suspend the transaction in question, or it may impose restrictions on the accounts used during the suspicious activities.

The CCP has recently been reviewed and amended. Under the former version, the police were generally responsible for the whole investigation. With the entry into force of the new CCP in 2004 (in particular, sections 32, 212 and 213), this has largely been reorganised with the Prosecutor's Office directing the criminal proceedings and the police performing the investigations under its control.[9] Only in cases of urgency would the police act on their own initiative.

Sanctions and sentencing

In general, the sanctions imposed by the court depend on the seriousness of the crime committed. For criminal offences in the first degree committed by natural persons the maximum punishment is imprisonment for a term of more than five years or life imprisonment. For legal persons the most severe sanction is compulsory dissolution. Criminal offences in the second degree are punished with imprisonment for a term of up to five years for natural persons and a pecuniary punishment for legal persons (section 4 of the PC).

Chapter 3 of Estonian Penal Code sets out 'Types and Terms of Punishments' for legal persons. It provides for four types of sanctions: pecuniary punishment, dissolution, fines, and confiscation of assets.

Sanctions for criminal offences

Pecuniary punishment

Under section 44(8) of the Penal Code, the court may impose a pecuniary punishment of 50,000 to 250 million EEK (Estonian krooni) (approximately €3,195–€15,975,000)[10] on the legal person. A pecuniary punishment may be imposed on a legal person also as a supplementary punishment together with compulsory dissolution.

Dissolution of the legal person

Under section 46, a court may impose compulsory dissolution on a legal person, 'if commission of criminal offences has become part of the activities of the legal person'.

Sanctions for misdemeanours

Fines

Under section 47(2), a court or an extra-judicial body may impose a fine of 500 to 50,000 EEK, which is approximately €32–€3,195, on a legal person who is found to have committed a misdemeanour. In the case of an offence related to the rules of competition, the court may impose a fine of 500 EEK (approximately €32); cf. section 47(3) of PC.

Confiscation

Under section 83(2), a court may order confiscation of the substance or items which were the direct object of the commission of an intentional offence, and of the objects used or acquired in the offence if these belong to the offender at the time of the judgment.

In relation to specific offences (i.e. economic and financial crimes), section 394(2) of the Penal Code provides for aggravated sanctions, i.e. two to ten years imprisonment, for the laundering of proceeds committed (1) by a group; (2) at least twice; (3) on a large-scale basis; or (4) by a criminal organisation.

Conclusion

According to legal experts, the most pressing problems regarding corporate criminal liability in Estonia are the issue of establishing responsibility of the legal person when the offence was committed under its authority by a regular employee or an agent (rather than a member of a body or senior official), and the need to identify a leading person even in cases of misdemeanours (where this requirement can cause delay and increase costs).[11] In general, the test of liability (stated in section 14 of the PC) remains somewhat difficult to meet, due to the lack of clarity concerning the applicability of the two main criteria, and in particular the one concerning the requirement that the offence be committed by 'a body or senior official'.

Another problematic aspect of the Estonian law of corporate crime relates to jurisdiction. The rule on jurisdiction based on the nationality criterion is not applicable to legal persons, as it applies to Estonian 'citizens' and only natural persons can be citizens.[12] A legal person can be convicted of criminal acts abroad only if the perpetrator is an Estonian senior official. According to OECD inspectors, Estonian authorities acknowledge these issues and intend to address them through amendments to the existing law. Another problematic aspect concerning jurisdiction is that section 7 (1) of the Penal Code requires dual criminality for offences committed abroad by or against Estonian citizens (or against legal persons registered in Estonia).[13] Therefore, in such cases prosecution is possible only if the act is punishable in the foreign state as well, which represents a constraint compared with Article 17 1.b of the European Convention anti-bribery.

Although Estonia was one of the first countries to sign up to the 1997 Convention on Combating Bribery,[14] according to a Transparency International report from 2008, the country is among those states (18 in total) where there is little or no enforcement of anti-corruption laws.[15] Up to June 2008, there had been no cases or investigations. However, there are legal reform proposals pending that could contribute to improved foreign bribery enforcement. Draft amendments to the Penal Code and the Code of Penal Procedure regarding the definition of a foreign public official, the definition of the offence of bribery, the jurisdiction and corporate liability, and illicit grounds for termination of prosecution were submitted to Parliament in 2008.

The Amendment Act to the Penal Code, Code of Criminal Procedure and Competition Act entered into force on 27 February 2010. It includes new provisions on sanctions and a new leniency programme. The Amendment Act makes the penalties considerably stricter than they were previously. The fine imposed on a legal person for taking part in anti-competitive agreements will be up to 5 per cent of the offender's past year's turnover. In case of hard-core cartels the fine will be up to 10 per cent and cannot be less than 5 per cent of the offender's past year's turnover.[16]

Notes

1 Dana Rone, *Legal Scientific Research on Institute of Criminal Liability of Legal Entities in Eight Countries – Nordic Countries (Finland, Sweden, Norway, Iceland and Denmark) and Baltic Countries (Latvia, Lithuania and Estonia)*, report prepared for the Ministry of Justice of the Republic of Latvia, March 2006, www.tm.gov.lv, p. 35.
2 The English version of the Estonian Penal Code is available online at: *www.nottingham. ac.uk/shared/shared_hrlcicju*/Estonia/Penal_Code__English_.*doc*
3 Ibid.
4 OECD Phase 1 Report on Estonia, March 2006, available online at http://www.oecd. org/infobycountry/0,3380,en_2649_37447_1_70387_119663_1_37447,00.html, p. 24.
5 Ibid., pp. 12–13.
6 Dona Rone, cf. supra, note 1, p. 34.
7 The English version of the Estonian Code of Criminal Procedure is available online at: http://www.legaltext.ee/text/en/X60027K4.htm
8 OECD Phase 1 Report, cf. supra, note 4, p. 20.
9 Ibid.
10 We used the exchange rates in place as of February 2006, quoted in the OECD Phase 1 Report, cf. supra, note 4, p. 25.
11 Dona Rone, cf. supra, note 1, p. 35.
12 OECD Phase 1 Report, cf. supra, note 4, p. 35.
13 Cf. *Evaluation Report on Estonia, Theme I: Incriminations*, Third Round, published by the Council of Europe's Group of States against Corruption, 4 April 2008, and available at http://www.coe.int/t/dghl/monitoring/greco/evaluations/round3/ GrecoEval3(2007)5_Estonia_One_EN.pdf, p. 19.
14 OECD Phase 1 Report, cf. supra, note 4, p. 2.
15 Fritz Heimann and Gillian Dell, *Progress Report 2008: Enforcement of the OECD Convention on Combating Bribery of Foreign Public Officials*, Transparency International, 24 June 2008, http://sup.kathimerini.gr/xtra/media/files/meletes/econ/offic240608.pdf, pp. 11–12, 21.
16 See the European Commission's brief on the new amendments, available at http:// ec.europa.eu/competition/ecn/brief/02_2010/ee_leniency.pdf

16 Country report: Finland

James Gobert

Introduction

Prior to 1995, Finnish law did not recognise corporate criminal liability. However, in 1995, as part of its reform of the criminal law, the Finnish legislature established criminal liability for legal persons. Section 9 of Chapter 1 PC – titled 'Scope of application of the criminal law of Finland' – states that

> If, under this chapter, Finnish law applies to the offence, Finnish law applies also to the determination of corporate criminal liability.[1]

In keeping with Finnish jurisprudential principles, under which criminal law is resorted to only when (1) legal rights that merit protection are at stake; (2) no more morally acceptable and equally (or nearly equally) effective remedy is available; and (3) the benefits of criminal sanctions are no greater than its disadvantages,[2] a cautious approach was taken.

Under the new law, a company can be prosecuted in the same way as can an individual. A company may be subjected to a fine authorised by the Penal Code if the prosecutor requests that such a fine be imposed. Private complaints by victims of corporate illegality may also be brought.

Scope and test of liability

Chapter 9 of the Finnish Penal Code deals specifically with corporate criminal liability. Under section 1.1,

> A corporation, foundation or other legal entity in whose operations an offence has been committed may on the request of the public prosecutor be sentenced to a corporate fine if such a sanction has been provided in this Code.

In Finnish law, the concept of 'legal entity' includes companies (partnerships, limited partnership companies, limited liability companies), commercial and non-commercial associations, foundations, and analogous legal bodies (e.g. cooperative societies).[3] The rules regarding liability in Civil Law are used to determine the organisations to which the criminal law will be applied.[4] A company may be held liable for an offence where a corporate fine has, by statute, been authorised for the offence.

Criminal liability does not extend to public authorities, including the police, the prosecution and other state agencies. However, if the state is only involved indirectly in an offence, as where it has subcontracted a building project to a construction company, it may be liable for an offence committed by the company.

Under Finnish law, legal entities may be held criminally liable for a range of offences, including bribery, fraud, obtaining subsidies through fraudulent means, competition offences, smuggling and environmental crimes.[5]

A company may be liable for an offence based on its own fault or vicariously, when the offence is committed by a director, senior manager or somebody who is authorised to exercise decision-making authority on behalf of the company. The individual in question may be either the perpetrator/principal or an accessory/ accomplice to the crime. In either case the company may be liable vicariously. If an individual is not authorised to act on behalf of the company, or is not acting for the benefit of the company, the company will not be vicariously liable for the individual's offence.[6]

For an offence of an individual to be imputed to the company, the offence must be committed either intentionally, knowingly or negligently. The individual's *mens rea* will be attributed to the company.

The rationale behind vicarious liability is not that the individual in question is the *alter ego* or personification of the company (although he or she may be). Rather, it is that the individual is the vehicle through which the company's offence is committed.

Proof of *mens rea* or 'fault' may be essential before a company can be convicted. It has been argued that the principle of respect for 'human dignity' set out in the Finnish Constitution justifies this requirement.[7]

Fault may consist of either an act of commission or an omission. In respect of the latter, managers who negligently fail to exercise the care and diligence required to prevent an offence (or in the words of the statute, have 'allowed the offence to be committed'), can expose the company to criminal liability. An offence of omission is deemed to have occurred either where the offender should have acted and didn't, or where the consequences of the failure to act occurred.

It might be observed that often in cases involving an omission it will be impossible to determine whose responsibility it was to see that a system was in place that would have prevented the resulting harm. Under Finnish law identification of such individuals is not necessary. The Finnish Penal Code recognises the concept of 'anonymous culpa'.[8] Anonymous culpa can be found when an individual offender cannot be identified or is not subject to legal sanction because of a personal defence. The rationale behind this provision is that sometimes it may be apparent that a legal person has not fulfilled its duty of care, or has allowed the commission of an offence, even if an individual offender remains unidentified.

The basis for a finding of corporate 'fault' is quite diverse. It may consist of the negligent selection of personnel, the negligent training of staff, or the failure to supervise staff properly. As previously mentioned, fault may also consist in not having in place a system to prevent offences, or in failing to control timely actions of employees.

A parent company will not usually be criminally liable for the offences of a subsidiary, as the two are considered to be independent entities in law. However, the parent company may be held liable if it has ordered the offence or if the offence was committed for its benefit. Overlapping management will be strong evidence of a common identity and may cause a court to conclude that for legal purposes the parent and subsidiary should be jointly liable.

Individual liability

As might be expected in a system where corporate liability can be derived from individual liability, a prosecution of both an individual and the company is possible under Finnish law. However, only the individual offender may be prosecuted if the company has exercised due diligence in hiring, training and supervising the offender. Internal guidelines and good record-keeping practices may be evidence of the company's due diligence.[9]

The individual may be prosecuted as either the principal or as an accessory to the crime. The individual's liability, however, must be based on a personal act or omission.

Whether the company will be prosecuted along with the individual does not necessarily depend on whether the company has benefitted from the crime. Rather it turns on where the major responsibility for the offence lies. Even if a decision is made not to prosecute the company, this does not mean that the company will be allowed to retain the benefits of the crime. The sanction of forfeiture, to be subsequently discussed, may allow for recovery of any instrumentality or property used in the offence or any proceeds gained from the offence.[10]

If both company and individual are prosecuted, the two usually will be tried together. If the statute of limitations precludes prosecution of the individual, the charge against the company will also fail.[11]

Investigation and prosecution

A company that is subject to criminal penalty may be prosecuted in the same manner as an individual. Under the Criminal Investigations Act, the subject of an investigation must be notified 'as soon as possible'. Specific time limits are not set out in statute.

In keeping with the principle of *nemo tenetur se ipsum accusare*, a company which is the object of a criminal investigation is not obliged to assist the police. Other protections guaranteed by the European Convention on Human Rights are also available to the company.

Finnish law recognises both 'complainant' and non-complainant offences. If an injured party chooses not to report an offence designated as a 'complainant' offence, criminal charges will not be forthcoming unless the prosecutor finds there is a strong public interest in bringing a prosecution. On the one hand, this approach keeps the criminal justice system from being overloaded with minor offences in which there is little public interest. A self-screening mechanism is at work in that, unless the injured party feels sufficiently strongly to complain, the case will die a quiet death. However, the problem with this approach is that companies will often exert explicit or (more likely) implicit pressure on employees injured as a result of the company's fault not to report the offence. Indeed, there may be self-censorship by employees who fear the loss of their job if they were to file a report. Even serious offences may as a result not come to the attention of the authorities.

The investigation of serious offences may be initiated by the police or prosecutor. After the investigation has been completed, the prosecutor will be responsible for determining whether formal charges will be brought. The prosecutor may decline to bring charges where the company's level of fault or the resulting harm is minimal and the company has taken steps to prevent future violations.

Even in the case of non-complainant offences, the prosecutor may decide that there is an insufficient public interest at stake to warrant a prosecution. The prosecutor may also decide not to prosecute a company where the involvement of corporate management in the commission of the offence has been slight or the resulting harm is relatively minor. Non-prosecution is especially likely to occur if the company has taken prompt steps to prevent any repetition of the offence.

Under the Coercive Measures Act, the investigating authority or the court may take steps necessary to prevent the company from avoiding a subsequent fine or divesting itself of property that may be subject to forfeiture. Sometimes the orders in question may be necessary to preserve evidence. The relevant measures include a prohibition of the transfer of funds, confiscation of assets and attachment of property.

Sanctions and sentencing

The normal penalty for a corporate offender will be a lump-sum fine. The fine must be authorised under Finnish law. Chapter 9 of the Penal Code sets out offences for which companies can be fined. Among the offences which will attract a fine are negligent homicide or injury, fraud, money laundering, tax-related offences, crimes involving unfair competition, forgery, bribery, crimes against the environment and work safety offences. Not atypically, these crimes will have both a simple and an aggravated version. It is also a punishable offence to be a 'criminal organisation' or to be involved in terrorist activities.

The sentencing process is initiated by a request from the public prosecutor to the court to impose a fine on the company under its discretion under the Penal Code. However, a court may decline to impose a fine where the company's lack of due diligence was minimal or corporate fault was not significant. Likewise, a fine may be waived if the court finds that the fault of an individual offender was disproportionate in comparison to that of the company. Usually, it is a precondition for the waiving of charges against the legal person that the latter has voluntarily taken all necessary measures to prevent new offences.[12] The relative fault of individual and company is especially likely to be considered when the individual in question owns a significant number of shares in the company.

The minimum corporate fine is €850 and the maximum €850,000. In setting a fine, a court will consider several factors:[13] (1) the nature of the company's fault – intentional offences are considered more serious than negligent offences, and grossly negligent offences are not surprisingly deemed more serious than those involving 'ordinary' negligence; (2) the nature and extent of the harm – the greater the harm, the higher the fine, although some types of offences, such as pollution, are deemed inherently serious regardless of the amount of the damage; (3) the degree to which management was involved in the offence – the higher the position of the offender within the company, the greater will be the fine; and (4) the financial situation of the company – factors to be considered here are the size, earnings, solvency and profitability of the company; fines should not be so high as threaten the continuing existence of the company or lead to the risk of employee redundancies.

Chapter. 9 section 4 PC states that a court may consider the following mitigating factors when sentencing a legal entity: the degree of participation of management in the offence; the seriousness of the offence; the consequences of the offence to the corporation; and the measures taken by the offender to prevent further offences or remedy the effects of the offence.

In practice, corporate fines have tended to be low. Tolvanen reports that the average fine in 2005 was €6,813 and questions whether such fines adequately signify the moral gravity of the corporate offence.[14] It is also doubtful whether fines at this level will have much of a deterrent effect, although the reputational damage of a conviction should not be discounted. Where the company in good faith has taken prompt steps to prevent future offences, has voluntarily compensated the victims of the offence, or has taken remedial measures to cure or undo the harm caused, a court may be more inclined to be lenient in fixing the amount of the fine. Cooperation in the investigation may also count in a company's favour. Any administrative fine (see below) ordered will also be taken into account in determining the amount of the penal fine.

Like most countries, Finnish authorities have given little thought to penalties other than fines. Obviously a company cannot be imprisoned but community service sentences and corporate probation have proved to be effective sanctions elsewhere. However, these are not authorised under Finnish law.

In addition to a fine, Chapter 10 of the Finnish Penal Code allows for forfeiture of illegally obtained assets. Forfeiture extends to both the proceeds of the crime and any instrumentality or property used in committing the crime. Forfeiture is mandatory when the company has benefitted from the offence. If the precise amount of the forfeiture is unquantifiable or cannot be determined, a court is permitted to impose a forfeiture based on its estimate of the likely benefit to the company or individual.

Apart from penalties authorised by the Penal Code, laws may allow for administrative proceedings (which are independent of the criminal action) and administrative fines. Administrative fines may be 'conditional' (conditioned on future compliance with the law) or unconditional (penalising past misconduct). Both the Companies Act and the Securities Market Act allow for such administrative penalties.

Administrative penalties may also be imposed to ensure compliance with EU directives, such as those relating to unfair competition. In respect of unfair competitive practices the maximum administrative fine may not exceed 10 per cent of the company's previous year's turnover or a maximum of €200,000. The minimum administrative fine is €500.

Finnish law also allows civil compensation to be awarded to the victim of a corporate crime in the context of the criminal proceedings. Where the harm has been caused deliberately, damages in full will be allowed. Otherwise the damages awarded may be affected by the financial status of the offender and other relevant considerations. However, compensation is often ordered out of moneys that would otherwise be subject to forfeiture, in which case forfeiture will not be ordered.

Since the introduction of corporate criminal liability in Finnish law in 1995, legal entities have only been subject to it in five cases (as of 2006), most of which involved environmental offences.[15]

Notes

1 Finnish Penal Code, http://www.finlex.fi/pdf/saadkaan/E8890039.PDF
2 Matti Tolvanen (2009) Trust, Business Ethics and Crime Prevention: Corporate Criminal Liability in Finland (Mykolas Romeris University reviewed research papers 'Jurisprudence').
3 Dana Rone, *Legal Scientific Research on Institute of Criminal Liability of Legal Entities in Eight Countries*, 2006, p. 14.
4 Ibid.
5 See Rone, supra, note 3, p. 12.
6 See Penal Code, ch. 9, sections 2–3.
7 See Tolvanen, supra, note 2.
8 See Penal Code, ch. 9, section 2.2.
9 See Lex Mundi, Criminal Liability of Companies Survey: Finland, http://www.lexmundi.com/lexmundi/Criminal_Liability_Survey_by_Jurisdiction.asp?SnID=534038719
10 See sanctions section.
11 See Penal Code, ch. 9, section 9.1.
12 See Rone, supra, note 3, p. 15.
13 See generally Penal Code, ch. 9, section 6.
14 See Tolvanen, supra, note 2.
15 Cf. Rone, supra, note 3, p. 15.

17 Country report: France

Pascal Beauvais

Introduction

In 1994, the French Criminal Code introduced the concept of criminal liability for legal persons.[1] The category of legal persons includes companies, associations, unions, and public entities (public companies and institutions, local communities). One of the features of French law is the fact that the criminal liability *stricto sensu* can, in certain fields, combine with a system of repressive administrative sanctions.

Historically, French law only considered criminal liability for actual physical persons. Therefore, the doctrine of legal persons was based on the 'fiction' theory presenting a legal person, such as a corporation, as a fictive person. This seemed to be in contradiction with the concept of criminal liability, whose application implied 'real' acts and a 'real' personal will.

Eventually, the 'fiction' theory was replaced by the 'real' theory, which considers that some organisations have a collective will, separate from that of the natural persons which comprise it, and requires the recognition of a legal entity capable of representing the personal and specific interests of the group. The phasing out of the 'fiction' theory was to lead to a redefinition of the principle of criminal non-liability of legal persons, especially since the development of the industrial economy resulted in the emergence of serious flaws appearing to be attributable to corporations.

Nonetheless, it was not until 1994 that the new Criminal Code was enacted. Article 121-2 established the principle of criminal liability of legal persons, foreseeing that 'legal persons, with the exception of the State, are criminally liable for the offences committed on their account by their organs or representatives'.

The scope and test of corporate criminal liability

Companies which because of their legal structure are not qualified as legal persons are not subject to criminal liability. Thus, simple companies, partnerships or group companies cannot be held criminally liable. On the other hand, foreign corporations can be held criminally responsible, since under French law they are considered to be legal persons.

Until the introduction of the 2004 law, the legislator had chosen to apply to legal persons the principle of specificity and liability. Legal persons were criminally liable only in the case of offences for which the law or the rule had explicitly and specifically envisaged such a liability. In 2004, the legislator abandoned this principle: therefore all criminal offences could, from then onwards, engage the criminal liability of corporations.

The French legislator had the choice between two mechanisms of criminal liability for legal persons: direct or indirect.[2] The mechanism of direct criminal liability is generally retained in civil and administrative matters: it defines the incriminating behaviour in relation to the legal person and attributes it directly to the legal person.

But the French law only retains indirect criminal liability. Indeed, according to F. Desportes, 'article 121-2 of the Criminal Code does not consider that a legal person can tangibly commit an offence. Rather, it defines the parameters in which a violation committed by a physical person can be attributed to a legal person'.[3] Therefore, the components of the offence are not to be determined in relation to the legal person but in relation to the natural person, organ or representative.

The criminal liability of a legal person is retained only if one of its organs or representatives – i.e., a natural person – is found to have committed an offence.

Regardless of whether the criminal liability of the natural person is actually charged or not, it is sufficient for the judge to determine that the offence was committed by the organ or representative of the legal person.[4] The Supreme Court currently tends to admit a more direct responsibility of the legal person, which does not require the precise identification of the individual who committed the offence as long as it appears from the case that the infringement could only have been committed by an organ or a representative. For non-intentional crimes, when there is no other possibility that an organ or a representative has committed the offence, the French judge makes a presumption that the organ or the representative has committed the offence.

The organs of the legal person are those defined by the legislation concerning the legal person (e.g., manager of the limited liability company SARL, or general director of an anonymous company SA). Determining the representative of the legal person is more difficult: according to case law – as discussed – it refers to employees who hold a position delegated with powers.[5]

The offence must also be committed on behalf of the legal person. Case law considers that the offence is committed 'on behalf of the legal person' when the offence is committed in the exercise of activities related to the operations and objectives of the organization, even if the legal person had no interest in it, and even if it resulted in no benefit to it.

With the exception of some non-intentional crimes, article 121-2 of the Criminal Code provides the combination of criminal responsibility of the individual and the legal person.

Sanctions and sentencing for corporations

The main penalty for corporations is a fine, the amount of which is equal to five times that for individuals. If the crime is one for which no fine is provided for in respect of individuals, the fine incurred by legal persons will be of €1,000,000.

In addition, legal persons can incur specific sentences, provided for by article 131-39 of the Criminal Code: dissolution, a permanent ban for 5 years to exercise a professional activity, placement under judicial supervision for 5 years, the final closure of the establishment or temporary closure for 5 years, a ban on public offering (either permanent or for 5 years), a prohibition to issue checks or use credit cards, and publicity of the court decision. Dissolution can only be imposed for the most serious offences and is possible only when the corporation was created or diverted from its purpose in order to commit the offence.

Investigation and prosecution procedures

Criminal proceedings for legal persons are governed by specific rules.[6]

First, the corporation must be represented, throughout the proceedings, by an individual. According to article 706-43 of the Criminal Procedure Code, 'criminal proceedings are initiated against the legal person in the form of the person of its legal representative at the time of the prosecution. The latter represents the legal person at all the stages of the proceedings'. However, to avoid conflicts of interest, the individual representative cannot be prosecuted criminally for the same or related facts as the legal person. In this case, 'the representative may seize the president of the district court for the purposes of judicially appointing a proxy to represent the legal person'.

For practical reasons, in order to facilitate the representation of very large corporations where legal departments are responsible for monitoring this type of procedure, 'the legal person may also be represented by any person granted a power of attorney for this purpose in accordance with the law or its articles of association'.

Finally, in order to avoid default procedures, in the absence of a legal representative, the president of the district court can appoint a judicial officer to represent the legal person.

Secondly, the representative of the legal person prosecuted may never be subjected to any coercive measure other than those applicable to witnesses.

According to the principle of discretionary prosecution, it is possible to simultaneously charge the legal person and the natural person, organ or representative of the legal person for the same crime.

If an investigation is opened, the legal person under investigation may be placed under judicial control by a magistrate under section 706-45 of the Criminal Procedure Code. The investigating judge may impose one or more of the following obligations:

• Depositing a security, the amount of which, payment time, and whether made in one or more instalments, are determined by the investigating judge;

- The creation of personal or real guarantees designed to uphold the victim's rights, within a time limit, for a length of time and an amount to be determined by the investigating judge;
- A prohibition to draw cheques other than those which allow the certified withdrawal of funds by the drawer from the drawee, and a prohibition to use credit cards;
- A prohibition on exercising certain professional or social activities, where the offence was committed during the carrying out, or at the time of these activities, and where it is feared that a new offence may be committed;
- Placement under the supervision of a judicial proxy appointed by the investigating judge for a renewable six-month period, in respect to the activity in the course of which the offence was committed.

The prohibitions provided for by paragraphs 3 and 4 may be ordered by the investigating judge only in so far as they are available penalties against the legal person.

The violation of judicial review not being punishable by detention (as in the case of individuals), the Criminal Procedure Code makes it an autonomous offence.

Other provisions require that employees' representatives must be notified of the hearing date. The Court may hear these particular representatives, in order for them to be informed of the consequences of its decision.

The combination of criminal liability with the system of administrative sanctions

Under French law corporations can, for the same offence, be punished cumulatively through criminal law *stricto sensu* and by administrative law enforcement systems, considered as penal law according to Article 6 of the European Convention on Human Rights. This combination of penal and administrative sanctions can be found in competition law and the law of financial markets.

In competition law, violations of cartel and abuse of dominance are both sanctioned by the criminal court and punished by the Competition Authority, an independent administrative authority that can impose hefty fines.

In stock exchange law, offences pertaining to transparency and equality in the financial markets (price manipulation, insider trading) are both sanctioned by the criminal court and punished by the *Autorité des Marchés Financiers (AMF)*, another independent administrative authority that can impose onerous fines.

This dual system of law enforcement, criminal and administrative, has been validated by the *Conseil Constitutionnel* subject to the constitutional principle of proportionality: cumulative penalties may not exceed the maximum provided by one or the other of the two laws (Decision 88 DC-248, 14 January 1989, the CSA, Decision 89-260 of 28 July 1989, the Securities and Exchange Commission). While it is arguable that double punishment is contrary to the principle of *non bis in idem* embodied in Protocol No. 7 of the European Convention on Human

Rights (according to which a person cannot be punished twice for the same offence), France expressed a reservation on this point, which allows it to combine administrative and criminal sanctions.

However, the concept of double punishment has been criticized by a growing number of observers who believe that the law should be reformed.[7]

Conclusions

In 2008, the Sub-Directorate of Statistics, Studies and Documentation of the Ministry of Justice conducted the first large statistical study on the criminal liability of legal persons ('Les condamnations de personnes morales de 2003 à 2005', D. Baux, O. Timbart, Ministère de la justice, SG/SDSE). This study revealed that 976 crimes committed by legal persons had led to convictions and sanctions in 2005, 42 per cent of which were in the Paris region, the main economic French hub.

In 2005, legal persons were subjected to a single sentence, usually a fine, in eight out of ten judgments (82 per cent). When the sentence contained several sentences, in most cases, in addition to the fine, an order to publicise the court's decision was also imposed.

In 2005, the average amount of a corporate fine was €10,916. The majority of convictions involved labour and social security offences (28 per cent of convictions). The offence of illegal work largely dominates in this category.

Unintentional homicides and injuries comprised 25 per cent of all convictions. Two-thirds of these arose from work-related accidents.

Following closely were breaches of legislation on competition and price (17 per cent), which primarily involve misleading advertising (half of the total), transactions without invoices, and unfair selling techniques.

Finally, 11 per cent of convictions were for fraud and counterfeiting, which mainly cover the offence of misrepresentation of the product.

Notes

1 See R. Merle, A. Vitu, Traité de droit criminel, T1, éditions Cujas, 1997, p. 805 et s.
2 See F. Desportes, article 121–2 Responsabilité pénale des personnes morales, Jurisclasseur Code pénal, fasc.11, 2001, n° 105 et sq.
3 Ibid.
4 Cass. Crim. 1 December 1998.
5 See Note. Crim. 1 December 1998 and Crim. 30 May 2000.
6 See generally F. Desportes, F. Le Gunehec, JurisClasseur Procédure pénale, articles 706-41 to 706-46.
7 See La dépénalisation de la vie des affaires, Groupe de travail présidé par Jean-Marie Coulon, Rapport au Garde des Sceaux, Collection des Rapports officiels, Documentation française, Janvier 2008.

18 Country report: Ireland

Edward Fitzgerald

Introduction

In Ireland, Section 11(i) of the Interpretation Act 1937 provides that 'references to a person in relation to an offence (whether punishable on indictment or on summary conviction) shall, unless the contrary intention appears, be construed as including references to a body corporate'. This section enables the prosecution of a company for any crime that could be committed by a natural person.

The courts have used both a test of 'identification' and a form of derivative managerial liability in determining the criminal liability of a legal person.[1] Specific tests covering statutory offences can also be found in various statutes.[2]

The scope and test of corporate criminal liability

Legal persons include private, public and statutory bodies subject to the laws and regulations governing the operation of companies in Ireland.

As exemplified in subsection 9 (1) of the Prevention of Corruption Act 2001, two conditions are required to establish the criminal liability of a legal person: (i) the legal person has to commit the offence itself; and (ii) the offence needs to be committed, either with the consent or connivance or with the wilful neglect of a director, manager, secretary, or other officer of the body corporate, or any person 'purporting to act' in such a capacity.[3]

The law in Ireland relating to legal persons is heavily influenced by English common law principles. As in the UK, in the absence of a statute, the test of corporate criminal liability is the so-called 'identification' test, under which only offences of persons who are deemed to be part of the 'controlling mind and will of the company' (or who, in other words, are 'identified' with the company) give rise to the criminal liability of the company.

The leading authority in England on the 'identification' doctrine is generally deemed to be the decision of the House of Lords in *Tesco Supermarkets Ltd. v Nattrass*.[4] Under *Nattrass*, directors, managing directors and senior managers who can speak for and act on behalf of the company constitute its 'controlling mind and will'. If such an individual were to commit a crime it could be imputed to the company. It is not necessary that the company benefit from the crime as liability is predicated on the standing of the perpetrator within the corporate hierarchy and not whether he/she acts to benefit the company.[5]

In Ireland, the 'identification' doctrine has been criticised because it gives too much discretion to the trial judge.[6] The problem is that whoever is identified with the company almost invariably needs to be determined on an ad hoc, case-by-case basis. It was suggested by Mr Justice Hinchy in *King v AG*[7] that this vagueness might be unconstitutional.

The concerns expressed by Mr Justice Hinchy were repeated in the Report of the Irish Law Reform Commission on corporate killing.[8] The Report states that the 'current state of the law may fall afoul of the legality principle' because it fails to provide 'clear and precise legislative rules which effectively eliminate the need for creative interpretation by judges'.

A related objection to the 'identification' doctrine is that it is too easily circumvented. It would seem that by placing junior personnel in the company in charge of a dangerous activity, responsibility might be said not to lie with a person who was part of the company 'directing mind and will', thereby avoiding imputation to the company of any offence that might occur in the course of carrying out the activity. While Irish jurisprudence allows corporate liability for acts of a *de jure* director who does not hold an official position in the company, it may be even more difficult to determine who is a *de jure* director than who constitutes the company's 'directing mind and will'.

Liability of directors and corporate officers

Section 9 of the Prevention of Corruption Act 2001 provides:

> (1) Where an offence under the Prevention of Corruption Acts, 1889 to 2001, has been committed by a body corporate and is proved to have been committed with the consent or connivance of or to be attributable to any wilful neglect on the part of a person being a director, manager, secretary or other officer of the body corporate, or a person who was purporting to act in any such capacity, that person as well as the body corporate shall be guilty of an offence and be liable to be proceeded against and punished as if he or she were guilty of the first-mentioned offence.

The same rule applies when the company is managed by its members:

> (2) Where the affairs of a body corporate are managed by its members, subsection (1) shall apply in relation to the acts and defaults of a member in connection with his or her functions of management as if he or she were a director or manager of the body corporate.[9]

When an offence has been committed by a body corporate and it is proven to have been committed with the consent or connivance, or as a result of the wilful neglect of a director, manager, secretary or other officer of the company, both the individual and the company may be prosecuted.[10]

Investigation and prosecution

Investigation

Within the Irish criminal justice system investigations are generally undertaken by the police (*An Garda Síochána*).[11] The Director of Public Prosecutions (DPP) has no formal investigative authority but may advise in respect of an investigation. The police can initiate an investigation following a complaint from any person, including a victim or a competitor, or as a result of independent information coming to their attention.[12]

To suspend an investigation, the police would generally need to refer the matter to the DPP for direction. However, the police have the discretion to terminate an investigation without referral to the DPP where no material evidence of an offence is found.[13]

The police have the ability to use special investigative techniques, such as undercover operations, informants, video-surveillance and controlled deliveries. The interception of telecommunications is allowed only for criminal investigations of serious offences punishable (in the case of a natural person) by imprisonment for a term of five or more years.[14]

Sections 63 and 64 of the Criminal Justice Act (1994) as amended by section 39 of the Criminal Justice (Terrorist Offences) Act (2005) allow the police to serve a court order to compel the production of material, search premises and obtain information in relation to an investigation. In a case where money laundering or a predicate offence is being investigated, the material that can be obtained includes bank records, customer identification records, and other records maintained by financial institutions.[15] Items subject to legal privilege are excluded.

In addition to the police, specialised units operate within the national police force to detect and prevent certain types of crimes. For example, the Garda Bureau of Fraud Investigation (GBFI)[16] deals with all serious fraud and money laundering cases, the National Bureau of Criminal Investigation[17] investigates serious and organised crime on a national and international basis, and the Money Laundering Investigation Unit[18] is responsible for recording, evaluating, analysing and investigating disclosures relating to suspicious financial transactions.

Other specialised investigating authorities include the Competition Authority, which investigates offences against the Competition Acts; the investigation branch of the Revenue Commissioners, which investigates revenue offences; the Health and Safety Authority, which investigates offences relating to safety and welfare at work; and the Office of Director of Corporate Enforcement (ODCE), which deals with offences violating Company Law.

The Revenue Commissioners' Investigations and Prosecutions Division[19] manages and co-ordinates all of the Revenue's prosecution activity involving serious cases of fraud and tax evasion. In addition, the Revenue Solicitor's Division provides comprehensive legal support services, including the conduct of litigation and appeals and the prosecution of criminal offences. Like the police, the Revenue

Commissioners' Investigations and Prosecutions Division can employ undercover operations, informants, video-surveillance and controlled deliveries.

The Company Law Enforcement Act (2001) established the Office of the Director of Corporate Enforcement (ODCE).[20] Under this Act, the Director is legally responsible for encouraging compliance with company law and for investigating and enforcing suspected breaches of the legislation. In the case of suspected breaches, the Director has three main options available: (i) to invite the persons in default to pay an administrative fine in lieu of facing a summary prosecution before the courts,[21] (ii) to initiate a summary prosecution for a suspected breach of the Companies Acts, and (iii) to refer a case to the DPP for decision as to whether a prosecution on indictment should be commenced.[22]

Prosecution

In Ireland, virtually all 'serious' offences are brought under the authority of the DPP.[23] Prosecutions for corruption, including foreign bribery, require the consent of the DPP and are brought in the name of the DPP. In certain minor cases the DPP has agreed that the Garda (police) can commence a prosecution without first seeking its formal permission.

The DPP has the discretion whether or not to institute a prosecution. In exercising this discretion, the DPP will go through a two-stage evaluation. First, the DPP will decide whether the evidence submitted establishes a *prima facie* case of guilt and there is reasonable prospect of securing a conviction. If it is determined that a *prima facie* case does not exist, the case is terminated unless further evidence emerges at a later date. Assuming a *prima facie* case has been made out, the DPP has to consider whether the prosecution is in the 'public interest'.[24]

Further guidelines on prosecutions have been issued by the Office of the DPP.[25] In general terms, the more serious the offence and the stronger the evidence to support it, the less likely that some other factor will outweigh the public interest in bringing the prosecution. In addition, the guidelines provide a list of factors that may be considered in determining whether the public interest requires a prosecution. These include both aggravating and mitigating factors. Relevant factors include whether the consequences of a prosecution or a conviction would be disproportionately harsh or oppressive in the particular circumstances of the offender (section 4.18.d), the attitude of the victim or the family of a victim of the alleged offence to a prosecution (section 4.18.e), and whether the likely length and expense of a trial would be disproportionate to the seriousness of the alleged offence and the strength of the evidence (section 4.18.g).

Sanctions and sentencing

We noted previously that under Section 11(i) of the Interpretation Act 1937 the term 'person' includes both natural and legal persons. Consequently, sanctions under particular statutes, such as the Prevention of Corruption Act 2001 and the Criminal Justice (Theft and Fraud) Offences Act 2001 which are directed to natural persons are also applicable to legal persons. However, in light of the paucity of prosecutions concerns remain as to whether the sanctions imposed in practice are indeed effective, proportionate and dissuasive.

The sanction against a convicted company will typically consist of a fine, which will be unlimited for serious offences. In addition, under the Criminal Justice Act 1994, criminal confiscation of the benefits derived from the crime may also be ordered. The Proceeds of Crime Act 1996 (POCA) also allows confiscation of the proceeds of an offence, including any property obtained or received as a result of the offence.

The Irish law on bribery distinguishes between active and passive bribery, and between bribery of a foreign and a domestic official. For a natural person the penalty for bribery may be a fine or a term of imprisonment of up to 10 years; in the case of a legal person, an unlimited fine on indictment or a fine of up to €3,000 for summary offences may be imposed.[26] A natural person convicted of bribery may also be subject to a civil disqualification order, preventing the offender from holding future directorships.[27] As there had been no prosecutions or convictions for foreign bribery in Ireland as of the time of the latest OECD review (2007), determining the level of fines in practice is problematic.[28]

The offence under section 43 of the Criminal Justice (Theft and Fraud Offences) Act 2001, which covers the specific offence of active corruption of an EU official with damage to the EU's financial interests, carries a penalty of a maximum of 5 years imprisonment (for natural persons) and/or an unlimited fine (for legal persons).[29]

The penalties under section 31(2) of the Criminal Justice Act (CJA) 1994 apply to both natural and legal persons. A person found guilty of an offence of money laundering on conviction or indictment is liable to a fine or to imprisonment for a term not exceeding 14 years, or to both. There is no maximum stated level of fine applicable for conviction on indictment.[30]

Future directions

In 2005, the Irish Law Reform Commission published a report dealing with the liability of companies for deaths arising from gross negligence[31] and recommended the creation of an offence of 'corporate manslaughter'. The company would be allowed a defence where it had taken all reasonable measures to prevent risks to human life. Whether or not it had done so would entail consideration of factors such as the way corporate activities were managed or organised by the company's senior managers, corporate decision-making rules, corporate communication systems, and whether the company was operating under a licence. The offence would apply to both public and private sector corporate bodies ('undertakings') as well as unincorporated entities. The offence could only be prosecuted pursuant to an indictment.

If convicted of corporate manslaughter, an unlimited fine could be imposed on the offender. The Report also envisaged ancillary penalties such as community service orders and adverse publicity orders.

The Commission did not ignore the role of natural persons, as has been done in England.[32] It recommended a separate offence of 'grossly negligent management causing death' which would apply to high managerial agents (directors, managers and other similar persons acting on behalf of the undertaking). The penalty for this offence would be a maximum penalty of 12 years imprisonment and disqualification from holding a high management office for up to 15 years.

Currently under consideration by the Irish Parliament is the 2008 Prevention of Corruption (Amendment) Bill. It is designed to provide greater clarity and greater consistency in this area of the law. At present the relevant law is contained in two different statutes, the Prevention of Corruption Act 2001 and the Criminal Justice (Theft and Fraud Offences) Act 2001, which differ in some significant respects.[33] Consolidation and harmonisation would seem desirable.

Notes

1   OECD Corporate Killing Report – Ireland: Phase 2 (2007) p. 54.
2   See, e.g., Prevention of Corruption Act 2001; Criminal Justice (Theft and Fraud Offences) Act 2001.
3   OECD report – Ireland: Phase 2 (2007).
4   [1971] 2 All E.R. 127.
5   See *Moore v Bresler* [1944] 2 All ER 515.
6   OECD report, cf. supra, note 1.
7   [1981] IR 233.
8   Report: Corporate Killing (Ireland, Law Reform Commission, LRC 77-2005).
9   OECD report, cf. supra note 1.
10 Ibid.
11 Except for certain duties which arise under the Garda (Complaints) Act, 1986 where an investigation is being carried out into an alleged offence by a member of the Garda, the Director of Public Prosecutions has no investigative function.
12 OECD report, cf. supra, note 1, p. 32.
13 A decision of the police to suspend, terminate, or not to initiate an investigation is appealable to a superior officer of the police force in the first instance. If such a decision is upheld without a good reason, it could be subject to judicial intervention.
14 The powers are contained under Sections 1, 4 and 5 of Interception of Postal Packets and Telecommunications Messages (Regulation) Act (1993).
15 OECD report, cf. supra, note 1, p. 32.
16 The Garda Bureau of Fraud Investigation was established in 1995.
17 The National Bureau of Criminal Investigation was established in 1997.
18 The Money Laundering Investigation Unit was established in 1995.
19 OECD report, cf. supra, note 1, p. 30.
20 The staff complement of the ODCE consists of 30 together with 6 Garda officers seconded from the GBFI to provide investigative support.
21 Irish authorities have indicated that this provision is yet to be instituted.
22 Company Law Enforcement Act s. 12.1.
23 OECD report – Ireland: Phase 1, p. 23.
24 OECD report – Ireland: Phase 1, p. 23.
25 *Guidelines for Prosecutions* (2006; originally issued in 2001).
26 OECD report, cf. supra, note 1, p. 59.
27 Ibid p.7.

28 OECD report, cf. supra, note 1, p. 8.
29 Ibid.
30 OECD report, cf. supra, note 1, p. 65.
31 *Report on Corporate Killing* (LRC 77-2005).
32 See Corporate Manslaughter and Corporate Homicide Act 2007 s. 18.
33 See OECD report, cf. supra, note 1, p. 47.

19 Country report: Italy

Cristina de Maglie

Introduction

Historically, the Italian legal system has always been diffident toward the principle of *corporate criminal liability*. There were deep-seated reasons for this, as well as for the attachment of Italian law to the dogma: '*societas delinquere non potest*', which can be found in the Italian Constitution.

Article 27, paragraph 1, of the Constitution establishes the principle of the personal nature of criminal liability. Until fairly recently it has been viewed as 'an insuperable obstacle' to the legitimization of criminal liability for legal entities. The reasons for this impassable barrier, which *de facto* covered the most aggressive and unscrupulous corporations with a net of immunity, have for some time now been authoritatively asserted.

Criminal law, it is stated, has always possessed an 'undeniable ethical imprint'. Even more than in the case of the concept of guilt, the concept of the personal nature of criminal liability presupposes a set of physiopsychic factors that can only be identified in physical persons. Criminal imputation requires a psychological connection, a guilty intent; 'personal' is exclusively the liability that is filtered through subjective components.

In other words, criminal imputation necessarily presupposes 'a person' with an individual 'history' who reflects on committing the crime. If the principle of corporate criminal liability is admitted, the personal nature of the criminal act that emerges in article 27 would be irremediably violated, without taking into account the fact that, by nature, legal persons are incapable of *suffering* the consequences of the criminal act. Moreover, the lack of a structured personality – which would permit evaluations of the juristic person's past and prognoses regarding the future – would frustrate any *re-educational* aspiration of article 27.

In other words, the principle of culpability did *not* permit the courts to *substitute* the subject that commits the crime for the one that suffers the criminal consequences. Moreover, applying a criminal sanction to the juristic person would negatively and unjustly impact innocent third parties as well (the overspill effect) (e.g. minor partners extraneous or even opposed to the decisions in question), with a macroscopic waste of the well-accepted principle based on which everyone has to suffer the consequences of their actions.[1]

These objections were dealt with in the 2001 reform. Legislative decree n. 231/2001 introduced into Italian law a model of *direct administrative responsibility* for collective entities. There were several *international* spurs to the legislation: the OECD Conventions and the European Union's convention on the protection of its financial interests (also known as the 'PIF Convention') in 1997 in terms of *national* impulses. Article 11 of the delegated law n. 300/2000 – which dealt with the 'rules concerning the administrative liability of legal persons, of companies and associations even without legal status' – is carried out by the legislative decree.

As stated in the report accompanying the decree, reform 'could no longer be put off'. The 2000 preliminary reform project for the criminal code – the so-called Grosso project – opened the way, dedicating an entire section (section VII) to the liability of legal persons. The attached report to the Grosso project indicated the reasons *external* and *internal* to the system that were creating pressure to make corporations criminally liable: on the one hand, the comparative analysis shows that the criminal liability of legal persons is, so to speak, an obliged choice due to the need for the harmonization and coordination of Italian law with most European legal systems. On the other hand, the criminal liability of legal persons is *not* incompatible with the basic principles of the rule of law, but instead responds to the need for the rationality, equity, transparency, and equilibrium of the system.

Interestingly, the project, which introduced the *direct* liability of legal persons, chose *not* to define this liability as a criminal liability, which would have represented a *'tertium genus* ... anchored to criminal assumptions and governed by the strong guarantees of criminal law'. The ideological gap left by the Grosso project provided the grounds for the legislative decree, which calls for a timely and multifaceted regulatory framework for the direct liability of legal persons: this represents a truly complex and complete microsystem whose 85 articles thoroughly deal with the problem of the liability of organizations, in terms of both substance and procedure. A strong message has thus been sent to theorists and legal experts, not only because the ideological resistance to the principle *'societas delinquere potest'* appears increasingly weaker, but also because, with the creation of a microsystem dedicated to legal persons, the premises have been set forth for the construction of a 'corporate criminal law' that is independent of and detached from the criminal code.[2]

Crucial in the analysis of the new law is the determination of the *nature* of corporate liability. The legislative decree plainly speaks of the 'administrative liability' of legal persons. But this represents an administrative liability that is different in several places from the general system of administrative liability outlined in law n. 689/1981. The report accompanying the decree refers to 'a *tertium genus'* that unites the essential aspects of the criminal and administrative systems in the attempt to adapt the reasons behind preventive effectiveness with those, even more important, 'behind maximum guarantees'.

These labels – which arguably stem from a 'fuzzy logic' – have profoundly irritated the guardians of the purity of the traditional dogma, who have ventured into long discussions about the 'real legal nature' – criminal or administrative – of corporate liability: a never-ending debate that risks equating problems concerning the mere construction of the language of legal science with dogmatic, substantive problems.

There is thus mention of 'liability defined as administrative but which in reality is *criminal* to all extents and purposes'; of an 'institution that, in its structure and function, is administrative in name only, appearing, with a probability that borders on certainty, as a masking of the criminal liability of the juristic person ...; of 'labelling fraud'; of the '*substantially criminal nature* of corporate liability'; of 'a third track for criminal law alongside punishment and safety measures'.

In effect, the supporters of the criminal nature of corporate liability rely on the *direct* and tenuous link between the liability of the organization and the commission of the *crime*. The relative *cognition* of this liability, left entirely to the judgement of the *criminal court*, is an important indication that we are dealing with categories and guarantees of criminal law and availing ourselves of *all* its coercive instruments.

The counterargument is that the system outlined in legislative decree 231 presents *other* and *no less important* aspects from which to deduce, with equal certainty, the *administrative nature* of the liability. The *choice* of the label of 'administrative liability', which must be taken seriously since it expresses the will of the legislator, and the structural consideration – that it is the name of the sanction that determines the nature of the sanction and not vice versa (in addition to other arguments that can be made) – suggests the *non-criminal* nature of corporate liability.[3]

Consider, for example, the *statute of limitation* system outlined in the decree, which is completely different from penal mechanisms. Consider also the sanctions called for in the case of corporate affairs – breakups, mergers, transformations, and bestowal – completely tied to the civil law regarding changes in the obligations of the company that is the object or subject of the modification.

In conclusion, the above analysis indicates the difficulty of placing the 2001 reforms squarely within the category of either the penal or administrative law. If we do not wish to accept the ambiguous label of *tertium genus* but cannot manage to rid ourselves of the obsession to classify, we can use the formula 'liability for criminal offence': this expresses the problem regarding the legal framework which the new laws seek to remedy and evokes the preceptive and sanctionary content of the new institutions. This represents a 'dogmatically neutral' formula.[4]

The problem of classifying the 2001 reforms may have been settled by the recent stance taken by the supreme court of Cassation. The court stated: 'Notwithstanding the *nomen juris*, the new, nominally administrative liability conceals its substantially criminal nature' (Cass. n. 3615/2007).

The scope and test of corporate criminal liability

Comparative experience reveals different systematic solutions to the issue of the scope of corporate criminal liability. These range from a complete equating of legal and physical persons – provided for, for example, in the Dutch penal code – to the adoption of the so-called 'principle of specialty' adopted by the French legislator in 1994.[5]

The legislative decree in question originally provided for the administrative liability of the corporation *exclusively* for the crimes of bribery, corruption and fraud. This was a declaredly minimalist choice that strongly diminished the practical impact of the laws.

However, after 2001 a series of reforms widened the range of crimes for which corporations are liable. Law n.61/2002 extended the liability of organizations to financial crimes as well; law n.62/2005 provided for liability in market abuse; law n.409/2001 established liability for fraud involving money, credit cards and revenue stamps. Moreover, more recent reforms provide for the liability of juristic persons for terrorism crimes (law n.7/2003); slavery (law n. 228/2003); female genital mutilation (law n.7/2006); the handling of stolen goods and money laundering (2007); and involuntary manslaughter and serious or very serious personal injuries committed in violation of workplace safety laws (2007) that protect against personal injury. There are also pending proposals that would extend corporate liability to environmental crimes.

Which *juristic persons* are the object of the laws? The delegated law provides indications in two separate places. First, article 11, paragraph 1, establishes the 'administrative liability of legal persons and corporations, associations or organizations without a legal status that do not carry out functions of constitutional import'; paragraph 2 also provides that 'legal persons refer to organizations with a legal status, except for the state and other public authorities that exercise public powers'.

The legislative decree has in this way translated the prescriptions of the delegating authority. It has above all provided for laws entailing liability even for subjects not having a legal status, formalizing once and for all the elimination of the traditional historical opposition between legal and non-legal status groups: even the latter – as the most recent debate has revealed – are considered to be subjects of the law.

In choosing a legislative technique that mirrors that used by the French criminal code, paragraph 3 of article 1 identifies exceptions to corporate criminal liability. As in the French system, the State and other territorial authorities are exempted from liability. Also exempted are organizations that carry out functions of constitutional import: that is, political parties and unions. Finally, 'non-economic public authorities' are excluded as well: the government has thus broadened the range of exclusions intended by the delegating law.

Article 5 sets the criteria for the abscription of the *actus reus* regarding the administrative liability of the organization.[6]

In indicating the physical persons who have committed a crime from whom derives the attribution of the *actus reus* to the corporation, the legislative decree proposes the *organic theory* model: this choice is in line with art. 27 of the Constitution. As far as the principle of personal responsibility is concerned, even in its 'minimal' interpretation, the identity of the author of the crime and the receiver of the sanction is assured when the physical person who has committed the crime is a subject that has acted 'in the interests or to the advantage of the organization'. In fact, the proof of the existence of a relevant link between the individual and the juristic person permits the identification of the organization as the absolute protagonist for all events concerning the social and economic life of the company, and thus also as the source of risk regarding the crime. The administrative sanction directed at the juristic person impacts the same centre of interests that has given rise to the crime.[7]

As concerns the typology of physical persons identified as the agents acting on behalf of the juristic person, the decree provides a twofold equiparation. First, the decree officially recognizes as liable for the organization's actions both the so-called top managers – who carry out representative, administrative or executive functions for the organization or one of its units – and those who have a subordinate role: the juristic person is even ultimately responsible for the actions of a simple employee. The vast US case law provides convincing support for this approach.

The second important equiparation concerns those who *formally* carry out the executive role and those who *de facto* exercise it. Here the government has applied the well-known 'functional theory', giving relevance to the concrete execution of top-level functions. The unions remain outside the legal framework in this regard, as they are considered subjects that 'do not exercise a pervasive control over the organization'.

Paragraph 2 of article 5 establishes a cause for the exclusion of the liability of the juristic person when its agent has committed the crime solely for his own advantage or that of third parties. The provision considers the possibility of a breach of the identification principle: in order to attribute the *actus reus* to the organization, the agent has to have committed it while aware – at least partly – of the advantages for the organization. If this *at least possible aim* does not emerge, then there is no sense in sanctioning the juristic person.

Articles 6 and 7 couple the liability of the juristic person to requirements that are appropriate for formulating a culpability judgment. The *fault of the organization* model prescribed by the law is meant to fulfil a basic *preventive* role, embodied in the carrot–stick approach: in this case the juristic person must put in place special preventive protocols – the compliance and ethics programmes in the US system – destined to prevent the criminal conduct. If the organization 'has adopted and effectively carried out' such 'organization models' before the commission of the crime, it can be excluded from liability; otherwise, it faces heavy and invasive sanctions.[8]

In detail, the legislative decree provides for two forms of 'organizational culpability' depending on whether the crime is committed by the high-level personnel of the organization or merely by an employee: the role of the physical person inside the organization has led the delegated authority to differentiate the law. The first hypothesis provided for in art. 6,[9] defined as '*culpability* deriving from the choice of *corporate policy*', calls for an inversion of the burden of proof. According to the report, we start from the assumption that, for crimes committed by a top manager, the requirement of organizational fault is integrated. Since, physiologically-speaking, top management expresses corporate policy, they are fully identified with the organization. If this is not the case, then the juristic person must prove his extraneousness to the crime by demonstrating that:

a   effective preventive compliance programmes have been adopted and applied to prevent crimes from being committed;
b   in order to guarantee the maximum efficiency of the organizational models a special control committee has been set up inside the organization, with full supervisory autonomy;
c   top management has committed the crime by 'fraudulently evading' the preventive compliance programmes;
d   there have been no omissions or negligence in the operation of the control committee.

The organizational models aimed at top management must take into account the nature and extension of the functions carried out by the juristic person and outline the requisites of the 'protocols for the formation and implementing of organizational decisions'.

Article 7 instead regulates the assumption of *'organizational culpability'*. Here, too, the heart of the regulations is the predisposition of 'effective organizational models' aimed at preventing crimes.[10]

An important qualification to criminal liability is that the juristic person is not liable if, before the commission of the crime, it had adopted an effective model of organization, management and control capable of preventing such types of crimes.

It is clear that the requirement for the *effectiveness* of the compliance programme does not equate to its omnipotence. It is not expected to always and absolutely prevent crimes; instead, it is asked to contain those requisites of efficiency, practicability and functionality that are reasonably able to minimize the sources of risk. In order to ensure that this efficiency is at its maximum, the model must be tailored to the organization for which it is intended and take into account its activities; in order to guarantee the proper functioning of the model, periodic controls are called for as well as programme changes in response to changes in the organization. Moreover, a disciplinary apparatus is provided to sanction any violations of the compliance programme provisions.

Article 8 completes the set of criteria for imputation, confirming the principle of 'autonomy of organizational liability'.[11] This is a fundamental rule that considers how the organizational processes are carried out inside post-modern corporations where *decentralization* has replaced traditional organizational models, which were propped up by a rigid bureaucratic framework whose effect was often to make it difficult to identify the *individual* physical person as well as to determine that individual's personal responsibility. Thus it is a good idea to avoid adopting *par ricochét* techniques, such as those contained in the 1994 French criminal code, which hold that in order to attribute liability to the organization it is indispensable to identify the physical person, through whom the law is obliged to pass in order to determine organizational liability, thereby impeding the manoeuvrability and practicability of the mechanism. The Italian legislator is to be commended for specifying that the liability of the juristic person is *independent* of that of the physical person who acts on behalf of the organization.

Sanctions and sentencing

The system of sanctions set out in the legislative decree has an 'essentially binary' structure, since it is centred on *fines* and *interdictive sanctions.* Completing this sanctionary pair is *forfeiture* and the *publication* of the judgment.

Fines are *always* calculated – and herein lies its great novelty – through the *shares* mechanism, thereby abandoning the obsolete system of the single-phase sentencing model. The shares system, successfully experimented with in many European countries, permits fitting the punishment to the crime through a *two-phase model*: in the first phase, the judge determines the *number* of shares, linking this to the objective and subjective seriousness of the offence; in the second, the amount of the share is determined based on the organization's economic capacity. This is a sentencing model that keeps distinct the *liability* of the juristic person for the crime and its *sensitivity* to the punishment. The latter is calculated mainly on the basis of the offender's economic capabilities, which is more suited to achieving the purposes of general and special prevention.

Article 12 of the decree establishes when the pecuniary punishment may be reduced. The decree provides for the mitigating factor of the 'tenuity of the crime', which, based on criminological and criminal policy considerations, is divided into two distinct forms: 1) the case in which the crime has been committed in the main interests of the author/physical person or third parties, without any appreciable advantage accruing to the juristic person; 2) when there has been reparatory conduct characterized by the adoption of organizational models capable of preventing future crimes, and where such models have been set up *before* the opening of the trial.

The *interdictive sanctions* of article 13 are applied *only* with regard to the offences they are expressly intended for, and only when certain conditions exist. Article 9 lists these conditions: the interdiction of the activity; the suspension or revocation of authorization, licences or concessions which aided in the commission of the crime; a prohibition on contracting with the public administration; the exclusion of financial facilitations, financing, contributions or subsidies; a prohibition on advertising goods and services. These are highly restrictive temporary or permanent sanctions that can strongly condition the activities of the juristic person, or even bring these to a complete halt.

Article 15 of the decree merits special attention. This article considers cases where the interdictive sanctions are applied to legal persons carrying out a public service or a service of public utility, when the interruption of such activities can cause serious problems for the collectivity, or when the application of the interdictive sanctions can have important negative consequences for employment, given the size of the company and the economic conditions in the territory in which it is located.

These cases represent a form of *probation* with a markedly special-preventive significance. In fact, the officer – whose powers are set by the judge – is charged with reorganizing the *corporate governance* of the organization and setting up an effective *compliance programme*.

Article 19 regulates *forfeiture*, which is conceived of as an obligatory, autonomous and valorized sanction whose aim is to more effectively fight against economic crimes. This sanction is conceived of in terms of both the classic structure of forfeiture – the forfeiture of the product or profit from the crime – and its modern form – forfeiture of an equivalent value.

The sanctionary system is completed by a series of regulations regarding recidivism, complicity in the crime, the statute of limitation, and the violation of the interdictive sanctions.

Is corporate criminal liability necessary?

The principle of corporate criminal liability remains deeply controversial. The criticisms can be summed up as follows: the criminal liability of legal persons is not necessary, since in terms of effectiveness other branches of the law are able to achieve the same objectives of criminal law, in particular the aim of crime prevention.

It is worthwhile recalling the words of Lawrence Friedman, who in 2000 wrote an important essay significantly entitled: 'In defense of corporate criminal liability'.[12]

Legal persons, Friedman states, are *reactive* to the full range of effects that connote retributive theory, since they possess: a) a specific identity that is manifested autonomously in the social area and which is clearly distinguished from that of the individuals that make up the juristic person; this identity differs from company to company and derives from the *culture* that each juristic person possesses, and it reflects the internal customs of the organization, the way *corporate governance* is managed, and its explicit or tacit objectives; b) a capacity to express moral judgements in public as well as points of view which are original and independent of those of the component individuals: judgements that commit the juristic person as a single subject with an integral identity and that permit the juristic person to 'participate in a concrete manner in creating and defining social norms'.[13]

This leads to an important conclusion: because they have a well-defined identity inside the collectivity to which their behaviour can easily be traced, organizations may *suffer* from *moral condemnation*, which is a fundamental and exclusive effect of *criminal law*. Only criminal law is capable of leaving a *stigma*: the other branches of the law have a 'different language and different social meanings' which are not able to communicate moral condemnation; only criminal law, through its rules, manages to express the *particular* and *superior* value that certain goods possess: 'in other words, the nature of liability must underscore that, in that circumstance, the value of the victim or good has no price'.[14]

In other words, the message of strong censure and solemn moral condemnation inherent in criminal law *cannot* be found in any other instrument of social control by the legal system. Even pecuniary sanctions, stripped of their criminal connotations and applied – with the same financial value – as a *non*-criminal sanction, could be viewed, by both the juristic person that suffers the sanction as well as the collectivity, as merely the price to pay to manoeuvre easily and unscrupulously in the business world.

On the other hand, it is more generally known that a trend has emerged in legal doctrine that attributes to modern criminal law a merely symbolic role (understood in the positive sense). We live in a society with a paucity of authentic alternative ideologies, characterized by the loss of traditional moral reference points (family, religion, etc.). The disintegration of social ethics, understood as an autonomous category of reference for the collectivity, has had the effect of investing criminal law with functions that traditionally do not belong to it and that have, until now, not been considered as pertaining to its exclusive sphere of reference. Today criminal policy requires not so much that criminal law impact the moral code of the collectivity, but that it shape it completely.

Thus, without going so far as adopting the extreme tendency that invests modern criminal law with a merely symbolic function, it is worth pointing out, along with Friedman, the risks connected with renouncing recourse to criminal law and its expressive power to combat corporate crime, for reasons of mere effectiveness.

The above considerations should lead us to conclude that the reaction to the legal system could vary *not* on the basis of the legal 'good' that is offended but on what *type of author* has committed the crime: 'For example, the value of human life and health,' Friedman concludes, 'would be perceived as less sacrosanct if attacked by a juristic person than in the case of aggression perpetrated by individuals.'[15]

Conclusion

After almost ten years there are not enough cases available to give a final judgement on the effectiveness of the laws in this area. Furthermore, despite the fact that more recent laws have broadened the list of offences which corporations can be held liable for, the list remains relatively small and does not reflect the full range of economic misconduct in which corporations have engaged. In addition, the sanctioning apparatus is weakened by the inconsistent ways in which it can be applied. The interdictive sanctions for legal persons are called for only in exceptional cases, and the pecuniary penalties are decidedly low compared with those in other countries such as the USA.

The above criticisms notwithstanding, the principle of criminal liability for legal persons represents a major advance in the law. One can only hope that in future this principle will become more deeply rooted in Italy as well.[16]

References

Alessandri (1984), *Reati d'impresa e modelli sanzionatori.*

de Maglie (2001), 'Principi generali e criteri di attribuzione della responsabilitá', *Diritto penale e processo* 1348.

de Maglie (2002), *L'etica e il mercato: la responsabilitá penale delle societá.*

de Maglie (2005), 'Models of Corporate Criminal Liability in Comparative Law', *Wash. U. Global Stud. L. Rev.* 547.

Gobert and Mugnai (2002), 'Coping with Corporate Criminality. Some lessons from Italy', *Crim. L. Rev.* 619.

Marinucci (2008), 'Il diritto penale dell'impresa: il futuro e'gia' cominciato', *Riv. it. dir. proc. pen.* 1465.

Paliero (2008), 'La societa'punita: del *come*, del *perche'*, e del *per cosa*', *Riv. dir. proc. pen.* 1516.

Romano (1995), 'Societas delinquere non potest (Nel ricordo di Franco Bricola)', *Riv. it dir. proc. pen.* 1931.

Notes

1 Romano (1995, 1931 et seq.); Alessandri (1984).
2 de Maglie (2002, 326 et seq.); de Maglie (2001, 1348 et seq.).
3 Gobert and Mugnai (2002, 619 et seq.).
4 Paliero (2008, 1516 et seq.).
5 de Maglie (2005, 547 et seq.).
6 Art. 5. Organizational liability:
   1. The organization is liable for crimes committed in its interest or advantage: a) by persons having a representative, administrative or management role in the organization or one of its organizational units with financial and functional authority, as well by persons who exercise (even *de facto*) management and control functions for the same; b) by persons under the direction or control of one of the subjects mentioned in a).
   2. The organization has no liability if the persons indicated in paragraph 1 have acted exclusively in their own interests or in those of third parties.
7 de Maglie (2002, 331); de Maglie (2001, 1350).
8 de Maglie (2002, 333); de Maglie (2001, 1351).
9 Art. 6. Subjects in top-level positions and organizational models of the collective entity:
   1. If the crime was committed by the persons indicated in article 5, paragraph 1, letter a), the organization is not liable if it can prove that: a) before the commission of the crime the management body had adopted and efficiently implemented organizational and management models suitable for preventing crimes of the type that occurred; b) the oversight task regarding the functioning of the afore-mentioned models and the compliance regarding the models for the latter's updating was entrusted to an organizational body with autonomous decision-making and control powers; c) the persons have committed the crime by fraudulently eluding the organizational and management models; d) there have been no omissions or insufficiencies in oversight activities by the body mentioned in letter b).
   2. Regarding the extension of the delegated powers and the risk of the commission of crimes, the models set out in letter a), paragraph 1, must respond to the following needs: a) identify the activities that can provide the occasion for the commmission of crimes; b) provide for specific protocols to plan the determination and carrying out of organizational decisions relating to the crimes to be prevented; c) identify ways to manage financial resources that are suitable to impeding the commission of crimes;

d) oblige the delegated body that is to oversee the functioning and observance of the models to provide information; e) introduce a disciplinary system with suitable sanctions in cases of failure to respect the measures indicated in the model.

3. The organizational and management models can be adopted, thereby meeting the needs expressed in paragraph 2, on the basis of codes of behaviour drafted by the organization's representative associations; these codes are then to be communicated to the justice ministry which, together with the competent ministries, can formulate, within thirty days, observations on the appropriateness of the models for preventing crimes.

4. For smaller organizations the tasks indicated in letter b), paragraph 1, can be carried out directly by the executive organ.

5. In any case, provision is made for the forfeiture of the profit earned by the organization from the crime, even in the form of an equivalent sum of money.

10 Art. 7. Subjects under someone else's direction, and organizational models of the collective entity:

1. In the case provided for in article 5, paragraph 1, letter b), the organization is liable if the commission of the crime was made possible by nonfeasance regarding the management or oversight obligations.

2. In any case, such provisions involving nonfeasance regarding the management or oversight obligations are not applicable if the organization, before the commission of the offence, had adopted and efficiently carried out a model of organization, management and control appropriate for preventing the types of crimes that occurred.

3. With regard to the nature and size of the organization as well as the type of activities it carries out, the model provides for suitable measures to guarantee the implementation of such activities in accordance with the law and to discover and eliminate in timely fashion risk situations.

4. The effective implementation of the model requires: a) a periodic check and, if necessary, a change in the model when significant violations of the prescriptions are uncovered, or when changes in the organization or its activities have taken place; b) a disciplinary system with suitable sanctions in case of nonfeasance regarding the measures indicated in the model.

11 Art. 8. Autonomy regarding the liability of the organization:

1. The organization is liable when: a) the author of the crime has not been identified or cannot be charged for its commission; b) the crime is extinguished for a reason other than amnesty.

2. Unless the law provides otherwise, no legal actions are undertaken against the organization when amnesty is granted for a crime for which it is liable and the accused has renounced its application.

3. The organization can waive the right to amnesty.

12 Friedman (2000, 833 et seq.).
13 Friedman (2000, 848).
14 Friedman (2000, 855).
15 Friedman (2000, 858).
16 Marinucci (2008, 1465 et seq.).

20 Country report: Lithuania

Deividas Soloveičikas

Introduction

Historically, Lithuanian criminal law did not recognize corporate criminal liability. This was perhaps not too surprising as the laws of Lithuania were influenced by Soviet criminal law. However, even after restoration of its independence, Lithuania was slow to accept the concept of *corporate culpa*.

The modern era of corporate criminal liability began in Lithuania in 2002 when the then existing criminal code, originally adopted in 1961, was amended to introduce criminal liability for companies. The new criminal code, adopted in 2003, culminated a decade of reform of Lithuanian criminal law as a whole. Since then, the code has been amended several times in respect of corporate criminal liability and on each occasion the law has been strengthened by either adding more criminal activities or expanding the list of actions or omissions for which companies could be sanctioned.

The impetus for reform of the Lithuanian law of corporate criminal liability came from the state's obligations under international treaties such as the Criminal Law Convention on Corruption, ratified by Lithuania in 2002,[1] and the UN Convention against Transnational Organized Crime, also ratified by Lithuania in 2002,[2] as well as various international treaties of the European Union. By its decision of 8 June 2009[3] (hereinafter referred to as the 'Decision of the Constitutional Court') the Constitutional Court of the Republic of Lithuania ruled that corporate criminal liability as well as the general concept of criminal fault was not contrary to the supreme law of the state, i.e. the Constitution of Lithuania.

Except for the present author, few scholars have written on the theme of corporate criminal liability in Lithuania; nor have there been many scientific researches in this field. Nevertheless, one can see the beginning of at least theoretical and doctrinal analysis of corporate criminal liability in Lithuania. The main obstacle to implementation of the new law in practice appears to be the resistance of indigenous lawyers who find the new law alien to that which they have known and applied for most of their working lives.

This report will include information on overall legal regulation of corporate criminal liability, the investigation and prosecution of legal persons, and the sanctions which can be applied following the conviction of a company.

Criminal liability of companies and their principals in Lithuania

The primary source of criminal liability of legal entities in Lithuania is Art. 20 of the Criminal Code of the Republic of Lithuania (hereinafter referred to as 'the Code').[4] However, the types of organizations that might be subject to prosecution for criminal activity are described in the *civil* code of the Republic of Lithuania (hereinafter referred to as 'CC'). The main features of a 'legal person', as set out in Art. 2.33 CC–Art. 2.35 CC and Art. 2.50(4) CC, are the right to conduct business under one's own name, the capacity to own assets, having legally recognized rights and being subject to legal obligations. In short, in the eyes of the civil courts, companies have legal personality and are treated much the same as natural persons as far as civil legal relationships are concerned.

When it comes to the criminal law, however, continental lawyers and even many scholars still find it difficult to discard the idea that only natural persons can perpetrate a crime. The principle of attribution to legal entities of the fault of natural persons is still not fully accepted in Lithuania, though it now is more of a practical than a purely legal issue. To pave the way for full corporate criminal liability in Lithuania, the parallel between the role of the legal person in civil and criminal law, i.e. as a holder of rights, obligations and responsibility for breaches of the law, will need to be better appreciated.[5]

Lithuanian company law under the CC and other laws divide legal persons into public and private. Public legal persons are incorporated by the state or municipality and have as their main purpose the satisfaction of public needs.[6] The main purpose of private legal persons is the gain of profit and commercial benefit. Whether a company is public or private is important for criminal law purposes, as not all companies may be liable for a particular criminal offence. The state itself as well as municipalities, their authorities and international organizations, cannot be the subject of a prosecution (Art. 20(5) of the Code).

Article 20(1) of the Code envisages that legal persons shall be liable for criminal activities only to the extent as provided for by the criminal law. In other words, criminal liability is not all-inclusive. In order to prosecute a legal person for behaviour forbidden by the Code such a prosecution must be directly authorized in the Code. Each separate paragraph of the particular Article of the Code will include a provision which says that legal persons shall be held liable for the commission of the crime provided for in the Article.

As noted above, the types of criminal activities for which legal persons can be prosecuted has been broadened substantially in recent years. Generally speaking, legal persons in Lithuania can now be criminally liable even for rape. More generally, legal persons can be prosecuted for offences against the independence of the state, territorial integrity and constitutional order; offences against human freedom, children and family privacy; and crimes against property and ownership (including fraud, damage of property and assets, etc.), intellectual property, IT, economics and business order, and the finance system (including tax evasion, smuggling, etc.). Hence, the list of criminal activities for which companies can be prosecuted is really quite long. At least at a theoretical level, legal entities are approaching the same level of criminal accountability as natural persons.

Article 20 of the Code encapsulates the main doctrines of corporate criminal liability: the indirect liability of corporation under the so-called *respondeat superior* doctrine elaborated by the US courts, and the 'identification' doctrine developed mainly by the English judges. Article 20(3) of the Code provides:

> A legal entity may be held liable for criminal acts also where they have been committed by an employee or authorised representative of the legal entity as a result of insufficient supervision or control by the person indicated in paragraph 2 of this Article.

As can be seen from the wording of the text, the Code recognizes indirect liability of fault to a company through attribution of the actions and fault (or *actus reus* and *mens rea*) of an employee of the company or an authorized person (who is not a senior manager of the legal entity). So the first condition for the application of *respondeat superior* in Lithuania is that the criminal offence must be perpetrated by an employee or authorized person. To determine who is an employee or authorized person one needs to consult, respectively, the Labour code or the CC. It does not matter whether representation of the company is disclosed or not.

A second condition is that the criminal offence must be committed for the benefit of the company. The latter requirement is construed broadly.[7] In light of Art. 20 of the Code, 'benefit' refers to any benefit the legal person might gain due to the perpetration of the offence, including financial or other material gain, whether direct or indirect. Benefit is also considered to exist if the crime is perpetrated in pursuit of an interest which is important or attractive for the legal person. Hence, 'benefit' includes the receipt of credit, a subsidy, or the avoidance of taxes and economic sanctions, as well as when the legal person is awarded a public contract, receives an assignment, etc.

The third condition for the application of Art. 20(3) is insufficient supervision or control by the senior manager described in the paragraph that precedes this Article. The status of this person will be discussed later in this article, but for now the innovative role of 'supervision' should be emphasized. It introduces into Lithuanian criminal law the important concept of 'due diligence' which, as a defence, effectively precludes prosecution of a company which has exercised due diligence to prevent crimes but whose efforts have been foiled by a 'maverick' employee or agent. Due diligence needs to be exercised on a continuous basis.

Insufficient supervision may consist of not having any code of conduct or corporate ethics that would condemn criminal behaviour or, if such a code exists, not informing employees and agents of their responsibilities under it. Insufficient supervision may also inhere in failing to provide proper training for staff. Under Lithuanian criminal law insufficient supervision turns into the criminal one only when the company is seriously at fault in failing to take action and prevent its employees and agents from perpetrating a crime.[8]

As mentioned previously, the Code recognizes the doctrine of 'identification' as a means for holding a company liable where a senior manager of the company commits a crime for the benefit of the legal person. Article 20(2) states:

> A legal entity shall be held liable for the criminal acts committed by a natural person solely where a criminal act was committed for the benefit or in the interests of the legal entity by a natural person acting independently or on behalf of the legal entity, provided that he, while occupying an executive position in the legal entity, was entitled:
> 1) To represent the legal entity, or
> 2) To take decisions on behalf of the legal entity, or
> 3) To control activities of the legal entity.

It should first be noted that this provision repeats the requirement that the criminal actions of the corporate executive need to be for the benefit of the company, while adding the additional element that the criminal act may also be 'in the 'interests' of the company. This wording suggests that the doctrine of identification might be applied on a broader basis than the concept of indirect liability, as the latter appears limited to instances of crimes which were committed for the benefit of the company.

Secondly, the quoted paragraph refers directly to natural persons who occupy an executive position in the company who perpetrate criminal activity on behalf of the company. These include persons who have a statutory right to represent the legal person under the articles of association, joint venture agreement, etc. Thus, persons such as the managing directors of the firm, members of a board of directors or other supervisory board, and corporate officers and senior managers will fall within this section. In addition, persons having a right to take decisions on behalf of the legal entity might include those who *de facto* can control the company and are authorized to manage it or a particular part of the corporation or its commercial activity. This suggests that a company can be prosecuted even in cases when, for example, an individual is not a senior manager, but is delegated functions which in practice make him/her the equivalent of such a person.

The above conclusion is reinforced by the provision allowing corporate criminal liability in cases when a crime is committed by persons controlling the activities of a legal entity. This would appear to embody the doctrine of aggregation, which is recognized in the case-law of the USA and the Netherlands, but which has been rejected in England. However, as the Code is silent on this point there is no authoritative answer as to whether the doctrine of aggregation will in fact be applied in Lithuania. In the opinion of the author it may be applied *de lege lata*, although in practice such application may be frustrated by the psychological constraints of legal practitioners. As mentioned in the introduction to this chapter, most lawyers have difficulty accepting the basic idea that a legal entity might be subject to criminal liability, especially when criminal fault (or *mens rea*) is required. In light of the fact that an understanding of the process of attributing the fault of a natural person to a legal one has been slow to develop, it is hard to imagine that it would be any easier for practitioners to acknowledge the possibility of finding corporate *culpa* in the aggregated actions of a number of individuals. The only point to be made is that this possibility is not precluded by Lithuanian criminal legislation.

Article 20(4) of the Code provides that criminal liability of a legal entity shall not excuse from criminal liability a natural person who has committed, organized, instigated or assisted in commission of the criminal act. This provision has a twofold significance. First, it again makes clear that a company is a *sui generis* perpetrator, a separate liability holder not to be equated with the employee, agent or other natural person who is the 'hands and brains' of the company. The Decision of the Constitutional Court explained:

> It has to be noted in the present context that the peculiarities of corporate criminal liability establish the relevant conditions and circumstances for its criminal liability in the Criminal Code, inter alia including that according to the Criminal Code corporate criminal liability takes place only when criminal activity is perpetrated by the natural person for the benefit of it or for its interests (or solely for its interests), who has the particular features which related him (her) with the legal person.[9]

Secondly, the provisions of Art. 20(4) are directed towards the individual liability of natural persons who act on behalf of the company and for its benefit when perpetrating the criminal offence. Accordingly, principals, employees, agents, etc. also are held to be criminally liable together with the legal person for which they have acted.

It should be noted, however, that the legal person and the natural person who acted on its behalf are not considered to be accomplices. Nor do they have to be prosecuted for the same offence. Under principles of Lithuanian criminal law doctrine as well as the jurisprudence of the Constitutional Court of the Republic of Lithuania, in implementing the concept of corporate criminal liability the foundational principle of *non bis in idem* is not to be ignored, since corporate criminal liability is separate from the liability of individuals.

Investigation and prosecution

Investigation of a corporate crime does not differ substantially from the investigation of a criminal offence perpetrated by an individual. Prosecution is carried out in accord with the Criminal Procedure Code of the Republic of Lithuania (hereinafter referred to as 'Criminal Procedure Code'),[10] which regulates all stages of the criminal process. In a nutshell, the criminal procedure is structured in such a way that the entire process is carried out by the investigation authorities, which are in turn supervised by the prosecutor.

The investigatory body that will carry out an investigation will depend on the nature of the criminal activity to be investigated. For example, distinctive institutions investigate the criminal offences of corruption and tax evasion. Whatever the nature of the particular investigation, however, it almost always will be supervised by the prosecutor. The prosecutor's office (which consists of three levels in Lithuania) is engaged not only in the supervision of investigative authorities and concrete procedural actions in particular criminal cases but also in the investigation of criminal activities and prosecution of the perpetrators in the state courts.

A criminal investigation will be commenced if the grounds envisaged in the Criminal Procedure Code to start an investigation and prosecution (e.g. information available to the investigation authorities on corporate criminal activity, application made by any other person, etc.) are present. A separate section of the Code (Art. 387) regulates corporate crime investigations and also provides that in cases when a prosecution is started against both a company and an individual the cases should be investigated jointly.

Article 388 of the Criminal Procedure Code stipulates that the person representing the firm during a criminal procedure might be the employee or the manager of the company as well as an advocate, who may be appointed by the state. Prosecutors claim that advocates, especially those appointed by the state, may have no real interest in defending the company to the fullest possible extent, and often acquiesce in charges which do not correspond to fair and proper criminal procedures. Thus, the issue or representation of companies charged with crimes appears to have become something of a 'hot spot' in criminal procedure at the moment in Lithuania.

When a company is being investigated and prosecuted, the prosecution may apply to have the activities of the company suspended and limited.

Sanctions and sentencing

Article 43 (1) of the Code provides that the following penalties may be imposed upon a legal entity convicted of a criminal act:

1) Fine;
2) Limitation of operation of the legal entity;
3) Winding up of the legal entity.

The sanctions are listed in order from the least to the most severe. A court should apply a more severe sanction only if it determines that a less severe sanction would not be appropriate. Only one penalty may be imposed for one criminal act, and no penalties other than those specified may be imposed. Having imposed a penalty upon a legal entity, a court may also choose to announce its judgment in the media.

Finally, Section 4 of Article 43 provides:

4. The sanctions of articles of the Special Part of this Code shall not specify the penalties to which legal entities are subject. Whereas imposing a penalty

upon a legal entity, a court shall refer to the list of penalties specified in paragraph 1 of this Article.

A court may impose a fine on a company for any offence committed under the Code, including instances where the Code creates criminal liability but does not specify a penalty. Article 47(2) states that a fine shall be calculated in the amounts of the minimum standard of living (MSL). Fines range from a minimum of one MSL (currently LTL 130, which is the equivalent of €36.23) to a maximum 50,000 MSLs (€1,811,500).

The winding up of the company is the most radical and severe penalty which may be imposed on a company convicted of a criminal offence. Such an order constitutes a virtual 'death penalty' for a company. It envisages a total shut down of the company as well as an end to its business activity. Article 53 of the Code provides that when imposing this penalty, a court shall order the legal entity to terminate, within a time limit specified by the court, its entire economic, commercial, financial or professional activity and to shut down all of its divisions and departments. The civil rights and obligations of the company may not be transferred to any other persons. Lithuanian criminal law does not include a formal provision that this kind of penalty must be imposed only in exclusive cases.

While a court may order the winding up of all of a convicted company's activities, it may less restrictively limit its order to certain activities or to structural subdivision(s) of the company. The effect of the latter order would be to place a compulsory constraint on the way that the offender organizes or carries on its business or on the operation of a subdivision which the court finds to have been responsible for the company's offence. Such an order may be for a limited or unlimited period ranging from one to five years. If a corporation was granted a licence or a permission to carry on a certain activity, such as a licence to provide insurance services, the public institution which issued the licence must, following a court order of prohibition, declare the license to be invalid. While a strict reading of Art. 52 suggests that it may not envisage limitations or restrictions on a firm's doing business with public authorities, or upon its advertising goods or services, its use of a trade mark or its ability to conclude certain contracts, such an interpretation would be undesirable, as it would create a loophole within the scheme of sanctions.

The penalty of public announcement of the company's offence in the media (Art. 43(2)) strikes at a company's public reputation and is designed to serve a deterrent function. The possible negative financial consequences of such a pronouncement, especially if it should lead to a consumer boycott of the company's products, may cost the offender far more in revenues than the maximum fine that the court might have imposed.

Media includes radio, television, newspapers, journals, booklets, etc. It is not clear, however, from the wording of the text of the Code, whether this is a penalty in its own right, the means of announcing a penalty, or a measure designed to enforce some other penalty imposed by the court. This might be considered a shortcoming since announcing the company's offence in the media might be a more effective measure if recognized as a separate penalty in its own right.

Conclusion

Lithuanian criminal legislation has adapted the concept of corporate criminal liability quite wisely. It has included within the Criminal Code all the main doctrines needed to effectuate the attribution of criminal liability to legal persons. However, the regulations are still largely theoretical. This is fairly normal with any new legislation, especially in a country that lacks practical experience in regulating the conditions of corporate *culpa*.

The implementation of corporate criminal liability into the national criminal laws was not dictated by the felt need for such liability; rather, it was more a function of Lithuania's membership in various international organizations and to its being a signatory to many transnational treaties and conventions that included the obligation to regulate corporate criminal liability within the state. On the other hand, it is valuable to add these innovative regulations during a period of growing globalization. In the context of a global community it is hard to predict when establishing the norms of corporate criminal liability within the state might be really useful. Therefore, the introduction of such laws into the Lithuanian criminal justice system should be viewed as a positive step.

The legal regulation of corporate criminal liability and the implementation of the relevant doctrines in practice are still work in progress. There were gaps in the transposition and implementation of international law into the national criminal laws of Lithuania, and, as a result, there are aspects of legal regulation of companies which will have to be adapted to the concept of corporate liability as now embodied in Lithuanian law. For instance, mitigating and aggravating conditions are still oriented towards individuals although there is a list of conditions that must be applied to legal persons as well. The practical implementation of corporate criminal liability would undoubtedly benefit from a deeper theoretical understanding of the concept. However, the legal trend is promising and one may be cautiously optimistic about the future development of Lithuanian law in this area.

Notes

1 Valstybės žinios, 2002, No. 23-851.
2 Valstybės žinios, 2002, No. 51-1929.
3 The decision of the Constitutional Court of The Republic of Lithuania of 8 June 2009 regarding the correspondence of paras. 1, 2, 3 of Art. 20, Art. 20(5), Art. 43(4) of the Criminal Code of the Republic of Lithuania to the Constitution of the Republic of Lithuania, 2009, No. 69-2798.
4 *Law on the Approval and Entry into Force of the Criminal Code. Criminal Cod*e, Valstybės žinios, 2000, No. VIII-1968.
5 See Soloveičikas, Deividas, Legal Person as a Perpetrator: Developments from Company Law to Criminal Law, Teisė, Vol. 48, 2003, P. 144.

6 Art. 2.34(2) CC.
7 A broad interpretation, however, may not be taken if it would result in the criminal liability of a natural person.
8 Soloveičikas, Deividas, Modern Doctrines on Realisation of Corporate Criminal Liability, Teisė, Vol. 46, 2003, P. 139 (in Lithuanian).
9 n. 3 above.
10 *Law on the Approval and Entry into Force of the Criminal Procedure Code. Criminal Procedure Code*, Valstybės žinios, 2002, No. IX-785.

21 Country report: Luxembourg

Ana-Maria Pascal and Janis Dillon

Introduction

Prior to February 2010, Luxembourg law did not recognise any form of corporate criminal liability. Criminal liability was strictly personal and therefore only the natural person could be prosecuted, not the company. Likewise, a sentence could be imposed only on the natural person who committed the offence and not on the legal person. The natural person would be liable not as a representative of the company but as the principal offender.

This historical lack of corporate criminal liability in Luxembourg is said to derive from the ancient principle *societas delinquere non potest* ('a legal entity cannot be blameworthy'), which prevents legal entities from incurring any criminal liability.[1]

Although a company could not be held liable for criminal offences, it could still be liable towards third parties for any civil consequences of such criminal acts.[2] Legal persons could therefore be ordered to pay damages and/or interest to persons who had suffered a loss due to an offence committed by them, or at their request.

Under Article 203 of the amended law of 10 August 1915 on commercial companies, it was also possible to dissolve and liquidate companies which had engaged in criminal activities.[3] However, the Luxembourg *Conseil d'Etat* acknowledged that the sanction of dissolving a company might in some cases be inappropriate or disproportionate to the offence committed and agreed that Luxembourg law needed to be supplemented by the introduction of criminal liability of legal persons into Luxembourg law.

In early 2010, Luxembourg legislation was changed so as to include criminal liability for legal persons (see the final part of this Report).

Liability of directors and corporate officials

While a company could not be held criminally liable (before March 2010), its directors or any other individual representing the company could be subjected to criminal liability for corporate acts that cause illegal harm. For example, there are a number of specific provisions concerning health and safety at work, according to which company directors can be held personally criminally liable. In cases involving a worker's injury or death, directors can be prosecuted for battery or even manslaughter.[4]

The courts must try to identify the physical person who actually committed the offence under the corporate cover. If that person can be identified, their criminal liability alone will be sought. The general test for personal criminal liability is laid down in Article 66 of the Criminal Code, which states that

> The following shall be punished as the perpetrators of a criminal offence:
> (i)   persons who commit an offence or cooperate directly in committing it;
> (ii) persons who in any way whatsoever aid or abet those committing an offence if it could not have been committed without their assistance;
> (iii) persons who, through gifts, promises, threats, abuse of authority or power, plots or deception, directly cause an offence;
> (iv) persons who, either through speeches in meetings or in public places, or through posters, or through writings, whether printed or not, that are sold or distributed, directly cause an offence to be committed, without prejudice to the last two provisions of Article 1 of the Act of 20 July 1869.

Under Luxembourg law, proving intent is an essential condition for establishing that an offence has been committed. This means that the perpetrator must have committed the offence freely and wilfully, unless there is a formal provision to the contrary in the Criminal Code or unless it is contradicted by the nature of the offence.

If the court cannot determine the identity of the physical person(s) who actually committed the offence, they may hold the person at the top of the company management (usually the managing director, chief executive officer, relevant departmental manager, general council or, more exceptionally, members of the board of directors) criminally liable for the offence.[5]

Article 157.4 of the 1915 law on commercial companies stipulates that criminal actions against directors have a specific limitation period of 1, 3, or 10 years, depending on the seriousness of the offence.[6]

In addition, the Luxembourg Criminal Code provides that some offences involving civil liability (i.e. forgery, fraudulent misrepresentation with the intention of causing economic loss, or breach of trust) may also constitute criminal offences for which directors are liable.[7]

However, according to the European Commission, the scope of criminal liability for company directors and officers remains fairly unclear under Luxembourg law, as it does not recognise the need for specific rules on directors' criminal liability, but rather relies on general rules of participation.[8]

Investigation and prosecution

The responsibility for conducting criminal investigations in Luxembourg lies with the national police (Police Grand-Ducale), under the authority of the Minister of Interior Affairs. The national police force is divided into central and regional services. The former, called the Judicial Police Service (SPJ), comprises eight sections, including the general crime section, the organised crime section, and the economic and financial crime section. There are six regional services, each with its own research and criminal investigation unit.[9]

The prosecuting authorities in Luxembourg have a wide range of means of investigation at their disposal, depending on whether the evidence is being sought during the preliminary enquiry or during the examination phase. In the case of an offence that is subject to a preliminary investigation, the Code of Criminal Procedure provides for a great variety of investigative means including on-site inspections, searches and seizures, taking evidence from witnesses, interrogatories, cross-examination and expert testimony.[10]

In addition to these general means of investigation, there are some specific techniques that may be used if the offence at stake is punishable by imprisonment above a certain threshold (usually two years or more). One such technique is communication monitoring (cf. Article 8.1 of the Code of Criminal Procedure).

Prosecution

In Luxembourg, it is the public prosecutors who generally initiate a criminal prosecution. There are two main prosecution offices placed under the authority of State prosecutors. One is attached to the district court of Luxembourg, the other to the district court of Diekirch.

Criminal proceedings are based on the principle of *opportunité des poursuites*, i.e. discretionary prosecution, according to which it is up to the prosecuting authorities to receive complaints and reports of offences, as well as any report made by the police or a public official pursuant to Article 23.2 of the Code of Criminal Procedure. Public prosecutors decide whether or not to take action when a complaint is lodged or an offence is reported. Although the Minister may order the Prosecutor General to initiate action, in practice this power is exercised only exceptionally.

According to OECD literature, Luxembourg criminal law includes an instrument which makes it possible to override the public prosecutors' decision not to bring criminal proceedings because of insufficient evidence. That instrument, known as a 'civil party petition' (*constitution de partie civile*) allows an injured party the opportunity to have criminal proceedings initiated, if he/she can demonstrate real personal and direct injury. If, however, the prosecutor decides to launch criminal proceedings, he/she may, depending on the seriousness of the offence, conduct a preliminary enquiry and lay charges directly before the court or, if the case is serious enough to require arrests, searches, seizures and other such measures, he/she may refer it to an investigating magistrate (*juge d'instruction*). According to Article 49 of the Code of Criminal Procedure, 'The preparatory investigation is *obligatory* in criminal cases and optional in lesser offences'.[11]

After a case is referred to an investigating magistrate, the prosecutor is barred from conducting further investigation. If the investigating magistrate is satisfied that the information is complete, he/she will order the investigation closed. The case is then handed over to the State prosecutor, who advises the district court of his/her conclusion, which will be either to refer the case to the court for trial, or to dismiss it.

Sanctions and sentencing

When legal persons could not be held criminally liable under Luxembourg law (prior to February 2010), there was no need for criminal sanctions applicable to companies.

In respect of sentencing company directors and officers, sanctions are determined by judges, depending on the circumstances of each case. In addition to fines and compensation, the following penalties may be imposed on company directors:

- Disqualification: Article 10 of the Criminal Code provides that persons sentenced to imprisonment for more than 5 years are mandatorily deprived of public titles, grades, functions, positions and offices.
- Loss of official rights: Articles 11 and 12 of the Criminal Code state that persons sentenced to imprisonment for 5–10 years may lose the right to hold public functions; vote or stand for election; wear decorations; be an expert, witness or certifier of official instruments; give evidence; be a member of a family council; possess arms; or be employed in an educational establishment.
- Extradition: Article 2 of the European Convention on Extradition of 13 December 1957 provides that persons committing offences punishable by deprivation of liberty for a maximum period of at least one year may be extradited.

The new law on corporate criminal liability (no 5718/2010)

In 2001 a Justice Ministry Working Group was established to prepare a draft bill that would clearly introduce criminal liability for legal persons under Luxembourg law.

This bill, modelled on the French legislation, was placed before Parliament on 20 April 2007 (Bill 5718). It was aimed to amend both the Criminal Code (which would then include a section on penalties for legal persons) and the Criminal Procedure Code (which would then include a section on proceedings against legal entities).

For almost two years, the draft Bill was before the Conseil d'Etat and the Public Prosecutor's Offices for opinion. In February 2010, the Luxembourg Parliament finally adopted the new law, which entered into force at the end of March 2010.[12]

Details of the new law on corporate criminal liability[13]

The new law introduces general criminal liability for legal persons in Luxembourg legislation. The aim is that legal entities may be held criminally liable in the same way as natural persons.

The scope of the new act is very wide in both *ratione materiae* and *ratione personae*. The law will apply to all types of legal persons (both public and private), with the exception of the State and municipalities, and to all types of offences covered by the Criminal Code and by special laws.

Furthermore, the new law makes legal entities criminally liable for offences committed, on their account, by their board of directors or representatives. However, it provides that the criminal liability of a legal person is independent from that of the natural persons who committed the offence on its behalf, or who were accomplices thereto.

The test of liability is twofold: the offence must have been committed (a) by a legal body or a member of the legal bodies of the legal entity; and (b) in the name and in the interest of the legal entity. Examples of 'legal bodies' of a company include its board of directors, auditor, manager(s) and the general assembly of shareholders.

Under the terms of the new law, the main criminal sanction for legal persons is a fine. Companies and other legal entities can incur fines of up to three times those incurred by natural persons. Legal persons convicted, for example, of bribing foreign officials are liable to a fine of up to €375,000. The other principle sanction is dissolution, which may be imposed (under article 37 of the Criminal Code) when the very *raison d'être* of the legal person was to commit the crime at stake.

The new law also provides for supplementary sanctions, such as confiscation of assets, temporary or permanent closing down of company activities, publicity orders, a ban on exercising certain professional activities, exclusion from entitlement to public benefits. Interestingly, the list does not include prohibition to raise funds or to access capital markets, as it does under French law.

Notes

1 *Directors' Liability: A Worldwide Review*, ch 28: 'Luxembourg' by Guy Harles and Danièle Nosbusch (Kluwer Law International, 2006 on behalf of the International Bar Association).
2 'Getting the Deal Through – Anti-corruption Regulation 2008: Luxembourg' prepared by Kleyr Collarini Grasso, 2008.
3 Ibid.
4 'Directors', Officers' and Managers' Personal Liability: The Legal Position in Luxembourg' Bonn Schmitt Steichen, p 15.
5 *Directors' Liability*, Harles and Nosbusch, cf. supra, note 1.
6 Bonn Schmitt Steichen, cf. supra, note 4, p 17.
7 *Directors' Liability*, Harles and Nosbusch, cf. supra, note 1.
8 Second Report from the Commission, 'Implementation of the Convention on the Protection of the European Communities' Financial Interests', Brussels, 14 February 2008.

9 See the OECD Phase 2 Report on Luxembourg, June 2004, http://www.oecd.org/dataoecd/55/4/32017636.pdf, para 75.

10 Ibid., paras. 80–1.

11 Ibid., paras 63–4.

12 See http://www.lexology.com/library/detail.aspx?g=4a30169c-9758-4b3d-970a-840cdbeca726

13 See the OECD Phase 2bis Report on the Application of the Convention on Combating Bribery of Foreign Public Officials in International Business Transactions and the 1997 Recommendation on Combating Bribery in International Business Transactions (20 March 2008), Part C, http://www.oecd.org/dataoecd/4/21/40322335.pdf, and 'Draft Bill on the Criminal Liability of Legal Entities' Arendt & Medernach, 15 October 2006.

22 Country report: The Netherlands

Melanie Ramkissoon

Introduction

Since 1976, when Article 51 was added to the Dutch Penal Code, a legal person can be held criminally liable for the same offences and with the same sanctions as a natural person.[1] This enactment was preceded by passage of the Economic Offences Act in 1951, which allowed the prosecution of a legal person for an economic offence.

Originally, the courts required that the legal person must have committed the offence through a natural person who either had the power to control its activities, or was part of the normal activity of the legal person, and acted for its benefit (without having directive power). However, this raised concerns about the possibility of proceeding against a legal person in certain types of complex cases. An example would be where the natural person cannot be identified, as in complex foreign bribery cases involving multi-layered corporate structures, where it is difficult to determine the degree of someone's control over the legal person's activities. Modern companies often have decentralised corporate structures where decision-making takes place at different levels. A second problematic area was where the natural person 'in control', although identified, could not be convicted under Dutch law because of a lack of jurisdiction (i.e. a foreign manager residing abroad committing foreign bribery), or incapacity (i.e. death of the natural person).[2] These problems have now been addressed, with the introduction of article 51.

Scope and test of corporate criminal liability

The main statutes and codes dealing with corporate criminal liability in the Netherlands are as follows:

- Dutch Penal Code (*Wetboek van Strafrecht*) (DPC);
- Dutch Code of Criminal Procedure (*Wetbooek van Strafvordering*) (DCCP);
- Economic Offences Act (*Wet Econmische Delicten*) (EOA);
- General Tax Act (*Algemene Wet inzake Rijksbelastingen*) (GTA); and
- Dutch Corporate Governance Code (Tabaksblad Code).

Article 51 of the DPC provides that, where a criminal offence is proved to have been committed by a legal person, criminal proceedings may be instituted against the legal person and/or against those who ordered or directed the commission of the offence.

Legal persons

Legal persons appear to be broadly defined in Dutch law. Included in this category are the State, provinces, municipalities, regulatory bodies, government bodies (article 1); religious associations (article 2); other associations, cooperatives, insurance societies, companies limited by shares, and limited liability companies (article 3).

The following are also considered to be legal persons: partnerships, unincorporated companies, special funds, and ship-owning firms. Indeed, it would seem that the only type of organisation that is not considered to be a legal person is the one-man business.[3]

Natural persons

A natural person and a legal person can both be convicted for the same offence. A natural person may be responsible for crimes committed by a legal person when the former is in a position to direct the latter's activities, and either fails to take action to prevent the illegal activity or accepts the risk of the illegal activity taking place or both.

The natural person need not necessarily occupy a high position in the organisation. Nor, under Article 51.2(2), is it required that the persons in charge be formal directors or owners of the legal person.

In Dutch law, there are no strict criteria for determining when a person is in *de facto* control of an organisation. According to the Supreme Court, a person is considered to be acting as a manager where he/she holds authority and has significant influence over others in the organisation, or a part/activity of the organisation. He/she can even be someone outside the organisation; a legal relationship between the natural person and the legal person is not required, as long as the former can be shown to have a considerable degree of power, influence and responsibility over the latter.

According to Dutch authorities quoted by OECD officials a 'person in charge' is criminally liable where his/her 'intentions (are) directed towards the prohibited actions', where he/she 'consciously accepts the considerable possibility that the prohibited acts will take place', or where he/she fails to take steps to 'prevent the prohibited acts that he/she was competent and reasonably obliged to take'.[4]

While a person who orders the commission of the criminal act will be liable, proof does not have to extend this far. In one case the Supreme Court ruled that a mere suggestion, as opposed to an explicit order, by a manager to perpetrate the unlawful act was sufficient to trigger criminal liability.

Under Dutch law, proof of specific knowledge of the criminal act which has taken place is not required. All that must be shown is that the natural person is aware (has general knowledge) of the criminal activity in question being committed within the context of the company.

Liability of directors and corporate officers

In the Netherlands, company directors and officers are sometimes prosecuted based on different criteria from those explained in the previous section. Article 47 of the DPC stipulates that a company director/manager can be held criminally liable as a co-perpetrator without having physically participated in a criminal activity. It states that:

> the following persons are liable as principals:
> i.   Those who commit a criminal offence, either personally or jointly with another **or** others, who caused an innocent person to commit a criminal offence.
> ii.   Those who, through gifts, promises, abuse of authority, use of violence, threats of deception or providing the opportunity, means or information, intentionally solicit the commission of an offence.

Criminal liability based on joint commission (article 47.1.i) refers to a person having knowingly and wilfully contributed to the commission of the offence. Actual involvement in the offence is not necessary, and no explicit agreements need to have been made. Someone may be deemed to have contributed to the criminal act simply by being present at its commission and not distancing himself/herself from it.[5]

Investigation and prosecution

The police usually initiate a preliminary investigation when there is an indication that a crime has been committed. They may arrest and interrogate a suspect based on a reasonable suspicion that the person in question may have committed an offence.[6]

For bribery offences, there are a number of investigative authorities: the Police, the Fiscal and Economic Intelligence and Investigation Service (FIOD-ECD), and the National Police Internal Investigation Department (*Rijksrecherche*). Any police office can open a criminal investigation, including for corruption offences, but the main responsibility rests with the *Rijksrecherche*.[7]

Economic and tax crimes are investigated by the FIOD-ECD, a special investigation service of the Tax and Customs Administration, created for this purpose. Tax authorities must report to the Head of the FIOD-ECD when they discover potential crimes in the course of their work. However, in cases of potential money laundering, tax authorities must report directly to the Dutch financial intelligence unit, the FIU Netherlands/MOT-BLOM.

After the police have carried out an investigation, they will prepare a report for the prosecutor's office. A case is transferred to these authorities when sufficient evidence has been obtained to justify a decision to prosecute.[8]

The public prosecutor is the official responsible for leading the criminal investigation and may instruct the police as to how to carry out the investigation. All special powers of investigation can be utilised, once a warrant has been issued by the public prosecutor. Special authorisation from the examining magistrate is only required if confidential communications are to be recorded, in cases of home search,[9] and in cases of wiretapping.[10]

The DCCP provides for a wide range of investigative methods. Under the Special Powers of Investigation Act (Wet BOB), covert and undercover investigations (infiltration) are permissible, as are pseudo-purchases, pretending to provide a service, and systematically obtaining intelligence about suspects.[11]

The Wet BOB covers all types of surveillance, as well as the recording of confidential communications.[12] The authorised investigative methods may be used in the investigation of either natural or legal persons. Some investigative techniques, of course, such as pre-trial detention, make no sense in the case of a legal person.

Prosecution

Under Article 167 of the DCCP, the Public Prosecutor's office determines whether or not to bring charges in a given case. In making that decision, a prosecutor will take two main factors into account: first, whether there is enough evidence to secure a conviction and second, whether the prosecution is in the public interest. Other factors that may also be taken into consideration include:

- the seriousness of the offence,
- the amount of negative publicity for the legal person that would be prosecuted,
- any developments in the company since the offence took place or was discovered, and
- the cooperation of the company in the criminal investigation.[13]

In some instances prosecutions may be brought only against the natural person, even if a legal person may be involved in the offence. Considerations that may warrant this approach include the difficulty of proving the legal person's involvement and the relatively modest penalties available even if liability of the legal person was to be established. In respect of the latter point, it might be noted that judges routinely impose lower fines than requested by the prosecution and frequently decline to order confiscation.[14]

Sanctions and sentencing

Under Article 9 of the DPC, the following sanctions may be imposed on a legal person: a fine, forfeiture, withdrawal of certain rights, public disclosure of the sentence, and compensation of the victims.

The specific sanction will vary depending on the seriousness of the offence and whether or not the crime was committed intentionally. For example, the maximum fine for forgery (art. 225 DPC), money laundering (art. 420bis DPC), and participation in a criminal organisation (art. 140 DPC) is €67,000. For tax fraud (art. 68 GTA) the maximum fine is €16,750. In most serious cases of economic crime, the court may order winding up the business (art. 7.c. EOA).

Natural persons found to have committed a crime are subject to a prison sentence. A defendant convicted of forgery or participation in a criminal organisation can be sentenced to a maximum of 6 years imprisonment; for theft, tax fraud or money laundering, the maximum sentence is 4 years imprisonment; and for embezzlement, it is 5 years imprisonment. The penalty for false representation in order to obtain an unlawful gain is up to 3 years imprisonment.

According to DPC provisions for foreign bribery, the same fines apply to natural and legal persons. Maximum fines amount to €11,250 for breaches of articles 177 (where the purpose of the bribe was not to obtain a breach of duty) and 178(1) (where the bribe was paid to influence a judge's decision) of the Penal Code, and to €67,000 for breaches of articles 177a and 178(2), where the bribe was paid to obtain a breach of duty or a conviction in a criminal case respectively. With specific regard to legal persons, article 23(7) of the DPC provides for a possible increase in the fine in cases 'where the category defined for the offence does not allow appropriate punishment'. In such cases, the fine may be up to €45,000 for the lower offences, and €670,000 for the aggravated offences.[15]

Notes

1 Houthoff Buruma, *Criminal Liability of Companies Survey Netherlands*, Lex Mundi Ltd. 2008, p. 1.
2 Ibid.
3 Cf. OECD Phase 2 Report, http://www.oecd.org/dataoecd/14/49/36993012.pdf, p. 58 (last accessed 25/02/2010).
4 Cf. OECD Phase 1 Report, http://www.oecd.org/dataoecd/39/43/2020264.pdf, p. 12 (last accessed 21/05/2010).
5 Houthoff Buruma, supra note 1, p. 11.
6 OECD Phase 1 Report, p. 20.
7 OECD Phase 2 Report, supra note 3, p. 35.
8 Cf. Alexis Aronowitz, 'The Netherlands', in *The World Factbook of Criminal Justice Systems*, US Department of Justice; Bureau of Justice Statistics, 1993. This document is available online at: http://www.ojp.usdoj.gov/bjs/pub/ascii/wfbcjnet.txt
9 See the Factsheet from the Dutch Ministry of Justice on the Special Powers of Investigation Act at http://www.justitie.nl/english/Publications/factsheets/bob.asp.
10 OECD Phase 1 Report, p. 20.
11 Articles 126h–j of the Code of Criminal Procedure.
12 Ibid., Articles 126g, k, m.
13 Houthoff Buruma, supra note 1, p. 7.
14 OECD Phase 2 Report, supra note 3, p. 60.
15 OECD Phase 2 Report, p. 60.

23 Country report: Poland

Ana-Maria Pascal

Introduction

In the early 2000s, Poland had only a system of administrative liability for legal persons in place. A number of features of that system caused concern for European officials, including the requirement, in most cases, of a prior conviction of the natural person, the exclusion of parallel criminal and administrative proceedings,[1] and sanctions that were based on the revenue of the legal person in the previous year. The issues were analysed by the Institute of Justice (a scientific branch of the Ministry of Justice) in 2001 with a view to establishing criminal liability in the near future. Subsequently, the Law of 28 October 2002 on Liability of Collective Entities for Acts Prohibited under Penalty (hereafter 'the Law') was enacted. As the title suggests, the Law is applicable to collective entities, which includes legal persons. This law was introduced in the context of Poland's efforts to meet the criteria for EU membership, as well as other international obligations such as the OECD Convention.

Following a challenge by the Polish Constitutional Tribunal, which found a number of key provisions of the Law to be unconstitutional, Parliament introduced some amendments to the law in 2005, aimed at clarifying those aspects which had previously been open to interpretation. The Law itself constitutes a significant step forward in tackling corporate crime in Poland. However, its effectiveness in practice is yet to be established, especially insofar as the new provisions are concerned, given the relatively short amount of time which has passed since the introduction of the 2005 amendments.[2]

The scope and test of liability

Scope of liability

Collective entities appear to be broadly defined under the 2002 Law.[3] Article 2 distinguishes between two types of collective entities: (a) legal persons and/or organisations without legal personality for which specific legal provisions grant legal capacity, and (b) commercial companies, local government units, associations, entrepreneurs other than a natural person, and foreign organisational entities.

The scope of this definition is obviously wide, covering the more common forms of legal entities, as well as state-owned and state-controlled entities. Moreover, the term 'collective entity' also applies to organisations without formal personality in law (i.e. non-business associations of people and property, partnerships etc.).

Test of liability

The main provisions on how corporate criminal liability is to be established are contained in articles 3, 4, 5 and 16 of the Law on Liability of Collective Entities. The general approach involves vicarious liability: the company is liable for offences committed by a natural person in the name or on behalf of the collective entity.

Article 3 of the Law provides:

> The collective entity shall be liable for a prohibited act consisting in conduct of a natural person who:
>
> (1)   acts in the name or on behalf of the collective entity under the authority or duty to represent it …, or whenever such person abuses the authority or neglects the duty,
> (2)   is allowed to act as the result of abuse of the authority or neglecting of the duty by the person referred to in point 1 above,
> (3)   acts in the name or on behalf of the collective entity on consent or at the knowledge of the person referred to in point 1,
> (4)   *repealed* – if such conduct did or could have given the collective entity an advantage, even of non-financial nature.

Two features of vicarious liability in Polish law are worth noting. First, the collective entity's liability is not dependent on actions of senior management. Liability can be based on the conduct of all persons (i.e. employees, contractors, agents, personnel in a subsidiary company, etc.) that have a relationship with the company.[4]

Second, there can be no liability of a collective entity until a conviction of the natural person is secured. The Statement accompanying the 2005 amendments to the Law provides that 'proceedings (the stage of proceedings before the court) in cases of the liability of a collective entity can commence *only after* a valid and final judgement is rendered in proceedings related to a punishable prohibited act'.

Under article 4 of the Law, the natural person must have committed one of the offences listed under article 16 of the Law on Liability of Collective Entities, and this must be acknowledged in a valid judgment. Thus, if an individual perpetrator cannot be identified, is deceased or has taken flight, or where the court has no jurisdiction over him/her, or liability of the natural person cannot be established, the collective entity cannot be prosecuted. This may be the most problematic aspect of Polish law on corporate crime.

Article 5 provides that a collective entity will be held liable if the offence has been committed as a result of 'at least absence of due diligence in electing the natural person referred to in articles 3.2 or 3.3, or of at least the absence of due supervision over this person, by an authority or a representative of the collective entity'. The Statement accompanying the 2005 amendments to the Law describes this formulation as confirming that an unlawful act of a natural person will trigger liability of the collective entity where the act occurred as a result of negligence on the part of the leading person or representative of the collective entity. Therefore, it would appear that article 5 provides the basis for prosecuting a legal entity where the offence was committed as a result of either a lack of due diligence in selection of, or a lack of supervision over, the individual perpetrator.[5] The responsibility for this absence of due diligence or supervision rests with 'an authority or a representative of the collective entity', not necessarily the leading person referred to in article 3.1. Given the wide variety of types of organisations, the meaning and applicability of the terms 'authority' or 'representative' will need to be established on a case-by-case basis.

The list of offences covered by the Law is set out in article 16. It includes economic and financial crimes, environmental offences, and violations of intellectual property.

Investigation and prosecution

The proceedings concerning the criminal liability of collective entities are governed by the regulations of the Code of Criminal Procedure (articles 303 onwards)[6] and the Law on Liability of Collective Entities (in particular, articles 22–43).

The Code of Criminal Procedure stipulates that:

Article 305. § 1. Having received notice of an offence, the agency authorised to conduct the preparatory proceedings shall be obligated to issue immediately an order on instituting or the refusal to institute an investigation or inquiry.

...

Article 309. § 1. An investigation shall be conducted in cases of crimes and misdemeanours specified in Articles 152 through 154 etc.

§ 2. An investigation should be completed within three months.

Article 310. § 1. In cases where investigation is not mandatory, an inquiry is conducted.

§ 2. An inquiry should be completed within one month. The state prosecutor who supervises the inquiry may extend this period for up to 3 months.

...

Article 311. § 1. The investigation shall be conducted by the state prosecutor.

§ 2. The Police shall conduct the investigation unless it is being conducted by the state prosecutor.

...

Article 331. § 1. Within 14 days of the conclusion of the investigation or inquiry, or receiving an indictment prepared in summary proceedings, the state prosecutor shall file an indictment to the court or shall issue an order on the discontinuance or suspension of the preparatory proceedings, or on a supplementary investigation or inquiry.

The Law on Liability of Collective Entities provides further details concerning the investigation and prosecution process when legal persons are held liable.

Article 23 states that the burden of proof rests with the party that files the evidence, typically the public prosecutor or the injured party (cf. art. 27). All matters of liability of collective entities fall under the jurisdiction of the regional court where the crime has been committed (art. 24), but the Court of Appeal may, at the request of the local court and due to the seriousness of the case, refer the matter to be tried by the provincial court (art. 25). Under article 36, the collective entity will be represented in the proceedings by a member of its body authorised to represent it.

Article 36.1 stipulates that the court will determine the facts and legal issues within the scope of the motion independently and using its sole discretion. However, it expressly states that the judgments referred to in article 4 (against the natural person) are binding. Therefore, in proceedings against the collective entity, it is not open to the court, the prosecution or the defence to seek to re-try or challenge the judgment secured against the natural person.

Sanctions and sentencing

The penalties provided under the Law for collective entities are summarised by Jaroslav Kruk, a senior partner in a Polish law firm:[7]

- fines between 1.000 PLN and 20.000.000 PLN (approximately €250–€5 million), but no more than 10 per cent of the company revenue in the tax year when the offence was committed;
- forfeiture of objects and/or financial gains resulting from the offence;
- bans on advertising, using public funds, applying for public procurement contracts, pursuing business activities, as well as public pronouncement of the ruling.

The new Law establishes fixed thresholds for the fines applicable to collective entities (art. 7), as stated above. The maximum fine is based on the revenue generated during the year when the offence was committed. The aim is to take into account the size and financial situation of the collective entity concerned. However, anomalies can easily occur. For example, a company showing no or little revenue during the year of the offence might not be punishable at all, or receive a very low fine, despite the fact that its level of assets at the time of sentencing is more buoyant. In particular, a newly established company may not receive any fine at all.

There are as yet not many cases to demonstrate the practice and considerations of the courts in imposing sanctions on collective entities. However, articles 10 and 12 of the Law stipulate the factors to be taken into account when determining the appropriate sentence. Under article 10,

When adjudicating the fine, imposing the bans or pronouncing the ruling in public, the court shall consider in particular the weight of irregularities in electing or supervising mentioned in article 5, the size of the advantages actually or potentially obtained by the collective entity, its financial situation, the social consequences of the penalty, and the impact of any punishment on the future functioning of the collective entity.

Article 12 allows the court to waive a fine, if the offence committed has not brought any financial benefit to the collective entity. In such cases the court will limit itself to imposing other sanctions, such as forfeiture, bans or publicity orders.

Under article 8, a collective entity convicted under the Law on Collective Entities may be subject to the forfeiture of the items used in the perpetration of the offence, or the financial gains resulting (even indirectly) from the offence. When imposing this penalty, the court will recognise any valid judgment issued on the basis of article 52 of the Penal Code[8] or article 24.5 of the Fiscal Penal Code which states that the collective entity must refund the financial gains obtained through the offence of the natural person (art. 11.2 of the Law on Collective Entities).

Article 9 of the Law provides for a wide range of additional sanctions that the court can impose on collective entities, including bans on promoting or advertising its business activities, products or services; using grants, subsidies, or other forms of financial support originating from public funds; using aid provided by international organisations; applying for public procurement contracts; pursuing business activities, except where it could lead to bankruptcy or liquidation of the collective entity, or layoffs of employees; and public pronouncement of the ruling. The various bans may be imposed for a period of up to five years.

A sanction can be imposed on a collective entity up to 10 years after a decision concerning the natural persons has been issued. At the end of this period, the judgment is cancelled (art. 43).

Conclusion

Due to the constitutional challenge and subsequent amendments to the law in 2005, there has been only a short period of time to assess the practical operation of the new provisions. OECD officials believe that this could explain the systemic bias in favour of prosecuting the natural person under the Polish legal system.

Further, most cases to date relate to tax offences. This, according to a local prosecutor, signals 'a need to adapt minds and habits in Poland to the new concept of liability of collective entities' to ensure that criminal offences committed by collective entities are duly investigated and, where necessary, prosecuted.[9]

In its 2008 report, Transparency International expresses a number of concerns and makes specific recommendations about ways to address them. One such concern relates to enforcement. The Organised Crime Bureau of the National Prosecutor's Office coordinates all corruption cases. The TI report recommends that Poland should consider safeguards, including a division of the functions between the Ministry of Justice and the National Prosecutor to ensure that the exercise of investigative and prosecutorial power will not be prejudiced by Article 5 considerations, i.e. of national economic interest, the potential effect on relations with another state or the identity of the natural or legal person. The TI report also calls for the government to increase transparency, particularly in transactions of selling public/state owned property (privatisation, reprivatisation, selling state-owned land or real estate).[10]

Notes

1 Administrative proceedings against the legal person could only be instituted after a decision had been made in the criminal proceedings against the natural person.
2 OECD Phase 2 Report on Poland, February 2007, http://www.oecd.org/dataoecd/3/54/38030514.pdf, p. 52.
3 The Law on Liability of Collective Entities for Acts Prohibited under Penalty is available in English at http://www.oecd.org/document/50/0,3343, en_2649_34859_39779314_1_1_1_1,00.html
4 Cf. OECD Phase 2 Report, cf. supra, note 2, p. 53.
5 Ibid., p. 54.
6 Excerpts in English are available at http://www.legislationline.org/topics/country/10/topic/12
7 Jaroslav Kruk, 'Polish Criminal Law', 27 November 2009, at http://www.ilflaw.com/publications/, section 7: 'Liability of Collective Entities'.
8 Art. 52 of the Penal Code reads: 'In the event of sentencing for an offence which brought material benefits to a natural or legal person or an organisational unit not possessing the status of a legal person, and committed by a perpetrator who acted on its behalf or in its interest, the court shall obligate the entity which acquired the material benefit, to return it in whole or in part to the benefit of the State Treasury; this shall not affect the material benefit subject to return to another entity.' (See Annex 3 to the OECD Phase 2 Report, cf. supra, note 2, p. 74.)
9 OECD Phase 2 Report, cf. supra, note 2, p. 55.
10 Fritz Heimann and Gillian Dell, *Progress Report 2008: Enforcement of the OECD Convention on Combating Bribery of Foreign Public Officials*, Transparency International, 24 June 2008, http://sup.kathimerini.gr/xtra/media/files/meletes/econ/offic240608.pdf, pp. 31–32.

24 Country report: Portugal

Ana-Maria Pascal and Melanie Ramkissoon

Introduction

Criminal liability of legal persons was introduced in Portugal in 1984, as a means of combating financial crimes. The scope of liability is limited to specified economic offences such as bribery, tax fraud, false accounting and money-laundering. Article 3 of Decree-Law no. 28/84, which established the criminal responsibility of legal persons, provides:

1. Legal persons, companies and de facto associations are liable for the offences laid down in this Decree-Law when they are committed by their governing bodies or representatives on their behalf and in the collective interest.
2. They are not liable if the offender has acted against express orders or instructions from authorised persons.
3. The liability of the entities mentioned in no. 1 does not exclude the individual liability of the offenders and no. 3 of Article 2 is applicable, with the necessary adaptations.

In 2007, Portuguese authorities undertook a full revision of the country's Penal Code. The ensuing legislation (Act 59 of September 2007), which approves the new Code, includes provisions on corporate criminal liability. According to a European Council report, 'although the criminal liability of legal persons in cases of corruption was not completely lacking before, Act 59/2007 … gave it more general legal force'.[1] It also established a criminal register for legal persons and similar bodies (section 8), entitled 'Criminal Register for Collective Entities' which, since the introduction of the new law until the EC evaluation, had received 17 reports of convictions[2] of private companies.

Other recent legal initiatives are considered in the concluding section of this report.

Scope and test of corporate criminal liability

Scope of liability

Article 3.1 subjects 'legal persons, companies and de facto associations' to criminal liability. It covers both corporations and unincorporated associations, and does not depend on the entity in question having a legal personality. State-owned and state-controlled bodies also seem to be covered, since they are not explicitly excluded. However, while there have been some cases holding private companies liable for offences under the Decree-Law, there have been no cases involving a state-owned or a state-controlled entity.[3]

A legal person can be prosecuted for any offence covered by the Decree-Law, if the offence was committed by its governing body or representative, on its behalf, and in its collective interest. A legal person is not liable when the natural person committing the offence has acted contrary to express company orders or instructions.

Liability of the legal person does not preclude liability of an individual(s) for the same offence.

Test of liability

Article 3.1 establishes a form of derivative liability for legal persons. For a legal person to be liable under Article 3.1, the offence must be committed (i) by its 'governing body' or 'representative', (ii) on 'its behalf', and (iii) in its 'collective interest'. According to Portuguese authorities, any employee, regardless of his/her position in the company, can be the legal person's representative.

Although identification of the natural person who committed the offence (i.e. a 'governing body' or 'representative') is required in order to bring a prosecution against a legal person, conviction of the natural person is not.

The condition that the offence be committed 'on behalf of' and 'in the collective interest of' the legal person will be satisfied even if the crime is committed only in part for the benefit of the company. Thus, in 'dual motivation' cases, where a representative of a legal person commits a relevant offence with the aim of benefitting himself, but the company also benefits, there will be legal liability of both individual and legal person. Likewise, the requirement that the company benefit will be satisfied even if only the legal person's foreign branch or subsidiary benefits from the offence.

Under article 3.2, the legal person is not liable 'if the offender has acted contrary to express orders or instructions from authorised persons'. The latter category includes those who have decision-making or control powers within the organisation.

Article 3.1's reference to 'governing bodies or representatives' includes associates and shareholders, as well as persons who have more formal managerial powers. The relationship between such persons and the legal person must be clearly stipulated in the latter's constitution. However, the key element for establishing liability of the legal person is not the status of the representative within the organisation, but whether, in committing the offence, the representative was acting on the legal person's behalf and in its collective interest.

The scope of the above provisions is somewhat a matter of speculation as the case-law has not addressed in a detailed way the question of who can be the representative of the legal person or how that person is to be identified. More experience may be needed, for instance, to clarify whether acts committed by an employee or outside agent lacking a formal contract with the legal person can give rise to the latter's liability if the individual in question is acting on behalf of the legal person and in its collective interest.

Exactly what is meant by the 'collective' interest of the company also remains somewhat unclear. There are, for instance, criminal acts that do not directly result in net profits such as offering bribery to obtain tax breaks or custom clearance and it is not clear whether they can trigger the liability of the legal person. Consider, for example, the case of a parent company based in Portugal which gains an advantage as a result of a bribe paid by one of its foreign subsidiaries. It is submitted that the parent company should be liable if it ordered, consented to, or ratified the actions of the subsidiary. However, at present case-law is lacking.

Identifying the natural person

The specific identity of the natural person who committed the offence must be determined before the legal person can be prosecuted. Both the individual and the organisation will be investigated for the same offence, although the initial stage of the investigation may focus on the legal person alone. It is only at the conclusion of this investigation that the public prosecutor has to decide whether to charge the natural person(s) or the organisation. Both, however, can be charged, and, significantly, either can be convicted even if the other is acquitted. Of course, there might be problems in establishing the criminal liability of the legal person in a case where the identity of the natural person cannot be clearly determined.

Investigation and prosecution

In Portugal the Public Prosecutor's Office is responsible for an investigation and is authorised to instruct the police in carrying out the investigation (Article 263). The Judicial Police may also investigate corruption offences, but under the supervision of the Public Prosecutor's Office.

An investigation will generally be opened once the Public Prosecutor's Office has been informed of an alleged offence. If the police independently become aware that an offence has been committed, they must report it to the Public Prosecutor's Office whether or not the offender can be identified (Articles 241–243). During the investigation, the public prosecutor will direct that appropriate measures be taken to identify the offender and obtain evidence.

Recent developments in Portuguese legislation[4] include a new Organic Law of the Criminal Police (Law 37/2008), which provides for the creation of a National

Unit of Combat against Corruption, a series of proposals for the implementation of European Directives on the prevention of money laundering and terrorist financing (Law 25/2008), and a new law on cybercrime (Law 109/2009), which provides more effective investigative and cooperation measures to combat new criminal phenomena in cyberspace.

In order to commence a prosecution the Public Prosecutor's Office does not need the consent of the Attorney General or a formal victim complaint. In the absence of case-law, however, it is difficult to assess how public prosecutors and the courts will apply Article 3.1 of DL 28/84 in practice.

Sanctions and sentencing

Under Article 7.1 of the Decree-Law, the primary penalties for legal persons convicted of domestic and foreign bribery offences are a reprimand, a fine and dissolution.

Fines are calculated based on a day-fine system. Fines can range between 10 and 360 days. The daily amount is determined by the legal person's economic and financial situation, and the total number of days by the culpability of the offender and the circumstances of the offence. A court may decide only to 'reprimand' an offender if it believes that this would be sufficient to prevent the commission of future offences.

Under Article 7.6, dissolution of the legal person can be ordered in two instances: first, if the legal organisation was founded with the intention to commit the offence; and second, if repeated violations indicate an intention to use the legal person for the purpose of committing the offence.

Several accessory or ancillary penalties can also be imposed under Article 8. These include confiscation, temporary deprivation of the right to bid in public tenders, deprivation of the right to public subsidies, temporary or permanent closure, a temporary ban on the offender's engaging in commercial activities, and the publicising of the conviction.

Under Articles 2.3 and 3.3, legal and natural persons who have been convicted of an offence are jointly liable for the payment of fines, indemnities and other penalties imposed by the court.

Aggravating and mitigating circumstances are provided for in the general part of the Criminal Code and may result in, respectively, an increase or a reduction in the penalty. For example, the minimum term of imprisonment can be increased by 1/3 in the case of recidivism, and the maximum and minimum terms of imprisonment reduced by 1/3 in the case of mitigating circumstances.[5]

If a convicted legal person enters a merger or acquisition agreement with another company, the criminal penalties of the absorbed company may be transferred to the takeover company. It is not altogether clear, however, what happens if a merger results in the creation of a new legal entity, rather than in one company being absorbed by another.

In Portugal, legal persons are often sanctioned for offences included in DL 28/84, such as fraud in obtaining funding, loans, subsidies or goods, and tax-related offences. The average fine imposed in 2004 was €5,392 and in 2005 €10,280. Compared with the maximum fine permitted by law – €1.8 million – these averages appear too low either to deter violations or to signify the gravity of the offence.

Penalties are also provided for convicted natural persons. For example, under Article 256.1 of the Criminal Code, a natural person may be punished with imprisonment up to 3 years or a comparable fine if he/she produces a false document, forges a document, uses the signature of another person to produce a false document, or uses falsified documents, to cause damage to others or to obtain illegitimate benefits.[6]

Accessory sanctions

In addition to the primary penalties, a judge may also impose a range of accessory sanctions pursuant to Article 8 of DL 28/84. These include asset forfeiture, temporary interdiction on exercising certain activities or professions, temporary deprivation of the right to bid in public tenders and deprivation of the right to public subsidies.[7] These sanctions can be imposed on both natural and legal persons for any offence included in DL 28/84.

The effectiveness in practice of sanctions like 'temporary deprivation of the right to bid in public tenders' or 'temporary interdiction on exercising certain activities or professions' is difficult to assess. As no criminal records are kept on convicted legal persons, there is no ready means for checking on whether a legal person is eligible to bid on a particular tender. Similarly, while convicted company representatives can theoretically be banned from being included on a commercial register, the absence of centrally available information on businesses may frustrate enforcement of the sanction related to a ban to exercise certain activities.

Confiscation

Under Portuguese law, confiscation can be ordered in the case of both natural and legal persons. Confiscation is mandatory following conviction of foreign bribery.

Confiscation applies not only to the bribe offered, but also to any proceeds of the offence that threaten public safety, order or morals, or are likely to be used in the commission of future offences. Confiscation may also apply to any rewards offered to offenders, and to property or other benefits obtained by the offender. When moneys or other benefits targeted for confiscation have disappeared or have been converted into some other form, a confiscation of assets of equivalent value can be ordered.

Confiscation is not limited to the property of the convicted person. Under Article 110 CC, it may also apply to assets of third parties who have benefitted from the offence, or assets acquired as a result of the offence if the owners are aware of their unlawful provenance.

An important task of the prosecutor and the investigating judge is to ensure seizure of assets that can be the subject of a confiscation order. The rules governing such seizure (set out in Articles 46 and 49 of DL 28/84 and Article 178 CCP) apply equally to natural and legal persons. In practice, confiscation orders seem to be made relatively infrequently, although statistics are limited.

Recent developments

In 2008 a draft amendment to the existing law (in particular, to Article 11 CC) was adopted. It states that:

> 2.   Legal persons and equivalent entities, except the State; other state owned (public) legal persons and international organizations of public law are liable for the crimes foreseen in Articles 152-A ... when committed:
>   a)   on their behalf and in the collective interest by natural persons occupying a leadership position within the legal person's structure; or
>   b)   by whoever acts under the authority of the natural persons referred to in the previous subparagraph, on account of a violation of his/her duties of vigilance and control.
>   ...
> 4.   The organs and representatives of legal persons and whoever, within the legal person, has the authority to exercise the control of its activity are considered as occupying a leadership position.

This amendment, unlike the rather broad approach taken in Article 3 of DL 28/84, adopts a narrow basis of liability for legal persons: only offences of natural persons who occupy a 'leadership position' inside the company can trigger the liability of the company.[8] A leadership position is defined in terms of 'whoever, within the legal person, has the authority to exercise the control of its activity'. OECD officials have expressed the hope that this amendment will cause courts to revisit and reinterpret the vaguer provisions of the previous Article 3 (especially those regarding who could trigger the liability of the legal person).

On the other hand, the amendment also provides for a new conceptual grounding for the test of liability of legal persons. Liability may follow when the offence results from a dereliction of the duties of vigilance and control owed by a person in a leadership position. Thus, for example, a manager's failure to prevent bribery by a subordinate when the manager was in a position to do so – or the manager's failure to set up an internal control system which could have prevented the offence – can trigger the liability of the legal person in a domestic bribery case. Interestingly, the liability of legal persons for 'infringement of the duties of vigilance and control' will not apply to cases of foreign bribery, as the new Article 11 CC does not cover offences laid down in DL 28/84.

The difference in approach to domestic and foreign bribery would have little effect if the case-law were to develop in a way that legal persons could be criminally liable for bribery committed by any agent or employee if the offence was totally or in part designed to benefit the legal person. However, there is no indication that the amendment will be interpreted in this manner, and OECD officials have expressed concerns about the different standards governing the liability of legal persons for offences of domestic and foreign bribery.[9]

All other elements in the amendment remain the same, including the provision (previously, Article 3.2) relating to the circumstances in which legal persons may be exempt from criminal liability – namely:

6. The liability of legal persons and equivalent entities is excluded when the actor has acted against the orders or express instructions of the person responsible.

In all cases, the natural and the legal person can both still be held criminally liable for the same offence.

Notes

1 *Compliance Report on Portugal*, Second Round, published by the Council of Europe's Group of States Against Corruption (GRECO), 10 October 2008, and available at http://www.coe.int/t/dghl/monitoring/greco/evaluations/round2/GrecoRC2(2008)2_Portugal_EN.pdf, p. 14.
2 Ibid., p. 12.
3 Cf. OECD Phase 1 Report on Portugal (2002), http://www.oecd.org/dataoecd/51/59/2088284.pdf, p. 9. Five years later, there was still no case law development in this regard, cf. OECD Phase 2 Report on Portugal (2007), http://www.oecd.org/dataoecd/28/24/38320110.pdf, p. 47.
4 Cf. OECD Phase 2 Follow-up Report on Portugal (2010), http://www.oecd.org/dataoecd/31/47/44424102.pdf, pp. 39–40.
5 Ibid.
6 Ibid.
7 Cf. Articles 9 to 21 of DL 28/84.
8 See OECD Phase 2 Report on Portugal (cf. supra, note 1), p. 48 and OECD Phase 2 Follow-up Report on Portugal (cf. supra, note 2), pp. 28 et seq.
9 OECD Phase 2 Report on Portugal, cf. supra, note 1, p. 49.

25 Country report: Romania

Ana-Maria Pascal

Introduction

For more than a decade after the 1989 Revolution, companies could not be held criminally responsible in Romania. The 1997 Criminal Code (law no. 65 of 16 April 1997) did not allow it. In June 2004, however, a new Criminal Code was introduced, which established corporate criminal liability. The new Code came into effect a year later. In July 2006, some amendments were made, which are relevant for establishing criminal liability for companies (see below).[1]

The reasons that led to the introduction of corporate criminal liability in the Romanian legal system were both internal and external. The former had to do with the social-economic situation of a country in transition, where it was not unusual to see 'paper' companies being created for the sole purpose of covering up the crimes of (powerful) individuals, or in order to facilitate such crimes – usually of a financial nature (i.e. fraudulent auctions, unfair competition etc.). The external influences were mainly those coming from Brussels. Under the European Council's Recommendation no (88)18, ascension (as well as member) states have to implement effective, proportionate and dissuasive sanctions with respect to corporate criminal liability, irrespective of whether or not an individual perpetrator has been identified. Corporate culpa is kept distinct from culpa of natural persons. Two other factors that contributed to the Romanian reform in the mid-2000s were the European convention's anti-corruption and anti-environmental crimes (to be sanctioned either criminally or administratively) respectively. All these recommendations coming from Europe's main legislative centre contributed to the decision to legislate on corporate criminal liability in Romania.

The scope and test of corporate criminal liability

One of the features in the 2004 Code is the criminal liability of legal entities. Under article 45,[2] legal entities are 'criminally liable in the cases stipulated by the law, for crimes committed in their name or in their interest' by the corporate entity or its representatives. The state, as well as public authorities and institutions, are exempt from liability.

The Romanian criminal code establishes a system of general liability. It assumes that a legal person may perpetrate, in principle, any offence (see the list of examples below), through any of its employees, irrespective of the employee's position in the organisation. However, a parent company cannot be prosecuted for offences committed by a subsidiary, because under Romanian law the criminal liability is that of the subsidiary.

Scope of liability

Romanian law (art. 3 of 2004 Code) classifies crimes into felonies and misdemeanours, depending on their seriousness. The Code specifies the following offences for which legal entities may be held criminally liable:

- Manslaughter (articles 181.2, 184)
- Grievous bodily harm (articles 189, 192)
- Genetic manipulation (articles 193–7)
- Crimes against individual freedom (i.e. forced labour, human traffic, blackmail, violation of private correspondence, manufacture/use of interception devices) (articles 201–5, 211–15)
- Health and safety offences (articles 243–5)
- Treason, terrorism and crimes against national security (articles 271–5, 277, 279, 282–3, 285–7, 295–300)
- Fascist, racist or xenophobic offences (art. 289)
- Crimes against the freedom of expression of religious beliefs (art. 246)
- Breach of trust through fraudulent asset management, fraud on creditors, deceit (including fraudulent issuance of cheques or other payment instruments), money laundering (articles 257, 258, 260, 268)
- Bribery, traffic of influence (articles 309, 312)
- Embezzlement, destruction of official seals or quality merchandise, unfair competition (articles 326–8)
- Traffic of illegal immigrants (art. 331)
- Organised crime (articles 354–8)
- Adulteration of foodstuffs or other products, non-compliance with recyclable waste provisions, drug dealing (articles 382, 383, 386–94)
- Anti-environment offences (articles 395–405)
- Non-compliance with regulations concerning the production, use, and transport of armament and explosive materials (articles 406–10)
- Non-compliance with legal provisions regarding the authorisation of building works and quality in buildings (articles 411–14)
- Breach of intellectual property rights, IT data and systems (articles 415–27, 429–32, 434–8, 440–8)
- Fraud, unfair competition, non-compliance with legal provisions regarding import and export operations, (articles 452–6)
- Fiscal crimes (articles 459–61)
- Violation of the European Community's financial interests (articles 479–84).

Test of liability

There are three criteria on which a legal person may be charged with a criminal offence:

- the perpetration of the offence when performing the object of activity;
- the perpetration of the offence to the benefit of the legal person;
- the perpetration of the offence on behalf of the legal person.[3]

The first criterion refers to offences that are closely connected to the performance of the company's object of activity, thereby related to the general policy of the company or to its operations (i.e. work safety, competition, environment protection).

The second criterion refers to offences that fall outside the activities related to the performance of the company's object of activity, but which result in a benefit for the legal person. The benefit may take the form of a profit or the avoidance of a loss.

The last criterion refers to offences perpetrated during the process of organising the activity and operation of the legal person without being directly connected to its object of activity. Any breach of the internal norms of conduct by employees, which would not lead to the employees' criminal liability, will also not constitute an offence for the company. On the other hand, if the breach is the result of the perpetration of an offence, the company is criminally liable because the offence is imputable to it.

Mens rea is required to be proved because the criminal liability of a legal person is direct. It is established in the following way. The final part of article 19[1] of the 2006 Code provides that a legal person may be held liable 'where the offence has been perpetrated by means of the infringement provided by the criminal law'.

The subjective position of company officers is first considered.[4] The offence may be the result of either a deliberate decision by the legal person as a whole, or negligence on its part. The latter may consist, for example, of inadequate safety measures, poor management of the company's activities, or unreasonable budgetary restrictions that created the circumstances leading to the perpetration of the offence. For offences committed by a company representative, it is required that the company had been aware of his/her intention to perpetrate such offences or had encouraged such actions. However, the formal opposition of company officers to an unlawful practice does not exonerate the legal person itself from criminal liability.

Strict liability offences do not require proof of *mens rea*. Failures to act, on the other hand, must be shown to have been perpetrated deliberately in order to constitute an offence.

In order to hold a company criminally liable, it is not required to identify or convict a natural person. The company itself is liable for offences which were the result, for instance, of a faulty decision, an omission in the way it organises its operations, or deficient safety measures. Since charging a legal person with an offence is based on the assumption that certain measures that could have prevented the perpetration of the offence were not taken, the company may not be charged if it can be shown that its activities are effectively managed and any deviation from the company's code of conduct is internally sanctioned.

Investigation and prosecution

Romania has established specialist agencies to investigate some offences, while others are investigated and prosecuted by the police and the Prosecutor's Office. For instance, health and safety offences are investigated by an agency called Inspectoratul Teritorial de Munca (ITM), the Local Labour Inspectorate, which is the equivalent of the Health and Safety Executive in the UK.

In the years leading up to negotiations for EU membership and the attendant pressures on Romania to harmonise its laws on breaches of intellectual property (IP) rights with existing EU law and practice, police departments and the Prosecutor's Office focused increasingly on IP matters. These offences were usually investigated by Customs and the police, who became willing to investigate claims more thoroughly. Special departments were created in the police, the Prosecutor's Office and custom authorities, which began to take a very proactive role in enforcing IP rights at the national borders.

A new law (no 344) was introduced in 2005 setting out detailed measures to enforce IP rights within customs proceedings. The legal framework for the protection and enforcement of IP rights now includes the EU IP Rights Enforcement Directive 2004/48/EC, the Government Ordinance on Enforcing IP Rights 100/2005, the Romanian Criminal and Civil Codes, and special laws on Trademarks (84/1998), Patent (64/1991), Design & Models (129/1992), Copyright and Related Rights (8/1996).

In the case of breaches of IP rights,[5] owners tend to resort to criminal prosecution as a means of enforcing their rights when they don't have information on the manufacturer/importer of the counterfeits or in cases where there is large-scale counterfeiting of products which could have a significant impact on the market. Due to certain amendments of the relevant legislation, a complaint is no longer required from the rights holder in order to take action in criminal cases. However, the full cooperation of the owner is required in proceedings in order to ascertain whether the relevant goods are counterfeit. A lack of cooperation on the part of the rights holder can result in either no penalty or relatively insignificant penalties being imposed on the infringer.

During the investigative stage of an IP offence, the prosecutor may take various preventive measures including seizure of the assets and bank accounts of alleged infringers (if applicable) and seizure of counterfeits (if applicable – for instance, in cases of breaches of IP protection laws). Investigation strategies include online investigations; interim measures taken by Customs, the Courts or the Prosecutor's Office aimed at putting an immediate stop to the counterfeiting activity; consultation with local licensees; obtaining advice from expert local counsel; evidence-gathering by the local investigators; and full collaboration of the rights holder.

After the investigation is completed and the case is sent to court, the court can order imprisonment or fines, damages for losses suffered by the owner – provided the owner has submitted a request for damages – and expenses incurred by the Romanian state in the course of the criminal proceedings.

Sanctions and sentencing

Under the Romanian Code, a number of penalties may be imposed for crimes committed by legal entities, including fines, complementary penalties and precautionary measures.

The single *main sentence* that can be imposed on a legal person is a fine ranging between RON 2,500 and RON 2,000,000 (approximately €750–€606,000), according to amended articles 53[1] and 53[2] of the 2006 Criminal Code. In the 2004 Code (art. 59), the range of fines for legal persons was between RON 1,000 and RON 1,000,000, which means that the level of main sentences effectively doubled over a two-year period.

Under article 71[1] of the 2006 Code, where the law provides a maximum sentence of 10 years imprisonment or a fine for a natural person, the range of fines that can be imposed on a legal person is RON 5,000–RON 600,000 (approximately €1,650–€198,000). Where the law provides life imprisonment or more than 10 years imprisonment for the natural person, the range of fines that can be imposed on the legal person is RON 10,000–RON 900,000 (approximately €3,300–€297,000).

There are, however, certain mitigating or aggravating circumstances, such as bankruptcy, which allow the minimum or maximum fine to be amended by the judge, albeit within the limits provided by the Code.

One of the 2006 amendments to the Code (viz., article 40[1]) specifies that, in case of multiple offences, the court will set a fine for each of the offences and apply the highest of these respective fines – which, if needed, can be increased by a third of the maximum allowed for that particular case.

The penalty for natural persons depends on the seriousness of the offence. For felonies the maximum penalty is life detention or a sentence of imprisonment from 15 to 30 years. For misdemeanours the penalty is imprisonment ranging from 15 days to 1 year or from 1 year to 15 years; a fine of between RON 100–RON 50,000 (approximately €33–€16.500); or service in the community of between 100 and 500 hours. In the 2004 Code (art. 58), this was 'a fine in the form of fine-days, from 5 days to 360 days, each day corresponding to an amount of between RON 10–100', which amounts to a total of RON 50–RON 36,000. Again, the increase over a two-year period is almost twofold.

In addition to a fine, the court may impose one or more *complementary penalties* on the legal person. These include suspension of the legal person's activity for a period of 1 to 3 years; prohibition to participate in public procurement procedures for a period of 1 to 5 years; prohibition of access to certain financial sources for a period of 1 to 5 years; posting of the conviction sentence or its publication in the media; dissolution of the legal entity. With the exception of dissolution, all other complementary penalties can be imposed cumulatively, totally or partially.

The *precautionary measures* are more straightforward. Special seizure may be ordered and enforced with regard to goods that are closely related to the offence. The seized goods must meet one of the following conditions:[6]

- They must have been obtained through the perpetration of a criminal offence;
- They must have been used for the perpetration of an offence if they belong to the perpetrator; if they belong to another person, that person must have been aware of the purpose for which they were used;
- They must have been produced with a view to perpetrating an offence, if they belong to the perpetrator; if they belong to another person, the production must have been performed by the owner or by the perpetrator and with the full awareness of the owner;
- They must have been offered with a view to cause the perpetration of an offence or to reward the perpetrator;
- They must have been acquired by perpetrating a criminal offence, if they are not returned to the aggrieved person and if they do not serve as a remedy for such person;
- It must be prohibited by law to own the goods in question.

Some precautionary measures that may be taken against a natural person are not appropriate for a legal person. These would include detainment and the obligation not to leave the country. The procedures applied to legal persons also differ from those which apply to natural persons.

Recent statistics on sanctions imposed for health and safety offences

Both the number and the value of sanctions imposed for health and safety offences have increased in recent years. Since the introduction in 2006 of the Romanian Health & Safety at Work Act, the annual total of fines increased from RON 40,800,000 (€13,464,000) in 2006 to RON 55,500,000 (€18,315,000) in 2008. For the first six months of 2009, the total was RON 21,500,000 (€7,095,000). Most of these fines were imposed following the Local Labour Inspectorate (ITM)'s proactive approach to construction, transport, commerce and agriculture offences.

The increase in the level of fines, as well as in investigation/prosecution levels, reflects the worrying situation on the ground – where more than 450 people die at work every year. According to ITM's records (which cannot account for what is estimated to be a high number of unreported incidents), 422 persons died at work in 2006, 474 in 2007, and 419 in 2008. Investigations reveal that in most cases, both the employer and the employee are responsible. The ITM revealed that 93.2 per cent of the incidents were caused by failures on the part of the deceased person (i.e. failure to obey the terms of the contract or to undertake operations correctly), while 62.7 per cent were caused by failures on the part of the employer (i.e. failure of guidance, supervision and control, as well as poor risk evaluation and failure to provide the necessary safety equipment and training).

The worst recent incident, in which 13 people lost their lives and 15 were injured in two mine explosions, took place on 15 November 2008 at Petrila. The Local Labour Inspectorate's investigation lasted seven months and found that five company officials were responsible for the accident – one former director and four managers. The Labour Inspectorate also imposed 14 sanctions on the mining company, and a fine of RON 152,000 (€50,160). Three of the company officials (the former director and two managers) are facing criminal charges of manslaughter and breaches of health and safety legislation. The trial started on 15 June 2010, at Targu Jiu Tribunal, where the first employee witnesses declared that they had not reported any problems encountered during their work to their superiors, for fear of being transferred.

Conclusion

The fact that the Romanian Criminal Code has been continuously updated during the last decade, with a greater emphasis on the criminal liability of legal persons, demonstrates the commitment of legislators to tackle corporate crime. The constant updating of the level of fines and the continuous diversification of sanctions also shows a willingness to promote increased accountability.

It is, however, too early to comment on how vigorously the new laws will be enforced. There is as yet limited implementation in practice. The criminal liability of legal entities was introduced only six years ago (and the respective law only came into force five years ago). As the KPMG authors conclude:

> The adoption of these criminal norms by the Romanian law system will certainly be a challenge for theoreticians but in particular for the criminal law practitioners. We believe that such innovation will also be a challenge to the theoreticians and practitioners of commercial law, given that numerous crimes may be committed under the umbrella of business and corporate activities. The introduction of legal entities' criminal liability will also have an impact on the shareholders and management of such legal entities, at least by inducing them to exhibit a higher level of prudence.[7]

Let us hope that such a positive impact will extend beyond the world of corporate management and legal practitioners, and that legislators will, in the future, consider amending the Codes so as to include public and not-for-profit organizations as well.

Notes

1 The Criminal Code of 29 June 2004 (hereafter the 2004 Code) is available online at http://www.dsclex.ro/coduri/cod_penal.htm, and the new Criminal Code with Amendments as of 12 July 2006 (hereafter the 2006 Code) is available online at http://www.dsclex.ro/legislatie/2006/iulie2006/mo2006_601.htm#l278. The key sections are article 45 in the 2004 Code and articles 19(1), 40(1), 40(2), 53(1) and 53(2) in the 2006 Code.

2 In the 2004 Code: 'Art. 45 (1) Juridical persons, with the exception of the state, public authorities and public institutions, will be held criminally liable in the cases stipulated by the law, for crimes committed in their name or in their interest, by their representatives. (2) The criminal liability of the legal person does not exonerate the criminal liability of the natural person who contributed to the perpetration of the offence'. In the 2006 Code: 'Art. 19(1). – (1) Juridical persons, with the exception of the state, public authorities and public institutions undertaking activities which cannot be undertaken by private companies, will be held criminally responsible for the crimes committed during their activities or in the name or for the interest of the legal person, if the crime constitutes an offence under penal law. (2) Criminal liability of legal persons does not exonerate the criminal liability of the natural person who contributed, in any way, to the perpetration of the offence.'

3 See article 19¹ of the 2006 Criminal Code, cf. supra, note 1.

4 Cf. *Criminal Liability of Companies Survey: Romania*, a report by Emil Bivolaru and Traian Isaila, Nestor Nestor Diculescu Kingston Petersen, Lex Mundi Publications, 2008, pp. 6–7, available at http://www.lexmundi.com/images/lexmundi/PDF/Business_Crimes/Crim_Liability_Romania.pdf

5 See Dragos M. Vilau (partner, Vilau & Mitel Ltd), the Romanian section of the 'Anti-counterfeiting 2008 Global Guide', http://www.worldtrademarkreview.com/issues/Article.ashx?g=4b3d5013-58e7-427c-b198-e06b10c13003

6 See Lex Mundi Survey on Romania, cf. supra, note 4, p. 5.

7 KPMG, *Legal News Flash*, January 2005, Issue 27, available at http://www.roembus.org/Economic/doingbusiness/ln1_criminal%20code_ian05_eng.pdf, p. 2.

26 Country report: Slovenia

Janis Dillon

Introduction

Under article 33 of the Slovenian Penal Code, 'the liability of a legal person for criminal offences which the perpetrator commits in its name, on its behalf or in its favour shall be provided for by statute'. This is not *stricto sensu* criminal liability, as legal persons are not considered to meet the principle of subjective guilt. It is rather liability for criminal acts. But the general part of the Penal Code and the Code of Criminal Procedure do apply to legal persons.[1]

Scope and test of corporate criminal liability

The 1999 Liability of Legal Persons for Criminal Offences Act (the '1999 Act') does not define the concept of 'legal person'. Nor indeed does any other piece of Slovenian legislation. However, some clarification of the scope of liability of legal persons is provided by Articles 2 and 3 of the 1999 Act.

All common types of legal entities are covered under the 1999 Act, including limited liability companies, unlimited companies, partnerships, joint stock companies, as well as foundations and other not-for-profit organisations. State-owned and state-controlled entities are also considered to be 'legal persons'. However, article 2(1) of the 1999 Act provides that the State, public administration bodies and local self-governing communities cannot be held liable for any criminal offences. All other legal entities, including state-owned companies, can be held criminally liable in the same way as any legal persons (be those public or private) that are not exercising state duties.[2]

Jurisdiction

Article 3 provides that both domestic and foreign legal persons are liable for criminal offences committed in Slovenia. Slovenian legal persons are also liable for criminal offences committed abroad, if these are crimes 'against the Republic of Slovenia, a citizen thereof, or a domestic legal person' or 'against a foreign state, foreign citizen or foreign legal person'.

Test of liability

The test of liability is explained in Article 4 of the 1999 Act, titled 'Grounds for the Liability of a Legal Person'. It provides that:

A legal person shall be liable for a criminal offence committed by the perpetrator in the name of, on behalf of, or in favour of the legal person:
1. If the committed criminal offence means carrying out an illegal resolution, order or endorsement of its management or supervisory bodies;
2. If its management or supervisory bodies influenced the perpetrator or enabled him to commit the criminal offence;
3. If it has at is disposal illegally obtained property gains or uses objects gained through a criminal offence;
4. If its management or supervisory bodies have omitted obligatory supervision of the legality of the actions of employees subordinate to them.

Therefore, a key factor in establishing liability is that the criminal offence is committed by the natural person in the name of, on behalf of, or in favour of the legal person. In other words, liability is not confined to the actions of senior management; instead, it is framed in such a way as to apply to all those (employees, contractors, representatives, etc.) who have a relationship with the legal person.

According to prosecution authorities, in most cases, the actual perpetrator is either a manager or an employee of a legal person responsible for the criminal offence. Management or supervisory bodies have to be involved in the perpetration of the offence, in order to trigger the liability of the legal person, as paragraphs 1, 2 and 4 of Article 4 provide. Let us explore the degree of this involvement.

Paragraphs 1 and 2 of the article describe situations where the management or supervisory bodies of the legal person are actively involved in the perpetration of the offence, by (a) 'carrying out an illegal resolution, order or endorsement of its management or supervisory bodies', or (b) influencing the perpetrator or enabling him/her to commit the criminal offence. In the first case, the perpetrator is merely a tool of management or the supervisory body. In the second, the role of the management is to solicit or instigate the offence.[3]

Paragraph 4 of Article 4 describes a situation where the management or supervisory bodies of the legal person are passively involved in the perpetration of the offence, by having 'omitted obligatory supervision of the legality of the actions of employees subordinated to them'.

The Act does not, however, define the concepts of 'management or supervisory bodies'. This may be intentional, so as to preserve the wide range of meanings for these terms, thereby allowing them to cover the various company structures that exist. In most cases, they will cover directors, managers, and supervisory boards that have the authority to manage and supervise the activities of the legal person. However, in some cases, courts will have to assess if a particular individual or body has such powers on the basis of existing acts and regulations, relevant for a given legal person. According to the OECD phase 2 report (para 158), Slovenian authorities indicate that these terms could also cover persons to whom executive authority has been delegated (i.e. persons empowered to act on behalf of the legal person). The application and scope of the various elements of Article 4 have yet to be fully considered by the courts.

Article 5 of the 1999 Act lists the various limits of the corporate criminal liability, as follows:

(1) Under the conditions under the preceding article a legal person shall also be liable for a criminal offence if the perpetrator is not criminally liable for the committed criminal offence.

(2) The liability of a legal person does not preclude the criminal liability of natural persons or responsible persons for the committed criminal offence.

(3) A legal person may only be liable for criminal offences committed out of negligence under the conditions from Point 4 of Article 4 of this Act. In this case the legal person may be given a reduced sentence.

(4) If a legal person has no other body besides the perpetrator who could lead or supervise the perpetrator, the legal person shall be liable for the committed criminal offence within the limits of the perpetrator's guilt.

According to the above, where corporate criminal liability is established, a legal person shall be held liable despite the fact that the perpetrator is not criminally liable (for instance, due to insanity or other circumstances excluding criminal liability), or in a case where the physical perpetrator has been acquitted. However, a legal person cannot be held liable unless the individual offender has been identified: the identification of the offender is a prerequisite for establishing (a) criminal liability, and (b) that the harm has not, for example, occurred by accident.[4]

Liability of directors and corporate officers

As stated above, the liability of a legal person does not exclude the liability of any natural person who may be the perpetrator of the criminal act. There is, however, an automatic professional exclusion: under Articles 246 and 449 of the Companies Act, individuals who have been sentenced because of a criminal act connected with the economy or legal transactions, etc. cannot be board members or managers in capital companies, and managers in limited liability companies. This exclusion may apply, according to OECD officials, to bribery.[5]

Investigation and prosecution

Under Slovenian law, both the police, the prosecution authority and, in many cases, investigative judges, are all involved in the investigation of crimes. It is the duty of state prosecutors to file criminal charges and perform all procedural acts under the criminal proceedings on behalf of the state. Some offences (such as the foreign bribery offence) are subject to prosecution *ex officio*.

If there is reason to suspect that a criminal offence has been committed, the police must take the necessary steps for finding the perpetrator, i.e. detecting and preserving evidence, and gathering all information that may be useful during the criminal proceedings. Following their investigation, the police must submit a criminal report to the prosecutor, who may request additional investigative work to be undertaken. Under Article 148(10) of the Code of Criminal Procedure (the 'CCP'), the police must submit a report to the state prosecutor even in cases where the information gathered during their investigation provides no basis for a crime report.

Article 145 of the CCP stipulates that all state agencies and organisations with public authority must report any criminal offences of which they have notice to the state prosecutor, indicating all evidence known to them. Members of the public may also bring any information related to criminal offences to the attention of law enforcement authorities. If a crime is reported directly to a court or, more commonly, to the police, the respective report must also be forwarded to the competent state prosecutor.

If there is enough evidence to establish that a criminal offence has been committed, the prosecutor must file a request for judicial investigation either with an investigating judge, or directly with the court. Where a legal person is involved in the crime, the identification of a natural person as the perpetrator of the offence is required.

Once the investigative judge establishes that an offence has been committed, he/she will send the file to the prosecutor, who may ask for the investigation to be supplemented, or decide to prosecute the case or not.

Prosecution

As stated above, identification of a natural person involved in the perpetration of the offence is normally required in order to carry out proceedings against a legal person. However, if proceedings cannot be carried out against the natural person who perpetrated the offence, due to illness, death or because the person had taken flight to escape justice, proceedings against the legal person are still possible. Nevertheless, the requirement remains that prosecution authorities must not only identify a natural person that was the actual perpetrator, but they must also have sufficient evidence to prove the direct intent of the natural person to commit the crime, before the legal person can be held responsible.

In practice, few convictions have been secured under the Liability of Legal Persons Act, despite a significant number of investigations and indictments since its enactment in 1999. Indeed, according to OECD officials, police and prosecutors indicated that a large number of cases against legal persons had not progressed beyond the investigation or indictment stage. Although court delays were often considered a challenge, the priority and capability of law enforcement authorities in investigating legal persons was described by many respondents as being at the heart of the problem.[6]

Proceedings against legal persons

The conviction of a natural person is not a prerequisite for the liability of the legal person (Article 5(1) of the 1999 Act) and, according to Slovenian authorities, cases where the legal person is convicted although the natural person has been acquitted may arise. However, the identification of a perpetrator is required, in order to trigger the liability of a legal person. The responsibilities can be cumulative, since the liability of a legal person does not exclude that of natural persons for the committed offence (Article 5(2) of the Act). According to Article 27, criminal proceedings against the legal and natural persons are initiated and carried out together, and a single judgment is given. (This is called 'unity of procedure' in the Act.) However, when legal obstacles (such as, immunity from prosecution) arise with regard to the natural person, proceedings against legal persons may still be initiated.

Article 5(4) stipulates an exception where the perpetrator of the offence is a director or manager of the legal person: 'If a legal person has nobody else apart from the perpetrator, who could lead or supervise the latter, the legal person shall be liable for the committed criminal offence within the limits of the perpetrator's guilt.' According to Slovenian authorities, this provision applies exclusively to 'single-person companies'.

Sanctions and sentencing

General rules on sentencing are set out in Article 41 of the Penal Code and Article 16 on the 1999 Act.

Article 41 of the Penal Code applies to both natural and legal persons. It states that the perpetrator shall be sentenced according to the gravity of their offence. The sentencing court must consider all mitigating and aggravating factors, in particular: the degree of the offender's culpability; the motive for which the offence was committed; the seriousness of the danger, damage or injury caused; the perpetrator's past behaviour; their financial situation; their conduct after committing the offence; and any circumstances which are relevant for establishing the character of the perpetrator.

Article 16 of the 1999 Act stipulates that, in determining the sentence for a legal person, the court should also take into account the economic situation of the latter. To this effect, factors such as profit, size, number of employees, assets and position in the market should be considered.

In Slovenian law, the following sentences may be imposed on legal persons found to have committed a criminal offence:

a   A fine: where the sentence for natural persons is more than 3 years imprisonment, the fine imposed on a legal person may range between €10,434 and €626,040 or up to 200 times the amount of the damage caused or proceeds obtained as a result of the criminal offence (articles 13 and 26 of the Liability of Legal Persons Act). Where the sentence for natural persons is less than 3 years imprisonment, the fine imposed on a legal person may be between €2,089 and €313,020 or up to 100 times the amount of the damage caused or proceeds obtained as a result of the criminal offence (articles 13 and 26 of the Liability of Legal Persons Act).[7]

b   Expropriation of assets: according to Article 14, half or more of the legal person's assets or its entire property may be expropriated. This sentence may be imposed for criminal offences which, for natural persons, carry a sentence of five years imprisonment or more.

c   Winding-up of the legal person: according to Article 15, this sentence may be ordered if the activity of the legal person was entirely or predominantly used for the carrying out of criminal offences. When applying this sentence, the court must also propose the initiation of liquidation proceedings.

According to OECD officials, since the entry into force of the 1999 Act, there has been only one conviction of a legal person for a criminal offence (money laundering), and, as such, Slovenian judges have limited experience in sanctioning legal persons.[8]

Notes

1   OECD report 'Slovenia – Phase 1: Report on Implementation of the OECD Anti-Bribery Convention' section 2, para 49.
2   Council of Europe, GRECO report (2003) 'Evaluation Report on Slovenia', para 62.
3   See the OECD report on Slovenia, Phase 1, para 56.
4   See the GRECO report (op cit), para 56.
5   OECD report 'Slovenia – Phase 1' section 3, para 97.
6   See the OECD phase 2 report on Slovenia, para 163.
7   All figures are based on the official exchange rate at the time of the introduction of the euro on 1 January 2007.
8   OECD report 'Slovenia – Phase 2' section C.6.a, para 169.

27 Country report: Spain

Melanie Ramkissoon

Introduction

Although the Spanish legal system does not recognise criminal liability of legal persons *per se*, legal entities can be held jointly and severally liable for fines imposed on their managers who are convicted of offences occurring during the course of carrying out the legal person's business. In criminal proceedings, moreover, legal persons can also be held civilly liable for damages caused by the criminal behaviour.[1]

The Spanish Criminal Code further identifies several 'ancillary consequences' which can be applied to companies and are designed to prevent the commission of future offences. These measures are discussed in greater detail in the final part of this Report.

Scope and test of corporate criminal liability

In 2003, articles 445(2) and 31(2) were added to the Spanish Penal Code. Together, they impose a form of criminal liability for legal persons, which allows sanctions to be applied to the legal person in cases of foreign bribery. Permissible sanctions include fines, the winding up or dissolution of the legal person, and prohibitions on its activities.

Under article 445(2) PC, when an individual who is acting on behalf of the legal person is convicted of foreign bribery, a judge can impose on the legal person the sanctions provided for in art. 129 PC. The need for a guilty 'person' means that conviction of an individual is required before any penalties can be imposed on the legal person.

Article 31(2) establishes joint and several liability of legal persons with regard to fines imposed on company managers who are convicted under article 31(1). When a manager is convicted and sentenced under art. 31(1), the liability of the legal person would seem to follow automatically unless the manager could be shown to have been on a 'frolic of his own'.

The ancillary consequences (discussed in the final part of this Report) can only be applied in proceedings for specified offences. These include economic and financial crimes (against the market and/or consumers; money laundering;

money forgery; corruption; price-fixing and bid-rigging in public auctions); environmental crimes; criminal offences against workers' rights; health and safety and drug-related offences; unlawful association; and intellectual property crimes.[2]

Liability of directors and corporate officials

Article 31 of the Penal Code provides for a secondary criminal liability in relation to the manager of a legal person, based on the liability of the legal person:

> Any person acting as an administrator (manager) in fact or in law for a corporate body or on behalf of in legal or voluntary representation of another person shall be personally liable, even though he does not possess the conditions, qualities or relations that the relevant concept of the crime or offence requires in order to be the perpetrator of it, should such circumstances be present for the organisation or person on whose behalf or in whose representation he acts.

The effect of the above provision is that, when a criminal offence is committed through an organisation, criminal liability is attached to one or more of its managers, but not to the legal person itself. There is no rule specifying who within the company should bear responsibility for the offence. However, evidence of criminal intent (or gross negligence) is required in order to hold the defendant liable for a criminal act. Thus the manager likely to be held responsible for the offence will be an individual who occupied a decision-making position within the company that took part in the offence.

At the same time, administrative penalties can be imposed on a legal person for offences attributable to directors, managers or employees of the legal person. However, the criminal and administrative proceedings are separate.

Investigation and prosecution

The investigating agencies

The main state bodies responsible for investigation and prosecution of business-related offences are: the State Prosecution Service (SPS), the Anti-Corruption Prosecution Office (ACPO), and the police.[3]

The SPS consists of prosecution services attached to various courts, as well as some special prosecution services and general offices. The head of the SPS is the State Attorney General, nominated by the Government. The investigatory powers of the SPS include the ability to compel the attendance and detain suspects, as well as to require both suspects and witnesses to answer questions. The SPS can also instruct the police and public authorities to provide reports. A judicial order, however, is required before fundamental rights (except for detention) can be infringed.

The ACPO is a specialist service authorised to investigate and prosecute cases of economic crime and corruption. Although it is part of the SPS, the ACPO differs from other public prosecution offices in that it has support units permanently assigned to it. On the other hand, the ACPO does not have any legal powers beyond those available to regular prosecutors. While the latter investigate most domestic corruption cases, the ACPO deals with cases of 'special significance'.

In 1996 the SPS issued an instruction note concerning the 'special significance' criterion. The Instruction identifies certain types of cases as *prima facie* cases of 'special significance' that can be initiated by the ACPO without the need for approval by the SPS. For all other cases (see the list in art. 18ter EOMF), the SPS will determine whether there is 'special significance' warranting an ACPO investigation. The criteria set out in the Instruction are meant only as a guideline and it is up to the SPS to establish whether a particular case should be investigated and prosecuted by the ACPO or not.

For instance, most foreign bribery cases normally require an SPS decision regarding their 'special significance' status for ACPO jurisdiction. OECD examiners have noted that the reference to bribery in art. 18ter EOMF, which allows the SPS to identify foreign bribery cases as cases of special significance, would seem to indicate a need to increase awareness about this particular offence.[4]

The investigation

An investigation will usually begin with the filing of a report or a criminal complaint with the police, a prosecutor, or a judge. However, prosecutors may also open cases on their own initiative. In some instances prosecutions by the SPS or ACPO have been triggered by press reports.

An investigation will take place prior to the commencement of judicial proceedings. In 2003, an amendment to the Penal Code (art. 5) placed two significant restrictions on such investigations. First, the duration of an investigation by either the SPS or ACPO was to be limited to six months from the date of receipt of the complaint, unless extended by a decree and opinion from the SPS. Second, a requirement was added that, in the course of the initial investigation, the prosecutor must take a declaration from the suspect, who may review the dossier of the proceedings.

The effect of the latter provision is that the prosecution can no longer maintain the secrecy of the initial investigation. ACPO prosecutors have pointedly noted that if a suspect is given access to the complete dossier during the initial investigation of an economic or corruption crime, the effectiveness of the investigation could be seriously undermined.

After a prosecutorial investigation has been completed, the prosecutor can either decide there is insufficient evidence of an offence and close the investigation or, if there is sufficient evidence of an offence, request an examining magistrate to carry out a judicial investigation. In the latter circumstances, the prosecutor will provide the magistrate with the evidence obtained up to that point, and make the arrested person available.

Before leaving the topic of investigations, it should be noted that in some regions, such as Catalonia and the Basque Country, the Civil Guard and the National Police have set up their own police forces. They both have units specifically assigned to the ACPO and specialising in anti-corruption activities.

Sanctions and sentencing

Sanctions under articles 129, 127, and 445(2) PC

Article 129 of the Spanish Criminal Code provides that five ancillary sanctions or 'consequences' may be imposed on legal persons by Spanish criminal courts:

a   Shutdown of the legal person's premises or establishments for a period of up to five years;
b   Winding-up of the legal person;
c   Suspension of the legal person's activities for a period of up to five years;
d   Prohibition to conduct future business or commercial operations related to the offence. This prohibition may be temporary or permanent. If temporary, it must not exceed a period of five years;
e   Placement of the legal person under judicial administration in order to safeguard the rights of employees or creditors for however long is necessary, but not exceeding a period of five years.

Article 445(2) PC provides that, where a natural person is convicted of foreign bribery while acting on behalf of a legal person, the latter can be subject to the sanctions provided in article 129 PC.

In addition to the above sanctions, article 127 of the Spanish Criminal Code allows seizure of the assets of any criminal offence committed with a *mens rea* other than negligence, as well as seizure of the subsequent earnings and instruments used to commit the offence, such as weapons or vehicles. If seizure of these assets is not possible, the court may order the seizure of other assets of the offender of equivalent value.[5]

A number of concerns about articles 445(2) and 129 PC have been expressed.[6] First, article 129 PC does not establish any monetary sanctions against legal persons, which is highly atypical. In virtually all states which impose criminal liability on legal persons, the main penalty following a conviction is a fine, and in many states that is the only penalty available. Second is the fact that sanctions under both articles 445 and 129 are discretionary. No situations or circumstances are identified where a sanction would be mandatory. Third, the articulated purpose of the sanctions in article 129 is 'the prevention of the continuation of the activity and the effects of the same'. There is no reference to general deterrence. Finally, sanctions such as closing down a company or appointing an administrator may be unrealistic in cases involving foreign bribery.

Sanctions under article 31 PC

Art. 31(2) PC provides for joint and several liability of legal persons with regard to fines imposed on managers who are convicted under art. 31(1) PC. The provision seems to apply only to special personal offences and not to the foreign bribery offence referred to in art. 445. Even if art. 31 were found to extend to foreign bribery, its applicability to legal persons would arguably be weak. The liability of the legal person is limited to joint and several liability for a fine imposed on a natural person. The fine designated for a natural person may be insufficient to be an effective or dissuasive deterrent in the case of a legal person. In cases of bribery, fines for individuals are limited to a maximum of three times the bribe, which may constitute a significant amount for the individual, but a small fraction of a company's annual profit.

Post scriptum[7]

In the summer of 2010, the Spanish Parliament approved a new law (nr. 5/2010 of June 22, effective December 23, 2010), introducing criminal liability for legal entities, in addition to any individual liabilities. According to this amendment to the Criminal Code, legal entities (with the exception of state, public bodies, political parties and syndicates) can be held criminally liable for offences committed by employees or company executives in the name of or on behalf of and to the benefit of the company. The new law provides for the following types of sentences: fines, dissolution of the company, suspension of its activity for up to 5 years, loss of right to public subsidies and judicial management. The only situation in which a legal entity can be exempt from criminal liability is if it is able to prove that it had appropriate internal controls in place to prevent criminal offences from being committed.

Notes

1 Esteban Astarloa, Uria Menéndez, 'Criminal Liability of Companies Survey: Spain', at p. 1, in Lex Mundi Publications 2008 (last accessed 24/02/2010), available online at   http://www.lexmundi.com/images/lexmundi/PDF/Business_Crimes/Crim_Liability_Spain.pdf
2 See Astarloa, supra note 1 at p. 2.
3 Cf. OECD Phase 2 report p. 19 etc, http://www.oecd.org/dataoecd/8/38/41590651.pdf (last accessed on 24/02/2010).
4 See OECD Phase 2 Report, supra note 3 at p. 4.
5 See Astarloa, supra note 1, at 2–3.
6 See OECD Phase 2 Report, supra note 3 at 43 etc.
7 We thank Mr Juan Damián Moreno for his assistance in finding out information about the new law establishing corporate criminal liability in Spain (Spanish Criminal Code Amendment-Act 5-2010 JUNE 22). See Miguel Angel Rodriguez-Sahagun and Ricardo Norena, 'New Spanish Criminal Liability of Companies', in *Doing Business in Spain*, pp. 123–125.

28 Country report: UK

James Gobert

Introduction

Unlike most Continental European states, the UK lacks a unified criminal code. This has led to a state of affairs where statutes imposing criminal sanctions on companies have been enacted into law on a piecemeal and sporadic basis. The relevant statutes are not necessarily even to be found within the body of the 'criminal law'. For example, there are many provisions in the Companies Act 2006 that have criminal penalties attached to them, although this is certainly not primarily designed to be a criminal statute. There is also a large body of quasi-criminal or regulatory statutes that impose criminal sanctions on companies for violations. The Health & Safety at Work etc. Act 1974 is an example of such a regulatory law.

Finally, there are the 'pure' criminal statutes, passed from time to time, where Parliament's intent is to create criminal liability, either specifically for companies, or for individuals but where liability to companies can be argued by analogy. Falling into the category of crimes aimed specifically at companies is the Corporate Manslaughter and Corporate Homicide Act 2007 (hereinafter CMCHA). In contrast, the Bribery Act 2010 creates liability for both individuals and companies, while the Fraud Act 2006, primarily directed at individuals, also envisages conviction of companies. The reader will note that each of these statutes is subject-matter specific.

If this dazzling array of statutes were not sufficiently confusing, there is no common thread regarding the test of corporate criminal liability. Sometimes, such as in laws dealing with pollution, liability is strict or absolute, and no *mens rea* needs to be proved. In other areas, corporate liability is vicarious, deriving from the fact that a director, corporate officer or senior manager in the company has committed an offence which is then imputed to the company. In such instances the fault of the company will turn on the elements of the crime as set out in the relevant statute relating to the individual offender. And in some instances, such as in the CMCHA and the Bribery Act 2010, the statute in question sets out its own test of corporate liability but only for the limited purposes of the statute. When no test of corporate liability is set out in a statute, or a company is prosecuted for an offence (such as causing grievous bodily harm) which does not specifically refer to companies as being within its ambit, the courts will fall back on the common law[1] 'identification' test of liability. Under this default position, a company is liable for an offence committed by an individual who can be characterised as (being part of) its 'directing mind and will'. In effect, the identification test imposes derivative liability on the company; the company's liability derives from that of a person who is identified with the company and who commits a criminal offence.

The wide diversity in the test of corporate liability is mirrored in respect of the individual liability of its directors and officers. Under many regulatory laws (e.g. the Health and Safety at Work etc. Act 1974), and some criminal laws (e.g. the Fraud Act 2006 and the Bribery Act 2010), a director can be held liable for the same offence as the company if he/she consented to or connived in the corporate offence. In sharp contrast, under the CMCHA, such accessorial liability is specifically rejected by section 18 of the statute. In the absence of a specific statutory provision, the question of whether a director or corporate officer can be held liable as an accessory to the company's offence will turn on the court's interpretation of the general principles of accessorial liability contained in the Accessories and Abettors Act 1861, which was enacted with natural persons in mind.[2]

The focus of the preceding paragraph was on individual liability for *complicity* in the company's offence. Separate from such accessorial liability, a director, officer or corporate official may be independently liable for violating the relevant substantive law. Thus, for instance, a CEO who orders a company employee to destroy a house in which the CEO (but not the employee) knows that there are inhabitants, and the inhabitants are killed, may be charged with murder, regardless of whether the company is prosecuted for manslaughter. Indeed, corporate manslaughter. There is no crime of corporate murder because in English law there is a mandatory life sentence for one convicted of murder and a company cannot be imprisoned.

Who investigates an alleged corporate crime will also vary depending on the crime charged. For example, in the case of workplace injuries and deaths (which may constitute either a simple or aggravated form of battery or, in the case of a death, manslaughter), the initial investigation will be conducted by the Health and Safety Executive, a regulatory body specifically established by statute to investigate work-related accidents. More generally, and in the absence of a specialised agency, the police will be responsible for investigating criminal offences. In some instances a protocol, such as exists in the health and safety area,[3] may allow for a joint or coordinated investigation involving both the police and a regulatory body. Finally, sanctions for companies found to have violated the criminal law may again vary tremendously, depending on the relevant statute. Some statutes have precise penalties or penalties whose upper limit is fixed. Other statutes allow the courts to impose an unlimited fine, with the precise amount in a given case being determined by precedents and guidelines established by judges,[4] or by parameters set by Parliament. The CMCHA, for instance, provides for a wide range of penalties, including remedial orders (also available under the Health and Safety at Work etc. Act 1974) and, more innovatively, publicity orders.

The test of corporate criminal liability

In the absence of a specific test of criminal liability set out in statute, examples of which we will look at subsequently, a company can be held liable for an offence committed by a person who can be characterised as being part of the 'directing mind and will' of the company; or what is commonly referred to as the 'identification' doctrine. The House of Lords' decision in *Tesco Supermarkets Ltd. v. Nattrass*[5] is generally considered to contain the authoritative statement of this test. The House of Lords, while not identifying who was the 'directing mind(s)' of Tesco, held that the branch manager of a supermarket did not fall within this category and was therefore 'another person' for purposes of the defence set out in the relevant section of the Trade Descriptions Act alleged to have been violated.

Interestingly, and contrary to the rule in almost every other jurisdiction that has considered the issue, a company can be held liable under the 'identification' doctrine for an offence of a corporate officer even though the officer was acting against the company's interests. In *Moore v Bresler Ltd* the secretary of a company had privately sold the company's products with the intent to defraud the company. In order to conceal his fault, he had submitted false documents to the Revenue relating to the tax on the items sold. When these violations came to light, both the secretary and the company were charged with violating the Finance (No 2) Act 1940. Not surprisingly, the company argued in its defence that not only was its secretary not acting pursuant to its directions, but also that the company itself was the victim of the offence. This fact notwithstanding, the court held that the relevant question was whether the company secretary was acting within his authority. If so, his acts were the acts of the company, and his offence could be imputed to the company. Whether or not the secretary was acting in the best interests of the company or solely in his own personal interest was irrelevant.

An ambitious attempt to expand and re-locate the identification doctrine within a broader scheme of liability was undertaken by Lord Hoffman in *Meridian Global Funds Management Asia Ltd. v Securities Commission.*[6] He asserted that the identification doctrine was a sub-category of a broader test which turned on the *attribution* of authority. Under Lord Hoffman's approach, an individual's acts or state of mind could be attributed to the company where the individual in question had the authority to act on behalf of the company with respect to the transaction in question. Whether or not the individual had such authority was to be discovered by examining (a) the company's 'primary rules of attribution' as contained in its constitution and articles of association, (b) any primary rules of attribution implied by Company Law, and (c) general principles, including rules of agency and estoppel. Lord Hoffmann further stated that a court could find a 'special rule' of attribution where it was clear that the statute was intended to apply to companies, and it was not inappropriate to hold that the individual offender's acts, knowledge or state of mind could count as those of the company *for purposes of the particular statute*. While many thought that *Meridian* signalled a new dawn in respect of the test of corporate criminal liability, the Court of Appeal in

A-G's Ref. (No. 2 of 1999)[7] held *Meridian* inapplicable in the context of a corporate manslaughter prosecution.

The 'identification' doctrine will provide the test of corporate criminal liability when no test is set out in the governing statute. Increasingly, however, one encounters statutes that have their own *sui generis* test of corporate liability. For example, Section 2 of the Health and Safety at Work etc. Act 1974 provides:

> (1) It shall be the duty of every employer to ensure, so far as is reasonably practicable, the health, safety and welfare at work of all his employees.

Similarly, under section 3:

> (1) It shall be the duty of every employer to conduct his undertaking in such a way as to ensure, so far as is reasonably practicable, that persons not in his employment who may be affected thereby are not thereby exposed to risks to their health or safety.

Notice that, while purporting to impose absolute duties on employers, each of these provisions has a built-in defence; namely that the employer has taken 'reasonably practicable' steps to avoid the harm.

An entirely different test of corporate liability can be found in the CMCHA, even though this Act envisages liability for deaths that would otherwise fall within the Health and Safety at Work etc. Act 1974. The basic offence under the CMCHA is set out in section 1 of the Act:

> (1) An organisation to which this section applies is guilty of an offence if the way in which its activities are managed or organised—
>   (a) causes a person's death, and
>   (b) amounts to a gross breach of a relevant duty of care owed by the organisation to the deceased.

However, in s. 1(3) of the Act one can see lingering echoes of the 'identification' doctrine in that the gross negligence causing the death needs to be traceable back to the company's senior managers.

> (3) An organisation is guilty of an offence under this section only if the way in which its activities are managed or organised by its senior management is a substantial element in the breach referred to in subsection (1).

Nonetheless, one can discern a gloss on the identification doctrine in the reference to senior management defined in terms of persons (note the plural) who play significant roles in either making decisions about how the whole or a substantial part of the company's activities are to be managed, or the actual managing of the whole or a substantial part of those activities. This formulation implicitly recognises the possibility of 'aggregated' fault as a basis of corporate liability, a position previously rejected by the courts.[8]

If one looks closely enough, one can also find imbedded in the CMCHA the Australian concept of 'corporate culture'.[9] However, a faulty corporate culture (demonstrated by a company's attitudes, policies, systems or accepted practices)[10] only becomes relevant when a health and safety violation serves as the basis of an offence, and even then it is only of evidentiary significance.

An arguably more progressive test of corporate liability can be found in the Bribery Act 2010. Under section 7 of this Act, a company can be guilty for failing to prevent bribery. No proof of a positive act on the part of the company is required; it is sufficient that it failed to take the necessary steps to prevent the bribery. However, it is a defence for the company to prove that it had adequate procedures in place, designed to prevent persons associated with the company from engaging in bribery.

What this cursory examination highlights is the lack of a uniform test of corporate criminal liability within English law. In order to determine the test of corporate liability in a given case, one must first identify the crime charged; second, check the relevant statute to see if it provides a test of fault; and third, and if it does not, apply the 'identification' test, perhaps with the added gloss of *Meridian.*

Liability of directors and corporate officers

Most regulatory offences have provisions for holding directors and officers of offending companies liable for their company's offence when they have consented or connived in the commission of the offence. Illustrative is Section 37 of the Health and Safety at Work etc. Act 1974:

> Where an offence ... by a body corporate is proved to have been committed with the consent and connivance of, or to have been attributable to any neglect on the part of any director, manager, secretary or other similar officer of the body corporate ... , he as well as the body corporate shall be guilty of that offence ... [11]

More traditional criminal offences contain comparable provisions regarding individual liability. To give but two examples, Section 12 of the Fraud Act 2006 provides:

> (2) If the offence is proved to have been committed with the consent or connivance of—
>   (a) a director, manager, secretary or other similar officer of the body corporate, or
>   (b) a person who was purporting to act in any such capacity, he (as well as the body corporate) is guilty of the offence and liable to be proceeded against and punished accordingly.

(3)   If the affairs of a body corporate are managed by its members, subsection (2) applies in relation to the acts and defaults of a member in connection with his functions of management as if he were a director of the body corporate.

and, similarly, Section 14 the Bribery Act 2010:

(2)   If the offence is proved to have been committed with the consent or connivance of—
(a)   a senior officer of the body corporate or Scottish partnership, or
(b)   a person purporting to act in such a capacity, the senior officer or person (as well as the body corporate or partnership) is guilty of the offence and liable to be proceeded against and punished accordingly.

The most glaring exception to this general principle of accessorial liability of corporate officers and directors can be found in s. 18 of the CMCHA:

(1)   An individual cannot be guilty of aiding, abetting, counselling or procuring the commission of an offence of corporate manslaughter.

It is hard to understand why it was felt that corporate manslaughter was deserving of this exceptional treatment, especially given that the basis of a company's liability can be found in the gross breach of a relevant duty by senior managers. The exemption seems strikingly at odds with the general recognition in regulatory schemes of the accessorial role of directors, corporate officers and senior managers in their company's offence, as well as the principle of vicarious fault underpinning the 'identification' doctrine and retained in respect of other corporate crimes. Of course, the individuals in question could still be prosecuted for gross negligence manslaughter independent of their company's liability for corporate manslaughter. However, such a charge would be difficult to make stick. Among elements of the offence which a prosecutor might have difficulty proving would be (1) a duty of care to the victim; (2) breach of that duty that amounted to gross negligence; and (3) that the breach was not too remote cause of the death.

Investigation and prosecution

Historically, criminal offences were investigated by the police. However, with the rise in corporate crimes, specialist agencies are often created to conduct investigations. For example, the (soon to be replaced) Financial Services Authority had a broad investigative remit in respect of offences relating to financial services, the Serious Organised Crime Agency (SOCA) has responsibility for the investigation of serious offences involving organised crime including money laundering, and the more narrowly focused Serious Fraud Office will investigate cases of serious fraud.

Specialist investigatory agencies also feature prominently in the enforcement of regulatory laws. The HSE (Health and Safety Executive), which has responsibility for workplace offences, is probably the most well known of these agencies.[12] Another highly active agency is Her Majesty's Revenue and Customs (HMRC), which investigates crimes that fall under the various Customs and Excise Acts. HMRC has wide-ranging powers including those of arrest, entry, search and detention. The British Transport Police has investigatory authority to police the railway and light railroad systems of Great Britain. Their jurisdiction is determined by the locus of the crime rather than the type of offence committed. The Civil Aviation Authority (Air Traffic Standards Division) and the Maritime and Coastguard Agency (Marine Accident Investigation Branch) operate similarly.

The rationale for specialist investigatory agencies in the corporate crime field is that, by dealing with such cases on a regular basis, the agency is able to build up an expertise that the typical local constabulary cannot. A specialist agency may also have more experience dealing directly with corporate executives, even if, on the whole, the police have greater experience in interviewing witnesses. Nor is it all that obvious that the police want the responsibility for investigating corporate crimes, when they already have their hands full with such mainstream offences as assaults, thefts, burglaries, rapes, criminal damage, etc. committed by natural persons.

The problem with specialist agencies is that they are dependent upon government funding. A pro-business government can easily eviscerate an agency by starving it of funds and manpower. Under recent Labour governments, for example, there was a dramatic reduction in the budget of the HSE, and, implicitly, its effectiveness in conducting workplace inspections. The present coalition government in the UK has signalled its intent to abolish the FSA or strip it of many of its powers.

While, since its inception, the Crown Prosecution Service has had primary responsibility for prosecuting serious criminal offences, many regulatory agencies, such as the HSE and FSA, retain the authority to bring a prosecution in their own name. Typically in such circumstances the agency will instruct a barrister of its choosing.

Increasingly, specialist agencies, the police and prosecuting authorities have recognised the value of cooperation. For example, there now is a protocol relating to work-related deaths between the police, local authorities, the Health and Safety Executive, the British Transport Police and the Crown Prosecution Service.[13] Joint investigations may be conducted, with the police or an agency taking the lead. Alternatively, either the police or an agency may transfer to the other responsibility for an existing investigation.

Sanctions and sentencing

Neither Parliament nor the English judiciary has shown much in the way of imagination when it comes to sentencing of companies convicted of a criminal offence, or company directors and officers convicted of aiding and abetting the criminal offence of their company. Likewise the Serious Fraud Office has an interdisciplinary staff which includes lawyers, accountants, computer experts and trained fraud investigators.

Sentencing of companies

The typical sentence imposed on a company convicted of a criminal offence, subject to exceptions that will be discussed subsequently, is a fine. For serious offences, the fine has no upper limit, but there is likewise no minimum. Unlike in many European countries, there is no unit system involving a mathematical calculation to determine the appropriate amount of the fine. Rather, the trial court, having heard the evidence and received supplementary information (following a conviction) relating to the appropriate sentence, is deemed to be in the best position to impose whatever fine it considers appropriate.

Historically, this discretionary approach led to very low fines, some verging on the derisory. In *R v British Steel Plc*,[14] for instance, a multi-million pound steel company was fined £100 after it was found to have committed a health and safety violation that resulted in the death of a worker; and in *Alphacell Ltd. v Woodward*[15] a company which had polluted a river was fined £24.

The prevailing pattern of fines caused unease even among the judges. In *R. v Howe & Sons (Engineers) Ltd*[16] the Court of Appeal set out guidelines on what constitutes an appropriate fine for a health and safety violation. The Court indicated that it was prepared to ignore precedent because in its view fines in previous cases had been set too low.[17]

The *Howe* Court stated that in general terms a fine should reflect the gravity of the offence and the means of the offender. The Court then proceeded to identify several specific factors that should be taken into account in sentencing:

- the extent of the violation
- how far short of the appropriate standard the company had fallen
- the degree of risk and the extent of the danger that had been created
- whether the violation was deliberate
- whether the violation was an isolated lapse or a continuing breach
- the defendant's resources
- the effect of a fine on the defendant's business.

The Court also identified several aggravating and mitigating factors that a sentencing court might consider. Aggravating factors included the fact that a death had resulted from the violation, that there had been a failure to heed past warnings, and that the breach had been deliberate with a view to making a profit. Mitigating factors included a prompt admission of responsibility, a timely plea of guilty, remedial measures taken after the deficiencies were drawn to the company's attention, and a good safety record.

Even after the *Howe* decision, fines in HSE cases remained disturbingly low. The average fine in 2006–07 for a health and safety violation was £15,370. However, if fines in excess of £100,000 were disregarded, this average fine would drop to £8,723.[18]

The fundamental danger of fines is that they can easily come to be viewed as a cost of doing business, an expense to be passed on to the company's customers, or to be recouped by making innocent workers redundant. Among critics there was a strong sense that penalties other than fines needed to be developed for corporate offenders.

As far back as 1988, the Committee of Ministers of the Council of Europe made sweeping recommendations for possible penalties for companies found to have committed a criminal offence. The proposed penalties were:

- a warning, reprimand, recognisance;
- a decision declaratory of responsibility, but no sanction;
- a fine or other pecuniary sanction;
- confiscation of property which was used in the commission of the offence or represented the gains derived from the illegal activity;
- a prohibition on certain activities, in particular exclusion from doing business with public authorities;
- an exclusion from fiscal advantages and subsidies;
- a prohibition upon advertising goods or services;
- an annulment of licences;
- removal of managers;
- appointment of a provisional caretaker management by the judicial authority;
- closure of the enterprise;
- winding-up of the enterprise;
- compensation and/or restitution to the victim;
- restoration of the former state;
- publication of the decision imposing a sanction or measure.

Very few of these proposed sanctions have been given serious consideration in the UK, let alone being enacted into law. However, a step in this direction was taken in the CMCHA, where section 9 of the Act allows a court to make a remedial order, designed to prevent future violations, and section 10 authorises publicity orders. The latter are potentially extremely powerful because, once the public becomes aware of the company's offence, it may engage in a boycott of its products. The damage to the offender's reputation and the resulting loss in revenue may far exceed any fine that even a court inclined to be punitive might have imposed.

In 2010 the Sentencing Guidelines Council issued guidelines for sentencing in cases of corporate manslaughter. The Council indicated that fines should seldom be less than £500,000 and normally should be measured in millions of pounds. The Council also indicated that a publicity order should be made in virtually all cases. Finally, as in *Howe*, the SGC identified general factors affecting the seriousness of the offence, aggravating factors and mitigating factors.

Among the general factors to be considered are the foreseeability of serious injury, the frequency of the breach within the organisation, and the level in the organisation's hierarchy where the fault lay. Aggravating factors included the extent and seriousness of the harm caused, whether the company had a history of 'near misses' in similar circumstances, whether there was any evidence of cost-cutting practices at the expense of safety within the company, and whether there was a deliberate failure to comply with appropriate licensing requirements. The list of mitigating factors included a prompt acceptance of responsibility, a high level of cooperation with investigating authorities, genuine efforts to remedy the effects of the offence and a good health and safety record.

Sentencing of corporate executives

The problem that courts encounter with sentencing corporate executives convicted of being an accessory to their company's crime is not so much the range of punishments, because individuals can be imprisoned, but rather that the traditional factors judges consider in sentencing individuals all argue against imprisonment. The convicted corporate director will usually not be violent, and is unlikely to have a criminal record or to pose a danger to the public if released. Conversely, the offender will often be able to point to a strong record of public and community service. Under these circumstances it is hard to identify a purpose that would be served by imprisonment other than the deterrence of similarly situated corporate executives. Unfortunately, the executives at whom such deterrence is aimed may consider themselves unlikely ever to be caught.

Again the way forwards may lie in introducing more creative sanctions. One possibility would be to put the defendant's skills and expertise to use for the public good. The potential of community orders for a corporate executive is far greater than for a street offender. For example, in *US v Mitsubishi Intl Corp*,[19] the trial judge ordered the convicted corporate officer to help design a rehabilitation programme for ex-offenders.

One sanction available under English law for convicted corporate directors and officers is disqualification. Under the Corporate Directors Disqualification Act, 1986, a director can be barred from serving in a similar capacity in the future once having been convicted of an indictable offence concerned with the 'promotion, formation, management, or liquidation of a company'. In a 2000 Report, the Home Office suggested that this might not be an inappropriate penalty for a corporate executive found to have been complicit in manslaughter committed by the director's company, although in the event, it will be recalled, the CMCHA rejected liability for individuals who had contributed to their company's offence.

Notes

1　'Common law' refers to law created by the courts rather than law which is set out in a statute or Code.
2　See James Gobert, 'Squaring the circle: The relationship between individual and organisational fault' (this volume).
3　See Anne Alvesalo-Kuusi, 'Investigating safety crimes in Finland' (this volume).
4　See *R. v Howe & Sons (Engineers) Ltd* [1999] 2 All ER 249.
5　[1972] AC 153, HL.
6　[1995] 3 All ER 918, Privy Council.
7　[2000] 2 Cr. App. 207, CA.

8   See *R. v H.M. Coroner for East Kent, ex parte Spooner* [1989] 88 Cr. App. R. 10.
9   See CMCHA section 8(3). See generally Rick Sarre, 'Penalising poor corporate "culture": Is this the key to safer corporate activity?' (this volume).
10 CMCHA section 8(3)(a).
11 Health and Safety at Work etc. Act s.37 (1974). The potential for using this section to fill the gap left by the 2007 Act is explored in F. Wright, 'Criminal Liability of Directors and Senior Managers for Deaths at Work' [2007] Crim. LR 949.
12 See Health and Safety at Work etc. Act 1974 s. 18.
13 http://www.hse.gov.uk/pubns/misc491.pdf (last accessed 13/05/2010).
14 [1995] ICR 586.
15 [1975] 2 All ER 475.
16 [1999] 2 All ER 249.
17 Id. 253.
18 http://www.hse.gov.uk/statistics/overall/hssh0607.pdf (last accessed 13/05/2010).
19 677 F.2d 78 (9th Cir. 1982).

Part IVb

Country reports

Countries with administrative liability

29 Country report: Czech Republic

Melanie Ramkissoon

Introduction

Czech law is based on the principle of individual criminal liability and does not recognise collective criminal liability. In the case of legal persons, it is always a natural person acting on behalf of the legal person who will be held accountable for criminal offences. However, legal persons bear civil and administrative liability and may be sanctioned accordingly.

Civil liability for bribery under the Commercial Code

In the Czech Republic, bribery is dealt with under the Commercial Code (art. 44.2e), where bribery is considered to be a form of unfair competition. Under section 53 of the Code, victims of unfair competition may demand that the perpetrator abstain from further illegal action and offer satisfaction in money or damages. The court may also order the perpetrator to surrender any unjustified enrichment.

Practical limitations

While the above provision should theoretically apply to legal persons, OECD inspectors signal several obstacles to its enforcement:

> First, the action must be brought by a victim of the crime. A provision that allowed a public prosecutor to bring an action has been repealed. Unfortunately, Czech jurisprudence is not clear on who a 'victim' is in a crime of foreign bribery. … Second, even if a foreign state or a non-Czech company may bring an action, it may not be practical to do so. Commencing private litigation in a foreign state is very costly and time consuming. It can therefore be justified only in cases involving large sums of money. Third, there are limits to the jurisdiction of Czech courts to hear foreign bribery cases under the Civil Code. According to an official of the Ministry of Justice, for a Czech court to assert jurisdiction, there must be some connection between the case and the Czech Republic. For example, a court may refuse to hear a case

if the only connection is that the briber is a Czech company. Given these practical limitations, the lead examiners do not believe that the Civil Code offers effective, proportionate and dissuasive sanctions against legal persons for foreign bribery.[1]

Equally unsettling is the fact that the above provision only applies to cases of bribery between competitors, where an employee of one company bribes an employee of another, competing organisation. Thus, the provisions of the Commercial Code may well not apply to foreign bribery cases.

Liability of directors and corporate officials

Under Czech law, only natural persons can be held criminally liable. The following two examples illustrate the type of offences for which individual company officials can face criminal charges.

The offence of money laundering

Prior to 2002, sections 251 and 251a of the Czech Criminal Code set out the law on money laundering. The former dealt with concealment, and the transfer or use of assets acquired through criminal offences; the latter addressed authorising another person to disguise the origin of an asset acquired by means of a crime. In July 2002, section 251a was repealed and two new provisions were added: section 252 on negligent money laundering, and 252a on concealment or deceit concerning the source of any benefits acquired by criminal activity.

The offence of false accounting

False accounting may also attract criminal sanctions for company representatives. Under section 125 of the Criminal Code, the failure to maintain accounts despite an obligation to do so, keeping accounts with false or substantially distorted data, and destroying and concealing accounts are all criminal offences. However, these provisions only apply to offences that can be proven to have jeopardised property rights of another person, or proper tax assessment.

Investigation and prosecution

The main law enforcement body responsible for investigating crimes in the Czech Republic is the police. Within the force, the Criminal Police and Investigation Service (CPIS) are responsible for conducting investigations. Two specialised units of the CPIS are allocated to economic and financial offences.

The Unit for Combating Corruption and Financial Crime (ÚOKFK) has nationwide competence over investigations into corruption. Set up in 2003 and based in Prague, this unit has regional branches throughout the country. The

ÚOKFK is sub-divided into two sections: the Department on Corruption and Protection of EU Interests, and the Department on Serious Economic Crimes.

The Unit for Detection of Illegal Proceeds and Tax Crime (ÚONVDK), set up in July 2004, deals with investigations into tax crimes, money laundering and financing of terrorism.

Prosecution

There is no specialised body to prosecute money laundering cases, but according to Czech authorities, there are prosecutors who specialise in this area in most prosecutors' offices.

The Public Prosecutor's Office is responsible for prosecuting false accounting under the Czech Criminal Code.

Territorial Financial Authorities (TFOs) are responsible for imposing fines for breaches of the Accounting Act, 563/1991, sections 37(6) and (7). There are 222 TFOs throughout the country and their primary task is collecting taxes. Their enforcement work focuses on ensuring compliance with fiscal laws; enforcement of accounting standards in general is secondary. Anti-corruption activities are allocated even lower priority. In the view of OECD examiners, enforcement of the Accounting Act is therefore inadequate.

The investigation and prosecution process includes several phases. First, the police and public prosecutors will have to receive a report that a crime has been committed. The police will then verify the facts and attempt to identify a suspect. If unable to do so, the case will be dismissed. If a suspect is identified, the police will open the prosecution with a resolution describing the offence at stake and its legal designation. Subsequently, the police will initiate an investigation to collect further evidence for trial. Upon completion of their investigation, the police will transfer the file to the prosecutor, who decides whether or not to proceed with the case.[2]

Sanctions and sentencing

Sanctions for money laundering

Under article 252a of the Criminal Code, money laundering is punishable by two years imprisonment and/or a fine of CZK 2,000 to 5 million (approximately €70 to €175,000). Other available sanctions include confiscation and prohibition from engaging in certain activities. The term of imprisonment can increase to up to five years if the offender belongs to an organised group or if he/she acquired a benefit of CZK 500,000 (€17,500) or more as a result of the crime. The penalty can be further increased to up to eight years and forfeiture of property if the offender has abused his/her position when committing the crime, or if he/she acquired a benefit of CZK 5 million (€175,000) as a result of the crime.

Sanctions for false accounting

Under article 125 of the Criminal Code, false accounting is punishable by imprisonment for a period of between six months and three years, a prohibition to engage in certain activities, and/or a fine of up to CZK 5 million (approximately €175,000). The term of imprisonment can increase to up to five years if the offence led to 'extremely grave consequences', such as damage to another person's property.

Under the Accounting Act, false accounting is punishable by a fine of up to CZK 500,000 (approximately €17,500), which may be increased to CZK 1 million (€35,000). Czech authorities admit that these sanctions are not dissuasive enough.

According to OECD reports, sanctions imposed for breaches of the Accounting Act have been low. Between 2000 and 2004, the average fine was approximately CZK 13,000 (€460) against natural persons and CZK 30,000 (€1,100) against legal persons.

Sanctions for foreign bribery

Foreign bribery is punishable by imprisonment for 1–5 years, a fine of CZK 2,000 to 5 million (approximately €70 to €175,000) and/or prohibition to engage in certain activities.

Administrative sanctions may include disentitlement to public benefits (e.g. export credit or support) and disqualification from participation in public procurement and privatisation.

Between 2002 and 2005 there were 328 convictions for domestic bribery. Only 29 of cases resulted in jail sentences, 16 of which were for less than one year. Almost a third of the convictions resulted in suspended sentences, while another third resulted in fines. Prohibition from engaging in certain activities or to undertake any public work was ordered in only 17 and 24 cases respectively.

Conclusion and future directions

In June 2004, the Czech government submitted a draft bill to Parliament, to introduce criminal liability for legal persons. The range of sanctions stipulated in the bill included fines, forfeiture of proceeds of a crime, a ban on receiving public subsidies and participating in public procurement, cancellation of licence to operate, publicity order, confiscation of property and winding up of the legal person.

In November 2004, however, the bill was rejected. According to Czech officials, the scope of liability was considered to be too wide. Other reasons invoked for rejecting the bill were that imposing criminal sanctions on legal persons would potentially punish innocent parties such as shareholder groups, and that imposing individual sanctions was sufficient.

OECD examiners have expressed serious concerns about the pace of legislative reform in the Czech Republic. No visible progress has been made in the years since Parliament rejected the 2004 draft bill.

Notes

1 OECD phase 2 report on Czech Republic, October 2006, para 174–6.
2 See the Criminal Procedure Code, sections 12(10), 157–167, 174.

30 Country report: Germany

Klaus Rogall

This paper applies to serious criminal offences committed by companies, involving death or serious injury (whether to workers or third parties) and significant financial loss (in particular money laundering, corruption, and fraud).

Introduction

The responsibility of legal persons and associations of persons (*Verbände*/ 'corporations'/'personnes morales') is regulated by the law for violations of good order, i.e. regulatory offences (OWiG) in Germany. The development of fines against legal persons and associations of persons originates in the legal practice of the 1920s. At that time there were specific provisions in different laws. The fines for which legal persons and associations of persons are liable under the OWiG (*Verbandsgeldbuße*) were finally normalised in § 30 OWiG, thus standardising the highly different provisions for fines against legal persons and associations of persons scattered in numerous laws.

The test of corporate criminal liability

The OWiG was enacted in 1952 and has been changed a total of 46 times to date. The last version dates from 2007. The law serves for the punishment of an injustice which is not considered to be punishable and as a result cannot or should not be punished as an indictable offence or misdemeanour. Before 1952, offences of this type could be reprimanded as 'misdemeanours' (criminal law) or punishable with a fine (administrative criminal law). These possibilities no longer exist. It should be added that the difference between 'real' criminal law and administrative 'criminal law' has a long tradition in Germany, which can be traced back to the Middle Ages.

The OWiG contains a material part ('General Part' and within the 'Specific Part' there are few 'single' regulatory offences – over 99 per cent of the other regulatory offences are found outside of the OWiG) and its own procedural law. The OWiG is always applicable when the offences under a federal law, state law or local law are punishable by fines (the regular legal consequences and envisaged sanctions in the OWiG). The OWiG is also a type of 'framework law'.

The responsibilities of legal persons and associations of persons are stipulated in §§ 9, 30 and 130 OWiG. The central norm is given in § 30 OWiG. These norms have the following wording:

Act on Regulatory Offences
CHAPTER TWO
BASIS FOR SANCTIONING
Section 9 [Acting for Another]
(1) If someone acts
    1.   as an entity authorised to represent a legal person or as a member of such an entity,
    2.   as a partner authorised to represent a commercial partnership, or
    3.   as a statutory representative of another, then a statute, pursuant to which special personal attributes, relationships or circumstances (special personal characteristics) form the basis of sanctioning, shall also be applicable to the representative if these characteristics do not indeed pertain to him, but to the person represented.
(2) If the owner of a business or someone otherwise so authorised
    1.   commissions a person to manage a business, in whole or in part, or
    2.   expressly commissions a person to perform on his own responsibility duties which are incumbent on the owner of the business, and if this person acts on the basis of this commission, then a statute pursuant to which special personal characteristics are the basis of sanctioning shall also be applicable to the person commissioned if these characteristics do not indeed pertain to him, but to the owner of the business. Within the meaning of the first sentence, an enterprise shall be the equivalent of a business. If someone acts on the basis of a corresponding commission for an agency which performs duties of public administration, then the first sentence shall apply *mutatis mutandis*.
(3) Subsections 1 and 2 shall also apply if the legal act which was intended to form the basis of the power of representation or the agency is void.

CHAPTER SIX
FORFEITURE; REGULATORY FINE IMPOSED ON LEGAL PERSONS AND ASSOCIATIONS OF PERSONS
Section 30 [Regulatory Fine Imposed on Legal Persons and on Associations of Persons]
(1) Where someone acting
    1.   as an entity authorised to represent a legal person or as a member of such an entity,
    2.   as chairman of the executive committee of an association without legal capacity or as a member of such committee,

3.   as a partner authorised to represent a partnership with legal capacity, or

4.   as the authorised representative with full power of attorney or in a managerial position as procura-holder or the authorised representative with a commercial power of attorney of a legal person or of an association of persons referred to in numbers 2 or 3,

5.   as another person responsible on behalf of the management of the operation or enterprise forming part of a legal person, or of an association of persons referred to in numbers 2 or 3, also covering supervision of the conduct of business or other exercise of controlling powers in a managerial position, has committed a criminal offence or a regulatory offence as a result of which duties incumbent on the legal person or on the association of persons have been violated, or where the legal person or the association of persons has been enriched or was intended to be enriched, a regulatory fine may be imposed on such person or association.

(2)   The regulatory fine shall amount

1.   in the case of a criminal offence committed with intent, to not more than €1 million,

2.   in the case of a criminal offence committed negligently, to not more than €500,000. Where there has been commission of a regulatory offence, the maximum regulatory fine that can be imposed shall be determined by the maximum regulatory fine imposable for the regulatory offence concerned. The second sentence shall also apply where there has been commission of an act simultaneously constituting a criminal offence and a regulatory offence, provided that the maximum regulatory fine imposable for the regulatory offence exceeds the maximum pursuant to the first sentence.

(3)   Section 17 subsection 4 and section 18 shall apply *mutatis mutandis*.

(4)   If criminal proceedings or regulatory fining proceedings are not commenced on account of the criminal offence or of the regulatory offence, or if such proceedings are discontinued, or if imposition of a criminal penalty is dispensed with, the regulatory fine may be assessed independently. Statutory provision may be made to the effect that a regulatory fine may be imposed in its own right in further cases as well. Independent assessment of a regulatory fine against the legal person or association of persons shall however be precluded where the criminal offence or the regulatory offence cannot be prosecuted for legal reasons; section 33 subsection 1 second sentence shall remain unaffected.

(5)   Assessment of a regulatory fine incurred by the legal person or association of persons shall, in respect of one and the same offence, preclude a forfeiture order, pursuant to sections 73 or 73a of the Penal Code or pursuant to section 29a, against such person or association of persons.

CHAPTER FOUR
VIOLATION OF OBLIGATORY SUPERVISION IN OPERATIONS AND ENTERPRISES

Section 130 [Violation of obligatory supervision]

(1) Whoever, as the owner of an operation or undertaking, intentionally or negligently omits to take the supervisory measures required to prevent contraventions, within the operation or undertaking, of duties incumbent on the owner and the violation of which carries a criminal penalty or a regulatory fine, shall be deemed to have committed a regulatory offence in a case where such contravention has been committed as would have been prevented, or made much more difficult, if there had been proper supervision. The required supervisory measures shall also comprise appointment, careful selection and surveillance of supervisory personnel.

(2) An operation or undertaking within the meaning of subsection 1 shall include a public enterprise.

(3) Where the breach of duty carries a criminal penalty, the regulatory offence may carry a regulatory fine not exceeding €1 million. Where the breach of duty carries a regulatory fine, the maximum regulatory fine for breach of the duty of supervision shall be determined by the maximum regulatory fine imposable for the breach of duty. The second sentence shall also apply in the case of a breach of duty carrying simultaneously a criminal penalty and a regulatory fine, provided that the maximum regulatory fine imposable for the breach of duty exceeds the maximum pursuant to the first sentence.

To which offences does this legal test apply?

The law is used for criminal offences or regulatory offences committed by an entity, a representative, proxy or another person with management or controlling powers (i.e. a representative) of the legal person or association of persons. It is only valid when in committing the criminal offence or minor offence.

Duties incumbent on the legal person or on the association of persons have been violated.

An enrichment of the legal person or the association of persons has been achieved or was intended.

An enrichment can also consist of the sparing of costs to the legal person or the association of persons.

To what organizations does the test apply?

§ 30 OWiG is essentially effective for all legal persons of public and private law. With regards to associations of persons, the effectiveness of § 30 OWiG is restricted to associations without legal capacity and commercial partnerships with legal capacity.

The imposition of a fine against a legal person or association of persons assumes that an entity, representative, proxy or another person with management or controlling powers has committed a criminal offence or regulatory offence which is substantiated in a closely described way to § 30 OWiG. In committing the offence, duties incumbent on the legal person or on the association of persons must have been violated (test 1) or the legal person or association of persons must have either been enriched or at least intended to be enriched by the action (test 2). In both cases the criminal offence or regulatory offence must be completely tortious and also culpably perpetrated.

A brief analysis of the strengths and weaknesses of the statute

It is not obviously clear how the responsibility of a legal person or association of persons can be theoretically understood using § 30 OWiG. Dispute exists as to whether § 30 OWiG only extends to the legal consequences of an offence committed by an individual or whether the provision is a norm of attribution, which attributes to the company the tort of a representative of a legal person or association of persons. It is also possible to understand § 30 OWiG as a legal norm which is testimony to crime and for this reason actually belongs to the provisions of crime and accessory to crime in the general part of criminal law. The lack of theoretical consideration of these questions leads to weaknesses in its legal use. As a result, the question of the limitations on the actions of legal persons and associations of persons remains a matter of dispute.

In addition, the basic duty to punish (a 'moral' reproach is not imposed outside of criminal law) through official administrative fines cannot be compared with the atonement character of a conviction and sentence as a socio-ethical non-value judgement. As a result, the regulatory fine sanctions on legal persons and associations of persons could convey a false impression to the public that they are related to insignificant misconduct.

In contrast, a strength of § 30 OWiG is the flexibility of the application of the law. In regulatory law the expediency principle (see below) is valid differently to that in criminal law. As a result, the best judgement of the administrative authority determines whether a process against a legal person or association of persons should be set into motion or not. Under a criminal law resolution the Office of the Public Prosecutor, which is not always an administrative authority, would have to intervene in every case. They could not, for example, disregard sanctions against the legal person or association of persons which lead to dissolution through insolvency.

Otherwise, the procedural law of the OWiG seems better suited to providing for the sanction of legal persons and associations of persons by practical means. This procedural law is simpler, faster and less acutely related to legal protection. Under a criminal law solution, a specific procedural law within the code of criminal procedure would probably have to be established.

For the parties involved, the advantage for them lies in that they are spared the charge of a criminal guilt and with it the label of being a 'criminal'.

In addition, this type of 'decriminalisation' reflects a modern legal-political trend.

Sanctions and sentencing

The provisions for the assessment of a fine against a legal person or association of persons require that the criminal offence or regulatory offence be committed by a representative of the legal person or association of persons who possesses the necessary competence for ascertaining its significance (Sinnbestimmung). 'Sinnbestimmung' is defined within the limits of corporate policy for decision-making, if and when the association behaves in a law-abiding manner. Which circle of representatives can act as an 'alter ego' of the legal person or association of persons comes into question and is exhaustively transcribed by law. Qualified actors are those authorised to represent a legal person or a member of such an entity, the chairman of the executive committee of an association without legal capacity or a member of such a committee, the partner authorised to represent a partnership with legal capacity, and in addition, general agents or current proxy holders in a management role and authorised signatories and similar persons covering the supervision of the conduct of the business of a legal person or association of persons (persons with management or controlling powers).

Essentially, a fine can only be imposed against a legal person or association of persons when a punishment or a penalty has been imposed against its representatives (standard process). However, in exceptional circumstances under the provisions of § 30 Paragraph 4 OWiG a fine can also be independently declared against the legal person or association of persons (independent process).

§ 30 only provides for the determination of a fine against a legal person or association of persons. The extent of the fine is dependent on whether a criminal offence or a regulatory offence has been charged (§ 30 Paragraph 2 S. 1 No. 1, 2 OWiG). For premeditated crimes, the fine is up to €1 million, for acts of negligence up to €500,000. If it is a regulatory offence, then the maximum fine is determined by the threatened maximum fine for that regulatory offence. For negligent regulatory offences, half of the scope of punishment for the action applies (§ 17 Paragraph 2 OWiG).

The fines for legal persons and associations of persons serve to confiscate illegal profits and in this way prevent dishonest profit seeking. § 30 Paragraph 3 OWiG explains the provision of § 17 Paragraph 4 OWiG for its appropriate use. The fines should exceed the economic advantage that the perpetrator obtained from the deed. For this purpose the legal maximum fine may be exceeded (§ 17 Paragraph 4 see 2 OWiG). Out of these specifications it follows that the economic advantage that flowed to the legal person or association of persons from the action should be calculated to be the lowest possible fine.

Example: The manager of a public limited company illegally disposed of waste. According to § 326 Criminal Code (StGB) he was sentenced to two years imprisonment which were suspended on probation. Through the illegal disposal, the public limited company saved disposal costs of up to €5 million.

The public limited company forfeited a fine of up to €1 million (cf. § 30 Paragraph 2 No. 1 OWiG). Suppose the fine could be settled at €300,000. It is optional to confiscate the economic advantage that the public limited company obtained through the action (§§ 30 Paragraph 3, 17 Paragraph 4 OWiG). As a result the fine against the public limited company can be fixed at a total of €5,300,000.

The assessment of penalties or fines for the entity etc. that committed the action depends on the general principles for the attribution of a sanction (§§ 46 StGB, 17 Paragraph 3 OWiG). Of particular significance is the importance of the action and the charge or rather the guilt attributed to the perpetrator.

According to effective law, the penalties for legal persons and associations of persons are not only sanctions or similar measures which can be imposed due to actions against the legal person or associations of persons. The dissolution of legal persons or associations of persons can (and in the area of criminal law, must) be arranged when the party involved in an illegal deed or a perpetrator of an offence acted for another party and through this acquired something. This is done so that the acquisition is removed (confiscated).

For particular offences against economic criminal law 1954 (WiStG 1954), instead of corporate dissolution, the payment of extra earnings can be ordered against a legal person or association of persons. According to law this is possible provided that the extra earnings have flowed to the legal person or association of persons out of an illegal action as defined by the WiStG.

§§ 75 StGB, 29 OWiG provide for the recovery of a legal person's own matters and rights that were developed by representatives of a legal person, a non-legal entity or a legal partnership due to a criminal offence or regulatory offence, or were needed for the perpetration or preparation of an action or have been predefined.

The disbanding of a legal person or association of persons (the 'death penalty') is as a sanction provided for neither in criminal law nor in regulatory law to date.

The prominent case in the last five years was settled on 8 October 2007 against Siemens with the imposition of a fine to the extent of €201 million. The State Court Munich justified the fine against the firm by stating that 'due to the calculated criminal acts by Reinhard S. Siemens had attained economic advantages, in particular market advantages, to the extent of at least 200 million Euros'. According to the findings of the court, from the end of 2001 until September 2004 the accused S., then commercial head of Siemens landline unit ICN, had 'in 77 cases bribed officials abroad in Libya, Nigeria and Russia for the purpose of obtaining contracts for Siemens and then collectively negotiated with others'.

Prosecution and proceedings

The prosecution of regulatory offences depends on the matter or the place where the regulatory offence is committed. Prosecution authorities are fundamentally the responsible administrative authorities. The relevant authority is legally defined for each case. For example, for offences against environmental regulations it is the responsible environmental authorities, for offences against cartel law it is the responsible cartel authorities.

The prosecution authority is the 'master' of the proceedings. According to the OWiG this is only not true when in exceptional circumstances the Office of Public Prosecution (§§ 40 ff. OWiG) or – for specific acts of prosecution – the court for the prosecution of regulatory offences is called upon (§ 35 Paragraph 1 OWiG). In exceptional circumstances the jurisdiction can also be reserved for the police.

In prosecution proceedings and also in accordance with § 30 OWiG the following expediency principle is valid: the prosecution and punishment of regulatory offences is outlined in § 47 Paragraph 1 Line 1 OWiG according to the best judgement of the administrative authority. Unlike in criminal proceedings, there is no compulsory prosecution. Upon discovering a regulatory offence the prosecution authority is only accountable for examining the facts of a case and to exercise their judgement to the effect of whether a prosecution and punishment is necessary. If this is not the case, the prosecution authority can refrain from instituting a proceeding or cease an already instituted proceeding (§ 47 Paragraph 1 Line 2). The public prosecutor and the judge can cease the summary proceedings due to unnecessary punishment. The possibility to cease proceedings reaches far further than in criminal law.

The proceedings are in two phases. There is a preliminary proceeding and a court proceeding. After examination of the case the responsible administrative authority allows for a fine when the existence of a regulatory offence is deemed to be evident, prosecution obstacles are lacking, and punishment with a fine seems necessary. If the party concerned has no objection against the fine, then this is final and can be enforced (§ 89 OWiG). This closes the proceeding. In this case, a court proceeding is not necessary.

If the party concerned objects, then a court proceeding comes before the magistrate's court (criminal court). The court independently examines the action of the party concerned. Essentially, the objective of the court proceeding is the allegation against the party concerned and not the fine. If the court considers a trial not to be required, the decision can be issued through a ruling, that is without a verbal hearing (cf. § 72 Paragraph 1 see 1 OWiG). A written proceeding is an exception. Usually, the main proceeding concludes due to a trial with a judgment. The party concerned can file an appeal against the judgment or ruling (§ 79 Paragraph 1 OWiG). If an appeal against the judgment or the resolution of the court is not possible or is unsuccessful, the decision about the case can be enforced through enforcement proceedings (§§ 89ff. OWiG).

Impact of liability and prosecution

There are no findings to date concerning the impact of prosecution/sentencing for these offences.

However, one could argue that the possibility of the imposition of a fine against a corporation and the accompanied reputation damage causes corporations to change their corporate culture to represent themselves as a 'good corporate citizen'.

The extensive consulting industry which has developed in recent years supports this hypothesis. Corporations invest a considerable amount of funds into legal advice to avoid legal proceedings ('compliance').

In Germany the question of transition to a criminal law system which also contains penal sanctions for legal persons and associations of persons has been discussed for a long time. Not only internal developments in the area of dogma, but most importantly models from abroad and European developments are required to show the way to a corporate criminal law system.

However, until now the federal government has strictly rejected the adoption of corporate criminal liability. They are of the opinion that a change in the system creates a considerable number of problems and in comparison with the present system of administrative fines it would offer no real advantages.

This is consistent with the predominant opinion in Germany that still assumes that corporations are

- not capable of acting
- not capable of being guilty and
- not capable of being sanctioned.

In fact, the regulatory law § 30 OWiG provides for a flexible, simple, fast and at the same time effective (deterrent) means of punishment. That speaks in favour of retaining the current legal situation.

As long as the punishment in terms of regulatory law is on the whole effective and deterrent, then the only argument for the adoption of corporate criminal liability lies in the consideration of the expressive function of the penalty. Corporate behaviour should be branded with the 'label' of socio-ethical disapproval. Depending on one's point of view this label is (at least in specific cases) necessary in order to orientate or calm the people, or on the contrary it is superfluous because the consequences for the effectiveness of safeguarding objects of legal protection are not discernible.

31 Country report: Sweden

Ana-Maria Pascal

Introduction

Under Swedish law, only natural persons are subject to criminal liability. A legal entity cannot commit a crime and cannot be subjected to criminal liability.

However, while a natural person(s) will be held responsible for a criminal offence, the Penal Code also stipulates that companies can be subjected to criminal sanctions (usually a fine) in cases where the offence has been committed in the context of a commercial activity.[1] Such a fine is not considered to be criminal punishment, as, again, Swedish jurisprudence does not allow for corporate criminal liability.

This mixed model, with criminal sanctions but no criminal liability for the legal person, is somewhat similar to the German model, also based on administrative (rather than criminal) liability. At the same time, the combination of administrative and criminal elements[2] reminds one of the situation in Italy, where a hybrid model is also in place for corporate liability. The Swedish model is indeed a new kind of *tertium genus*, significantly different from both the German and the Italian ones.

The scope and test of liability

Scope of liability

Chapter 36, section 7 of the Penal Code provides the key elements of this quasi-criminal liability which is a peculiarity of Swedish legislation. The liability is applied to any 'entrepreneur' for 'a crime committed in the exercise of business activities', if:

1   The crime has entailed gross disregard for the special obligations associated with the business activities or is otherwise of a serious kind, and
2   The entrepreneur has not done what could reasonably be required of him for prevention of the crime.

According to both Swedish authorities and relevant literature, 'entrepreneur' is a general term frequently used in different Swedish statutes, but without explicit definition. The uncodified definition of the term is 'any natural or legal person that professionally runs a business of an economic nature'. The term apparently covers state-owned and municipal trading companies.[3]

Test of liability

Determining whether a crime entails 'a gross disregard for the special obligations associated with the business activities' or is otherwise 'serious' involves consideration of the criminal activity as a whole. The economic aspects of the crime are of particular importance, including existing gains and future economic prospects created as a result of the crime.

The provisions of the first paragraph of section 7 do not apply 'if the crime was directed against the entrepreneur or if it would otherwise be manifestly unreasonable to impose a corporate fine'.

In July 2006, Sweden amended the Penal Code provisions on corporate fines (chapter 36, sections 7–10). The first requirement – that the crime should involve a gross disregard of the obligations associated with the company's business activity or otherwise be of a serious nature – was abolished. The second requirement – that the entrepreneur had not done what was reasonably expected of him to do in order to prevent the crime – was supplemented by the alternative requirement that the offence be committed either by a person in a leading position, or by someone who otherwise has a special responsibility of supervision or control of the business.[4] The provision about exemptions was also abolished.

Liability of directors and corporate officers

Since companies cannot be prosecuted under Swedish legislation, a legal representative of the company (usually, a 'managing director'), or a person to whom powers have been delegated, will be prosecuted. According to a 2007 report by the Centre for Corporate Accountability (UK), Swedish case law states that:

> The employers' responsibility for the work environment is borne primarily by the highest manager i.e. in a limited company usually by its Managing Director.[5]

As the authors of the report explain, the term 'managing director' can refer to a board member, but in practice, it is usually the most senior employee appointed by the board.

As indicated above, Swedish law allows delegation of the responsibility of directors to others within the organisation. For the delegation to be valid, a number of conditions must be satisfied: (1) there must be a need for delegation; (2) the delegate must have the requisite training and competence for the assignment involved and must hold a relatively independent position within the organisation;[6] and (3) there must be clarity of delegation.

The test of liability for workplace offences is based on intent or negligence. It is only when there is an intentional or negligent non-compliance with an injunction or prohibition ordered by the Work Environment Authority (WEA, the agency responsible for enforcement of health and safety legislation in Sweden), that prosecution can take place. 'Negligence usually means that one or more persons have omitted to take the measures which could have prevented the injury.'[7] WEA reports that in 2002, a total of 44 people were convicted and that the defendants included persons who held a wide range of positions, from supervisors, safety managers, and heads of department to managing directors.[8]

Investigation and prosecution

The two main enforcement authorities responsible for the investigation and prosecution of criminal matters are the police and the prosecution service. The National Police Board is the central administrative authority of the police service. Following a reform in January 2005, two agencies are in charge of the day-to-day administration of the prosecution service: the Swedish Prosecution Authority and the National Economic Crimes Bureau.[9] In 2003, a special agency, the National Anti-Corruption Unit, was created by the Prosecutor General for corruption-related offences. For money laundering offences, the designated authority is the National Police Board, although in practice the Financial Police (a division of the National Criminal Investigation Department which is part of the National Police Board) serve as the intelligence unit.[10]

Under chapter 23, sections 1–3 of the Code of Judicial Procedure,[11] a preliminary investigation must be initiated by either the police authority or the prosecution service as soon as there is cause to believe (usually, due to a report) that an offence subject to public prosecution has been committed. The prosecutor assumes responsibility for complicated investigations and in cases where 'special reasons' require the prosecutor's involvement.[12] The aim of the preliminary inquiry is to establish who may be reasonably suspected of the offence and whether sufficient reason exists for their prosecution (section 2).

Swedish legislation is based on the principle of mandatory prosecution. However, there are various exceptions which can lead to prosecution being waived, such as when the crime is not considered serious, when psychiatric care has been rendered, and when the suspect has committed another offence for which he/she will be sanctioned and no further sanction is deemed necessary.

Although the legal and natural persons are usually proceeded against together, it is also possible to proceed against the legal person independently, for instance where no natural person has been identified. According to OECD officials, this has happened in at least three cases – two involving environmental crimes, and the other a violation of safety regulations.[13]

Sanctions and sentencing

Where a violation of chapter 36, section 7 has been established, a fine of the corporate offender is mandatory. Under the old provisions of chapter 36, section 8, the level of corporate fines was very low, ranging between 10,000 and 3,000,000 Swedish crowns (SEK), approximately €1,000 to €330,000. In addition, bribery offences may also lead to disbarment from public procurement according to Chapter 10 of the Public Procurement Act.

Following the 2006 amendments to the Code, the minimum fine was lowered even more – to 5,000 SEK – while the maximum fine was increased to 10,000,000 SEK (€1.1 million). The 2006 amendments introduced a simplified procedure for imposing fines not exceeding 500,000 SEK (€55,000).[14]

Chapter 36 contains some guidelines on determining the appropriate fine in a particular case. Pursuant to section 9, 'special consideration shall be given to the nature and extent of the crime and to its relation to the business activity'. The Penal Code does not provide any guidelines for how to interpret this provision. However, Swedish authorities explain that, in addition to the guidelines in chapter 29 of the Penal Code ('On the Determination of Punishment and Exemption from Sanction'), some indication on this can be found in the Commentary to the Penal Code. It states that the extent and severity of the crime, the motive of the crime (especially economic gain), the position of the perpetrator and the significance of the affected public interest are all important in this determination. Moreover, whether the crime is committed with intent or through negligence, and whether it was committed at the request of management or without management's knowledge, are also factors to be considered. It is an unwritten rule that a corporate fine should be 50 per cent of the gain of the crime where it is committed with intent, and 10 to 30 per cent of the gain if it is committed through negligence.[15]

In addition, section 10 provides that

> A corporate fine may be remitted or set at less than it should have been under the provisions of Section 9:
> 1   if a sanction for the crime is imposed on the entrepreneur or a representative of the entrepreneur,
> 2   if the crime involves some other payment liability or a special legal effect for the entrepreneur,
> 3   if this is otherwise called for on special grounds.[16]

According to Swedish authorities, the first two grounds are aimed at avoiding the imposition of a double punishment where (a) the entrepreneur is a natural person or a very small joint-stock limited company in the case where the owner and the company representative is the same person, or (b) the entrepreneur must pay damages or administrative sanctions, which have the same effect as corporate fines (i.e. punishment).

The third ground relates to extraordinary circumstances, such as where application of the normal rules for the imposition of a corporate fine would result in the closure of the business or unemployment. According to authorities, however, the financial status of the entrepreneur is not normally a factor in determining the level of the corporate fine to be imposed.[17]

Conclusion and future directions

Despite the lack of total criminal liability for legal persons, Sweden has been deemed to have a good record in respect of addressing certain kinds of corporate offences, such as corruption, tax offences, and money laundering. According to a Transparency International (UK) report, in 2008 there were 15 investigations open, including 12 Oil-for-Food cases involving companies such as AstraZeneca, Atlas Copco, Scania and Volvo. Sweden also joined a multi-jurisdictional investigation into alleged bribery in relation to leasing/sales of Saab Gripen jets to Hungary and the Czech Republic.[18]

Other prosecutions have involved cases of unfair competition and bid-rigging. On 14 March 2005, two companies in the ventilation business were found by the City Court of Stockholm to have engaged in illegal anti-competitive co-operation in connection with two procurements. One of the companies was granted full leniency from fines.[19]

However, the overall impression of international observers is that legislation is still lacking in clarity, and that corporate fines are rarely imposed in Sweden. According to a report published by the Council of Europe Group of States against Corruption (GRECO) in February 2009, anti-corruption legislation:

> is very general in its wording, although some further guidance regarding the application of the law can be found in the preparatory works, and the existing case law is rather limited. As a result, it is difficult to foresee all consequences of the law. It appears that the current legislation, which has been subject to a number of successive amendments in order to comply with developing international standards and which is subject to domestic criticism, would benefit from a revision in order to become more comprehensive and clear in respect of public and private sector corruption and, above all, vis-à-vis the wider public. The revision of existing bribery legislation, which has been on the Government's agenda for some time, is strongly supported by the OECD.[20]

Transparency International's representative considers that, apart from cases of money laundering and tax offences, Sweden's record of prosecuting companies is weak.[21] Awareness of the existence of corporate fines is low both at board level and in the media. The general perception is that corporations are unlikely either to be held liable or to be sanctioned for their crimes.

Notes

1 Dana Rone, *Legal Scientific Research on Institute of Criminal Liability of Legal Entities in Eight Countries – Nordic Countries (Finland, Sweden, Norway, Iceland and Denmark) and Baltic Countries (Latvia, Lithuania and Estonia)*, report prepared for the Ministry of Justice of the Republic of Latvia, March 2006, www.tm.gov.lv, p. 16.
2 Philippe de Baets talks about 'a structural liaison between the administrative and penal pillars of a hybrid enforcement structure' that operates in Sweden (Philippe de Baets, 'The labour inspection of Belgium, the UK and Sweden in a comparative perspective', in *International Journal of the Sociology of Law*, 31 (2003), 35–53, p. 45).
3 OECD Phase 1 Report on Sweden, 27 June 2000, http://www.oecd.org/dataoecd/16/1/2389830.pdf, pp. 7–8. See also Dana Rone, cf. supra, p. 16, n. 22.
4 Dona Rone, cf. supra, note 1, p. 18.
5 Cf. 'International comparison of health & safety duties imposed on company directors', a report prepared by the Centre for Corporate Accountability for the Health and Safety Executive, 2007, http://www.essex.ac.uk/cwcn/directors.html , p. 53.
6 Case no A: 93-06-03, NJA 1993, S. 245, cited in the CCA report, p. 54.
7 Cf. CCA report, p. 59.
8 Ibid.
9 Cf. OECD Phase 2 Report on Sweden, 22 September 2005, http://www.oecd.org/dataoecd/20/8/35394676.pdf, p. 22.
10 Ibid., pp. 33–34.
11 The official English translation of the Code of Judicial Procedure is available on the Swedish Government's website, at http://www.sweden.gov.se/content/1/c4/15/40/472970fc.pdf
12 OECD Phase 1 Report, cf. supra, note 3, p. 15.
13 OECD Phase 2 Report, cf. supra, note 9, p. 47.
14 OCED Follow-up Report, November 2007, http://www.oecd.org/dataoecd/3/43/39905457.pdf, p. 5.
15 OECD Phase 1 Report, cf. supra, note 3, p. 10.
16 The official English translation of the Penal Code is available on the Swedish Government's website, at http://www.sweden.gov.se/content/1/c6/01/51/94/add334ba.pdf
17 OCED Phase 1 Report, cf. supra, note 3, pp. 9–10.
18 Fritz Heimann and Gillian Dell, *Progress Report 2008: Enforcement of the OECD Convention on Combating Bribery of Foreign Public Officials*, Transparency International, 24 June 2008, http://sup.kathimerini.gr/xtra/media/files/meletes/econ/offic240608.pdf, p. 34.
19 Cf. news published by the Practical Law Company, http://pensions.practicallaw.com/9-200-5572?q=*&qp=&qo=&qe, March 2005.
20 *Evaluation Report on Sweden, Theme I: Incriminations*, Third Round, published by the Council of Europe's Group of States Against Corruption (GRECO), 19 February 2009, and available at http://www.coe.int/t/dghl/monitoring/greco/evaluations/round3/GrecoEval3(2008)4_Sweden_One_EN.pdf, p. 16.
21 OECD Phase 2 Report, cf. supra, note 9, p. 46.

Index

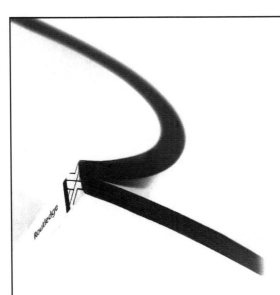